TAKING SIDES

Clashing Views on Controversial

ssues in Abnormal Psychology

TAKING SIDES

Clashing Views on Controversial
ssues in Abnormal Psychology

Selected, Edited, and with Introductions by

Richard P. Halgin
University of Massachusetts–Amherst

Dushkin/McGraw-Hill
A Division of The McGraw-Hill Companies

To my wonderful wife, Lucille, whose love and support provide me with immeasurable amounts of energy, and to our children, Daniel and Kerry, whose values and achievements have been inspiring.

Photo Acknowledgment
Cover image: © 2000 by PhotoDisc, Inc.

Cover Art Acknowledgment
Charles Vitelli

Library of Congress Cataloging-in-Publication Data
Main entry under title:
Taking sides: clashing views on controversial issues in abnormal psychology/selected, edited, and with introductions by Richard P. Halgin.—1st ed.
Includes bibliographical references and index.
1. Psychology, Pathological. I. Halgin, Richard P., *comp.*
616.89

0-07-237193-5
ISSN: 1527-604X

Printed on Recycled Paper

Preface

The field of abnormal psychology is inherently controversial because we lack a clear delineation between normal and abnormal behavior. Most phenomena in the realm of abnormal psychology fall along continua; the point on a continuum at which behavior moves from being considered "normal" to being considered "abnormal" varies considerably and is influenced by a number of factors. Consider the example of an active boy's behavior. His running around impulsively and shouting out aimless comments would be viewed as normal behavior on a playground but abnormal behavior in a quiet classroom. In a classroom setting, his behavior might be referred to as impulsive and hyperactive, possibly prompting his teacher to refer him to a mental health professional for therapy and medication to help him settle down and pay attention. Although such referrals are commonplace in American schools, some people contend that we pathologize the normal behavior of children when we view their high levels of energy as mental disorders. This is but one of the debates about which you will read in this book, and it is a good example of the kind of controversy found in the field of mental health.

There are many complex issues that arise in the field of abnormal psychology; in this book you will read about 20 controversial matters with which mental health experts struggle. Part 1 explores debates pertaining to the classification of mental disorders by considering whether or not the current diagnostic system is conceptually flawed and whether or not it is biased against women. Part 2 looks at psychological conditions about which there has been vehement disagreement in recent years, with some experts expressing intense skepticism about the validity of specific clinical problems that have been in the spotlight. Moving on to issues pertaining to treatment, Part 3 looks at differing viewpoints about the effectiveness of particular interventions. Part 4 explores pertinent social issues that interface with the field of abnormal psychology. The final part features a set of debates about ethical and legal issues that pertain to the field of mental health.

Most students who enroll in a course in abnormal psychology begin the semester with the belief that they will be learning about problems that affect "other people," rather than themselves. In a short period of time, however, they come to realize that they are reading about conditions that have much more personal salience than they had anticipated. Sooner or later, they recognize conditions that they or someone close to them have experienced, and their interest in the topic intensifies. In all likelihood, you will have a similar reaction as you read this book. To capture the essence of each debate, you will find it helpful to connect yourself in a personal way to the issue under consideration; you might imagine yourself dealing with the issue personally, or as the relative of a client with the particular problem, or even as a professional trying to provide mental health assistance.

99738

Plan of the book   To assist you in understanding the significance of each issue, every issue begins with an *introduction* that provides important background about the issue and summarizes the perspective in each of the pieces. Points and counterpoints are enumerated to help you appreciate the specific areas of disagreement between the two pieces. Each issue concludes with a set of *challenge questions* that can serve as the basis for further thought or discussion on the topic as well as a list of suggested additional readings. In addition, Internet site addresses (URLs) have been provided on the *On the Internet* page at the beginning of each part, which should prove useful as starting points for further research on the issues. At the back of the book is a listing of all the *contributors to this volume* with a brief biographical sketch of each of the prominent figures whose views are debated here.

A word to the instructor   An *Instructor's Manual With Test Questions* (multiple-choice and essay) is available through the publisher for the instructor using *Taking Sides* in the classroom. A general guidebook, *Using Taking Sides in the Classroom*, which discusses methods and techniques for integrating the pro-con approach into any classroom setting, is also available. An online version of *Using Taking Sides in the Classroom* and a correspondence service for *Taking Sides* adopters can be found at http://www.dushkin.com/usingts/.

   Taking Sides: Clashing Views on Controversial Issues in Abnormal Psychology is only one title in the Taking Sides series. If you are interested in seeing the table of contents for any of the other titles, please visit the Taking Sides Web site at http://www.dushkin.com/takingsides/.

Acknowledgments   Preparing the first edition of a volume such as this takes remarkable levels of creativity, energy, and conscientious attention to detail —attributes that accurately characterize my senior editorial assistant, Joseph Greer. From the very outset Joe's commitment to this project was exceptional in every way, as he began scouring the field in search of appropriate articles or issues for the book. He continued to play an indispensable role throughout the preparation of the volume and generously agreed to author the instructor's manual, which provides instructors with an articulate set of insights, discussion ideas, and test items. The collegial relationship and collaborative input provided by Joe helped make the preparation of this book an especially rewarding experience for me, and I feel greatly indebted to him.

   Special gratitude also goes to the undergraduate research assistants whose diligent efforts were essential to the completion of this project. Kerry Halgin and Alessandro Piselli played prominent roles in preparing the manuscript for production; they critically analyzed the pieces, gathered biographical information on the contributors, and enumerated the major points in the pieces. The sophisticated and thoughtful efforts of Kerry and Sandro were truly remarkable.

   Also playing important roles were Jill Hermanowski and Matthew Lakoma, who devoted countless hours reviewing hundreds of publications for appropriate articles and issues; their careful and thoughtful gathering of source materials was crucial to the timely completion of this book. Each of these four research assistants provided support that was exceptional.

Thanks also to Ted Knight and the staff at Dushkin/McGraw-Hill. Ted was wonderfully helpful and influential at every stage of this project. From the beginning he made it clear to me that the tasks would be much more challenging than I had initially anticipated, and he was right; yet with his impressive wisdom and experience, he provided valuable guidance all along the way.

Richard P. Halgin
University of Massachusetts-Amherst

Contents In Brief

Contents

Psychiatrist Frank W. Putnam contends that the diagnosis of multiple personality disorder meets the standards for the three basic forms of validity: content validity, construct validity, and criterion-related validity. Psychiatrist Paul R. McHugh denies the validity of multiple personality disorder, asserting that this condition is a socially created behavioral disorder induced by psychotherapists.

Issue 4.   Does Attention Deficit Disorder Exist?   54

Psychiatrist Edward M. Hallowell asserts that an appreciation for the complexity of attention deficit disorder (ADD) can provide valuable understanding about the workings of the brain and how this disorder affects the lives of millions of people. Educational consultant and former special education teacher Thomas Armstrong contends that the diagnosis of ADD has been blown out of proportion by the public and the professional community and is, in fact, a questionable diagnosis.

Issue 5.   Is Schizophrenia a Biological Disorder?   74

Clinical psychiatrist Nancy C. Andreasen emphasizes the significant advances that scientists have made in defining schizophrenia as a biological disorder that results from disturbances in brain circuitry. Psychologist Victor D. Sanua expresses alarm about the views of biologically oriented scientists who give insufficient attention to the role of stressful life experiences in causing and aggravating the symptoms of mental disorders such as schizophrenia.

Issue 6.   Does Post-Abortion Syndrome Exist?   86

Psychiatrist E. Joanne Angelo contends that women who have abortions are at risk of developing a lasting, serious syndrome consisting of several emotional and behavioral problems. Social activist Joyce Arthur asserts that a general consensus has been reached in the medical and scientific communities that most women who have abortions experience little or no psychological harm.

Psychiatrist Richard P. Kluft supports the notion that people can recover memories that have been long unavailable, and he cites several verified examples in which psychotherapy patients recalled previously inaccessible memories of traumatic events. Psychologist Elizabeth F. Loftus cites extensive laboratory research to support her conclusion that suggestion and imagination can create "memories" of events that never actually occurred.

PART 3 TREATMENT 119

Martin E. P. Seligman, a leading researcher in the field of psychotherapy, praises the study of psychotherapy conducted by researchers at the popular magazine *Consumer Reports*, which he says is the most extensive study on record demonstrating the effectiveness of psychotherapy. Psychotherapy researchers Neil S. Jacobson and Andrew Christensen criticize the *Consumer Reports* study on methodological grounds, asserting that it adds little to understanding the effectiveness of psychotherapy.

Psychologist and psychotherapy researcher Sol L. Garfield asserts that too much emphasis is being placed on the importance of using empirically supported or validated therapies for treating people with specific psychiatric disorders. Psychologist and psychotherapy researcher Philip C. Kendall contends that psychotherapists should rely on the knowledge derived from extensive research when they select treatments for clients with particular psychiatric disorders.

Physician Peter R. Breggin, founder of the International Center for the Study of Psychiatry and Psychology, asserts that behavior-modifying medications such as Ritalin are vastly overused by parents and teachers who have come to view normal childhood behaviors as pathological conditions warranting psychiatric interventions. Professor of psychiatry Russell Barkley views behavior disorders of childhood, such as attention deficit hyperactivity disorder (ADHD), as serious conditions warranting medical intervention in order to reduce the likelihood of social, academic, and emotional problems.

Psychiatrists Fred Ovsiew and Jonathan Bird assert that psychosurgery is an invaluable intervention for certain kinds of seriously disordered patients who have not responded to other forms of treatment, and they insist that failure to provide this intervention to those who need it would be ethically questionable. Neurosurgeon Frank T. Vertosick, Jr., argues that psychosurgical procedures rest on a shaky scientific foundation and involve procedures that cause irreversible injury to the brain.

PART 4   SOCIAL ISSUES   185

Psychology and communication researchers L. Rowell Huesmann and Jessica Moise assert that there is a clear relationship between aggression and children's viewing of media violence, and they point to several theoretical explanations for this connection. Psychology professor Jonathan L. Freedman disagrees with the conclusion of researchers that there is a relationship between aggression and children's viewing of media violence, and he argues that many conclusions in this area are based on methodologically flawed studies.

Sociology professor Diana E. H. Russell considers pornography profoundly harmful because it predisposes men to want to rape women and undermines internal and social inhibitions against acting out rape fantasies. Law professor Nadine Strossen contends that there is no credible research to support the claim that sexist, violent imagery leads to harmful behavior against women.

Educational psychology professor Jeffery P. Braden supports the *Bell Curve* theory, stating that educators can use its conclusions and recommendations to improve educational opportunities for students. Psychology professor Robert J. Sternberg dismisses the *Bell Curve* theory as being "bad science" that is theoretically and methodologically flawed and that plays into the societal tendency to blame social problems on things over which we have no control.

David B. Larson, president of the National Institute for Healthcare, maintains that religion can heal many ills, both physical and psychological, and that religiously committed people fare better psychologically in many facets of life than nonreligious people. Albert Ellis, president of the Institute for Rational-Emotive Therapy, expresses concern about religious commitment, particularly fanaticism, and he criticizes the research in this area as being biased.

Professor of psychiatry Howard H. Goldman discusses the benefits resulting from deinstitutionalization, a process that he believes has emerged from sound public policy. Psychiatrist E. Fuller Torrey calls the deinstitutionalization movement a disaster that has resulted in widespread homelessness among the mentally ill. He attributes this failed policy to social errors within the legal and academic realms.

PART 5 ETHICAL AND LEGAL ISSUES 277

Rhea K. Farberman, director of public communications for the American Psychological Association, makes the case that mental health professionals should be called upon to assess terminally ill persons requesting hastened death in order to ensure that decision making is rational and free of coercion. Psychiatrists Mark D. Sullivan, Linda Ganzini, and Stuart J. Youngner argue that the reliance on mental health professionals to be suicide gatekeepers involves an inappropriate use of clinical procedures to disguise society's ambivalence about suicide itself.

Psychologist Mark A. Yarhouse asserts that mental health professionals have an ethical responsibility to allow individuals to pursue treatment aimed at curbing same-sex attraction, stating that doing so affirms the client's dignity and autonomy. Psychologist Douglas C. Haldeman criticizes therapy involving sexual reorientation, insisting that there is no evidence that such treatments are effective and that they run the risk of further stigmatizing homosexuality.

Law professor Alan M. Dershowitz criticizes the "abuse excuse," a legal tactic by which criminal defendants claim a history of abuse as an excuse for violent retaliation. He asserts that it is dangerous to the very tenets of democracy, which presuppose personal accountability for choices and actions. Law professor Peter Arenella argues that Dershowitz grossly exaggerates the extent to which the "abuse excuse" is actually used in criminal law by highlighting a few high-profile, exceptional cases.

Physician Max Fink asserts that electroconvulsive therapy (ECT) is an effective intervention whose use has been limited as a result of social stigma and philosophical bias, which have been reinforced by intimidation from the pharmaceutical and managed care industries. Physician Leonard R. Frank criticizes the use of ECT because of its disturbing side effects, some of which he personally has suffered, and asserts that its resurgence in popularity is economically based.

Introduction

What's "Abnormal" About Abnormal Psychology?

Richard P. Halgin

The field of abnormal psychology lends itself well to a discussion of controversial issues because of the inherent difficulty involved in defining the concept of "abnormal." The definition of abnormality is contingent on a myriad of influences that include cultural, historical, geographical, societal, interpersonal, and intrapersonal factors. What is considered everyday behavior in one culture might be regarded as bizarre in another. What was acceptable at one point in time might seem absurd in contemporary society. What seems customary in one region, even in one section of a large city, might be viewed as outrageous elsewhere. Even on a very personal level, one person's typical style of emotional expression might be experienced by another person as odd and disruptive. This introductory essay looks at some of the complex issues involved in defining and understanding abnormality and, in doing so, will set the stage for the controversial issues that follow. With this theoretical foundation, you will be better equipped to tackle the thorny issues in this volume and to develop an approach for reaching your own conclusions about these controversies.

Defining Abnormality

One of the best ways to begin a discussion of the complexity of defining abnormality is by considering our own behavior. Think about an outlandish costume that you wore to a Halloween party and the fun you had engaging in this completely normal behavior. Now imagine wearing the same costume to class the following day, and think about the reactions you would have received. What seemed so normal on the evening of October 31 would have been considered bizarre on the morning of November 1. Only a day later, in a different context, you would have been regarded as abnormal, and your behavior would have been viewed as both disturbed and disturbing. Consider another example: Recall a time in which you were intensely emotional, perhaps weeping profusely at a funeral. If you were to display similar emotionality a few days later in a class discussion, your behavior would cause considerable stir, and your classmates would be taken aback by the intensity of your emotions. Now consider a common behavior that is completely acceptable and expected in American culture, such as shaking a person's hand upon meeting. Did you know that in some cultures such behavior is regarded as rude and unacceptable? These simple examples highlight the ways in which the concept of "normal" is contingent on many factors. Because of the wide variability in definitions of what is abnormal, psychologists have spelled out criteria that can be used in determining abnormal human behavior. These criteria fall into four categories: distress, impairment, risk to self or other people, and socially and culturally unacceptable behavior.

Distress

I begin with the most personal criterion of abnormality because the experience of inner emotional distress is a universal phenomenon and a powerful way in which every person at some point in life feels different from everyone around them. Distress, the experience of emotional pain, is experienced in many ways, such as depression, anxiety, and cognitive confusion. When people feel any of these responses to an extreme degree, they feel abnormal, and they typically look for ways to alleviate their feelings of inner pain. Some of the issues in this book illustrate the various ways in which different people respond to similar life events. For example, Issue 6 explores the emotional impact of abortion on women who undergo this procedure, with the controversy focusing on the extent to which abortion might evoke intense experiences of lasting emotional distress.

Impairment

People who are intensely distressed are likely to find it difficult to fulfill the everyday responsibilities of life. When people are very depressed or anxious, they typically have a difficult time concentrating on their studies, attending to their work responsibilities, or even interacting with other people. Impairment involves a reduction in a person's ability to function at an optimal or even an average level. Although distress and impairment often go hand in hand, they do not always; a person can be seriously impaired but feel no particular distress. This is often the case with substance abuse, in which people are incapable of the basic tasks of physical coordination and cognitive clarity but feel euphoric. Some of the debates in this book address the issue of impairment and the difficulty in assessing the extent to which people are impaired. For example, Issue 17 focuses on physician-assisted suicide, with particular attention to the role of mental health professionals in determining a person's competency to choose suicide. One aspect of the controversy pertains to the issue of whether or not a terminally ill person is too impaired to make a rational life-ending decision.

Risk to Self or Others

Sometimes people act in ways that cause risk to themselves or others. In this context, risk refers to danger or threat to the well-being of a person. In the case of suicide or self-mutilating behavior, the personal risk is evident. In the case of outwardly directed violence, rape, or even emotional exploitation, the risk is to other people. Although the issue of risk to self or others might not seem controversial on the surface, there are many facets of risk that provoke debate. For example, does an individual have the right to engage in self-injurious, perhaps even life-ending, behavior, or does society have a right, even a responsibility, to intervene? The choice of suicide, even by terminally ill people, has prompted heated debate in our society, but so have less-extreme issues, such as the choice to view pornography. The issue of pornography is especially controversial because some experts believe that viewing sexually explicit—particularly sexually violent—stimuli places individuals at risk of engaging in the violent behaviors that they observe in pornographic media. This controversy, addressed in Issue 13, raises not only questions pertaining to risk to other people but also question of whether or not indulgence in pornography might result in personal psychological risk.

Socially and Culturally Unacceptable Behavior

Another criterion for defining abnormality pertains to the social or cultural context in which behavior occurs. In some instances, behavior that is regarded as odd within a given culture, society, or subgroup is common elsewhere. For example, some people from Mediterranean cultures believe in a phenomenon called *mal de ojo,* or "evil eye," in which the ill will of one person can negatively affect another. According to this belief, receiving the evil eye from a person can cause a range of disturbing physical and emotional symptoms; consequently, individuals in these cultures often take steps to ward off the power of another person's evil eye. Such beliefs might be regarded as strangely superstitious, almost delusional, in American culture, but they are considered common elsewhere. Even more subtle contexts can influence the extent to which a behavior is defined as abnormal, as illustrated by the example of the Halloween costume mentioned previously. This book features issues related to social and cultural variables, such as the extent to which the black-white IQ gap is attributable to race or to problems of assessment (Issue 14). There is also a debate about the extent to which religious commitment improves or impairs mental health functioning in people (Issue 15).

What Causes Abnormality?

In trying to understand why people act and feel in ways that are regarded as abnormal, social scientists consider three dimensions: biological, psychological, and sociocultural. Rather than viewing these dimensions as independent, however, experts discuss the relative contribution of each dimension in influencing human behavior, and they use the term *biopsychosocial* to capture these intertwining forces. In the context of abnormality, the biopsychosocial conceptualization of human behavior conveys the sense that abnormal behavior arises from a complex set of determinants in the body, the mind, and the social context.

Biological Causes

During the past several decades scientists have made tremendous progress in discovering ways in which human behavior is influenced by a range of biological variables. In the realm of abnormal psychology, the contributions of the biological sciences have been especially impressive, as researchers have developed increasing understanding of the ways in which abnormal behavior is determined by bodily physiology and genetic makeup. As is the case with many medical disorders, various mental disorders, such as depression, run in families. Mental health researchers have made great efforts to understand why certain mental illnesses are passed from one generation to another and also to understand why certain disorders are not inherited even in identical twin pairs when one of the twins has the condition and the other does not.

In addition to understanding the role of genetics, mental health experts also consider the ways in which physical functioning can cause or aggravate the experience of psychological symptoms. Experts know that many medical conditions can cause a person to feel or act in ways that are abnormal. For example, a medical abnormality in the thyroid gland can cause wide variations in mood and emotionality. Brain damage resulting from a head trauma, even a slight one, can result in bizarre behavior and intense emotionality. Similarly, the use of drugs or alcohol can cause people to act in extreme ways that neither they nor those who know them well would have ever imagined. Even exposure to environmental stimuli, such as toxic substances or allergens, can cause people to experience disturbing emotional changes and to act in odd or bizarre ways. Several issues in this book explore conditions in which biology plays a prominent causative role. For example, attention deficit disorder (ADD) is regarded as a disorder of the brain that interferes with a person's ability to pay attention or to control behavior (see Issue 4).

Psychological Causes

Biology does not tell the entire story about the causes of mental disorders; many forms of emotional disturbance arise as a result of troubling life experiences. The experiences of life, even seemingly insignificant ones, can leave lasting marks on a person. In cases in which an experience involves trauma, such as rape or abuse, the impact can be emotionally disruptive throughout life, affecting a person's thoughts, behaviors, and even dreams.

In trying to understand the psychological causes of abnormality, social scientists and mental health clinicians consider a person's experiences. Not only do they focus on interpersonal interactions with other people that may have left a mark, but they also consider the inner life of the individual—thoughts and feelings that may cause distress or impairment. Some conditions arise from distorted perceptions and faulty ways of thinking. For example, highly sensitive people may misconstrue innocent comments by acquaintances that cause obsessional worry about being disliked or demeaned. As a result, these people may respond to their acquaintances in hostile ways that perpetuate interpersonal difficulties and inner distress.

For several of the issues in this book, psychological forces play a significant causative role. For example, Issue 3 considers the personality disturbances of people who have suffered traumatic life experiences and the controversies surrounding the possibility that trauma might be repressed or might cause the development of multiple personalities.

Sociocultural Causes

The term *sociocultural* refers to the various circles of social influence in the lives of people. The most immediate circle is composed of people with whom we interact in our immediate environment; for college students, this includes roommates, classmates, and coworkers. Moving beyond the immediate circle are people who inhabit the extended circle of relationships, such as family members back home or friends from high school. A third circle is composed of the people in our environments with whom we interact minimally and rarely by name, such as residents of our community or campus, whose standards, expectations, and behaviors influence our lives. A fourth circle is the much wider culture in which people live, such as American society.

Abnormal behavior can emerge from experiences in any of these social contexts. Troubled relationships with a roommate or family member can cause intense emotional distress. Involvement in an abusive relationship may initiate an interpersonal style in which the abused person becomes repeatedly caught up with people who are hurtful or damaging. Political turmoil, even on a relatively local level, can evoke emotions ranging from intense anxiety to incapacitating fear.

This book discusses several conditions in which sociocultural factors are significant. For example, Issue 2 focuses on the potential role of gender bias in the diagnosis of mental disorders. Other issues address the ways in which pornography may be responsible for the extent of violence against women (Issue 13) and the ways in which psychological testing may be rooted in racial bias and play a role in perpetuating discrimination (Issue 14).

The Biopsychosocial Perspective

From the discussion so far, it should be evident that most aspects of human behavior are determined by a complex of causes involving an interaction of biological, psychological, and sociocultural factors. As you read about the clinical conditions and mental disorders discussed in this book, it will be useful for you to keep the biopsychosocial perspective in mind, even in those discussions in which the authors seem narrowly focused. For example, a condition may be put forth as being biologically caused, leading the reader to believe that other influences play little or no role. Another condition may be presented as being so psychologically based that it is difficult to fathom the role that biology might play in causing or aggravating the condition. Other issues may be discussed almost exclusively in sociocultural terms, with minimal attention to the roles of biological and psychological factors. An intelligent discussion in the field of abnormal psychology is one that explores the relative importance of biological, psychological, and sociocultural influences. An intelligent discussion in the field of abnormal psychology is also one that avoids reductionistic thinking, in which simplistic explanations are offered for complex human problems.

Why We View Behavior As "Abnormal"

In addition to understanding how to define abnormality and what causes abnormal behavior, it is important to understand how members of society view people who are abnormal and how this view affects people with emotional problems and mental disorders. Many people in our society discriminate against and reject mentally disturbed people. In so doing, they aggravate one of the most profound aspects of dealing with mental disorder—the experience of stigma. A stigma is a label that causes certain people to be regarded as different and defective and to be set apart from mainstream members of society. Today, several decades after sociologist Erving Goffman brought the phenomenon of stigma to public attention, there is ample evidence in American society that people with mental disorders are regarded as different and are often deprived of the basic human right to respectful treatment.

It is common for people with serious psychological disorders, especially those who have been hospitalized, to experience profound and long-lasting emotional and social effects. People who suffer from serious psychological problems tend to think less of themselves because of these experiences, and they often come to believe many of the myths about themselves that are perpetuated in a society that lacks understanding about the nature of mental illness and psychological problems.

Although tremendous efforts have been undertaken to humanize the experiences of people with psychological problems and mental disorders, deeply rooted societal reactions still present obstacles for many emotionally distressed people. Controversies continue to rage about the systems of diagnosis and assessment used by mental health professionals, about the validity of certain clinical conditions, and about the efficacy of various psychotherapeutic and medical interventions. As you read both sides of the debates in this book, it is important that you keep in mind the strong personal beliefs that influence, and possibly bias, the statements of each writer and to consider the ways in which various societal forces are intertwined with the comments of the author.

The most powerful force within the field of mental health during the twentieth century was the medical model, upon which many forms of intervention are based. This book frequently mentions a system of diagnosis developed by the American Psychiatric Association that has been revised several times during the past 50 years. This system is published in a book called the *Diagnostic and Statistical Manual of Mental Disorders*. The most recent version is the fourth edition, which is commonly abbreviated *DSM-IV*. In this medical model diagnostic system, mental disorders are construed as diseases that require treatment. There are both advantages and disadvantages to this approach.

Not only does *DSM-IV* rely on the medical model, but it also uses a categorical approach. A categorical approach assumes that diseases fit into distinct categories. For example, the medical disease pneumonia is a condition that fits into the category of diseases involving the respiratory system. In corresponding fashion, conditions involving mood fit into the category of mood disorders, conditions involving anxiety fit into the category of anxiety disorders, and so on. However, as the authors of *DSM-IV* admit, there are limitations to the categorical approach. For one thing, psychological disorders are not neatly separable from each other or from normal functioning. For example, where is the dividing line between normal sadness and clinical depression? Furthermore, many disorders seem linked to each other in fundamental ways. In a state of agitated depression, for example, an individual suffers from both anxiety and saddened mood.

Several of the conditions and interventions discussed in this book have been debated for years. As you read about these issues, it will be helpful for you to keep in mind the context in which these debates have arisen. Some debates arise because of turf battles between professions. For example, psychiatrists may be more inclined to endorse the diagnostic system of the American Psychiatric Association (*DSM-IV*) and to support biological explanations and somatic interventions for mental disorders. Psychologists, on the other hand, may urge mental health professionals to take a broader point of view and to proceed more cautiously in turning to biological explanations and causes.

The Influence of Theoretical Perspective on the Choice of Intervention

Although impressive advances have been achieved in determining why people develop various mental disorders, understanding of how best to treat their conditions remains limited and also powerfully influenced by the ideological biases of many clinicians and researchers. For much of the twentieth century, various interventions emerged from markedly different schools of thought, each approach being tied to one of the three major realms—biological, psychological, or sociocultural. But how are biological, psychological, and sociocultural frameworks used in determining choice of intervention?

Within the biological perspective, disturbances in emotions, behavior, and cognitive processes are viewed as being caused by abnormalities in the functioning of the body, such as the brain and nervous system or the endocrine system. Treatments involve a range of somatic therapies, the most common of which is medication, the most extreme of which involves psychosurgery. Several issues in this book focus on debates about reliance on biological explanations and interventions, such as the issues on ADD (Issue 4), schizophrenia (Issue 5), psychosurgery (Issue 11), and electroconvulsive therapy (Issue 20).

The realm of psychological theories contains numerous approaches, although three schools of thought emerged as most prominent during the second half of the twentieth century: psychodynamic, humanistic, and behavioral. Proponents of the psychodynamic perspective emphasize unconscious determinants of behavior and recommend the use of techniques involving exploration of the developmental causes of behavior and the interpretation of unconscious influences on thoughts, feelings, and behavior. This is pertinent to the debate over repressed memories (Issue 7), which involves clinicians who believe that people are inclined to "forget" traumatic experiences in order to defend themselves from the disruptive anxiety they would otherwise experience.

At the core of the humanistic perspective is the belief that human motivation is based on an inherent tendency to strive for self-fulfillment and meaning in life. Humanistic therapists use a client-centered approach in which they strive to treat clients with unconditional positive regard and empathy. Mental health professionals are called upon to act in ways that are more client-centered as they deal with issues ranging from distress about sexual orientation (Issue 18) to matters involving a client's choice to end life due to a debilitating illness (Issue 17).

According to the behavioral perspective, abnormality is caused by faulty learning experiences, with a subset of behavioral theory focusing on cognitive functions, such as maladaptive thought processes. Because behaviorists and cognitive theorists believe that disturbance results from faulty learning or distorted thinking, intervention focuses on teaching clients more adaptive ways of thinking and behaving. Some of the discussions in this book focus on the ways in which behavioral and cognitive approaches might be preferable to medical approaches to conditions such as ADD (Issue 4) and distress related to sexual orientation (Issue 18).

Clinicians working within sociocultural models emphasize the ways that individuals are influenced by people, social institutions, and social forces. According to this viewpoint, psychological problems can emerge from social contexts ranging from the family to society. In a corresponding vein, treatments are determined by the nature of the group. Thus, problems rooted within family systems would be treated with family therapy; societal problems caused by discrimination or inadequate care of the mentally ill would be dealt with through enactment of social policy initiatives. Several issues in this volume touch upon sociocultural influences, such as those pertaining to the deinstitutionalization of the mentally ill (Issue 16), the effects of pornography (Issue 13), the impact of IQ testing on members of minority groups (Issue 14), and the extent to which society has encouraged the use of flimsy excuses for unacceptable behavior (Issue 19).

Keeping the Issues in Perspective

In evaluating the content of the writings in this book, it is important to keep in mind who the writers are and what their agendas might be. Most of the contributors are distinguished figures in the fields of mental health, ethics, and law. They are regarded as clear and influential thinkers who have important messages to convey. However, it would be naive to think that any writer, particularly when addressing a controversial topic, is free of bias.

It is best to read each issue with an understanding of the forces that might influence the development of a particular bias. For example, as physicians, psychiatrists have been trained in the medical model, with its focus on biological causes for problems and somatic interventions. Nonphysician mental health professionals may be more inclined to focus on interpersonal and intrapersonal causes and interventions. Lawyers and ethicists are more likely to be further removed from questions of etiology, focusing instead on what they believe is justified according to the law or right according to ethical standards.

As you read about the issues facing mental health clinicians and researchers, you are certain to be struck by the challenges that these professionals face. You may also be struck by the powerful emotion expressed by the authors who discuss their views on topics in this field. Because psychological stresses and problems are an inherent part of human existence, many discussions about abnormal psychology are emotionally charged. At some point in life, most people have a brush with serious emotional problems, either directly or indirectly. This is a frightening prospect for many people, one that engenders worried expectations and intense reactions. By acknowledging our vulnerability to disruptive emotional experiences, however, we can think about the ways in which we would want clinicians to treat us. As you read the issues in this book, place yourself in the position of an individual in the process of being assessed, diagnosed, and treated for an emotional difficulty or mental disorder.

Before you take a side in each debate, consider how the issue might be personally relevant to you at some point in life. You may be surprised to discover that you respond in different ways to issues that might have special salience to yourself, as opposed to random people somewhere else. By imagining yourself being personally affected by a professional's controversial opinion regarding one or more of the debates in this book, you will find yourself immersed in the discussions about issues for which there is no clear right or wrong.

On the Internet . . .   DUSHKIN ONLINE

DSM-IV Questions and Answers

At this site, the American Psychological Association provides questions and answers concerning the *DSM-IV.*

http://www.psych.org/clin_res/q_a.html

Teaching on Gender Issues

This paper, which was developed in collaboration with the Canadian Psychiatric Association Education Council and approved by the Canadian Psychiatric Association Board of Directors, discusses the importance of psychiatrists' recognizing gender differences when teaching about gender issues.

http://www.cpa-apc.org/pubs/papers/eguide32.htm

PART 1

Classification and Diagnosis

*I*n recent decades mental health experts have devoted considerable effort to developing a system for the classification and diagnosis of mental disorders. The system that is currently in use is called the Diagnostic and Statistical Manual of Mental Disorders, 4th ed. This comprehensive book, which provides a list and description of all mental disorders, has engendered considerable controversy, with some critics asserting that the system is seriously flawed and others contending that it contains biases, particularly about women.

- Is the *DSM-IV* a Useful Classification System?

- Is There Gender Bias in the *DSM-IV*?

ISSUE 1

Is the *DSM-IV* a Useful Classification System?

YES: Allen Frances, Michael B. First, and Harold Alan Pincus, from "DSM-IV: Its Value and Limitations," *Harvard Mental Health Letter* (June 1995)

NO: Herb Kutchins and Stuart A. Kirk, from "DSM-IV: Does Bigger and Newer Mean Better?" *Harvard Mental Health Letter* (May 1995)

ISSUE SUMMARY

YES: Psychiatrists Allen Frances, Michael B. First, and Harold Alan Pincus contend that although the *Diagnostic and Statistical Manual of Mental Disorders*, 4th ed. *(DSM-IV)* has certain limitations, it represents a vast improvement over previously used systems and incorporates the most up-to-date knowledge available.

NO: Professor of social work Herb Kutchins and professor of social welfare Stuart A. Kirk assert that the American Psychiatric Association's diagnostic system, particularly the current edition, *DSM-IV*, is so flawed that its utility should be seriously questioned.

When making a diagnosis, mental health professionals use standard terms and definitions, which are contained in the *Diagnostic and Statistical Manual of Mental Disorders (DSM)*. Since the publication of the first edition of this manual in 1952 by the American Psychiatric Association (APA), there have been several revisions: *DSM-II, DSM-III, DSM-III-R,* and *DSM-IV*. With each revision the authors of the *DSM* have tried to incorporate the most current knowledge about each mental disorder and have relied increasingly on empirical methods in their efforts to increase the reliability and validity of diagnostic labels.

For the first edition of the *DSM*, leading psychiatrists in the APA made the first systematic attempt to spell out diagnostic criteria for mental disorders. Although their efforts were well intentioned, mental health practitioners soon came to realize that these diagnostic criteria were vague and unreliable. The authors of the second edition, which was published in 1968, made an important change in the system when they based the system on the *International Classification of Diseases (ICD)*. Although the authors of the second edition made an effort to avoid theoretical bias, it soon became apparent that this system was actually based on psychoanalytic concepts. The publication of *DSM-III* in 1980 was heralded as a major improvement over its predecessors because this volume contained more precise rating criteria and better definitions for disorders. In 1987 the revision *DSM-III-R* was published as an interim manual until a more complete overhaul, *DSM-IV*, could be published in 1994.

Although the efforts of the APA to develop an efficient and reasonable diagnostic system might seem noncontroversial, each edition has provoked a storm of controversy and vehement debate. Certain issues have taken on the aura of political campaigns, with vocal activists lobbying on behalf of emotionally charged issues. For example, in 1980 the authors of *DSM-III* removed homosexuality from the list of psychological disorders, following 10 years of debate, with the realization that it was absurd to pathologize people on the basis of sexual orientation. In that same edition posttraumatic stress disorder was added in response to pressure from Vietnam veterans who urged mental health professionals to recognize the constellation of symptoms experienced by thousands of survivors of traumatic events, such as combat.

Allen Frances, Michael B. First, and Harold Alan Pincus are prominent psychiatrists who were centrally involved in the development of *DSM-IV*. In the following selection, they assert that the current version of the *DSM* consists of a clear and comprehensive summary of the most up-to-date knowledge available, which coincides with international classification systems for all medical disorders.

Herb Kutchins and Stuart A. Kirk are outspoken critics of the APA's diagnostic manuals. They view the *DSM* as a highly politicized money-making publication that is laden with problems of reliability and validity. In the second selection, Kutchins and Kirk assert that *DSM-IV* is complicated and imprecise and lacks a unified theoretical framework.

POINT

- *DSM-IV* provides a comprehensive summary of what is known about mental disorders, and it is simple and clear to use.
- Decisions about controversial diagnoses have been made by relying on open discussion and empirical data rather than mere opinion.
- *DSM-IV* relies on empirical data and represents an important advance from earlier editions.
- *DSM-IV* represents the most careful and comprehensive scientific analysis of diagnoses ever conducted.

COUNTERPOINT

- *DSM-IV* is an excessively complicated manual, it is too long, and it lacks important features needed to make the system user-friendly.
- Decisions about controversial diagnoses have been unduly influenced by political forces.
- *DSM-IV* lacks a consistent conceptual framework, with inadequate articulation of the underlying principles.
- Scientific standards pertaining to reliability and validity have been compromised in *DSM-IV*.

Allen Frances, Michael B. First,
and Harold Alan Pincus

 **YES**

DSM-IV: Its Value and Limitations

Our years of work on *DSM-IV* [*Diagnostic and Statistical Manual of Mental Disorders*, 4th ed.] have made us acutely aware of its imperfections, and we want to discuss them here. But first we will respond to the criticisms of [Herb] Kutchins and [Stuart A.] Kirk, which are superficial and easily refuted. They complain, first, that *DSM-IV* is too long and complex. It is longer than DSM-III-R] [a revised version of *DSM-III*], but that is because we have tried to provide a fuller summary of what is known about mental disorders. Psychiatric diagnosis is inherently complex. Our goal was not to make it simple but to make it clear, and we believe we have succeeded fairly well. The manual had to be long to serve its purpose; most readers use it as a reference and expect it to be detailed and authoritative. To meet their needs, we expanded the discussion of ways to distinguish a disorder from others that resemble it (differential diagnosis). We also added more information on variations associated with age, gender, and culture; on physical examinations and laboratory findings; and on common comorbid (accompanying) medical and psychiatric conditions.

Kutchins and Kirk say that *DSM-IV* lacks the support of a consistent conceptual framework or adequate scientific evidence. Here they offer two inconsistent complaints. While questioning the scientific credibility of *DSM-IV,* they long for the days when *DSM* was influenced by theoretical formulations that were not (and could not possibly be) based on empirical data. In fact, the field lacks a widely accepted overarching theory (or theories) confirmed by scientific data. But the preparation of *DSM-IV* benefitted from the impressive amount of data now available to inform diagnostic decisions.

The empirical review took place in three stages. In the first stage 150 work groups identified issues from the published literature on mental disorders, and each group laid out these issues for review by 50 to 100 experts. In the second stage 45 sets of data derived from earlier studies were reanalyzed to answer questions addressed inadequately in the published literature. In the final stage 12 focused field trials with new patients compared various ways of defining mental disorders for reliability and utility. All the issues and options under consideration were widely known to the research and clinical communities. A *DSM-IV* options book was published in 1991 to stimulate further suggestions and data. As Kutchins and Kirk note, we succeeded in avoiding angry contro-versies—not, as they imply, by some political maneuver, but by relying on open discussion and empirical data rather than mere opinion.

Carefully Done

Kutchins and Kirk incorrectly state that the DSM task force "barely men-tioned reliability." In fact, no more careful and comprehensive analysis of the reliability of psychiatric diagnoses has ever been conducted. In the fo-cused field trials more than 6,000 patients were evaluated at 70 sites by several hundred raters. Kutchins and Kirk have apparently confused these field trials, completed several years ago during the preparation of *DSM-IV,* with a different reliability project that is now under way. This project was never intended to influence the making of *DSM-IV*. Its aim is to develop a videotape library of diagnostic interviews so that the reliability of *DSM-IV* diagnoses can be evaluated consistently at various times and places through-out the world, in clinical practice as well as research settings. The project will attempt to determine how reliability is influenced by the identity of the clinician, the nature of the material presented, and the diagnostic criteria themselves. . . .

Kutchins and Kirk are also inaccurate in their account of the relationship between *DSM-IV* and ICD, the international classification of general medical disorders. *DSM-IV* is fully compatible, not only with the ICD-9-CM system now used in the United States, but also with the ICD-10 revision that will eventually be implemented. Compatibility with ICD-10 was in fact one of the require-ments we set for *DSM-IV*. The United States Government has now delayed the implementation of ICD-10 until well after the year 2000, mainly because it will be expensive to reprogram the medical records systems and analyze the impact of these changes on Medicare payments. Therefore we have worked hard to insure that all *DSM-IV* codes are valid under ICD-9-CM as well as ICD-10.

The genuine limitations of *DSM-IV* are less trivial than those inaccurately described by Kutchins and Kirk. We have discussed those limitations in great detail in earlier publications, in *DSM-IV* itself, and in the *DSM-IV Guidebook.* . . . We will summarize some of the most important points here.

First, the manual does not provide a definition that clearly distinguishes mental disorders from normality and that works in every clinical situation. The term "mental disorder," as opposed to "physical disorder," implies an anachro-nistic mind-body dualism, but we have persisted in using the term because we cannot find an adequate substitute. No definition adequately specifies the boundaries of this concept in all situations, but in that respect it resembles many other concepts in medicine and science. The definition of mental disor-der given in *DSM-IV* is not intended to determine which disorders should be included in the manual or where the line should be drawn between a mental disorder and a life problem.

Limited Understanding

DSM-IV is also inherently limited by its status as a descriptive system. It is not based on a deep understanding of mental disorders because in most cases we lack that understanding. Some *DSM-IV* diagnoses, such as dementia of the Alzheimer's type, are well enough understood to be called established diseases. A few other diagnoses have a causal rather than a purely descriptive basis: those that involve the direct physiological effect of a substance or medical condition (such as alcohol intoxication) and those that involve a reaction to stress (such as posttraumatic stress disorder). Still other diagnoses, such as the simple phobias, are no more than single symptoms.

But most disorders defined in *DSM-IV* are syndromes—symptoms that commonly occur together and are grouped in order to facilitate research, education, and treatment. The purpose is to identify patterns that share such features as degree of impairment, course of illness, family history, biological markers, comorbid disorders, and response to treatment. The predictive power of these associations makes a syndromal classification useful. Descriptive definitions of syndromes do not necessarily represent independent disease entities; they reflect the state of medical understanding at the time they are drafted, and require regular revision as that understanding evolves. Our aim is to define mental disorders in ways that correspond ever more closely to the underlying causes of pathology and targets of treatment. *DSM-IV* is an imperfect but indispensable tool for that purpose.

Another limitation of *DSM-IV* is inherent in the fact that, like all systems of medical diagnosis, it makes use of categories based on sets of criteria with defining features. This categorical approach to classification works best when all members of a class are nearly alike, the boundaries between classes are clear, and the different classes are mutually exclusive. But such categories necessarily impose artificial boundaries on a natural continuum, and some experts would prefer a dimensional model instead. Dimensional systems make use of features that can be measured quantitatively and work well in describing phenomena that are distributed continuously, without clear boundaries. This approach improves the reliability of diagnosis, and it preserves some information that is lost when everything must be classified in one category or another. But so far dimensional systems have not taken root in medicine, partly because dimensional descriptions are less vivid and familiar than categorical ones, and partly because there is no agreement on which dimensions to use. Dimensional approaches may become more widely accepted as we learn more about them.

Providing Guidance

DSM-IV should not be used as a book of recipes or taken as literally as some fundamentalists take the Bible. It is true that excessively flexible and idiosyncratic application of *DSM-IV* categories would reduce its usefulness as a common language for communication among professionals. But its classifications, criteria, and descriptions are meant to be used as guidelines, not applied mechanically. *DSM-IV* should be employed only by professionals with appropriate training and experience who are guided by clinical judgment. For example, a certain diagnosis may be justified even if not all the required symptoms are present, as long as the symptoms that are present are persistent and severe. Clinical judgment partially compensates for the lack of clear boundaries separating mental disorders from one another and from normality. It is often needed in deciding whether the patient's impairment or distress is sufficient to constitute a mental disorder, and to determine which *DSM-IV* category comes closest to describing the symptoms. Although the use of clinical judgment necessarily limits the reliability of diagnoses, there is no adequate alternative.

DSM-IV will often recommend multiple diagnoses for a single patient. Since the publication of *DSM-III* in 1980 new categories have repeatedly been introduced, old ones have been divided up, and criteria that exclude diagnoses have been removed. Thus many patients now meet the criteria for more than one mental disorder. This development is not objectionable as long as it is clearly understood that the diagnoses are tools for communication and research, not necessarily descriptions of independent disease entities or pathological processes. When a patient meets criteria for more than one diagnosis, they may be related in any of the following ways:

1. Condition A causes or predisposes to condition B;
2. Condition B causes or predisposes to condition A;
3. An underlying condition C causes or predisposes to both condition A and condition B;
4. Conditions A and B are part of a more complex unified syndrome that is yet to be defined;
5. Conditions A and B seem to occur together often because their definitions overlap;
6. Condition A and condition B often occur together by chance, because both are common.

The flaws in *DSM-IV* reflect the limitations of our present scientific knowledge about mental health and illness. The manual will eventually be superseded as new knowledge is acquired through the powerful tools of neuroscience and clinical research. *DSM-IV* may appear somewhat quaint and primitive once we understand more deeply the nature and causes of psychiatric disorders, but it will have fulfilled its intended function by facilitating the growth of that understanding.

DSM-IV: Does Bigger and Newer Mean Better?

The *Diagnostic and Statistical Manual of Mental Disorders,* Fourth Edition (*DSM-IV*) is the 1994 revision of a dull, complex, technical compendium of psychiatric conditions compiled by the American Psychiatric Association (APA). It contains no major discoveries or innovations, no basically new approach to mental illness. In fact, the APA has made every effort to avoid controversial departures from current psychiatric practice. Yet the publication of this manual was a major news event reported on the front page of *The New York Times.* To understand what is happening, we must look at the historical context.

Consistent, credible diagnosis has always been a problem in the field of mental health, and the APA published the first edition of *DSM* in 1952 in order to standardize psychiatric nomenclature. In 1968 it published a revision of the manual, *DSM-II,* that was designed to conform with the system used in the International Classification of Diseases (ICD). This was necessary because of an international agreement to use ICD as the official reporting system for all illnesses.

Everyone was dissatisfied with *DSM-II.* Few clinicians used it to plan treatment, and many researchers doubted its scientific value. In fact, the basic credibility of psychiatric diagnosis was under attack. In one study of state hospital patients, schizophrenia was found to have been substantially overreported. When outside experts evaluated the patients, many were rediagnosed as suffering from mood disorders. In another experiment a psychologist arranged to have sane people committed to a mental hospital by faking a single symptom. Once hospitalized, they dropped even that pretense without being unmasked by staff members (although other patients recognized the deception).

The APA soon had to confront a series of critics who complained that diagnostic decisions in *DSM* were influenced by political considerations. Gay activists objected to listing homosexuality as a mental illness, and in 1973 the APA decided to drop it from *DSM-II.* The decision was challenged and ultimately confirmed by a referendum of the membership in 1974. Meanwhile, Vietnam veterans were demonstrating for the adoption of the diagnosis of posttraumatic stress disorder so that they could qualify for psychiatric benefits. They finally succeeded with the publication of *DSM-III.* The irony was that in the very act of remedying two genuine grievances, the APA confirmed the charges of political influence on the formulation of diagnoses.

Getting Specific

In order to improve the scientific and professional value of the manual, a task force began work on a revision in the mid-'70s. When the new edition, *DSM-III*, was published in 1980 it contained a number of important new features. A major innovation was the introduction of specific criteria for each diagnosis instead of brief, vague descriptions. Another innovation was a multiaxial system consisting of five dimensions. Diagnosticians were asked to record clinical conditions (Axis I), personality and developmental disorders (Axis II), medical conditions (Axis III), the severity of psychosocial stressors (Axis IV), and the patient's highest level of adaptive functioning (Axis V). The editors of *DSM-III* also made an effort to confirm the reliability of psychiatric diagnoses. If a classification system is to be useful for clinical or research purposes, different clinicians must be able to agree on the diagnosis of a given patient. The *DSM-III* task force claimed that most of its diagnoses were highly reliable, although the evidence for this claim is questionable.

The new edition was heralded as a revolution in mental health practice and a "paradigm shift" in psychiatric thinking. Despite its size, complexity, and high price, it was an astonishing success—partly because insurance companies and government agencies that had become major sources of financing for mental health services demanded use of its diagnostic system.

Only three years after the publication of *DSM-III*, the APA initiated what was at first described as a minor revision that would rectify mistakes and incorporate new research findings. When the revision was published as *DSM-III-R* in 1987, it retained the basic design of *DSM-III*, but there were changes in more than half of the diagnoses, and no studies of the overall reliability of the new manual. The rush to revise the text aborted efforts of independent investigators to evaluate the usefulness of *DSM-III* in clinical practice, since research on the older version was now moot and an evaluation of *DSM-III-R* would be premature.

Meanwhile a new series of embarrassing public confrontations occurred, this time with feminists who objected to the inclusion of three new diagnoses: self-defeating personality disorder, paraphiliac rapism (later replaced by sadistic personality disorder), and what is now called premenstrual dysphoric disorder (PDD). Although the developers of the manual insisted that the new diagnoses had a scientific basis, they placed them in an appendix labeled "Needing Further Study." (Two of the diagnoses have been dropped from *DSM-IV* because of insufficient scientific evidence; PDD is still reserved for further study.)

After the publication of *DSM-III-R*, the APA almost immediately started work on the present edition, and Allen Frances, who was appointed to oversee the revision process, announced that the publication of *DSM-III-R* had been a mistake. The APA says that the newest edition, *DSM-IV*, is easier to use than older ones, but the claim is difficult to justify. *DSM-IV* is a volume of more than 900 pages, 50% longer than *DSM-III-R*, yet it adds only 13 new diagnoses and eliminates eight old ones. It no longer includes the index of symptoms that allowed users of *DSM-III-R* to move quickly from clinical observations to diagnoses. An appendix comparing *DSM-IV* to *DSM-III-R* is far less clear and precise than similar appendices in previous revisions. An appendix reviewing the mental disorders listed in the International Classification of Diseases has been dropped; this will make it more difficult to translate diagnoses between the two systems.

Confusing the Issue

The instructions for use of *DSM-IV* are often excessively complicated. For example, the chapter on substance-related disorders has been lengthened from 62 to 98 pages, and these disorders are also included in other parts of the manual. The change necessitates a time-consuming hunt for the appropriate diagnosis, and it may heighten disagreement among clinicians, thereby reducing reliability. A similar problem exists with respect to mental disorders that result from general medical conditions. These were previously called "organic," but the editors of the manual did not want to imply that other psychiatric disorders lacked an organic basis. They dropped the term "organic" and dispersed many of the medically-related conditions to various parts of the manual. This reorganization only complicates the task of locating these disorders; it does not resolve the underlying conceptual issue.

Its developers regard the new manual as more "user-friendly" mainly because they have simplified the operational criteria (the long lists of symptoms used to identify each disorder), and the use of the multiaxial system is no longer required. Certain criteria have been eliminated and instructions for applying the criteria have sometimes been simplified, although many other procedures have been made more complicated. But *DSM-IV* has also relaxed the rules to allow greater individual discretion. Users are told that they may employ clinical judgment to make a diagnosis even when the criteria have not been fully satisfied. Sacrificing precision in this way may seem convenient to some clinicians, but in the long run it could lead to lower reliability and sloppier practice. It would be a mistake to return to the days when there were no clear standards for psychiatric diagnoses. Although the manual should not be used mechanically, winking at the diagnostic criteria and ignoring the multiaxial system are not good alternatives.

Making Changes

The developers of *DSM-IV* acknowledged that many diagnoses in older versions lacked adequate scientific support, and they announced that extensive research would go into the revision. They now argue that the new manual has a more solid scientific basis than any previous one. Certainly more researchers and investigations have been involved; the names of more than 1,000 contributors occupy 26 pages of the manual. But all that activity does not necessarily guarantee scientific credibility. One fundamental deficiency of the manual is the lack of a consistent conceptual framework. *DSM-I* was strongly influenced by Freudian theories, and it described psychiatric disorders as reactions—schizophrenic reactions, affective reactions, psychoneurotic reactions, and so on. Although the scheme was not entirely consistent, it was at least related to a set of theoretical assumptions.

In later editions *DSM* has moved increasingly away from psychoanalytical thinking. The terms "reaction" and later, "neurosis" have been dropped, and the medical aspects of diagnosis have been increasingly emphasized. *DSM-IV* continues this trend, but underlying principles are not adequately articulated, and the resulting hodgepodge lacks a consistent rationale. Three hundred diagnoses, a larger number than ever before, are divided into 16 categories. Some of these categories are based on the presumed cause of the disorder, some on shared symptoms, and some on the patient's age. There is no consistent rationale for placing a disorder in one category rather than another.

Standards of reliability also continue to be a problem. Although reliability was the main scientific concern in developing *DSM-III,* the DSM-IV Task Force barely mentioned it when their work began. The APA belatedly proposed reliability trials for only 10 diagnoses. This research, which is now in progress, has been criticized because it is inadequate to test the overall reliability of the manual in everyday practice. Even if it does produce useful data, it obviously cannot affect *DSM-IV.* The approach appears to be one suggested in *Alice in Wonderland*—"sentence first, verdict afterward."

Another basic concern is the standard for evaluating the validity of diagnoses. The APA announced that new diagnoses had to meet more rigorous scientific tests for inclusion in *DSM-IV.* But most of the diagnoses have been carried over from earlier editions, and the APA admits that many of them do not meet the new standards. As a result, we cannot be sure which diagnoses have a solid scientific basis.

Because of the disruption that revisions of *DSM* cause in research and practice, and because of all the unsettled questions about the new revision, many professionals complained that the release of *DSM-IV* was premature. In response to critics who said that *DSM-IV* was rushed to publication, the APA repeatedly claimed that it had to publish a new edition to conform to the 1992 revision of the International Classification of Diseases, ICD-10. But ICD-10 has not yet been adopted by the United States. The latest estimate is that this will not happen until 2003. *DSM-IV,* like *DSM-III-R,* is keyed to ICD-9-CM. ICD-10 uses a very different coding system, and an appendix to *DSM-IV* covers some of the ICD-10 codes. When ICD-10 is recognized in this country, users will have to consult the main body of *DSM-IV* for a diagnosis before turning to that appendix. Even this cumbersome, confusing procedure does not entirely solve the problem. There are hundreds of directions that involve the use of ICD-9-CM throughout *DSM-IV,* and instructions about ICD-10 are incomplete and inadequate. Thus the manual will be obsolete when ICD-10 is adopted. Clinicians might have to abandon *DSM-IV* entirely and rely on ICD-10—unless the APA decides to publish another revision of *DSM.*

The APA manuals, so far, are a great success story, but we might consider the lesson of another such story, the triumph of the American automobile. After World War II Detroit seemed to have found the secret of unlimited sales by making each model bigger and more streamlined, with more accessories than the previous one. But the bigger cars were more expensive and harder to operate; they broke down more easily, consumed more energy and created more pollution. When American automakers ignored these problems, consumers stopped buying their cars.

DSM-IV is not only bigger than ever but has its own set of accessories—a "library" that includes a casebook, five projected volumes of research reports, several volumes describing clinical interviewing techniques, a study guide, a glossary, a computerized version of the manual, and more. We doubt that the road to continued success for psychiatry is a series of manuals, each in a new color coordinated with accessories, each bigger than the last, and each with built-in obsolescence that insures demand for the next model. Unless the APA confronts the issues discussed here, *DSM* may be cruising toward the same junkyard as the great fishtailed, portholed, chrome-grilled dinosaurs that were once regarded as the pinnacle of American ingenuity.

CHALLENGE QUESTIONS

Is the *DSM-IV* a Useful Classification System?

1. To what extent should the authors of the next edition of the *DSM* be concerned with vehemently expressed opinions about particular diagnostic labels?
2. What role does a diagnostic system such as that in *DSM-IV* play in the stigmatization of mental illness?
3. Compare the description of a particular diagnosis (e.g., schizophrenia) in an earlier *DSM* with the *DSM-IV* diagnostic criteria for that disorder. How would you characterize the changes that have been made in terms of clarity and usefulness?
4. To what extent does the linking between mental disorders and the *International Classification of Diseases* "medicalize" emotional problems?
5. What issues would you urge the American Psychiatric Association to consider as work is begun on *DSM-V*?

Suggested Readings

Barron, J. W. (Ed.) (1998). *Making diagnosis meaningful: Enhancing evaluation and treatment of psychological disorders.* Washington, DC: American Psychological Association.

Kutchins, H., & Kirk, S. A. (1997). *Making us crazy. DSM: The psychiatric bible and the creation of mental disorders.* New York, NY: The Free Press.

Sarbin, T. R. (1997). On the futility of psychiatric diagnostic manuals (DSMs) and the return of personal agency. *Applied & Preventative Psychology, 6,* 233–243.

Thakkar, J., & Ward, T. (1998). Culture and classification: The cross-cultural application of the DSM-IV. *Clinical Psychology Review, 18*(5), 501–529.

Tucker, G. J. (1998). Putting DSM-IV in perspective. *American Journal of Psychiatry, 155*(2), 159–161.

ISSUE 2

Is There Gender Bias in the *DSM-IV*?

YES: Terry A. Kupers, from "The Politics of Psychiatry: Gender and Sexual Preference in DSM-IV," in Mary Roth Walsh, ed., *Women, Men, and Gender: Ongoing Debates* (Yale University Press, 1997)

NO: Ruth Ross, Allen Frances, and Thomas A. Widiger, from "Gender Issues in DSM-IV," in Mary Roth Walsh, ed., *Women, Men, and Gender: Ongoing Debates* (Yale University Press, 1997)

ISSUE SUMMARY

YES: Forensic psychiatric consultant Terry A. Kupers asserts that several phenomena pertaining to gender and sexuality are pathologized in the diagnostic system of the *Diagnostic and Statistical Manual of Mental Disorders,* 4th ed. *(DSM-IV).*

NO: Ruth Ross, Allen Frances, and Thomas A. Widiger, coeditors of the American Psychiatric Association's *DSM-IV Sourcebook,* disagree with the notion of bias associated with gender and sexuality.

$\mathbf{D}$uring the last few decades of the twentieth century, Americans have become acutely aware of ways in which discrimination and bias pertaining to gender and sexuality have influenced culture. Much has been written about the ways in which societal disadvantages experienced by women have been emotionally costly. Some contend that it should come as no surprise that women are more likely than men to be diagnosed with mental disorders and are also more likely to seek professional help for their psychological problems. However, the issues of psychiatric diagnosis and help-seeking behavior are multifaceted, and sometimes they involve subtle bias.

Researchers and clinicians have been particularly interested in understanding the reasons why women are more likely than men to be assigned particular diagnoses, such as mood and personality disorders. Some experts have questioned whether or not there is a gender bias that results in feminine personality characteristics being perceived as pathological. Take the case of dependent personality disorder, a diagnosis with characteristics involving an excessive need to be taken care of, which leads to submissive, clinging behaviors and feelings of insecurity. Some theorists contend that women have been socialized to yield control to men and to develop a style of dependency. At some other point along the continuum of dependency, such behavior can be labeled as pathological, and the dependent individual is assigned the diagnosis of a personality disorder.

Terry A. Kupers argues in the following selection that the field of psychiatry has been influenced in overt and covert ways such that various political causes have been advanced, with the result being that society's concept of mental health, as well as categories of mental disorder, have been socially constructed. In other words, people in positions of power (in the case of psychiatry, mostly men) determine what constitutes mental disorder among those over whom they have power. For example, Kupers notes that just when middle-class women are entering the workplace in record numbers, increasing attention is being given to the emotionally charged label "premenstrual syndrome." According to Kupers, those in power can pathologize just about any characteristic noted among those who are not in power. Thus, excessive emotionality in women can be characterized as pathological, and so can excessive assertiveness.

In the second selection, Ruth Ross, Allen Frances, and Thomas A. Widiger acknowledge that a number of psychiatric disorders have markedly different rates of occurrence in women and men, but they are uncertain about whether these differences are actual or attributable to various biases. They note that a disorder such as dependent personality disorder involves stereotypical feminine traits, which could be mislabeled as personality disorder in a biased system, but they assert that the diagnosis actually involves maladaptive variants of these stereotypic feminine traits. Ross and her colleagues argue that the *DSM-IV* development process was characterized by serious attempts to base decisions on a fair and balanced interpretation of the available data pertaining to gender issues in diagnosis.

POINT

- The *DSM-IV* categories of mental disorder are socially constructed by people in power who determine what constitutes mental disorder in those over whom they have power.
- *DSM-IV* pathologizes normal phenomena found in women (e.g., menstrual cycles) while ignoring male characteristics that could just as easily be pathologized.
- The authors of *DSM-IV* yielded to pressures from feminist psychiatrists and psychologists who argued that certain diagnoses stigmatized and blamed victims of domestic abuse.
- Gender differences in the diagnosis of many conditions are well established and reflect diagnostic biases.

COUNTERPOINT

- The *DSM-IV* development process involved serious attempts to base decisions on fair and balanced interpretations of available data on gender-related issues in diagnosis.
- *DSM-IV* cautions against the imposition of gender-biased assumptions, especially when diagnosing personality disorders.
- The authors of *DSM-IV* relied on a thorough empirical study of controversial diagnoses (e.g., self-defeating personality disorder) before making a determination to drop these labels.
- There is no reason to believe that the appearance of given disorders should be spread equally between genders.

15

Terry A. Kupers

YES

The Politics of Psychiatry: Gender and Sexual Preference in DSM-IV

The fourth edition of the *Diagnostic and Statistical Manual of Mental Disorders* (DSM-IV), published by the American Psychiatric Association (APA) in 1994, contains the official list of diagnostic categories. It is touted as an improvement over previous editions, more precise in its descriptions of mental disorders, more rigorous in its criteria for establishing diagnoses. There is some effort to take gender and sexual orientation into consideration, as well as race and ethnicity. And there are claims of greater objectivity on account of the improvements, the detail, and the attention to cultural contexts. But is the new edition really an improvement, or merely a more rigorous rationalization for pathologizing nonmainstream behaviors and attitudes? And how successful have the authors been in transcending past gender biases? A meaningful discussion of these questions requires reading between the lines as well as attending to the social and historical context.

A Longer, More Detailed List of Diagnostic Categories

The first thing to note about the DSM-IV is its size, 886 pages. DSM-I (APA, 1952) contained 130 pages; DSM-II (APA, 1968) contained 134 pages; DSM-III (APA, 1980) contained 481 pages. (A revised DSM-III, DSM-III-R, was published in 1987, but I will leave it out of this summary for simplicity's sake.) In each edition there are new disorders, new groupings of disorders, some deletions, and various revisions in the way well-established disorders are viewed.

For instance, with the publication of the third edition in 1980, Panic Disorder, Post-traumatic Stress Disorder, Social Phobia, and Agoraphobia were added. The last two diagnoses had been lumped under the category Phobias in DSM-II; in DSM-III they, along with Panic Disorder and PTSD, became subtypes of the group of Anxiety Disorders. And with the publication of DSM-III some names were changed, for instance Manic-Depressive Disorder (DSM-II) became Bipolar Disorder (DSM-III); and some categories were dropped, notably homosexuality.

From Terry A. Kupers, "The Politics of Psychiatry: Gender and Sexual Preference in DSM-IV," in Mary Roth Walsh, ed., *Women, Men, and Gender: Ongoing Debates* (Yale University Press, 1997), pp. 340–347. Originally published in *masculinities*, vol. 3, no. 2 (1995). Copyright © 1995 by *masculinities*. Reprinted by permission.

Again, in DSM-IV, there are new categories (Substance-Induced Anxiety Disorder, Sibling Relational Problem, Physical and Sexual Abuse of Adult); there are name changes (Multiple Personality Disorder becomes Dissociative Identity Disorder); there are new groupings (Gender Identity Disorders subsumes what used to be three groupings: Gender Identity Disorder of Childhood, of Adolescence, and of Adulthood); and there are deletions (Passive-aggressive Personality Disorder, Transsexualism). Relatively few new categories were added to DSM-IV, the emphasis being on more detail in the descriptions, presumably to increase inter-rater reliability. And the fourth edition makes the diagnostic categories relatively less exclusive so that one does not need to be as careful to rule out one category in order to pin down the diagnosis of another. Consequently a given individual is more likely to be assigned two or more "comorbid" diagnoses, for instance Obsessive Compulsive Disorder with Depression or with Alcohol Dependence.

Two Explanations for a Longer, More Detailed DSM

Why has the DSM grown thicker, the list of disorders longer? There are two basic explanations, one built upon a positivist notion of scientific progress, the other on the notion that our concepts of mental health and mental disorder are socially and historically constructed.

According to the positivist model, which underlies the stance of orthodox psychiatry and rationalizes its current turn toward biologism (for a critique see Cohen, 1993), advancing technology, and newer research findings permit us to discover mental disorders which always existed, but went undetected until now because our understanding of the brain and mental functioning was not as sophisticated as it is today. Joel Kovel (1980) says it well: "Psychiatry's self-image (is) of a medical profession whose growth is a matter of increasing mastery over a phenomenon, mental illness, which is supposed to be always present, a part of nature passively awaiting the controlling hand of science" (p. 72). The emphasis in DSM-IV on extensive reviews of clinical and research literatures and the conduct of field trials with revised diagnostic categories reflect this assumption. The goal is to see how much consistency can be achieved among diagnosticians.

Then there is the rush to develop "Treatment Guidelines," keyed to DSM-IV categories. For instance, the APA recently released its "Practice Guidelines for the Treatment of Patients with Bipolar Disorder" (APA, 1994b). Treatment guidelines provide medical centers and third-party payers with a rationale for allowing some benefits and disallowing others. Thus scientific truth is defined in terms of consensus among certain clinicians, mainly psychiatrists who have clout in the APA, about the proper diagnosis and treatment of each disorder.

Confident that their opinions about the existence of mental disorders constitute a science that is advancing rapidly and unfalteringly, psychiatrists and their collaborators are not very likely to uncover the biases and social interests that determine the path of their scientific endeavors, for instance the fact that a significant part of their research is funded by pharmaceutical companies that would like very much to see them identify mental disorders for which the treatment of choice is a pharmaceutical agent.

The social/historical model holds that "the disorder and the remedy are both parts of the same social process, and that they form a unity subject to the total history of the society in which they take place" (Kovel, 1980, p. 72). Our concept of mental health as well as our categories of mental disorder are socially constructed, and people in power determine what constitutes mental disorder among those they have power over (Conrad, 1980; Foucault, 1965). Jean Baker Miller (1976), building on [G. W. F.] Hegel's Master/Slave dialectic, points out that in the interest of continuing domination, the dominant group is the model for "normal human relationships" while the subordinate group is viewed as inferior in one way or another (Blacks are intellectually inferior, women are "ruled by emotion"). Thomas and Sillen (1974) point out that slaves who ran away from their owners' plantations in the antebellum South received the diagnosis "drapetomania," literally, "flight-from-home madness" (p. 2).

Elizabeth Packard's husband declared in 1860 that her disagreement with his religious views was evidence of insanity; and because the laws of Illinois as well as the male asylum psychiatrist were on his side, he was able to have her locked in an asylum (Chesler, 1972). Hughes (1990) uncovers some of the gender biases in the testimony of families who had a member admitted to an asylum in late nineteenth-century Alabama. To skip to the present, it is merely coincidental that just when middle-class women are entering the workplace in record numbers, premenstrual syndrome is declared a form of mental disorder?

Social theory provides two related answers to the question of why the DSM grows longer and more detailed in successive editions. First, the growth of the mental health industry depends on the expansion of the list of diagnostic categories. The number of psychiatrists, psychologists, and psychotherapists has grown considerably in recent years, as has the variety of psychotropic medications. As clinicians examine and treat a larger proportion of the citizenry, more diagnoses are needed to justify the whole endeavor. I will return to this point in the section on childhood disorders.

Second, our consciousness and everyday lives have become increasingly regimented and administered over the past century, and as a result the average citizen is permitted fewer eccentricities before deviance is declared. The Industrial Revolution required a disciplined workforce capable of sufficient delayed gratification to endure long hours at hard labor for less than fair wages. Those who could not work had to be marginalized as criminals, beggars, or lunatics. This was the period when great leaps were made in the description of such psychotic conditions as dementia praecox, later to be renamed schizophrenia. Since the explosive growth of consumerism in the 1920s, newer, milder diagnoses are needed for those who are capable of working, who buy into the promise of ad campaigns that the purchase of one commodity after another will lead to happiness, and yet are unable to attain the kind of happiness portrayed in advertisements and films. The successful but still unhappy people must be neurotic; perhaps they need psychoanalysis, psychotherapy, a tranquilizer, or an antidepressant.

While the positivist model directs our attention toward the gathering of ever more empirical data analyses, the social/historical model permits us to understand the way social interests determine our views on psychopathology as well as our views on what constitutes scientific progress.

About Homosexuality

The debate about homosexuality in the late 1960s and early 1970s included mass demonstrations at annual meetings of the APA. The straight male leadership was forced to back down, voting in 1973 to delete the category of homosexuality from the official list of mental disorders. The change was reflected in the next edition, DSM-III, in 1980.

But the stigmatization did not end there. The official list of mental disorders is merely the tip of the iceberg when it comes to pathologizing. Psychoanalysts and psychotherapists pathologize constantly, deciding, for instance, when to intervene in the patient's story and make an interpretation. There is the decision to interpret something and not to interpret something else, and the clinician's views about normalcy and pathology determine her or his choices. In the 1920s, analysts repeatedly interpreted penis envy in women (for a summary of psychoanalytic views on gender, see Connell, 1994). Why did they not choose instead to interpret the pathology in men's defensive need to exclude women from the halls of power? In the 1960s, analysts interpreted the radical activism of young adults as a sign of psychopathology. Why did they not interpret the inactivism of others (including themselves) in the face of great social upheavals (Kupers, 1993b)?

I do not believe there is anything inherently wrong with pathologizing certain human characteristics. Sedgwick (1982) argues convincingly that the attempt by libertarians and radical therapists in the sixties to get rid of the entire concept of mental illness was misguided at best. The question is which human traits shall be pathologized. Throughout the history of the mental health professions, why has homosexuality consistently been the target for pathologizing while homophobia has never appeared among the list of mental disorders? The unstated biases reflected in these choices do not disappear just because one category of mental disorder is deleted.

Still, in the struggle to transcend homophobia, it is a positive development when homosexuality is removed from the list of mental disorders. In its place, in DSM-III (1980), a new category was added, Ego-Dystonic Homosexuality, designed for gays and lesbians who would prefer to be straight but were having trouble converting their desires. Since this category became, in practice, a substitute for the category of homosexuality, its deletion in DSM-IV is another positive step—likely motivated by the presence of more women and gays on the task force and work groups that developed DSM-IV. The APA even calls for all professional organizations and individuals "to do all that is possible to decrease the stigma related to homosexuality" (APA, 1993, p. 686).

But the pathologization of homosexuality remains. Consider this state-ment, made two years after the APA decided to stop diagnosing homosexuality, by Otto Kernberg (1975), a prominent psychoanalyst:

> We may classify male homosexuality along a continuum that differentiates the degree of severity of pathology of internalized object relations. First, there are cases of homosexuality with a predominance of genital, oedipal factors, in which the homosexual relation reflects a sexual submission to the parent of the same sex as a defense against oedipal rivalry.... In a second and more severe type, the male homosexual has a conflictual identification with an image of his mother and treats his homosexual objects as a representa-tion of his own infantile self.... In a third type of homosexual relation, the homosexual partner is "loved" as an extension of the patient's own pathological grandiose self.... This, the most severe type of homosexual in-volvement, is characteristic of homosexuality in the context of narcissistic personality structure proper, and constitutes the prognostically most severe type of homosexuality. (pp. 328–29)

I am not aware of any disclaimer of this formulation by Kernberg, who is listed as an adviser to the authors of DSM-IV. Even though the diagnosis of homosexuality is no longer officially sanctioned, a clinician, following Kern-berg and other prominent experts, might assign a gay man the DSM-IV diag-noses Gender Identity Disorder, Sexually Attracted to Males (APA, 1994a, p. 534) with Narcissistic Personality; or Transvestic Fetishism (p. 530) with Narcissis-tic Personality Disorder; and other clinicians would get the point. There is also continuing debate about whether the goal in treating homosexuals should be conversion to heterosexuality (Socarides, Kaufman, Gottlieb, & Isay, 1994). In other words, long after the category is removed from the official list and the APA advocates destigmatization, prominent clinicians continue to pathologize ho-mosexuality while showing no interest in creating a category for homophobia.

Women's Disorders

Women have evolved a strong voice within establishment psychiatry. The list of contributors to DSM-II (1968) contains the names of thirty-seven men and three women, whereas the equivalent list for DSM-IV (1994a) contains the names of twenty-six men and eleven women. (It is not as easy to determine how many gays and lesbians were involved.) As a result, there were rancorous debates about the pathologization of women's experiences and characteristics prior to the publication of DSM-IV. Two proposed diagnostic categories were at is-sue: "Self-defeating Personality" (for women who find themselves repeatedly victimized by abusive men) and "Late Luteal Phase Dysphoric Disorder" (the luteal phase of the menstrual cycle begins at ovulation and ends at menses, and this diagnosis is synonymous with PMS). Feminist psychiatrists and psycholo-gists argued that the former diagnosis stigmatized and blamed the victims of domestic abuse (Caplan, 1987). They prevailed: Self-defeating Personality was not included in DSM-IV. Meanwhile the categories Sexual Abuse of Adult (APA, 1994a, p. 682) and Physical Abuse of Adult (p. 682) were added to the official list, permitting the clinician to diagnose pathology in the perpetrator.

In regard to Late Luteal Phase Dysphoric Disorder, the question was why pathologize the woman's natural cycles? Why not pathologize instead men's need to avoid all signs of emotion and dependency while maintaining an obsessively steady pace (Spitzer et al., 1989)? I coined the term "pathological arrhythmicity" for this disorder in men (Kupers, 1993a). The debate about PMS was not as intense as the one about Self-defeating Personality. Some women clinicians claimed that a category for PMS might serve to increase sensitivity among male colleagues to the experiences of women. The debate ended in compromise: Premenstrual Dysphoric Disorder is included in an appendix of DSM-IV designated " . . . For Further Study."

But remember, the official manual is merely the tip of the iceberg when it comes to pathologizing. Penis envy was never an official diagnostic category, yet it was frequently diagnosed. Phyllis Chesler (1972) explains how the diagnosis of Hysteria in women has served to maintain their subordination: "Both psychotherapy and marriage enable women to express and defuse their anger by experiencing it as a form of emotional illness, by translating it into hysterical symptoms: frigidity, chronic depression, phobias, and the like" (p. 122). Hysteria is a rare diagnosis today, and women are more likely diagnosed Borderline Character Disorder, Multiple Personality Disorder (there is intense debate about the existence of this disorder, connected with the debate about "recovered memories" of childhood molestation), or Somatization Disorder. Judith Herman (1992) points out that among women assigned these modern diagnostic substitutes for hysteria are a significant number who were molested as girls, but these diagnoses divert attention away from the early traumas and focus the clinician's attention instead on the woman's personal flaws. She proposes that instead of diagnosing Borderline Character Disorder and Somatization Disorder in so many women today, we consider the diagnosis "Complex Post-traumatic Stress Disorder," the residual condition resulting from repeated childhood sexual and physical abuse. Thus far Complex PTSD has not made its way into the DSM.

Another relevant critique of the way women's characteristics are selectively pathologized comes from the staff of the Stone Center at Wellesley College (Jordan, Kaplan, Miller, Stiver, & Surrey, 1991). They believe that this culture's overvaluation of autonomy and independence leaves something to be desired in terms of community and the capacity to be intimate, and that a very male notion of independence and autonomy is at the core of traditional clinical descriptions of psychopathology. Women are pathologized because of their emphasis on connection and interdependence. They call for a redrawing of the line between psychopathology and mental health so that women's need for connection and community will be viewed as an admirable trait rather than a symptom.

The APA has not heeded this group's call. The category Dependent Personality Disorder remains in DSM-IV and is assigned disproportionately to women, while no equivalent category has been devised to describe the male dread of intimacy and dependency. The description of Dependent Personality Disorder contains the very bias that clinicians from the Stone Center are concerned about. Consider this sentence: "Individuals with this disorder have difficulty initiating projects or doing things independently" (APA, 1994a, p. 666). Often there is a choice between two contrasting ways to handle problems at work: one way being for the individual to come up with a totally independent solution and get credit for doing so at promotion time; another being for several coworkers to brainstorm, work together to figure out a solution collectively, and share the credit. It is as if official psychiatry has decided that individual action is preferred and the search for collaborative solutions (more usual for women workers in today's corporate culture) is pathological. Thus, in spite of improvements in DSM-IV regarding gender bias, many problems remain.

What About the Men?

I have already mentioned several diagnoses that might be included in a DSM but are not: homophobia, "pathological arrhythmicity," and the dread of dependency. There are other male behaviors we might wish to pathologize: dependence on pornography, workaholism, friendlessness, the need for sexual conquests, the tendency to react to aging by deserting one's same-age female partner and taking up with someone the age of one's children, and so forth.

There is a brief and very telling statement about the gender distribution of each mental disorder in DSM-IV. Disorders diagnosed more frequently in males include Conduct Disorder in boys and adolescents, Obsessive-Compulsive Personality Disorder (distinct from Obsessive-Compulsive Disorder, or OCD, which is distributed equally between the sexes), Narcissistic Personality Disorder, Paraphilias, Antisocial Personality Disorder, Intermittent Explosive Disorder, and Pathological Gambling. A comparable list of conditions diagnosed more often in women includes Histrionic Personality Disorder, some forms of Depression, Eating Disorders, Dissociative Identity Disorder, Kleptomania, Panic Disorder, Somatization Disorder, Agoraphobia, and Borderline Personality Disorder.

Could there be a clearer reflection of gender stereotypes? But why are the same qualities that compose the stereotypes—the unfeeling, action-oriented, sexually aggressive, misbehaving male; and the emotional, dependent, weight-conscious, frightened, and sickly woman—so much the basis for pathologizing each gender? Perhaps the diagnostic categories serve to create an upper limit for the very characteristics that are socially encouraged in each gender. Boys are encouraged to be active, rough, aggressive, sexually adventurous, steady, and rational. But when boys become too aggressive they are assigned the diagnosis Conduct Disorder or Intermittent Explosive Disorder, when men become too steady and rational they are diagnosed Obsessive-Compulsive Personality Disorder, when men break the rules too badly in the sexual realm they are considered Paraphiliacs, and so forth. It is a little like the college and pro football teams that encourage players to be hyperaggressive and then have to discipline some of them when they draw negative publicity by raping women after a game. The mental disorders typically assigned to men, like the fines assigned for the overly aggressive football players, serve to keep the lid on the very behaviors that are being encouraged. Similarly, women are encouraged from early childhood to be emotional and connected with others, but if they are too emotional they are diagnosed Histrionic Personality Disorder, and if they are too connected they are diagnosed Dependent Personality Disorder. There is little if any support for creating new, improved forms of masculinity and femininity in DSM-IV.

Childhood Disorders and the Shaping of Gender

The main thing to notice about the section of DSM-IV on childhood and adolescent disorders is that the list of disorders is growing. In DSM-II (1968) there were two subsections containing a total of seven disorders, whereas in DSM-IV (1994a) there are ten subsections and thirty-two disorders. Most of the enlargement occurred between DSM-II and DSM-III, the authors of DSM-IV being more interested in providing detailed descriptions for established disorders than in adding new ones to the official list. Still, the number of children who see mental health professionals and undergo psychotherapy or receive psychotropic medications is growing, and children are being taken to see professionals at younger ages.

Consider three childhood disorders from the list in DSM-IV: Attention Deficit/Hyperactivity Disorder (ADHD), Oppositional Defiant Disorder, and Gender Identity Disorder. What if Oscar Wilde had been given one or more of these diagnoses when he was six or eight years old? What if Ritalin had been prescribed to limit his energy level or he had been given Prozac to control his nonconformist notions about gender and sexuality? What if there had been a way at that time to predict which children might become gay or antisocial (research of this kind is proliferating today), and preventive treatment had been instituted? Would Wilde's vision have been the same, would he have created great literature? This is not to say that Wilde was mentally disordered, or that mental disorder is a prerequisite for works of genius. Rather I am selecting Wilde to illustrate the point that earlier diagnosis and treatment of mental disorders in children runs the risk of stigmatizing unusual men and women, creating less tolerance for experimentation in the realm of gender roles, and thereby limiting the historical possibilities for transforming gender relations.

Of course, in some children, for instance those who compulsively pull out their hair or those who cannot sit still long enough to finish a classroom assignment, professional intervention can have positive effects. I am not arguing that any particular child should be denied examination and treatment. But when children in unprecedented numbers are taken to see professionals, there are social ramifications. One is that approaches to social problems are reduced to the search for psychopathology in individual children. For instance, consider the difficulty teachers have maintaining order in classrooms containing ever-larger numbers of students as budgets for public instruction decline. The teacher cannot reduce the size of the class, but he or she can tell the parents of problematic children that their kids suffer from ADHD and need to be taking Ritalin. In general, it is when we despair about the prospects for social transformation—e.g., making public education a higher social priority—that we tend to reduce social problems to the pathology of individuals. Breggin and Breggin (1994) outline the dangers of this development, though they tend to polarize the discussion by minimizing the positive contributions of child psychiatry and psychotherapy.

Of course, there is money to be made from the quest for earlier detection of mental disorders in children. An even more alarming implication is that society has embarked on the early correction of all deviations from the "straight" path of development. As our lives as workers and consumers become more routinized, and as the gap between the rich and the poor grows wider, concerned parents begin to wonder if their children are going to be among the winners or the losers. This motivates them to watch for early signs of mental disorder and hurry their children off to a mental health professional at the first sign of hyperactivity, school failure, impulsive behavior, or gender impropriety.

There are class and race differences. Diagnosing children in the inner city with Conduct Disorder and Oppositional Defiant Disorder does not usually lead to quality treatment (the public mental health service system is shrinking rapidly); but the diagnoses do serve to rationalize the fact that low-income, inner city children are less likely than their middle-class cohorts to find fulfilling work and are more likely to wind up behind bars. People actually begin to believe it is the psychopathology of poor people, not social inequity, that causes unemployment and criminality. As we pathologize more "off-beat" qualities, we are inadvertently tightening the bounds around what is considered "normal" behavior for boys and girls. Nothing is said about this social inequity in DSM-IV, and this silence is quite worrisome.

Conclusion

The DSM-IV is definitely an improvement over previous editions. There is more participation by women in the work groups. Homosexuality has been deleted from the list of disorders, as has DSM-III's Ego-Dystonic Homosexuality; the proposal to add Self-defeating Personality has been defeated; and there are sections on racial and ethnic differences (that do not go far enough toward correcting racial bias in the diagnostic process . . .). Meanwhile, the DSM grows longer, the descriptions of mental disorders become more codified, and psychiatry has little or nothing to say about the social ramifications of its pathologizing.

Traditional psychiatry looks backward, diagnosing mental illness in those who do not fit yesterday's prescribed social roles. Emotionality as well as assertiveness in women, rebellion on the part of minority members, and homosexuality have all been pathologized. As previously stigmatized groups gain power within the mental health professions, diagnoses are modified. DSM-IV reflects admirable progress in terms of the inclusion of diverse groups and the concerted effort to minimize gender bias and homophobia wherever it can be identified. Still, the fourth edition of DSM continues to pathologize deviation from yesterday's gender roles.

Instead of a longer, more detailed list of mental disorders, we need a system of psychopathology that is informed by a vision of a better society. We could begin by envisioning that society, one in which gender equality reigns and there is no homophobia or any other form of domination. Then, by extrapolating backward from that vision, we could pathologize the qualities that would make a person dysfunctional in that more equitable and just social order. Racism, misogyny, and homophobia would head the list of psychopathologies. This kind of pathologizing might even serve to bring about the vision. Unfortunately, far from solving the problems of gender bias and homophobia, the improvements in DSM-IV will serve largely to appease potential dissenters as the mental health professions evolve an ever more conformist manual of psychopathology.

References

American Psychiatric Association. (1952). *Diagnostic and statistical manual of mental disorders.* Washington, D.C.: Author.

American Psychiatric Association. (1968). *Diagnostic and statistical manual of mental disorders* (2nd ed.). Washington, D.C.: Author.

American Psychiatric Association. (1980). *Diagnostic and statistical manual of mental disorders* (3rd ed.). Washington, D.C.: Author.

American Psychiatric Association. (1993). Position statement on homosexuality. *American Journal of Psychiatry, 150,* 686.

American Psychiatric Association. (1994a). *Diagnostic and statistical manual of mental disorders* (4th ed.). Washington, D.C.: Author.

American Psychiatric Association. (1994b). Practice guideline for the treatment of patients with bipolar disorder. *American Journal of Psychiatry, 151,* Supplement, 1–36.

Breggin, P. R., & Breggin, G. R. (1994). *The war against children.* New York: St. Martin's Press.

Caplan, P. J. (1987). The psychiatric association's failure to meet its own standards: The dangers of self-defeating personality disorder as a category. *Journal of Personality Disorders, 1,* 178–182.

Chesler, P. (1972). *Women and madness.* New York: Avon.

Cohen, C. (1993). The biomedicalization of psychiatry: A critical overview. *Community Mental Health Journal, 29,* 509–522.

Connell, R. W. (1994). Psychoanalysis on masculinity. In H. Brod & M. Kaufman (Eds.), *Theorizing masculinities* (pp. 11–38). Thousand Oaks, Calif.: Sage.

Conrad, P. (1980). On the medicalization of deviance and social control. In D. Ingleby (Ed.), *Critical psychiatry* (pp. 102–119). New York: Pantheon.

Foucault, M. (1965). *Madness and civilization.* New York: Pantheon.

Herman, J. (1992). *Trauma and recovery: The aftermath of violence—From domestic abuse to political terror.* New York: Basic Books.

Hughes, J. S. (1990). The madness of separate spheres: Insanity and masculinity in Victorian Alabama. In M. C. Carnes & C. Griffen (Eds.), *Meanings of manhood: Constructions of masculinity in Victorian America* (pp. 67–78). Chicago: University of Chicago Press.

Jordan, J., Kaplan, A., Miller, J. B., Stiver, I. P., and Surrey, J. L. (1991). *Women's growth in connection: Writings from the Stone Center.* New York: Guilford Press.

Kernberg, O. F. (1975). *Borderline conditions and pathological narcissism.* New York: Jason Aronson.

Kovel, J. (1980). The American mental health industry. In D. Ingleby (Ed.), *Critical psychiatry* (pp. 72–101). New York: Pantheon.

Kupers, T. A. (1993a). *Revisioning men's lives: Gender, intimacy and power.* New York: Guilford.

Kupers, T. A. (1993b). Psychotherapy, neutrality and the role of activism. *Community Mental Health Journal, 29,* 523–534.

Miller, J. B. (1976). *Toward a new psychology of women.* Boston: Beacon Press.

Sedgwick, P. (1982). *Psychopolitics: Laing, Foucault, Goffman, Szasz and the future of mass psychiatry.* New York: Harper & Row.

Socarides, C. W., Kaufman, B., Gottlieb, F., & Isay, R. (1994). Letters about reparative therapy. *American Journal of Psychiatry, 151,* 157–59.

Spitzer, R. L., Severino, S. K., Williams, J. B., & Parry, B. L. (1989). Late luteal phase dysphoric disorder and DSM-III-R. *American Journal of Psychiatry, 146,* 892–897.

Thomas, A., & Sillen, S. (1974). *Racism and psychiatry.* Secaucus, N.J.: Citadel.

Gender Issues in DSM-IV

How to Understand Differences in Gender Prevalences

A number of psychiatric disorders have markedly different rates of occurrence in women and men. It is not clear whether these differences are inherent to actual differences in psychopathology between women and men or are the artifactual result of biases in ascertainment, definition, or assessment (Brown 1986; Davidson and Abramovitz 1980; Deaux 1985; Earls 1987; Hamilton et al. 1986; Kaplan 1983; Lewine et al. 1984; Loring and Powell 1988; Russell 1985; Sherman 1980; Smith 1980; Snyder et al. 1985; Widiger and Nietzel 1984; Widiger and Settle 1987; Widiger and Spitzer 1991; Widom 1984; Zeldow 1984). Gender differences in treatment seeking or referral patterns may explain the different gender ratios that occur in community samples as opposed to more selected clinical samples. For example, there is a higher ratio of women with major depressive disorder in clinical than in epidemiological samples, perhaps because women are more likely to recognize and admit to depression. In contrast, there is a higher ratio of men with schizophrenia in clinical than in epidemiological samples, perhaps because men with schizophrenia are more disruptive and likely to require treatment intervention. However, there also appear to be data supporting the view that a higher rate of major depression in women is a real and not artifactual finding. Biases in definition may also play a role in gender differences in prevalence. There may also be gender differences in prevalence because of biases in the evaluator that may lead to misinterpretation of the diagnostic criteria. It is likely that there are also real differences in prevalence, at least for certain disorders (e.g., conduct disorder, antisocial personality disorder) that reflect real differences between women and men.

Gender and the Personality Disorder Criteria

Another extremely controversial issue has been the question of a possible gender bias within the DSM-III-R criteria sets, particularly for the diagnoses of histrionic personality disorder and dependent personality disorder (Hirschfeld

From Ruth Ross, Allen Frances, and Thomas A. Widiger, "Gender Issues in DSM-IV," in Mary Roth Walsh, ed., *Women, Men, and Gender: Ongoing Debates* (Yale University Press, 1997), pp. 348–357. Originally published in *Annual Review of Psychiatry*, vol. 14 (1995). Copyright © 1995 by American Psychiatric Press, Inc. Reprinted by permission.

et al. 1991, 1996; Pfohl 1996). Both of these personality disorders are diagnosed much more frequently in women than in men. Histrionic personality disorder and dependent personality disorder appear to involve, at least in part, stereotypic feminine traits (Kaplan 1983; Sprock et al. 1990; Walker 1994) that could be mislabeled as personality disorder in a gender-biased system. In contrast, others have argued that histrionic personality disorder and dependent personality disorder are diagnosed more frequently in women than in men not because of definition or assessment bias but precisely because these personality disorders involve maladaptive variants of stereotypic feminine traits, just as antisocial personality disorder and obsessive-compulsive personality disorder involve maladaptive variants of stereotypic masculine traits and are diagnosed more frequently in men (Widiger and Spitzer 1991; Widiger et al. 1994b; Williams and Spitzer 1983). There is no reason to assume that each personality disorder will occur with an equal frequency across genders. To the extent that some personality traits are more prevalent or predominant within one gender (e.g., Eagly and Crowley 1986; Eagly and Steffen 1986), one might expect personality disorders that represent maladaptive or excessive variants of these traits to be more prevalent within that gender. However, concerns about a possible gender bias are also understandable. The DSM-III/DSM-III-R personality disorder criteria were constructed, for the most part, by males with little input from systematic empirical research. It would not be surprising to find that male clinicians would have a lower threshold for the attribution of maladaptive feminine traits than for the attribution of maladaptive masculine traits.

It is also important to ensure that empirically derived criteria sets do not impel or exaggerate gender differences through research that is confined largely to one gender. This risk is perhaps easiest to demonstrate in the case of antisocial personality disorder. As a matter of convenience, studies on antisocial personality disorder have often been confined to males; as a result, the diagnostic criteria that performed best within these studies are criteria that work best for males with this disorder. For example, it is possible that the DSM-III-R criteria for antisocial personality disorder, with such behaviors as forcing someone into a sexual activity before age fifteen or beating one's spouse after the age of fifteen, were biased toward the manner in which males expressed antisocial personality traits. More males than females may indeed have antisocial personality disorder, but to the extent that the diagnostic criteria were based on research confined to male subjects, the criteria set may result in the underdiagnosis of females with this disorder. Moreover, there is evidence that antisocial personality traits in females may be misdiagnosed as histrionic (Ford and Widiger 1989; Hamilton et al. 1986).

The DSM-IV Personality Disorders Work Group addressed this problem in a variety of ways. The DSM-IV field trials on antisocial personality disorder were analyzed separately for males and for females to assess whether any proposed revisions would be detrimental to the diagnosis of antisocial personality disorder in females. In addition, individual criteria were revised to be more gender neutral. For example, the DSM-III-R histrionic personality disorder item "is inappropriately sexually seductive in appearance or behavior" (American Psychiatric Association 1987, p. 349) was revised to "interaction with others is often characterized by inappropriate sexually seductive or provocative behavior" (American Psychiatric Association 1994, p. 657). This item was revised to emphasize seductive or provocative behavior rather than just appearance, because normal sexual attractiveness can be readily confused with sexual seductiveness and because females may be more likely to be perceived as sexually seductive in appearance given the social pressure concerning physical attractiveness in females. Provocative or seductive behavior is perhaps less prone to gender-biased attributions than seductive appearance. Likewise, the criteria set for conduct disorder was revised in part to include antisocial behaviors that tend to occur in females (e.g., staying out at night despite parental prohibitions before age thirteen).

Gender variations in the expression of personality disorders are also discussed in the "Specific Culture, Age, and Gender Features" sections of the texts for these disorders. For example, in the discussion of histrionic personality disorder, it is noted that

> the behavioral expression of histrionic personality disorder may be influenced by sex role stereotypes. For example, a man with this disorder may dress and behave in a manner often identified as "macho" and may seek to be the center of attention by bragging about athletic skills, whereas a woman, for example, may choose very feminine clothes and talk about how much she impressed her dance instructor. (American Psychiatric Association 1994, p. 656)

The text discussions also caution against the imposition of gender-biased assumptions when making personality disorder diagnoses—for example, noting that "there has been some concern that antisocial personality disorder may be underdiagnosed in females, particularly because of the emphasis on aggressive items in the definition of conduct disorder" (American Psychiatric Association 1994, p. 647) or cautioning in the text for dependent personality disorder that "societies may differentially foster and discourage dependent behavior in males and females" (American Psychiatric Association 1994, p. 667).

To the extent that there are clearly established gender variations in the expression of a personality disorder (or any disorder), the authors of the future DSM-V may eventually consider developing separate criteria sets for each gender. This is already done for gender identity disorder, in which such differences are inherent in the disorder itself. However, there is currently insufficient research to support such an approach in DSM-IV.

Self-Defeating Personality Disorder

The inclusion of the self-defeating personality disorder (originally called masochistic personality disorder) in the appendix to DSM-III-R generated substantial controversy (Caplan 1987, 1991; Rosewater 1987; Walker 1987, 1994). In considering whether to continue to include self-defeating personality disorder in the DSM-IV appendix, the conceptual and empirical foundation for this proposed disorder was thoroughly studied by the DSM-IV Personality Disorders Work Group and by the Task Force on DSM-IV. As a culmination of its review process, the Personality Disorders Work Group recommended that self-defeating personality disorder not be included in the main body or the appendix of DM-IV (Widiger, in press).

The literature review for self-defeating personality disorder (Fiester, 1996) indicated that this newly proposed diagnosis has received very little research attention and that there have been only a few investigations of real patients (the few available studies have focused more on surveys or the diagnosis of illustrative written case examples). The work group was also concerned about the inherent difficulty of accurately diagnosing self-defeating personality disorder in the presence of a harsh environmental context or when other psychiatric disorders are present. The clinical studies suggested that self-defeating personality disorder would overlap a great deal with the eleven other personality disorders that are included in DSM-III-R. This is a serious problem because most clinicians and researchers believe that we are already burdened by the inclusion of too many personality disorders in DSM-III-R, creating a system that is cumbersome to use in clinical and research practice and usually results in multiple diagnoses.

However useful the concept of masochism remains in the practice of psychotherapy, the work group discussions revealed that there are structural problems that prevent the simple translation of the psychodynamic construct of masochism to the psychiatric diagnosis of personality disorder. The criteria set of self-defeating personality disorder was an attempt to provide a descriptive operationalization of the psychodynamic construct that unconscious forces may lead to a masochistic pattern of interpersonal relationships and behaviors. The analytic literature has attributed this masochistic pattern to a variety of unconscious motivations, including self-punishment consequent to superego pathology; an external reenactment of introjected early sadomasochistic relationships; self-directed aggression as a defense against sadism; and pathological narcissism. In the psychotherapy situation, the evaluation of these unconscious motivations usually requires a careful and prolonged assessment of the patient's transferential attitudes and behaviors in the treatment relationship. This judgment depends on a good deal of psychodynamic expertise and inference and usually can be confirmed only by the patient's masochistic treatment behavior, not just by the evaluation of problems presented in the diagnostic interview. The self-defeating personality disorder criteria represented an attempt to draft a set of behavioral and interpersonal criteria that would capture the surface manifestations of the presumed unconscious motivation for masochistic behavior. This turned out to be an inherently impossible task. One cannot convert this particular psychodynamic construct inferring unconscious masochistic motivation into a behavioral (and less inferential) criteria set that is not confounded by the individual's interactions with the environment. This effort failed because it cannot be done, not just because of any deficiencies in the specific self-defeating personality disorder criteria that were selected. It was not simply a matter of studying and improving the existing criteria set. The basic issue is that much "self-defeating" behavior occurs for reasons other than the specific "masochistic" unconscious motivations that are meant to be at the heart of the self-defeating personality disorder concept. It is usually impossible within the context of a general psychiatric evaluation to determine whether the individual's pattern of self-defeating behavior is an expression of unconscious motivation that would play out over and over again regardless of the environment in which the individual exists or whether the "self-defeating" pattern of behavior is an understandable and perhaps adaptive result of the need to survive in a harsh and punishing environment.

In addition many mental disorders are characterized by behaviors and symptoms that are "self-defeating" in their effect but not "masochistic" in their unconscious motivations. This is particularly true for chronic depression but is also true for many other psychiatric disorders. The concept of self-defeating personality disorder is inherently confounded with self-defeating aspects that are secondary consequences of other mental disorders. There were also no studies to document that the diagnosis described a behavior pattern that was not already adequately represented by an existing Axis I or Axis II diagnosis. Although self-defeating behaviors are encountered commonly enough in clinical practice, it is not clear that the self-defeating personality disorder diagnosis is specific in capturing the central or predominant pathology in most of these cases.

Another major concern that was factored into the consideration of the proposed self-defeating personality disorder diagnosis was that the diagnosis might be used to blame victims of (spouse) abuse for their own victimization (Fiester 1991; Widiger, 1995; Widiger and Frances 1989). The proposed criteria set did provide an exclusion criterion such that the items would not be considered present if they occurred exclusively in response to or in anticipation of being physically, sexually, or psychologically abused. However, many of the instruments that were developed to assess self-defeating personality disorder failed to consider this exclusion criterion, and many victims are reluctant to acknowledge the presence of actual abuse. The research on self-defeating personality disorder often failed to consider the occurrence and influence of victimization on the diagnosis (e.g., Spitzer et al. 1989), and the research on victimization has failed to assess adequately for the role and influence of self-defeating personality traits (e.g., Walker 1984).

Although there undoubtedly are individuals with self-defeating personality patterns, the utility and validity of the construct as a psychiatric diagnosis has not yet been established, and the Personality Disorders Work Group concluded that its provision within an appendix to DSM-IV would provide the diagnosis with a credibility or recognition that it did not yet warrant. A diagnosis that has the potential for misuse should be held to an especially high standard of validation before it is given any official credibility. Nevertheless, the concept of self-defeating unconscious motivations is sometimes useful in understanding or treating individuals encountered in clinical practice.

Sadistic Personality Disorder

Sadistic personality disorder was included in the appendix to DSM-III-R based almost completely on anecdotal case reports. In considering whether to continue to include this proposed diagnosis in the DSM-IV appendix, the Personality Disorders Work Group undertook a literature review on sadistic personality disorder (Fiester and Gay 1991). The group found that little research on sadistic personality disorder had been done and that the only published studies were by the original proponents of the disorder (i.e., Fiester and Gay 1991; Gay, in press; Spitzer et al. 1991). Based on the lack of systematic research supporting this diagnosis and the potential for misuse, the Personality Disorders Work Group recommended that it not be included in the appendix to DSM-IV (Widiger 1995).

Premenstrual Dysphoric Disorder

As mentioned earlier, the inclusion of late luteal phase dysphoric disorder, as it was then called, in the appendix to DSM-III-R produced one of the more heated controversies surrounding the publication of DSM-III-R (Chait 1986; Eckholm 1985; Hamilton and Gallant 1988; Holtzman 1988; Reid 1987). Proponents maintained that late luteal phase dysphoric disorder is a clinically significant condition that is supported by research and clinical literature and that its omission might lead to underdiagnosis, misdiagnosis, failure to give appropriate treatment, and stigmatization by blaming individual women with the problem for their symptoms. Opponents referred to the paucity of clinical and research literature and warned that inclusion might encourage inappropriate diagnosis and treatment and also had the potential to stigmatize women in general. There were concerns about whether there were sufficient data to generate a valid and reliable criteria set for this proposed disorder. Questions were also raised as to whether it was best conceptualized as a mental disorder (rather than an endocrinological or gynecological one) and whether a disorder related to male hormones should be included.

A Late Luteal Phase Work Group was formed and given responsibility for making a recommendation, based on empirical data, as to whether late luteal phase dysphoric disorder should continue to appear in the appendix of DSM-IV, should be included in the main body of the manual, should be included in the section for "Other Clinically Significant Conditions That May Be a Focus of Clinical Attention," or should be left out altogether (American Psychiatric Association 1991). To make a recommendation on this issue, the work group conducted an exhaustive literature review that included clinical and research studies on both premenstrual syndrome and late luteal phase dysphoric disorder. Because late luteal phase dysphoric disorder first appeared in the nomenclature in 1987, published studies using the proposed late luteal phase dysphoric disorder criteria from DSM-III-R were limited, but these increased in number during the period of the review from 1988 to 1992 (Gold et al., in press). The purpose of this literature review was to try to determine "if there is a clinically significant mental disorder associated with the menstrual cycle that can be separated from other mental disorders" (Gold, in press). More than five hundred articles on premenstrual syndrome and late luteal phase dysphoric disorder were reviewed, and information on prevalence, association with preexisting mental disorders, course of illness and prognosis, familial factors, biological and treatment studies, and social, forensic, and occupational issues were examined. The group identified a number of methodological problems in the literature: variable or unclearly specified definitions of premenstrual syndrome, small sample sizes, lack of control groups, prospective daily ratings not used, possibly biased sample selection, failure to delineate timing and duration of symptoms, and failure to collect adequate hormonal samples. Despite these problems, the work group determined that, based on the literature review, a relatively circumscribed group of women (perhaps 3%–5%) suffer from severe and clinically significant dysphoria related to the premenstrual period.

The work group also carried out a reanalysis of previously collected data from more than six hundred subjects from five sites (Hurt et al. 1992; Severino et al., in press). The results of this reanalysis supported the clinical usefulness of the criteria set for late luteal phase dysphoric disorder but suggested some changes in emphasis to reflect that the disturbance is most closely related to mood disorder and to emphasize the dysphoric nature of the symptoms. The revised proposed criteria require severe impairment and minimize physical symptoms.

The literature review and data reanalysis were widely circulated for comments and critique among thirty-six advisers who were selected to represent a range of different perspectives, including individuals who had done research on the disorder and others who were very concerned about its possible misuse. The group attempted to formulate criteria that would be optimal for research purposes and could also be easily and consistently applied by clinicians. They focused on where the disorder should be placed in the classification and what it should be called (Gold, in press). They concluded that the name *late luteal phase dysphoric disorder* was cumbersome and somewhat misleading (because the symptoms may not be related to the endocrinological changes of the late luteal phase) and proposed the name *premenstrual dysphoric disorder* (Gold, in press).

... The final decision of the Task Force on DSM-IV was to continue to include the disorder, renamed *premenstrual dysphoric disorder,* in the appendix to the manual, and not to make it part of the official nomenclature. It was decided to refer to premenstrual dysphoric disorder as an example of a depressive disorder not otherwise specified for purposes of differential diagnosis, rather than as an example of a mental disorder not otherwise specified, based on the fact that the data seem to support a strong mood component in the disorder. The appendix in which the criteria set for premenstrual dysphoric disorder is included is titled "Criteria Sets and Axes Provided for Further Study." The introduction to the appendix states that "the task force determined that there was insufficient information to warrant inclusion of these proposals as official categories or axes in DSM-IV" (American Psychiatric Association 1994, p. 703). It is noted that "the items, thresholds, and durations contained in the research criteria sets are intended to provide a common language for researchers and clinicians who are interested in studying these disorders. It is hoped that such research will help to determine the possible utility of these proposed categories and will result in refinement of the criteria sets" (American Psychiatric Association 1994, p. 703).

The decision to include premenstrual dysphoric disorder in the appendix to DSM-IV received widespread media attention (e.g., Alvardo 1993; Seligman and Gelman 1993; Spam 1993). In some cases, these accounts were fair and balanced accounts of the issues involved (Spam 1993). Unfortunately, many articles reported inaccurate information and contributed to the controversy by fostering the impression that the developers of DSM-IV were attempting to pathologize a large part of the female population. They often stated that premenstrual dysphoric disorder would be included in the main body of the manual as an official diagnosis or claimed that the much more common premenstrual syndrome would be considered a mental disorder in the DSM-IV diagnostic system.

However, the "Differential Diagnosis" section of the text that accompanies the proposed research criteria for premenstrual dysphoric disorder in the DSM-IV appendix states that

> the transient mood changes that many females experience around the time of their period should not be considered a mental disorder. Premenstrual dysphoric disorder should be considered only when the symptoms markedly interfere with work or school or with usual social activities and relationships with others (e.g., avoidance of social activities, decreased productivity and efficiency at work or school). Premenstrual dysphoric disorder can be distinguished from the far more common "premenstrual syndrome" by using prospective daily ratings and the strict criteria listed below. It differs from the "premenstrual syndrome" in its characteristic pattern of symptoms, their severity, and the resulting impairment. (American Psychiatric Association 1994, p. 716)

Although there is a lack of a consistent definition of premenstrual syndrome, the proposed research criteria set for premenstrual dysphoric disorder is an attempt to define a severe dysphoric disorder that causes clinically significant impairment and is not to be confused with the milder premenstrual syndrome. The text for premenstrual dysphoric disorder notes,

> it is estimated that at least 75% of women report minor or isolated premenstrual changes. Limited studies suggest an occurrence of "premenstrual syndrome" (variably defined) of 20%–50%, and that 3%–5% of women experience symptoms that may meet the criteria for this proposed disorder (American Psychiatric Association 1994, p. 716).

It was, in part, because of the tentative nature of the criteria that it was decided to continue to place premenstrual dysphoric disorder in the appendix so that further studies in larger populations could investigate the validity and reliability of the items selected and the ability of the criteria to discriminate these symptoms from milder premenstrual syndrome.

The proposed DSM-IV criteria set for premenstrual dysphoric disorder requires that five or more of the following symptoms (with at least one being one of the first four) be present most of the time during the last week of the luteal phase in most menstrual cycles during the past year (American Psychiatric Association 1994, p. 717):

> 1) feeling sad, hopeless, or self-deprecating; 2) feeling tense, anxious or "on edge"; 3) marked lability of mood interspersed with frequent tearfulness; 4) persistent irritability, anger, and increased interpersonal conflicts; 5) decreased interest in usual activities, which may be associated with withdrawal from social relationships; 6) difficulty concentrating; 7) feeling fatigued, lethargic, or lacking in energy; 8) marked changes in appetite, which may be associated with binge eating or craving certain foods; 9) hypersomnia or insomnia; 10) a subjective feeling of being overwhelmed or out of control; and 11) physical symptoms such as breast tenderness or swelling, headaches, or sensations of "bloating" or weight gain, with tightness of fit of clothing, shoes, or rings. There may also be joint or muscle pain. The symptoms may be accompanied by suicidal thoughts. (American Psychiatric Association 1994, p. 715)

The symptoms must begin to remit within a few days after the onset of the follicular phase and be absent in the week postmenses. The disturbance must markedly interfere with work or school or usual social activities and relationships with others and must not be merely an exacerbation of the symptoms of another mental disorder. The symptoms described in the criteria set must be confirmed by prospective daily ratings during at least two consecutive symptomatic cycles. The criteria set describes a pattern of symptoms that is far more severe and impairing than what is usually called premenstrual syndrome, despite the variations in definitions of premenstrual syndrome. DSM-IV states that the symptoms of premenstrual dysphoric disorder are "typically... of comparable severity (but not duration) to those of a major depressive episode" (American Psychiatric Association 1994, p. 715)....

Conclusion

For most of the diagnoses in DSM-IV, the emphasis on documentation and empirical data as the foundation for change resulted in remarkably little controversy. However, the gender issues related to diagnosis that have historically been subject to controversy continued to be the subject of disagreement during the development of DSM-IV. In part, this may have resulted from the fact that systematic research efforts on gender differences have begun only recently. However, the larger social questions these issues touch on made it more difficult to settle them on empirical grounds alone or even to reach a shared interpretation of the data that are available. Ultimately it is for others to judge, but we believe that the DSM-IV development process was characterized by serious attempts to base decisions on a fair and balanced interpretation of the available data on gender-related issues in diagnosis. It is hoped that the new section "Culture, Age, and Gender Features" that is included in the texts for many disorders will be helpful in alerting clinicians to gender-related differences in presentation and to possible gender-related pitfalls in making diagnoses. However, perhaps the most important gender-related accomplishment of DSM-IV has been to stimulate and encourage debate on issues related to gender and diagnosis. It is hoped that when possible problems related to gender are noted in the text for specific disorders, this will stimulate studies on those disorders that will inform the next revision of DSM and lead to more accurate diagnostic information.

The major questions concerning the relationship between gender and psychiatric diagnosis remain largely unanswered. It is not at all clear whether and to what extent marked differences in gender prevalence of certain diagnoses reflect true gender differences or are artifacts of ascertainment, definition, or assessment. For those gender differences that do stand up to improved methodological rigor in diagnosis, the next step will be to identify the mechanisms involved in these differences in psychopathology.

References

Alvardo, D. Furor over new diagnosis for PMS. San Jose Mercury News, May 22, 1993, p. 1A.

American Psychiatric Association. DSM-IV Options Book: Work in Progress (9/1/91). Washington, D.C., American Psychiatric Association, 1991.

American Psychiatric Association. Diagnostic and Statistical Manual of Mental Disorders, 3rd Edition, Revised. Washington, D.C., American Psychiatric Association, 1987.

American Psychiatric Association. Diagnostic and Statistical Manual of Mental Disorders, 4th Edition. Washington, D.C., American Psychiatric Association, 1994.

Brown, L. S. Gender-role analysis: A neglected component of psychological assessment. Psychotherapy 23:243–248, 1986.

Caplan, P. The psychiatric association's failure to meet its own standards: The dangers of self-defeating personality disorder as a category. Journal of Personality Disorders 1:178–182, 1987.

Caplan, P. J. How do they decide who is normal? The bizarre, but true, tale of the DSM process. Canadian Psychology 32:162–170, 1991.

Chait, L. R. Premenstrual syndrome and our sisters in crime: A feminist dilemma. Women's Rights Law Reporter 9:267–293, 1986.

Davidson, C. V., Abramovitz, S. I. Sex bias in clinical judgment: Later empirical returns. Psychology of Women Quarterly 4:377–395, 1980.

Deaux, K. Sex and gender. Ann. Rev. Psychol. 36:49–81, 1985.

Eagly, A. H., Crowley, M. Gender and helping behavior: A meta-analytic review of the social psychology literature. Psychol. Bull. 100:283–308, 1986.

Eagly, A. H., Steffen, V. J. Gender and aggressive behavior: A meta-analytic review of the social psychological literature. Psychol. Bull. 100:309–330, 1986.

Earls, F. Sex differences in psychiatric disorders: Origins and developmental influences. Psychiatric Developments 1:1–23, 1987.

Eckholm, E. Premenstrual problems seem to beset baboons. The New York Times, June 4, 1985, p. C2.

Fiester, S. J. Self-defeating personality disorder: A review of data and recommendations for DSM-IV. Journal of Personality Disorders 5:194–209, 1991.

Fiester, S. J. Self-defeating personality disorder, in DSM-IV Sourcebook, Vol 2. Edited by Widiger, T. A., Frances A. J., Pincus, H. A., et al. Washington, D.C., American Psychiatric Association, 1996.

Fiester, S. J., Gay, M. Sadistic personality disorder: A review of data and recommendations for DSM-IV. Journal of Personality Disorders 5:376–385, 1991.

Fiester, S. J., Gay, M. Sadistic personality disorder, in DSM-IV Sourcebook, Vol 2. Edited by Widiger, T. A., Frances, A. J., Pincus, H. A., et al. Washington, D.C., American Psychiatric Association, 1996.

Ford, M., Widiger, T. Sex bias in the diagnosis of histrionic and antisocial personality disorders. J. Consult. Clin. Psychol. 57:301–305, 1989.

Gallant, S. J. A., Hamilton, J. A. On a premenstrual psychiatric diagnosis: What's in a name? Professional Psychology: Research and Practice 19:271–278, 1988.

Gay, M. Sadistic personality disorder in a child abusing population. Child Abuse Negl. (in press).

Gold, J. H. Late luteal phase dysphoric disorder and the DSM-IV, in DSM-IV Sourcebook, Vol. 4. Edited by Widiger, T. A., Frances, A. J., Pincus, H. A., et al. Washington, D.C., American Psychiatric Association (1996).

Gold, J. H., Endicott, J., Parry, B. L., et al. Late luteal phase dysphoric disorder, in DSM-IV Sourcebook, Vol 2. Edited by Widiger, T. A., Frances, A. J., Pincus, H. A., et al. Washington, D.C., American Psychiatric Association (in press).

Hamilton, S., Rothbart, M., Dawes, R. M. Sex bias, diagnosis, and DSM-III. Sex Roles 15:269–274, 1986.

Hirschfeld, R. M. A., Shea, M. T., Weise, R. Dependent personality disorder: Perspectives for DSM-IV. Journal of Personality Disorders 5:135–149, 1991.

Hirschfeld, R. M. A., Shea, M. T., Talbot, K. M. Dependent personality disorder, in DSM-IV Sourcebook, Vol 2. Edited by Widiger, T. A., Frances, A. J., Pincus, H. A., et al. Washington, D.C., American Psychiatric Association, 1996.

Holtzman, E. Premenstrual syndrome as a legal defense, in The Premenstrual Syndromes. Edited by Gise, L. H., Kose, N. G., Berkowitz, R. L. New York, Churchill Livingstone, 1988, pp. 137–143.

Hurt, S. W., Schnurr, P. P., Severino, S. K., et al. Late luteal phase dysphoric disorder in 670 women evaluated for premenstrual complaints. Am. J. Psychiatry 149:525–530, 1992.

Kaplan, M. A woman's view of DSM-III. Am. Psychol. 38:786–792, 1983.

Lewine, R., Burbach, D., Meltzer, H. Y. Effect of diagnostic criteria on the ratio of male to female schizophrenic patients. Am. J. Psychiatry 141:84–87, 1984.

Loring, M., Powell, B. Gender, race, and DSM-III: A study of the objectivity of psychiatric diagnostic behavior. J. Health Soc. Behav. 29:1–22, 1988.

Pfohl, B. Histrionic personality disorder, in DSM-IV Sourcebook, Vol 2. Edited by Widiger, T. A., Frances, A. J., Pincus, H. A., et al. Washington, D. C., American Psychiatric Association, 1996.

Reid, R. L. Premenstrual syndrome. AACC ENDO 5:1–12, 1987.

Rosewater, L. B. A critical analysis of the proposed self-defeating personality disorder. Journal of Personality Disorders 1:190–195, 1987.

Russell, D. Psychiatric diagnosis and the oppression of women. Int. J. Soc. Psychiatry 31:298–305, 1985.

Seligman, J., Gelman, D. Is it sadness or madness? Psychiatrists clash over how to classify PMS. Newsweek, March 15, 1993, p. 66.

Severino, S. K. et al. Database reanalysis in DSM-IV Sourcebook, Vol 4. Edited by Widiger, T. A., Frances, A. J., Pincus, H. A., et al. Washington, D. C., American Psychiatric Association (in press).

Sherman, J. A. Therapist attitudes and sex-role stereotyping, in Women and Psychotherapy. Edited by Brodsky, A. M., Hare-Mustin, R. T. New York, Guilford Press, 1980, pp. 34–66.

Smith, M. L. Sex bias in counseling and psychotherapy. Psychol. Bull. 187:392–407, 1980.

Snyder, S., Goodpaster, W. A., Pitts, W. M., et al. Demography of psychiatric patients with borderline personality traits. Psychopathology 18:38–49, 1985.

Spam, P. Vicious cycle: The politics of periods. Washington Post, July 8, 1993, pp. C1–C2.

Spitzer, R. L., Williams, J. B. W., Kass, F., et al. National field trial of the DSM-III-R diagnostic criteria for self-defeating personality disorder. Am. J. Psychiatry 146:1561–1567, 1989.

Spitzer, R. L., Fiester, S. J., Gay, M., et al. Results of a survey of forensic psychiatrists on the validity of the sadistic personality disorder diagnosis. Am. J. Psychiatry 148:875–879, 1991.

Sprock, J., Blashfield, R. K., Smith, B. Gender weighting of DSM-III-R personality disorder criteria. Am. J. Psychiatry 147:586–590, 1990.

Walker, L. E. A. The Battered Woman Syndrome. New York, Springer, 1984.

Walker, L. W. A. Inadequacies of the masochistic personality disorder diagnosis for women. Journal of Personality Disorders 1:183–189, 1987.

Walker, L. E. A. Are personality disorders gender biased? in Controversial Issues in Mental Health. Edited by Kirk, S. A., Einbinder, S. D. Boston, Allyn & Bacon, 1994, pp. 22–30.

Widiger, T. A. Deletion of self-defeating and sadistic personality disorders, in DSM-IV Personality Disorders. Edited by Livesley, W. J. New York, Guilford, 1995.

Widiger, T. A., Frances, A. J. Controversies concerning the self-defeating personality disorder, in Self-Defeating Behaviors: Experimental Research, Clinical Impressions, and Practical Implications. Edited by Curtis, R. C. New York, Plenum, 1989, pp. 289–309.

Widiger, T., Nietzel, M. Kaplan's view of DSM-III: The data revisited. Am Psychol. 39:1319–1320, 1984.

Widiger, T., Settle, S. Broverman et al. revisited: An artifactual sex bias. J. Pers. Soc. Psychol. 53:463–469, 1987.

Widiger, T. A., Spitzer, R. L. Sex bias in the diagnosis of personality disorders: Conceptual and methodological issues. Clinical Psychology Review 11:1–22, 1991.

Widiger, T. A., Corbitt, E., Funtowicz, M. Rejoinder to Dr. Walker, in Controversial Issues in Mental Health. Edited by Kirk, S. A., Einbinder, S. D. Boston, Allyn & Bacon, 1994b, pp. 30–38.

Widom, C. W. Sex roles and psychopathology, in Sex Roles and Psychopathology. Edited by Widom, C. S. New York, Plenum, 1984, pp. 3–17.

Williams, J. B. W., Spitzer, R. L. The issue of sex bias in DSM-III: A critique of "A woman's view of DSM-III" by Marcie Kaplan. Am. Psychol. 38:793–798, 1983.

Zeldow, P. B. Sex roles, psychological assessment, and patient management, in Sex Roles and Psychopathology. Edited by Widom, C. S. New York, Plenum, 1984, pp. 355–374.

CHALLENGE QUESTIONS

Is There Gender Bias in the *DSM-IV*?

1. What recommendations with regard to gender would you make to the task force working on *DSM-V*?
2. Should each *DSM* diagnosis have a separate list of gender-related diagnostic criteria?
3. What are some of the social issues that influence the differential assignment of certain diagnoses, such as eating disorders, personality disorders, and depression?
4. What are some of the social issues that make women more likely than men to seek professional help for emotional problems?

Suggested Readings

Becker, D. (1997). *Through the looking glass: Women and borderline personality disorder.* Boulder, CO: Westview Press, A Division of HarperCollins Publishers, Inc.

Glickauf-Hughs, C., & Wells, M. (1998). Self-defeating personality disorder: A re-examination. *Psychotherapy Bulletin, 33*(4), 32–35.

Huprich, S. K., & Fine, M. A. (1997). Diagnoses under consideration—self-defeating and depressive personality disorders: Current status and clinical issues. *Journal of Contemporary Psychotherapy, 27*(4), 303–322.

Livesley, J. W. (Ed.) (1995). *The DSM-IV personality disorders.* New York, NY: The Guilford Press.

Widiger, T. A. (1998). Sex biases in the diagnoses of personality disorders. *Journal of Personality Disorders, 12*(2), 95–118.

On the Internet ...

The International Society for the Study of Dissociation

This is the Web site of the International Society for the Study of Dissociation (ISSD), a nonprofit group whose efforts focus on research and training for dissociative disorders.

http://www.issd.org

Sidran Foundation

The Sidran Foundation Web site provides online resources for the recognition and treatment of trauma-related stresses and disorders.

http://www.sidran.org

Children and Adults with Attention-Deficit/Hyperactivity Disorder

This is the Web site for Children and Adults with Attention-Deficit/Hyperactivity Disorder (CHADD), a nonprofit organization that supports people with ADHD through advocacy and education.

http://www.chadd.org

National Alliance for Research on Schizophrenia and Depression

This is an online resource for the study of brain disorders provided by the National Alliance for Research on Schizophrenia and Depression (NARSAD).

http://www.mhsource.com/narsad.html

National Abortion Federation

At this site the National Abortion Federation (NAF) reviews the research on the existence of post-abortion syndrome.

http://www.prochoice.org/facts/postab.html

Questions and Answers About Memories of Childhood Abuse

This site offers questions and answers from the American Psychological Association concerning the nature, prevalence, current research, and issues in recovered memory.

http://www.apa.org/pubinfo/mem.html

PART 2

Psychological Conditions

*A*t the heart of abnormal psychology are the psychological conditions and mental disorders for which people seek professional treatment. Although many conditions involve fairly clear sets of symptoms that can be recognized and treated by clinicians, other conditions are vaguer. In fact, some critics contend that there are conditions that are manufactured in the minds of some clients and reinforced by clinicians who are too eager to pathologize people. Particular controversy has emerged about the validity of conditions such as multiple personality disorder, attention deficit disorder, post-abortion syndrome, and the phenomenon of repressed memories. Questions have also arisen about the nature and causes of specific disorders such as schizophrenia.

- Is Multiple Personality Disorder a Valid Diagnosis?

- Does Attention Deficit Disorder Exist?

- Is Schizophrenia a Biological Disorder?

- Does Post-Abortion Syndrome Exist?

- Are Repressed Memories Valid?

ISSUE 3

Is Multiple Personality Disorder a Valid Diagnosis?

YES: Frank W. Putnam, from "Response to Article by Paul R. McHugh," *Journal of the American Academy of Child and Adolescent Psychiatry* (July 1995)

NO: Paul R. McHugh, from "Resolved: Multiple Personality Disorder Is an Individually and Socially Created Artifact," *Journal of the American Academy of Child and Adolescent Psychiatry* (July 1995)

ISSUE SUMMARY

YES: Psychiatrist Frank W. Putnam contends that the diagnosis of multiple personality disorder meets the standards for the three basic forms of validity: content validity, construct validity, and criterion-related validity.

NO: Psychiatrist Paul R. McHugh denies the validity of multiple personality disorder, asserting that this condition is a socially created behavioral disorder induced by psychotherapists.

M ental health experts have been fascinated for many years by the possibility that a person can develop seemingly independent personalities that are characterized by unique attributes and behaviors. For most of the past century, mental health experts used the label "multiple personality disorder" (MPD) to describe this kind of condition. During the past decade the official diagnostic term was changed to "dissociative identity disorder." Regardless of which term is used, the essence of the condition is that an individual possesses two or more distinct personality states, each with an enduring pattern of perceiving, relating to, and thinking about the environment and the self. At least two of these identities recurrently take control of the person's behavior, and the individual is unable to recall important personal information.

Relatively few cases of MPD were reported for most of the twentieth century, but that changed in 1980, when the authors of the *Diagnostic and Statistical Manual of Mental Disorders*, 3rd ed. (*DSM-III*) included this condition in the list of mental disorders. The disorder was characterized as a condition in which a person experiences a disorganization of the self that results in the experience of discrepant individuals residing within one's overall being. Along with this broadening of the diagnosis came a proliferation of cases of MPD. Interestingly, in the years prior to 1970, only a handful of cases had been reported, but in recent decades many thousands of cases have been documented.

With the astronomical increase in the number of diagnosed cases of MPD, clinicians and researchers began to wonder if the increase was due to the increased incidence of the disorder or to an artificial phenomenon due to the broadening of the definition of the disorder. Some skeptics raised the worrisome possibility that the condition is iatrogenic—that it can be generated in a client by a psychotherapist, often through the use of hypnosis. Although presumably well meaning, the psychotherapist might suggest to a client that long-standing psychological problems are the result of a fragmentation of personality, thus leading the client to act and think in ways reflective of seemingly independent identities.

In the following selection, Frank W. Putnam contends that MPD is indeed a valid diagnosis, and he asserts that there are no documented cases in which the full syndrome of MPD was induced by fascination or by hypnosis. Further, he contends that MPD—and its core pathological process, dissociation—can be detected and measured by reliable and valid structured interviews and scales.

In the second selection, Paul R. McHugh contends that many individuals who develop the characteristics of MPD are responding to the crude suggestion of therapists that they harbor some "alter" personalities. Responding to the therapist's suggestion, he concludes, the patient gets caught up in feeling pressured to act in ways that are consistent with the role of having several personalities.

POINT

- MPD is a valid diagnosis that meets the standards of the three basic forms of validity.
- The notion that MPD is iatrogenic is based on research with role-playing students in staged situations, which has little bearing on real-life clinical work.
- The clinical phenomenology of MPD has been delineated and replicated in numerous studies of more than 1,000 cases.

- MPD and its core pathological process, dissociation, can be detected and measured by reliable and valid structured interviews and scales.

COUNTERPOINT

- MPD is little more than a modern-day form of hysteria.
- MPD is a condition that is induced by therapists.

- Much of the expansion in the diagnosis of MPD is due to the fact that the condition is included in the *DSM*, which leads some practitioners to believe that MPD must exist because there are operational criteria available for making the diagnosis.
- Therapists elicit the expression of other personalities by presenting leading questions to the patient that reinforce the idea that the individual possesses separate personalities.

Frank W. Putnam  **YES**

Response to Article by Paul R. McHugh

For more than a century, the existence of multiple personality disorder (MPD) has provoked heated debate. That both the diagnosis and the controversy are still with us says something about the resiliency of both sides of the question. The similarities between the charges leveled in the current debate and those in the historical record suggest that things, unfortunately, have not changed very much in 100 years. It is unlikely that this exchange will resolve the matter, but perhaps we can move the question along to a higher level. The criticisms leveled at MPD are not credible when examined in the light of what we know about the etiologies of mental illness. Debate can be advanced by critiqueing the validity of MPD in the same manner in which the validity of other psychiatric diagnoses are assessed.

What are the criticisms of MPD? There are three basic criticisms made against this diagnosis. The first is that MPD is an iatrogenic disorder produced in patients by their psychiatrists. The second is that MPD is produced by its portrayal in the popular media. The third is that the numbers of MPD cases are increasing exponentially. The first and second charges are often lumped together and viewed as being responsible for the third.

The first accusation is historically the oldest and the most serious because it alleges therapeutic misconduct of the gravest nature. The psychiatrist's fascination with the patient's symptoms supposedly reinforces the behavior and produces the syndrome. A variation of this accusation charges that the condition is produced by the improper use of hypnosis. In either instance, the fact is that there are no cases reported in which the full clinical syndrome of MPD was induced either by fascination or by hypnosis. Experiments by Nicholas Spanos are sometimes cited as examples of the creation of MPD by role-playing students (Spanos, 1986). The reader is invited to compare the verbal responses of undergraduates responding to a staged situation with the psychiatric symptoms of MPD patients reported in the clinical literature. Two clinical studies examined the effects of using hypnosis on the symptoms and behaviors of MPD patients (Putnam et al., 1986; Ross, 1989). There were no significant differences between MPD cases diagnosed and treated with or without hypnosis. Since MPD appears in many patients with no history of hypnotic interventions, the misuse of hypnosis apparently is not responsible for the syndrome.

From Frank W. Putnam, "Response to Article by Paul R. McHugh," *Journal of the American Academy of Child and Adolescent Psychiatry*, vol. 34, no. 7 (July 1995). Copyright © 1995 by The American Academy of Child and Adolescent Psychiatry. Reprinted by permission of Lippincott Williams & Wilkins.

The second allegation, that MPD is induced by media portrayals, ignores extensive research on the effects of the media on behavior. More than 30 years of research on the relation of television viewing to violence informs us of just how difficult it is to find clear-cut effects produced by exposure to specific media imagery. Certainly there are media effects, but these effects are not simple and direct identifications. Rather they are indirect, cumulative, and heavily confounded by individual and situational variables (Friedlander, 1993). The depiction of violence in the media is vastly more common (perhaps it is even the norm for movies and television) than the portrayal of MPD. Yet, the critics of MPD would have us believe that the minuscule percentage of media time devoted to MPD is directly responsible for the increase in diagnosed cases. This would be an extraordinarily specific and powerful effect—far, far beyond anything found by the thousands of studies on violence conducted by media researchers.

The first and second accusations beg an important question. Why this disorder? If these individuals are so suggestible, why don't they develop other disorders? Why should suggestion effects be unique to MPD? Psychiatrists inquire about and exhibit interest in other symptoms. We do not believe that asking about hallucinations produces them in a patient. Why should asking about the existence of "other parts" of the self produce alter personalities? What is so magical about this question? With respect to media portrayals of mental illness, a random channel-walk through the soap opera and talk show circuits will convince one that many other symptoms and disorders fill the airwaves. Eating disorders, obsessive-compulsive disorder, bipolar illness, assorted phobias, sexual dysfunctions, autism, chronic fatigue syndrome, etc., etc., are discussed in graphic detail and glamorized after their own fashion. Why don't suggestible individuals identify with these conditions? Truly, if there is such a high degree of suggestive specificity to MPD, it is worthy of intensive investigation.

The third accusation, that cases of MPD are increasing "exponentially" or "logarithmically," shows little understanding of basic mathematics. Critics often cite inflated numbers of cases without any support for their figures. I have plotted the numbers of published cases year by year, and while it is true that they have increased significantly compared to prior decades, the rise in the slope is not nearly as dramatic as the critics' hyperbole suggests. Over the same period, other disorders, e.g., Lyme disease, obsessive-compulsive disorder, and chronic fatigue syndrome, have shown equal or faster rises in the numbers of published cases. This reflects a basic process in medicine associated with the compilation and dissemination of syndromal profiles. When symptoms that were once viewed as unrelated are organized into a coherent syndromal presentation and that information is widely disseminated, physicians begin to identify the condition more frequently. The rapid rise in the number of cases of "battered child syndrome" following the classic paper by Kempe and his colleagues is a very relevant example of this process in action. A related criticism is that a few clinicians are responsible for most of the diagnosed MPD cases. Again, a review of the MPD literature demonstrates a healthy diversity of authorship comparable with that found for other conditions.

The crucial question raised by this debate is: How should the validity of a psychiatric diagnosis be judged? Considerable thought has gone into this question. (For a more complete discussion, see *The Validity of Psychiatric Diagnosis* by Robins and Barrett, 1989.) Many psychiatrists endorse the model of diagnostic validity put forth by Robins and Guze in 1970 and subsequently amplified by others (Robins and Barrett, 1989). This model requires that psychiatric diagnoses satisfy aspects of three basic forms of validity: content validity, criterion-related validity, and construct validity. Content validity is probably the most fundamental form of validity for psychiatric diagnosis. It requires that the diagnostician be able to give a specific and detailed clinical description of the disorder. Criterion-related validity requires that laboratory tests, e.g., chemical, physiological, radiological, or reliable psychological tests, are consistent with the defined clinical picture. Construct validity requires that the disorder be delimited from other disorders (discriminant validity).

The clinical phenomenology of MPD has been delineated and repeatedly replicated in a series of studies of more than 1,000 cases. A review of the best of these studies demonstrates striking similarities in the symptoms of MPD patients across different sites and investigational methodologies (Coons et al., 1988; Putnam et al., 1986; Ross et al., 1990). They should convince the interested reader that a specific, unique, and reproducible clinical syndrome is being described. A small but growing body of literature on childhood and adolescent MPD links the adult syndrome with childhood precursors, establishing a developmental continuity of symptoms and pathology (Dell and Eisenhower, 1990; Hornstein and Putnam, 1992). The well-delineated, well-replicated set of dissociative symptoms that constitute the core clinical syndrome of MPD satisfies the requirements for content validity.

MPD and its core pathological process, dissociation, can be detected and measured by reliable and valid structured interviews and scales (Carlson et al., 1993; Steinberg et al., 1991). Published data on validity compare very favorably with accepted psychological instruments and satisfy the reliability requirement imposed by Robins and Guze for the inclusion of psychological tests as measures of criterion validity. These instruments have been translated into other languages and proven to discriminate MPD in other cultures. Discriminant validity studies have been conducted for the Dissociative Experiences Scale and the Structured Clinical Interview for DSM-III-R-Dissociative Module, both of which show good receiver operating characteristic curves, a standard method for evaluating the validity of a diagnostic test (Carlson et al., 1993; Steinberg et al., 1991). MPD is well discriminated from other disorders by reliable and valid tests and thus has good criterion-related and construct validates.

Multiple personality disorder has been with us from the beginnings of psychiatry (Ellenberger, 1970). At present we conceptualize this condition as a complex form of posttraumatic dissociative disorder, highly associated with a history of severe trauma usually beginning at an early age. I believe that research demonstrates that the diagnosis of MPD meets the standards of content validity, criterion-related validity, and construct validity considered necessary for the validity of a psychiatric diagnosis. The simplistic argument that MPD is individually and socially caused "hysteria" evades the much more important question of what is the best approach to helping these patients. Denying its existence or blaming psychiatrists and television for MPD patients' symptoms is not constructive. It is important to move beyond debate about the existence of the condition to more serious discussions of therapeutic issues.

References

Carlson EB, Putnam FW, Ross CA et al. (1993), *Validity of the Dissociative Experiences Scale* in screening for multiple personality disorder: a multicenter study. *Am J Psychiatry* 150:1030–1036

Coons PM, Bowman ES, Milstein V (1988), Multiple personality disorder: a clinical investigation of 50 cases. *J Nerv Ment Dis* 176:519–527

Dell PF, Eisenhower JW (1990), Adolescent multiple personality disorder. *J Am Acad Child Adolesc Psychiatry* 29:359–366

Ellenberger HF (1970), *The Discovery of the Unconscious: The History and Evolution of Dynamic Psychiatry.* New York: Basic Books

Friedlander BZ (1993), Community violence, children's development, and mass media: in pursuit of new insights, new goals and new strategies. In: *Children and Violence,* Reiss D, Richters JE, Radke–Yarrow M, Scharff D, eds. New York: Guilford Press, pp 66–81

Hornstein NL, Putnam FW (1992), Clinical phenomenology of child and adolescent dissociative disorders. *J Am Acad Child Adolesc Psychiatry* 31:1077–1085

Putnam FW, Guroff JJ, Silberman EK, Barban L, Post RM (1986), The clinical phenomenology of multiple personality disorder: review of 100 recent cases. *J Clin Psychiatry* 47:285–293

Robins LE, Barrett JE, ed. (1989), *The Validity of Psychiatric Diagnosis.* New York: Raven Press

Ross CA (1989), Effects of hypnosis on the features of multiple personality disorder. *Am J Clin Hypn* 32:99–106

Ross CA, Miller SD, Bjornson L, Reagor P, Fraser G, Anderson G (1990), Structured interview data on 102 cases of multiple personality disorder from four centers. *Am J Psychiatry* 147:596–601

Spanos NP (1986), Hypnosis, nonvolutional responding, and multiple personality: a social psychological perspective. *Prog Exp Pers Res* 14:1–62

Steinberg M, Rounsaville B, Cicchetti D (1991), Detection of dissociative disorders in psychiatric patients by a screening instrument and a structured diagnostic interview. *Am J Psychiatry* 149:1050–1054

Paul R. McHugh

 **NO**

Resolved: Multiple Personality Disorder Is an Individually and Socially Created Artifact

W here's hysteria now that we need it? With *DSM-IV* [*Diagnostic and Statistical Manual of Mental Disorders,* 4th ed.], psychiatrists have developed a common language and a common approach to diagnosis. But in the process of operationalizing diagnoses, we may have lost some concepts about patient behavior. The term "hysteria" disappeared when *DSM-III* was published; without it, psychiatrists have been deprived of a scientific concept essential to the development of new ideas: the null hypothesis. This loss hits home with the epidemic of multiple personality disorder (MPD).

The work of Talcott Parsons (1964), David Mechanic (1978), and Isidore Pilowsky (1969) taught psychiatrists to appreciate that phenomena such as hysterical paralyses, blindness, and pseudoseizures were actually behaviors with a goal: achieving the "sick role." Inspired by Parsons, Mechanic and Pilowsky used the term "abnormal illness behavior" in lieu of hysteria. Their approach eliminated the stigma of malingering that had been implied in hysteria and indicated that patients could take on such behavior without fraudulent intent. They were describing an old reality of medical experience.

Some people—experiencing emotional distress in the face of a variety of life circumstances and conflicts—complain to doctors about physical or psychological symptoms that they claim are signs of illness. Sometimes they display gross impairments of movement or consciousness; sometimes the features are subtle and changing. These complaints prompt doctors to launch investigations in laboratories, to conduct elaborate and sometimes dangerous studies of the brain or body, and to consult with experts, who examine the patient for esoteric disease. As the investigation proceeds, the patient may become still more persuaded that an illness is at work and begin to model the signs of disorder on the subtle suggestions of the physician's inquiry. For example, a patient with complaints of occasional lapses in alertness might—in the course of investigations that include visits to the epilepsy clinic and to the EEG laboratory

From Paul R. McHugh, "Resolved: Multiple Personality Disorder Is an Individually and Socially Created Artifact," *Journal of the American Academy of Child and Adolescent Psychiatry*, vol. 34, no. 7 (July 1995). Copyright © 1995 by The American Academy of Child and Adolescent Psychiatry. Reprinted by permission of Lippincott Williams & Wilkins.

for sleep studies, photic stimulation, and nasopharyngeal leads—gradually develop the frenzied thrashing movements of the limbs that require the protective attention of several nurses and hospital aides.

Eventually, with the patient no better and the investigations proving fruitless, a psychiatric consultant alert to the concept of hysteria and its contemporary link to the "sick role" might recognize that the patient's disorder is not an epileptic but a behavioral one. The patient is displaying movements that attract medical attention and provide the privileges of patienthood.

Talcott Parsons, the Harvard sociologist, pointed out in the 1950s that medicine was an organized component of our society intended to aid, through professional knowledge, the sick and the impaired. To accomplish this, certain individuals—physicians—are licensed by society to decide not only how to manage the sick, but to choose and distinguish the sick from other impaired people. Such an identification can provide these "sick" individuals with certain social privileges, i.e., rest, freedom from employment, and support from others during the reign of the condition. The person given the appellation "sick" by the social spokesman—the physician—was assumed by the society to respond to these privileges with other actions, i.e., cooperating with the intrusions of investigators of the illness and making every effort at rehabilitation so as to return to health. The hidden assumption is that the burdens and pains of illness act to drive the patient toward these cooperative actions with the physicians and thus to be happy to relinquish the few small pleasures that can be found in being treated as a victim of sickness.

However, because there are advantages to the sick role, there are some situations in which a person might seek this role without a "ticket of admission," a disease. This is hardly a remarkable idea as almost anyone has noticed the temptation to "call in sick" when troubles are afoot. But in some patients —those with emotional conflicts, weakened self-criticism, and high suggestibility—this temptation can be transformed, usually with some prompting, into the conviction that they are infirm. This kind of patient may, in fact, use more and more information from the medical profession's activities to amplify the expression of the infirmity.

Psychiatrists have known about these matters of social and psychological dynamics for more than 100 years. They were brought vividly to attention by the distinguished pupil of Jean-Martin Charcot, Joseph Babinski (he of the plantar response). Like Sigmund Freud and Pierre Janet, Babinski had observed Charcot manage patients with, what Charcot called, "hysteroepilepsy." But Babinski was convinced that hysteroepilepsy was not a new disorder. He believed that the women at Charcot's clinic were being persuaded—and not so subtly—to take on the features of epilepsy by the interest Charcot and his assistants expressed (Babinski and Froment, 1918). Babinski also believed that these women were vulnerable to this persuasion because of distressing states of mind provoked in their life circumstances and their roles as intriguing patients and the subject of attention from many distinguished physicians who offered them a haven of care.

Babinski was bringing the null hypothesis to Charcot and with it, not a rejection of these women as legitimate victims of some problem, but an appreciation that behaving as if epileptic obscured reality and made helping their actual problem difficult. Babinski wrote that just as hysteroepilepsy rested on persuasion, so a form of counterpersuasion could correct it. He demonstrated that these patients improved when they were taken from the wards and clinics where other afflicted women—epileptic and pseudoepileptic—were housed and when the attention of the staff was turned away from their seizures and onto their lives. These measures—isolation and countersuggestion—had the advantage of limiting the rewards for the behavior and of prompting a search for and treatment of the troubles in the personal life.

All this became embedded in the concept of hysteria and needs to be reapplied in the understanding of MPD. The patients I have seen have been referred to the Johns Hopkins Health System because elsewhere they have become stuck in the process of therapy. The histories are similar. They were mostly women who in the course of some distress sought psychiatric assistance. In the course of this assistance—and often early in the process—a therapist offered them a fairly crude suggestion that they might harbor some "alter" personalities. As an example of the crudity of the suggestions to the patient, I offer this published direction of how to both make the diagnosis and elicit "alters":

> The sine qua non of MPD is a second personality who at some time comes out and takes executive control of the patient's behavior. It may happen that an alter personality will reveal itself to you during this [assessment] process, but more likely it will not. So you may have to elicit an alter personality.... To begin the process of eliciting an alter, you can begin by indirect questioning such as, "Have you ever felt like another part of you does things that you can't control?" If she gives positive or ambiguous responses, ask for specific examples. You are trying to develop a picture of what the alter personality is like.... At this point, you might ask the host personality, "Does this set of feelings have a name?" Occasionally you will get a name. Often the host personality will not know. You can then focus on a particular event or set of behaviors and follow up on those. For instance, you can ask, "Can I talk to the part of you who is taking those long drives to the country?" (Buie, 1992, p. 3).

Once the patient permits the therapist to "talk to the part... who is taking those long drives," the patient is committed to having MPD and is forced to act in ways consistent with this role. The patient is then placed into care on units or in services—often titled "the dissociative service"—at the institution. She meets other patients with the same compliant responses to therapists' suggestions. She and the staff begin a continuous search for other "alters." With the discovery of the first "alter," the barrier of self-criticism and self-observation is breached. No obstacles to invention remain.

Countless numbers of personalities emerge over time. What began as two or three may develop to 99 or 100. The distressing symptoms continue as long as therapeutic attention is focused on finding more alters and sustaining the view that the problems relate to an "intriguing capacity" to dissociate or fractionate the self.

At Johns Hopkins, we see patients in whom MPD has been diagnosed because symptoms of depression have continued despite therapy elsewhere. Our referrals have been few and our experience, therefore, is only now building, probably because our views—that MPD may be a therapist-induced artifact—have only recently become generally known in our community (McHugh, 1995). We seem to challenge the widely accepted view and to "turn back the clock." The referrals that come to us often arrive with obstacles to our therapeutic plans. Patients and their referring therapists often wish to stay in regular contact (two to three times weekly) and to continue their work on MPD. At the same time, we at Hopkins are expected to treat the depression or some other supposed "side issue." We, however, following the isolation and countersuggestion approach, try to bring about, at least temporarily, a separation of the patient from the staff and the support groups that sustain the focus on "alters." We refuse to talk to "alters" but rather encourage our patients to review their present difficulties, thus applying the concept of "abnormal illness behavior" to their condition.

The advocates for MPD are in the same position as Charcot was when Babinski offered his proposal of the null hypothesis. As in any scientific discussion, it is not the responsibility of the proposers of the null hypothesis to prove its likelihood. That hypothesis simply claims that nothing special has been discovered. I claim the same in this debate. The investigators proposing a new entity must demonstrate that the null hypothesis should be rejected.

In most of the discussions by champions of MPD just the opposite occurs. Not only is the null hypothesis discarded without any compelling reason, but nonrelevant information is presented to justify a uniqueness to MPD. Perhaps the most common proposal is that MPD must exist in the way proposed because it is included in *DSM-IV* and operational criteria are available to make the diagnosis. This is a misunderstanding of *DSM-IV*. It provides a way in which a diagnosis can be reliably applied to a patient, but it does not in any way validate the existence of the condition or negate a null hypothesis about it.

Charcot had quite reliable ways of diagnosing hysteroepilepsy. It just did not exist as he thought it did, but rather it was a behavior seeking the sick role. It is my opinion that MPD is another behavioral disorder—a socially created artifact—in distressed people who are looking for help. The diagnosis and subsequent procedures for exploring MPD give them a coherent posture toward themselves and others as a particular kind of patient: "sick" certainly, "victim" possibly. This posture, if sustained, will obscure the real problems in their lives and render psychotherapy long, costly, and pointless. If the customary treatments of hysteria are provided, then we can expect that the multiple personality behaviors will be abandoned and proper rehabilitative attention can be given to the patient.

Hysteria as a concept has been neglected in *DSM-III* and *DSM-IV*, but it offers just what it has always offered: a challenge to proposals of new entities in psychiatry. Some diagnoses survive and others do not. MPD has run away with itself, and its proponents must now deal with this challenge. Charcot took such a challenge from his student. Everyone learned in the process.

References

Babinski J, Froment J (1918), *Hysteria or Pithiatism and Reflex Nervous Disorders in the Neurology of War*. Rolleston JD, trans; Buzzard EF, ed. London: University of London Press

Buie SE (1992), Introduction to the diagnosis of multiple personality disorder. *Grand Rounds Rev* (4):1–3

McHugh PR (1995), Witches, multiple personalities, and other psychiatric artifacts. *Nature Med* 1:110–114

Mechanic D (1978), Effects of psychological distress on perceptions of physical health and use of medical and psychiatric facilities. *J Hum Stress* 4:26–32

Parsons T (1964), *Social Structure and Personality*. New York: Free Press

Pilowsky I (1969), Abnormal illness behaviour. *Br J Med Psychol* 42:347–351

CHALLENGE QUESTIONS

Is Multiple Personality Disorder a Valid Diagnosis?

1. How might the notion of "iatrogenic disorder" be applied to other psychological conditions, such as anxiety disorders, mood disorders, or even learning disorders?
2. McHugh discusses the concept of hysteria. How did theorists such as Sigmund Freud and Jean Martin Charcot characterize hysterical conditions?
3. What factors might motivate some patients to report the experience of multiple personalities?
4. What factors might motivate some clinicians to reinforce the experience of multiple personalities?
5. What explanations other than multiple personality disorder might be used to explain the reports of some people that they have the experience of multiple personalities?
6. What treatment recommendations would you make to a clinician whose patient reports the experience of several personalities?

Suggested Readings

Kluft, R. P. (1995). Current controversies surrounding dissociative identify disorder. In L. Cohen, J. Berzoff, & M. Elin (Eds.), *Dissociative identity disorder: Theoretical and treatment controversies.* (pp. 347–377). Northvale, NJ: Jason Aronson.

Piper, A. J. (1998). Multiple personality disorder: Witchcraft survives in the twentieth century. *The Skeptical Inquirer, 22*(3), 44–50.

Piper, A. J. (1997). *Hoax and reality: The bizarre world of multiple personality disorder.* Northvale, NJ: Jason Aronson.

Ross, C. A. (1997) *Dissociative identity disorder: Diagnosis, clinical features, and treatment of multiple personality.* New York, NY: John Wiley & Sons, Inc.

Spanos, N. P. (1996). *Multiple identities & false memories: A sociocognitive perspective.* Washington, DC: American Psychological Association.

ISSUE 4

Does Attention Deficit Disorder Exist?

YES: Edward M. Hallowell, from "What I've Learned from ADD," *Psychology Today* (May–June 1997)

NO: Thomas Armstrong, from "ADD: Does It Really Exist?" *Phi Delta Kappan* (February 1996)

ISSUE SUMMARY

YES: Psychiatrist Edward M. Hallowell asserts that an appreciation for the complexity of attention deficit disorder (ADD) can provide valuable understanding about the workings of the brain and how this disorder affects the lives of millions of people.

NO: Educational consultant and former special education teacher Thomas Armstrong contends that the diagnosis of ADD has been blown out of proportion by the public and the professional community and is, in fact, a questionable diagnosis.

$\mathbf{A}$nyone who has set foot in an American classroom has observed a range of children whose behaviors and compliance span a relatively wide continuum. At one end are well-behaved children who listen attentively to their teachers, cooperate pleasantly with their peers, and follow instructions with patience and a sense of calm. At the other end are children who seem to be completely out of control. These children are both disturbed and disturbing. They show a constellation of behaviors characterized by inattention and hyperactivity. These children are referred to by teachers and special educators as having attention deficit disorder (ADD), or by the *Diagnostic and Statistical Manual of Mental Disorders,* 4th ed. *(DSM-IV)* label "attention deficit hyperactivity disorder" (ADHD). Their inattention is evidenced by a range of behaviors, including carelessness, distractibility, forgetfulness, and difficulty following through on tasks or organizing themselves. Their hyperactivity is characterized by restlessness, running around, difficulty playing with others, excessive talk, and other behaviors suggesting that they are "on the go."

A few decades ago these hyperactive and impulsive children might have been labeled as having "minimal brain dysfunction," a label that suggested that an underlying neurological problem was the basis for their disruptive behavior. As times have changed, so also have the labels, such that the terms *attention deficit disorder* and *attention deficit hyperactivity disorder* have become commonplace in describing children in every school in America. The numbers of children carrying diagnostic labels involving inattention have grown so rapidly that some critics have questioned whether or not many in our society have come to view this diagnosis as a simple label for a very complex problem. Questions have arisen about whether the symptoms of children identified as having ADD reflect neurological problems or social ills that stem from deficient parenting and problem-laden educational systems.

In the following selection, Edward M. Hallowell speaks from his personal experience as a person who was diagnosed with attention deficit disorder in 1981, when he suddenly was able to make sense of his impatience, distractibility, restlessness, proneness to procrastination, disturbingly brief attention span, and intense bursts of energy. Hallowell's personal experiences brought him to the conclusion that advances in understanding the workings of the brain could help researchers develop more compelling explanations for the seemingly out-of-control behaviors of millions of American children, as well as develop interventions to help the many people who are tormented by this extreme form of restless inattentiveness.

In the second selection, Thomas Armstrong asserts that conditions such as attention deficit disorder are part of a national phenomenon in which there has been a proliferation of relevant books, special assessments, learning programs, residential schools, parent advocacy groups, clinical services, and medications. He points out that prevalence estimates range widely, and he calls into question the nature of the assessments (such as behavior-rating scales) that are used to derive this diagnosis, scales that Armstrong views as too dependent on opinion. He asserts that careful scrutiny will demonstrate that there really is not much difference between children labeled ADD and "normal" children.

POINT	COUNTERPOINT
• Proper diagnosis and treatment of ADD allows sufferers to take responsibility more effectively and to become more productive and patient.	• ADD has become a diagnosed psychiatric disorder, and millions of children and adults run the risk of stigmatization from the application of this label.
• ADD has a biological basis, and millions of individuals with ADD have benefited spectacularly from medications that have relieved many disturbing symptoms.	• The evidence for ADD being a medical disorder is unclear, particularly in light of the variable nature of this condition.
• The scientifically based prevalence rate of ADD is 5 percent of the population.	• Prevalence estimates of ADD range from 1 percent to 20 percent of the population.
• ADD occurs along a spectrum, ranging from severe cases involving rampant disorganization and uncontrollable impulsivity to mild cases in which the symptoms are barely noticeable.	• Under rigorous scientific scrutiny, few if any differences are evident between children who are labeled ADD and those who are considered "normal."

Edward M. Hallowell

 **YES**

What I've Learned from ADD

When I discovered, in 1981, that I had attention deficit disorder (ADD), it was one of the great "Aha!" experiences of my life. Suddenly so many seemingly disparate parts of my personality made sense—the impatience, distractibility, restlessness, amazing ability to procrastinate, and extraordinarily brief attention span (here-one-moment-gone-the-next), not to mention the high bursts of energy and creativity and an indefinable, zany sense of life.

It was a pivotal moment for me, but the repercussions have been more powerful and wide-ranging than I could have imagined 16 years ago. Coming to understand ADD has been like stepping through a porthole into a wider world, expanding my view of my patients, friends, and family. I now know that many personality traits and psychological problems have a genuine basis in biology —not just ADD, but also depression, learning disorders, anxiety, panic attacks, and even shyness.

That insight has been tremendously freeing, for myself and my patients, and it has also led the mental health field to novel, effective treatments for brain disorders. I use the word "brain" intentionally, to emphasize that in many ways our personality is hardwired. Yet just as important is the fact that biology is only part of the story. We're all born with a set of genes, but how those genes get expressed depends largely on life experience and the way our environment interacts with our biology. If we understand this, we can "manage" our brains more deftly, using methods that range from medicine to lifestyle changes. Diagnosing and treating ADD—in my own life and those of hundreds of patients— has shown me just how remarkable these interventions can be. I have seen more than a few teetering marriages right themselves when the couple understood it was ADD, not bad character, causing their troubles. I have also seen many careers that had been languishing in the bin labeled "underachiever" suddenly take off after diagnosis and treatment of ADD. Scores of students have been able to rescue their academic careers after diagnosis and treatment. It is a powerful diagnosis: powerfully destructive when missed and powerfully constructive when correctly picked up.

ADD has taught me to look at people differently. These days, when I meet someone I often ask myself the question, "What kind of brain does he have?" as a way of trying to understand the person. I've learned that brains differ tremendously from person to person, and that some of the most interesting and productive people around have "funny" (i.e., highly idiosyncratic) brains. There is no normal, standard brain, any more than there is a normal, standard automobile, dress, or human face. Our old distinctions of "smart" and "stupid" don't even begin to describe the variety of differences in human brains; indeed, these distinctions trample over those differences.

Today we know more than ever about the brain—but in learning more we have realized how little we actually know. With sophisticated brain scans that map the activity of networks of neurons we can peer inside the once impenetrable armor of our skulls and learn just how brains act when they are seeing, thinking, remembering, and even malfunctioning. And yet the vast territory of the brain still stretches out before us uncharted, like the sixteenth-century maps of the New World we used to see in our fifth-grade history books. Although we are coining new terms all the time (like emotional intelligence or post-traumatic stress disorder or even attention deficit disorder), although we are discovering new neurotransmitters and brain peptides that reveal new connections and networks within the brain, and although we are revising or throwing out old theories as new ones leap into our screens, any honest discussion of mental life must begin with the confession, "There's so much we still don't know."

Disorder and Metaphor?

What do these philosophical flights of fancy have to do with ADD and me? A few years ago ADD burst upon the American scene the way psychiatric disorders sometimes do, emerging as a riveting new metaphor for our cultural milieu. In the 1930s we embraced neurasthenia; in the '50s W. H. Auden coined the term "the age of anxiety"; in the '70s Christopher Lasch dubbed us the "culture of narcissism." Now, in the '90s, ADD has emerged as a symbol of American life.... This may explain why *Driven to Distraction* and *Answers to Distraction,* two books I wrote a few years ago with Harvard psychiatrist John Ratey, M.D., found a surprisingly wide and vocal audience.

At the same time, there has been some misunderstanding because of the sudden popularity of ADD. Scientists rightly get upset when they see extravagant claims being made that studies cannot justify—claims, for instance, that up to 25 percent of our population suffers from ADD. (The true number is probably around 5 percent.) And ordinary people are annoyed because they feel this diagnosis has become a catchall excuse—clothed in neurological, scientific language—for any inappropriate behavior. ADD can seem to undercut our country's deep belief in the work ethic. "Why didn't you do your homework?" *"Because I have ADD."* "Why are you late?" *"Because I have ADD."* "Why haven't you paid your income tax in five years?" *"Because I have ADD."* "Why are you so obnoxious?" *"Because I have ADD."* But, in fact, once ADD is properly diagnosed and treated, the opposite happens: The sufferer is able to take responsibility more effectively and becomes more productive and patient. The student who always forgot his homework and was constantly penalized for doing so is able to remember his homework—after his ADD is treated. The same is true for the adult in the workplace, who, once his ADD is treated, is finally able to finish the project he has so "irresponsibly" neglected, or the academician who is at last able to complete her Ph.D. dissertation.

So what is this condition, and where has it been all these centuries? Is it just another fad, or is there some scientific basis to ADD?

ADD is not a new disorder, although it has not been clearly understood until recent years, and its definition will become even more refined as we learn more about it. Right now, we are like blind men describing an elephant. The elephant is there—this vast collection of people with varying attentional strengths and vulnerabilities. However, generating a definitive description, diagnostic workup, and treatment plan with replicable research findings still poses a challenge. As long ago as the 1940s, the term "minimal brain damage syndrome" was used to describe symptoms similar to what we now call ADD. Today, the standard manual of the mental health field, the DSM-IV, defines ADD as a syndrome of involuntary distractibility—a restless, constant wandering of the crucial beam of energy we call attention. That trait is the hallmark of this disorder. More specifically, the syndrome must include six or more symptoms of either inattention or hyperactivity and impulsivity—the latter variant is known as attention deficit disorder with hyperactivity, or ADHD. . . .

To define a disorder solely in terms of attention is a true leap forward, since for centuries nobody paid any attention to attention. Attention was viewed as a choice, and if your mind wandered, you were simply allowing it to do so. Symptoms of ADD—not unlike those of depression, mania, or anxiety disorders—were considered deep and moral flaws.

When people ask me where ADD has been all these years, I respond that it has been in classrooms and offices and homes all over the world, right under our noses all along, only it has been called by different names: laziness, stupidity, rottenness, and worthlessness. For decades children with ADD have been shamed, beaten, punished, and humiliated. They have been told they suffered from a deficit not of attention but of motivation and effort. That approach fails as miserably as trying to beat nearsightedness out of a child—and the damage carries over into adulthood.

It's All in Your Head

The evidence that ADD has a biological basis has mounted over the last 20 years. First, and most moving, there is the clinical evidence from the records of millions of patients who have met the diagnostic criteria and who have benefited spectacularly from standard treatment. These are human stories of salvaged lives. The fact that certain medications predictably relieve target symptoms of ADD means that these symptoms have roots in the physical world.

I recall watching an eighth grader named Noah receive a reward for "Most Improved" at graduation. This boy's mother had been told by an expert that Noah was so severely "disturbed" that she should look into residential placement. He was often in trouble at school. From my first meeting with Noah I was struck by his kindness and tenacity; no expert had understood that he suffered from ADD, as well as mild cerebral palsy. Like many ADDers he was intuitive, warm, and empathic. After coaching, teacher involvement, extra structure, and the medication Ritalin, Noah improved steadily, from the moment of diagnosis in sixth grade until graduation from eighth. As I watched him walk up to receive his award, awkward but proud, shake the hand of the principal, then turn and flash us all a grin, I felt inside a gigantic, "YES!" *Yes* for the triumph of this boy, *yes* for the triumph of knowledge and determination over misunderstanding, *yes* for all the children who in the future will not have to suffer. Standing in the back of the gym, leaning against the wall, I cried some of the happiest tears I've ever shed.

There is also intriguing biological evidence for the existence of ADD. One seems to inherit a susceptibility to this disorder, which appears to cluster in families just as manic-depression and other mental illnesses do. Though no scientist has been able to isolate a single causative gene in any mental disorder—and, in fact, we are coming to understand that a complex interaction of genes, neurotransmitters, hormones, and the environment comes into play in mental illness—there is solid evidence that vulnerability can be passed down through generations. One particularly careful, recent review in *The Journal of The American Academy of Child and Adolescent Psychiatry* supported the heritability of ADD based upon family and twin-adoption studies and analysis of gene inheritance.

Evidence of ADD may even show up in specific areas of the brain. In 1990, Alan Zametkin, M.D., a psychiatrist at the National Institute of Mental Health (NIMH), reported startling findings about the ADD brain in the *New England Journal of Medicine*. Zametkin measured sugar metabolism—a major indicator of brain activity—in the brains of 30 adults who had a childhood history of ADD, along with 30 normal individuals. PET scans (positron emission tomography) allowed Zametkin to determine just how much sugar each participant's brain was absorbing, and in what regions. Sufferers of ADD absorbed less sugar in the areas of the brain that regulate impulse control, attention, and mood. Another study, by NIMH researcher David Hauser, M.D., linked ADD to a rare thyroid condition called generalized resistance to thyroid hormone (GRTH). Seventy percent of individuals with GRTH suffer from ADD—an extraordinarily high correlation. Finally, recent brain scan studies have revealed both anatomical and functional differences in the brains of individuals with ADD—slight but real differences in the size of the corpus callosum (which serves as the switchboard that connects the two hemispheres of the brain), as well as differences in the size of the caudate nucleus, another switching station deep within the brain. These breakthrough studies lay the foundation for promising research, but much more work needs to be done before we may be able to use these findings to actually help us diagnose ADD. They simply point us in the direction of biology—and that pointer is powerful.

The Pivotal Movement

Nothing matters more in ADD than proper diagnosis. Even today this condition is so misunderstood that it is both missed and overdiagnosed. As the public's awareness of the disorder grows, more and more people represent themselves as experts in ADD. As one of my patients said to me, "ADD has become a growth industry." Not every self-proclaimed expert knows ADD from ABC. For instance, depression can cause someone to be distracted and inattentive (and in many cases depression and ADD even occur together). However, a constant pattern of ADD symptoms usually extends back to early childhood, while depression is usually episodic. Thyroid disease can also look very much like ADD, and only testing by a physician can rule this out. High IQ can also mask or delay the diagnosis of ADD.

If the proper care is taken, a diagnosis of ADD can be made with confidence and accuracy, even though there is no single proof-positive test. Like most disorders, ADD occurs on a wide spectrum. In severe cases an individual can barely function due to rampant disorganization or uncontrollable impulsivity, not to mention secondary symptoms such as low self-esteem or depression. Yet very mild cases of ADD can be barely noticeable, especially in a bright individual who has adapted well.

To me, the life history is the one, absolutely convincing "test," which is then supported by the criteria of the DSM-IV and by psychological testing. When someone tells me they've been called "space-shot," "daydreamer," and "out in left field" all their lives, I suspect they might have ADD. At our clinic in Concord, Massachusetts, we use an abbreviated neuropsychological battery that helps us confirm a diagnosis. The battery includes standard written tests that measure memory and logic, impulsivity, and ability to organize complex tasks. Score alone does not tell the whole story; the tester needs to watch the client to determine whether he or she becomes easily frustrated and distracted. We even include a simple motor test that measures how quickly a person can tap their finger. (Patients with ADD are very good at this; depressed patients are not.) Though these tests are helpful, they are by no means definitive. A very smart person without ADD may find these tests boring, and become distracted. On the other hand, one of the great ironies of this kind of testing is that three of the best non-medication treatments available for ADD—structure, motivation, and novelty—are actually built into the testing situation, and can temporarily camouflage ADD.

A diagnosis by itself can change a life. My own father suffered from manic-depression, and I used to wonder if I had inherited the same disorder. When I learned I had ADD, that fact alone made a huge difference to my life. Instead of thinking of myself as having a character flaw, a family legacy, or some potentially ominous "difference" between me and other people, I could see myself in terms of having a unique brain biology. This understanding freed me emotionally. In fact, I would much rather have ADD that not have it, since I love the positive qualities that go along with it—creativity, energy, and unpredictability. I have found tremendous support and goodwill in response to my acknowledging my own ADD and dyslexia. The only time talking about this diagnosis will get you in trouble is when you offer it as an excuse.

After a diagnosis of ADD, an individual and his or her family can understand and change behavior patterns that may have been a problem for many years. Treatment must be multifaceted, and includes:

• **Educating the individual** and his or her family, friends, and colleagues or schoolteachers about the disorder. Two of the largest national organizations providing this information are CHADD (Children and Adults with Attention Deficit Disorder; call (954) 587-3700) and ADDA (Attention Deficit Disorder Association; call (216) 350-9595).

• **Making lifestyle changes,** such as incorporating structure, exercise, mediation, and prayer into one's daily life. Structural approaches include using practical tools like lists, reminders, simple filing systems, appointment books, and strategically placed bulletin boards. These can help manage the inner chaos of the ADD life, but the structure should be simple. One patient of mine got so excited about the concept of structure he impulsively went out to Staples and spent several thousand dollars on complex organizing materials that he never used. An example of simple structure: I put my car keys in a basket next to my front door so that I do not have to start each day with a frantic search for them.

Exercise can help drain off anxiety and excess aggression. Regular meditation or prayer can help focus and relax the mind.

• **Coaching, therapy, and social training.** Often ADD sufferers complain that structure is boring. "If I could be structured, I wouldn't have ADD!" moaned one patient. A coach can be invaluable in helping people with ADD organize their life, and encouraging them to stay on track. If a psychotherapist is the coach, he or she needs to be actively involved in advising specific behavioral changes.

Therapy itself can help resolve old patterns of self-sabotage or low self-esteem, and may help couples address long-standing problems. For example, setting up a simple division of labor between partners can prevent numerous arguments. Social training can help those with ADD learn how to avoid social gaffes. And merely understanding the condition can promote more successful interactions.

• **Medication.** The medications used to treat ADD constitute one of the miracles of modern medicine. Drugs are beneficial in about 80 percent of ADDers, working like a pair of eyeglasses for the brain, enhancing and sharpening mental focus. Medications prescribed include stimulants like Ritalin or Dexedrine, tricyclic antidepressants like Tofranil and Elavil, and even some high-blood pressure medicines like Catapres.

All of these medications work by influencing levels of key neurotransmitters, particularly dopamine, epinephrine, and norepinephrine. It seems that the resulting change in neurotransmitter availability helps the brain inhibit extraneous stimuli—both internal and external. That allows the mind to focus more effectively. There is no standard dose; dosages can vary widely from person to person, independent of body size.

Ritalin, by far the most popular drug for the treatment of ADD, is safe and effective. Of course, Ritalin and other stimulants can be dangerous if used improperly. But Ritalin is not addictive. Nor is it a euphoric substance—people use drugs to get high, not to focus their minds. For example, you would not cite,

"I took Ritalin last night and read three books" as an example of getting high. Using stimulants to cram before exams, however, is as inadvisable as overdosing on coffee. Students do it, but they should be warned against it. Ritalin should only be taken under medical supervision and of course should not be sold, given away, or otherwise misused.

The diagnosis and treatment of ADD represent a triumph of science over human suffering—just one example of the many syndromes of the brain we are at last learning to address without scorn or hidden moral judgment. As we begin to bring mental suffering out of the stigmatized darkness it has inhabited for centuries and into the light of scientific understanding and effective treatment, we all have reason to rejoice.

NO ⬅

Thomas Armstrong

ADD: Does It Really Exist?

S everal years ago I worked for an organization that assisted teachers in using the arts in their classrooms. We were located in a large warehouse in Cambridge, Massachusetts, and several children from the surrounding lower-working-class neighborhood volunteered to help with routine jobs. I recall one child, Eddie, a 9-year-old African American youngster possessed of great vitality and energy, who was particularly valuable in helping out with many tasks. These jobs included going around the city with an adult supervisor, finding recycled materials that could be used by teachers in developing arts programs, and then organizing them and even field-testing them back at the headquarters. In the context of this arts organization, Eddie was a definite asset.

A few months after this experience, I became involved in a special program through Lesley College in Cambridge, where I was getting my master's degree in special education. This project involved studying special education programs designed to help students who were having problems learning or behaving in regular classrooms in several Boston-area school districts. During one visit to a Cambridge resource room, I unexpectedly ran into Eddie. Eddie was a real problem in this classroom. He couldn't stay in his seat, wandered around the room, talked out of turn, and basically made the teacher's life miserable. Eddie seemed like a fish out of water. In the context of this school's special education program, Eddie was anything but an asset. In retrospect, he appeared to fit the definition of a child with attention deficit disorder (ADD).[1]

Over the past 15 years, ADD has grown from a malady known only to a few cognitive researchers and special educators into a national phenomenon. Books on the subject have flooded the marketplace, as have special assessments, learning programs, residential schools, parent advocacy groups, clinical services, and medications to treat the "disorder." (The production of Ritalin or methylphenidate hydrochloride—the most common medication used to treat ADD—has increased 450% in the past four years, according to the Drug Enforcement Agency.[2]) The disorder has solid support as a discrete medical problem from the Department of Education, the American Psychiatric Association, and many other agencies.

I'm troubled by the speed with which both the public and the professional community have embraced ADD. Thinking back to my experience with Eddie

From Thomas Armstrong, "ADD: Does It Really Exist?" *Phi Delta Kappan*, vol. 77, no. 6 (February 1996). Copyright © 1996 by Thomas Armstrong. Reprinted by permission of the author.

and the disparity that existed between Eddie in the arts organization and Eddie in the special education classroom, I wonder whether this "disorder" really exists *in* the child at all, or whether, more properly, it exists in the relationships that are present between the child and his or her environment. Unlike other medical disorders, such as diabetes or pneumonia, this is a disorder that pops up in one setting only to disappear in another. A physician mother of a child labeled ADD wrote to me not long ago about her frustration with this protean diagnosis: "I began pointing out to people that my child is capable of long periods of concentration when he is watching his favorite sci-fi video or examining the inner workings of a pin-tumbler lock. I notice that the next year's definition states that some kids with ADD are capable of normal attention in certain specific circumstances. Poof. A few thousand more kids instantly fall into the definition."

There is in fact substantial evidence to suggest that children labeled ADD do not show symptoms of this disorder in several different real-life contexts. First, up to 80% of them don't appear to be ADD when in the physician's office.[3] They also seem to behave normally in other unfamiliar settings where there is a one-to-one interaction with an adult (and this is especially true when the adult happens to be their father).[4] Second, they appear to be indistinguishable from so-called normals when they are in classrooms or other learning environments where children can choose their own learning activities and pace themselves through those experiences.[5] Third, they seem to perform quite normally when they are *paid* to do specific activities designed to assess attention.[6] Fourth, and perhaps most significant, children labeled ADD behave and attend quite normally when they are involved in activities that *interest* them, that are *novel* in some way, or that involve high levels of *stimulation*.[7] Finally, as many as 70% of these children reach adulthood only to discover that the ADD has apparently just gone away.[8]

It's understandable, then, that prevalence figures for ADD vary widely—far more widely than the 3% to 5% figure that popular books and articles use as a standard. As Russell Barkley points out in his classic work on attention deficits, *Attention Deficit Hyperactivity Disorder: A Handbook for Diagnosis and Treatment,* the 3% to 5% figure "hinges on how one chooses to define ADHD, the population studied, the geographic locale of the survey, and even the degree of agreement required among parents, teachers and professionals.... Estimates vary between 1[% and] 20%."[9]

In fact, estimates fluctuate even more than Barkley suggests. In one epidemiological survey conducted in England, only two children out of 2,199 were diagnosed as hyperactive (.09%).[10] Conversely, in Israel, 28% of children were rated by teachers as hyperactive.[11] And in an earlier study conducted in the U.S., teachers rated 49.7% of boys as restless, 43.5% of boys as having a "short attention span," and 43.5% of boys as "inattentive to what others say."[12]

The Rating Game

These wildly divergent statistics call into question the assessments used to decide who is diagnosed as having ADD and who is not. Among the most frequently used tools for this purpose are behavior rating scales. These are typically checklists consisting of items that relate to the child's attention and behavior at home or at school. In one widely used assessment, teachers are asked to rate the child on a scale from 1 (almost never) to 5 (almost always) with regard to behavioral statements such as: "Fidgety (hands always busy)," "Restless (squirms in seat)," and "Follows a sequence of instructions." The problem with these scales is that they depend on *subjective judgments* by teachers and parents who may have a deep, and often subconscious, emotional investment in the outcome. After all, a diagnosis of ADD may lead to medication to keep a child compliant at home or may result in special education placement in the school to relieve a regular classroom teacher of having to teach a troublesome child.

Moreover, since these behavior rating scales depend on opinion rather than fact, there are no objective criteria through which to decide *how much* a child is demonstrating symptoms of ADD. What is the difference in terms of hard data, for example, between a child who scores a 5 on being fidgety and a child who scores a 4? Do the scores mean that the first child is one point more fidgety than the second? Of course not. The idea of assigning a number to a behavior trait raises the additional problem, addressed above, of context. The child may be a 5 on "fidgetiness" in some contexts (during worksheet time, for example) and a 1 at other times (during recess, during motivating activities, and at other highly stimulating times of the day). Who is to decide what the final number should be based on? If a teacher places more importance on workbook learning than on hands-on activities, such as building with blocks, the rating may be biased toward academic tasks, yet such an assessment would hardly paint an accurate picture of the child's total experience in school, let alone in life.

It's not surprising, then, to discover that there is often disagreement among parents, teachers, and professionals using these behavior rating scales as to who exactly is hyperactive or ADD. In one study, parent, teacher, and physician groups were asked to identify hyperactive children in a sample of 5,000 elementary school children. Approximately 5% were considered hyperactive by at least one of the groups, while only 1% were considered hyperactive by all three groups.[13] In another study using a well-known behavior rating scale, mothers and fathers agreed that their children were hyperactive only about 32% of the time, and the correspondence between parent and teacher ratings was even worse: they agreed only about 13% of the time.[14]

These behavior rating scales implicitly ask parents and teachers to compare a potential ADD child's attention and behavior to those of a "normal" child. But this raises the question, What is normal behavior? Do normal children fidget? Of course they do. Do normal children have trouble paying attention? Yes, under certain circumstances. Then exactly when does normal fidgeting turn into ADD fidgeting, and when does normal difficulty paying attention become ADD difficulty?

These questions have not been adequately addressed by professionals in the field, yet they remain pressing issues that seriously undermine the legitimacy of these behavior rating scales. Curiously, with all the focus being placed on children who score at the high end of the hyperactivity and distractibility continuum, virtually no one in the field talks about children who must statistically exist at the opposite end of the spectrum: children who are too focused, too compliant, too still, or too *hypo*active. Why don't we have special classes, medications, and treatments for these children as well?

A Brave New World of Soulless Tests

Another ADD diagnostic tool is a test that assigns children special "continuous performance tasks" (CPTs). These tasks usually involve repetitious actions that require the examinee to remain alert and attentive throughout the test. The earliest versions of these tasks were developed to select candidates for radar operations during World War II. Their use with children in today's world is highly questionable. One of the most popular of the current CPT instruments is the Gordon Diagnostic System (GDS). This Orwellian device consists of a plastic box with a large button on the front and an electronic display above it that flashes a series of random digits. The child is told to press the button every time a "1" is followed by a "9." The box then records the number of "hits" and "misses" made by the child. More complex versions involving multiple digits are used with older children and adults.

Quite apart from the fact that this task bears no resemblance to anything else that children will ever do in their lives, the GDS creates an "objective" score that is taken as an important measure of a child's ability to attend. In reality, it tells us only how a child will perform when attending to a repetitive series of meaningless numbers on a soulless task. Yet ADD expert Russell Barkley writes, "[The GDS] is the only CPT that has enough available evidence . . . to be adopted for clinical practice."[15] As a result, the GDS is used not only to diagnose ADD but also to determine and adjust medication doses in children with the label.

There is a broader difficulty with the use of *any* standardized assessment to identify children as having ADD. Most of the tests used (including behavior rating scales and continuous performance tasks) have attempted to be validated as indicators of ADD through a process that involves testing groups of children who have previously been labeled ADD and comparing their test results with those of groups of children who have been judged to be "normal." If the assessment shows that it can discriminate between these two groups to a significant degree, it is then touted as a valid indicator of ADD. However, one must ask how the initial group of ADD children originally came to be identified as ADD. The answer would have to be through an earlier test. And how do we know that the earlier test was a valid indicator of ADD? Because it was validated using two groups: ADD and normal. How do we know that *this* group of ADD children was in fact ADD? Through an even earlier test . . . and so on, ad infinitum. There is no Prime Mover in this chain of tests; no First Test for ADD that has been declared self-referential and infallible. Consequently, the validity of these tests must always remain in doubt.

In Search of a Deficit

Even if we admit that such tests *could* tell the difference between children labeled ADD and "normal" children, recent evidence suggests that there really aren't any significant differences between these two groups. Researchers at the Hospital for Sick Children in Toronto, for example, discovered that the performance of children who had been labeled ADD did not deteriorate over time on a continuous performance task any more than did that of a group of so-called normal children. They concluded that these "ADD children" did not appear to have a unique sustained attention deficit.[16]

In another study, conducted at the University of Groningen in the Netherlands, children were presented with irrelevant information on a task to see if they would become distracted from their central focus, which involved identifying groups of dots (focusing on groups of four dots and ignoring groups of three or five dots) on a piece of paper. So-called hyperactive children did not become distracted any more than so-called normal children, leading the researchers to conclude that there did not seem to be a focused attention deficit in these children.[17] Other studies have suggested that "ADD children" don't appear to have problems with short-term memory or with other factors that are important in paying attention.[18] Where, then, is the attention deficit?

A Model of Machines and Disease

The ADD myth is essentially a *paradigm* or world view that has certain assumptions about human beings at its core.[19] Unfortunately, the beliefs about human capacity addressed in the ADD paradigm are not terribly positive ones. It appears as if the ADD myth tacitly endorses the view that human beings function very much like machines.[20] From this perspective, ADD represents something very much like a mechanical breakdown. This underlying belief shows up most clearly in the kinds of explanations that parents, teachers, and professionals give to children labeled ADD about their problems. In one book for children titled *Otto Learns About His Medicine,* a red car named Otto goes to a mechanic after experiencing difficulties in car school. The mechanic says to Otto, "Your motor does go too fast," and he recommends a special car medicine.[21]

While attending a national conference on ADD, I heard experts share similar ways of explaining ADD to children, including comparisons to planes ("Your mind is like a big jet plane... you're having trouble in the cockpit), a car radio ("You have trouble filtering out noise"), and television ("You're experiencing difficulty with the channel selector"). These simplistic metaphors seem to imply that human beings really aren't very complex organisms and that one simply needs to find the right wrench, use the proper gas, or tinker with the appropriate circuit box—and all will be well. They are also just a short hop away from more insulting mechanical metaphors ("Your elevator doesn't go all the way to the top floor").

The other feature that strikes me as being at the heart of the ADD myth is the focus on *disease* and *disability.* I was particularly struck by this mindset while attending a workshop with a leading authority on ADD who started out his lecture by saying that he would treat ADD as a medical disorder with its own etiology (causes), pathogenesis (development), clinical features (symptoms), and epidemiology (prevalence). Proponents of this view talk about the fact that there is "no cure" for ADD and that parents need to go through a "grieving process" once they receive a "diagnosis."[22] ADD guru Russell Barkley commented in a recent address: "Although these children do not look physically disabled, they are neurologically handicapped nonetheless.... Remember, this is a disabled child."[23] Absent from this perspective is any mention of a child's potential or other manifestations of health—traits that are crucial in helping a child achieve success in life. In fact, the literature on the strengths, talents, and abilities of children labeled ADD is almost nonexistent.[24]

In Search of the ADD Brain

Naturally, in order to make the claim that ADD is a disease, there must be a medical or biological cause for it. Yet, as with everything else about ADD, no one is exactly sure what causes it. Possible biological causes that have been proposed include genetic factors, biochemical abnormalities (imbalances of such brain chemicals as serotonin, dopamine, and norepinephrine), neurological damage, lead poisoning, thyroid problems, prenatal exposure to various chemical agents, and delayed myelinization of the nerve pathways in the brain.[25]

In its search for a physical cause, the ADD movement reached a milestone with the 1990 publication in the *New England Journal of Medicine* of a study by Alan Zametkin and his colleagues at the National Institute of Mental Health.[26] This study appeared to link hyperactivity in adults with reduced metabolism of glucose (a prime energy source) in the premotor cortex and the superior prefrontal cortex—areas of the brain that are involved in the control of attention, planning, and motor activity. In other words, these areas of the brain were not working as hard as they should have been, according to Zametkin.

The media picked up on Zametkin's research and reported it nationally.[27] ADD proponents latched on to this study as "proof" of the medical basis for ADD. Pictures depicting the spread of glucose through a "normal" brain compared to a "hyperactive" brain began showing up in CH.A.D.D. (Children and Adults with Attention Deficit Disorder) literature and at the organization's conventions and meetings. One ADD advocate seemed to speak for many in the ADD movement when she wrote: "In November 1990, parents of children with ADD heaved a collective sigh of relief when Dr. Alan Zametkin released a report that hyperactivity (which is closely linked to ADD) results from an insufficient rate of glucose metabolism in the brain. Finally, commented a supporter, we have an answer to skeptics who pass this off as bratty behavior caused by poor parenting."[28]

What was *not* reported by the media or cheered by the ADD community was the study by Zametkin and others that came out three years later in the *Archives of General Psychiatry*. In an attempt to repeat the 1990 study with adolescents, the researchers found no significant differences between the brains of so-called hyperactive subjects and those of so-called normal subjects.[29] And in retrospect, the results of the first study didn't look so good either. When the original 1990 study was controlled for sex (there were more men in the hyperactive group than in the control group), there was no significant difference between groups.

A recent critique of Zametkin's research by faculty members at the University of Nebraska also pointed out that the study did not make clear whether the lower glucose rates found in "hyperactive brains" were a cause or a result of attention problems.[30] The critics pointed out that, if subjects were startled and then had their levels of adrenalin monitored, adrenalin levels would probably be quite high. We would not say, however, that these individuals had an adrenalin disorder. Rather, we'd look at the underlying conditions that led to abnormal adrenalin levels. Similarly, even if biochemical differences did exist in the so-called hyperactive brain, we ought to be looking at the nonbiological factors that could account for some of these differences, including stress, learning style, and temperament.

The Stigma of ADD

Unfortunately, there seems to be little desire in the professional community to engage in dialogue about the reality of attention deficit disorder; its presence on the American educational scene seems to be a fait accompli. This is regrettable, since ADD is a psychiatric disorder, and millions of children and adults run the risk of stigmatization from the application of this label.

In 1991, when such major educational organizations as the National Education Association (NEA), the National Association of School Psychologists (NASP), and the National Association for the Advancement of Colored People (NAACP) successfully opposed the authorization by Congress of ADD as a legally handicapping condition, NEA spokesperson Debra DeLee wrote, "Establishing a new category [ADD] based on behavioral characteristics alone, such as overactivity, impulsiveness, and inattentiveness, increases the likelihood of inappropriate labeling for racial, ethnic, and linguistic minority students."[31] And Peg Dawson, former NASP president, pointed out, "We don't think that a proliferation of labels is the best way to address the ADD issue. It's in the best interest of all children that we stop creating categories of exclusion and start responding to the needs of individual children."[32] ADD nevertheless continues to gain ground as the label du jour in American education. It's time to stop and take stock of this "disorder" and decide whether it really exists or is instead more a manifestation of society's need to *have* such a disorder.

Notes

1. In this article, I've used the generic term "attention deficit disorder" (ADD) rather than the American Psychiatric Association's current diagnostic category of "attention deficit hyperactivity disorder" (ADHD) because of its wider use in popular culture.

2. Ritalin production figures were provided in a personal communication from the Drug Enforcement Agency's public relations department.

3. Esther K. Sleator and Rina L. Ullmann, "Can the Physician Diagnose Hyperactivity in the Office?," *Pediatrics,* vol. 67, 1981, pp. 13–17.

4. Russell A. Barkley, *Attention Deficit Hyperactivity Disorder: A Handbook for Diagnosis and Treatment* (New York: Guilford, 1990), pp. 56–57.

5. R. G. Jacob, K. D. O'Leary, and C. Rosenblad, "Formal and Informal Classroom Settings: Effects on Hyperactivity," *Journal of Abnormal Child Psychology,* vol. 6, 1978, pp. 47–59; and Donald H. Sykes, Virginia J. Douglas, and Gert Morgenstern, "Sustained Attention in Hyperactive Children," *Journal of Child Psychology and Psychiatry,* vol. 14, 1973, pp. 213–20.

6. Diane McGuinness, *When Children Don't Learn* (New York: Basic Books, 1985), p. 205.

7. Sydney S. Zentall, "Behavioral Comparisons of Hyperactive and Normally Active Children in Natural Settings," *Journal of Abnormal Child Psychology,* vol. 8, 1980, pp. 93–109; and Sydney S. Zentall and Thomas R. Zentall, "Optimal Stimulation: A Model of Disordered Activity and Performance in Normal and Deviant Children," *Psychological Bulletin,* vol. 94, 1983, pp. 446–71.

8. Gabrielle Weiss et al., "Hyperactives as Young Adults," *Archives of General Psychiatry,* June 1979, pp. 675–81.

9. Barkley, p. 61.

10. Eric Taylor and Seija Sandberg, "Hyperactive Behavior in English Schoolchildren: A Questionnaire Survey," *Journal of Abnormal Child Psychology,* vol. 12, 1984, pp. 143–55.

11. Malka Margalit, "Diagnostic Application of the Conners Abbreviated Symptom Questionnaire," *Journal of Clinical Child Psychology,* vol. 12, 1983, pp. 355–57.

12. John S. Werry and Herbert C. Quay, "The Prevalence of Behavior Symptoms in Younger Elementary School Children," *American Journal of Orthopsychiatry,* vol. 41, 1971, pp. 136–43.

13. Nadine M. Lambert, Jonathan Sandoval, and Dana Sassone, "Prevalence of Hyperactivity in Elementary School Children as a Function of Social System Definers," *American Journal of Orthopsychiatry,* vol. 48, 1978, pp. 446–63.

14. McGuinness, pp. 188–89.

15. Barkley, p. 329.

16. Russell Schachar et al., "Attaining and Maintaining Preparation: A Comparison of Attention in Hyperactive, Normal, and Disturbed Control Children," *Journal of Abnormal Child Psychology,* vol. 16, 1988, pp. 361–78.

17. Jaab van der Meere and Joseph Sergeant, "Focused Attention in Pervasively Hyperactive Children," *Journal of Abnormal Child Psychology,* vol. 16, 1988, pp. 627–39.

18. See Esther Benezra and Virginia I. Douglas, "Short-Term Serial Recall in ADDH, Normal, and Reading-Disabled Boys," *Journal of Abnormal Child Psychology,* vol. 16, 1988, pp. 511–25; and Robert A. Rubinstein and Ronald T. Brown, "An Evaluation of the Validity of the Diagnostic Category of Attention Deficit Disorder," *American Journal of Orthopsychiatry,* vol. 54, 1984, pp. 398–414.

19. For an overview of the function of paradigms in scientific development, see Thomas Kuhn, *The Structure of Scientific Revolutions* (Chicago: University of Chicago Press, 1962).

20. For a look at the image of the machine as it affects special education perspectives in general, see Lois Heshusius, "At the Heart of the Advocacy Dilemma: A Mechanistic World View," *Exceptional Children,* vol. 49, 1982, pp. 6–11.

21. Matthew Galvin, *Otto Learns About His Medicine: A Story About Medication for Hyperactive Children* (New York: Magination Press, 1988).

22. See, for example, Lisa J. Bain, *A Parent's Guide to Attention Deficit Disorders* (New York: Delta, 1991), pp. 150–51.

23. Russell Barkley was quoted in a keynote address titled "Help Me, I'm Losing My Child!," included in the *Proceedings of CH.A.D.D. Fourth Annual Conference* (1992), available from Caset Associates Ltd., 3927 Old Lee Highway, Fairfax, VA 22030.

24. Most of the articles I've located in this area center on children labeled both "gifted" and "ADD." See, for example, James T. Webb and Diane Latimer, "ADHD and Children Who Are Gifted," *Exceptional Children*, vol. 60, 1993, pp. 183–84; and James Delisle, "ADD Gifted: How Many Labels Can One Child Take?," *The Gifted Child Today*, March/April 1995, pp. 42–43. One exception was Sydney Zentall, "Production Deficiencies in Elicited Language but Not in the Spontaneous Verbalizations of Hyperactive Children," *Journal of Abnormal Child Psychology*, vol. 16, 1988, pp. 657–73.

25. See Dorothea M. Ross and Sheila A. Ross, *Hyperactivity: Current Issues, Research, and Theory* (New York: John Wiley, 1982); and Cynthia A. Riccio et al., "Neurological Basis of Attention Deficit Hyperactivity Disorder," *Exceptional Children*, vol. 60, pp. 118–24.

26. A. J. Zametkin et al., "Cerebral Glucose Metabolism in Adults with Hyperactivity of Childhood Onset," *New England Journal of Medicine*, vol. 323, 1990, pp. 1361–66.

27. Some of the national media articles highlighting the Zametkin study include Philip Elmer-DeWitt, "Why Junior Won't Sit Still," *Time*, 26 November 1990, p. 59; Gina Kolata, "Hyperactivity Is Linked to Brain Abnormality," *New York Times*, 15 November 1990, p. A-1; and Sally Squires, "Brain Function Yields Physical Clue That Could Help Pinpoint Hyperactivity," *Washington Post*, 15 November 1990, p. A-18.

28. Jeanne Gehret, *Eagle Eyes: A Child's Guide to Paying Attention* (Fairport, N.Y.: Verbal Images Press, 1991).

29. Alan Zametkin et al., "Brain Metabolism in Teenagers with Attention-Deficit Hyperactivity Disorder," *Archives of General Psychiatry*, vol. 50, 1993, pp. 333–40.

30. Robert Reid, John W. Maag, and Stanley F. Vasa, "Attention Deficit Hyperactivity Disorder as a Disability Category: A Critique," *Exceptional Children*, vol. 60, 1993, p. 203.

31. Debra DeLee is quoted in a 29 March 1991 letter from the National Education Association to the Office of Special Education Programs, written in response to the federal government's Notice of Inquiry regarding ADD.

32. Peg Dawson is quoted in the *APA Monitor* (a publication of the American Psychological Association), November 1990.

CHALLENGE QUESTIONS

Does Attention Deficit Disorder Exist?

1. To what extent should conditions involving inattention and hyperactivity be regarded as medical, as opposed to emotional, disorders?
2. What are the minimum behavioral criteria that should be met before recommending that an inattentive or hyperactive individual be given a prescription of a medication such as Ritalin?
3. What might motivate some parents to urge educators and psychologists to diagnose their children with ADD?
4. What interventions other than medication should be instituted in the home and in the classroom to help the hyperactive child?
5. To what extent, if any, can the media be held responsible for cultivating hyperactivity and short attention spans among young people?

Suggested Readings

Armstrong, T. (1997). *The myth of the A.D.D. child: Fifty ways to improve your child's behavior and attention span without drugs, labels, or coercion.* New York, NY: Plume.

Barkley, R. A. (1998). *Attention-deficit hyperactivity disorder: A handbook for diagnosis and treatment.* New York, NY: The Guilford Press.

Barkley, R. A. (1999). Theories of attention-deficit/hyperactivity disorder. In H. C. Quay, & A. E. Hogan (Eds.), *Handbook of disruptive disorders.* (pp. 295–313). New York, NY: Kluwer Academic Plenum Publishers.

Hallowell, E., & Ratey, J. (1995). *Driven to distraction: Recognizing and coping with attention deficit disorder from childhood through adulthood.* New York, NY: Pantheon Books.

ISSUE 5

Is Schizophrenia a Biological Disorder?

YES: Nancy C. Andreasen, from "Linking Mind and Brain in the Study of Mental Illnesses," *Science* (March 1997)

NO: Victor D. Sanua, from "The Myth of the Organicity of Mental Disorders," *The Humanistic Psychologist* (Spring 1996)

ISSUE SUMMARY

YES: Clinical psychiatrist Nancy C. Andreasen emphasizes the significant advances that scientists have made in defining schizophrenia as a biological disorder that results from disturbances in brain circuitry.

NO: Psychologist Victor D. Sanua expresses alarm about the views of biologically oriented scientists who give insufficient attention to the role of stressful life experiences in causing and aggravating the symptoms of mental disorders such as schizophrenia.

Schizophrenia is an extremely disturbing mental disorder that causes havoc in the lives of millions of individuals as well as in the lives of those who are close to them. People with schizophrenia experience a disturbance at least six months in duration, with no less than one month of active symptoms, including at least two of the following: delusions, hallucinations, disorganized speech, disturbed or catatonic behavior, and negative symptoms such as flat affect or severe lack of motivation. Many misconceptions and stereotypes about this disorder have been around for decades. One mistaken notion is the idea that the only people with schizophrenia are homeless individuals who roam the streets of America talking to themselves and hearing voices; although some homeless people meet the criteria for schizophrenia, it is important to realize that this disorder affects people in all socioeconomic classes, ethnic groups, and walks of life. Throughout the twentieth century countless attempts have been made to explain the causes of this debilitating disorder, with numerous theories becoming popular only to be discredited as a result of scientific inquiry.

Theories about the causes of schizophrenia have traditionally fallen into two categories: biological and psychological, with vehement arguments being made for each. As research has accumulated, scientists have increasingly empha-sized the biological contributions, moving far from the psychological explana-tions. As we begin the twenty-first century, it is difficult to believe that one theory, considered tenable for years, targeted an individual's relationship with his or her mother as the basis for developing schizophrenia. In fact, the term *schizophrenogenic mother* was used to characterize a style in which a mother pre-sumably evoked symptoms of this disorder by placing her child in impossible emotional binds. Now that the field of mental health has moved to the biologi-cal end of the continuum with regard to causal explanations for schizophrenia, some critics believe that exclusively biological explanations are as absurd as the purely psychological explanations of the mid-twentieth century.

In the following selection, Nancy C. Andreasen argues that the cause of schizophrenia lies in abnormalities of the brain, with research pointing to the likelihood that symptoms of this disorder result from disruptions in brain cir-cuitry. She expresses enthusiasm about the possibility that scientists will be able to use sophisticated techniques such as neuroimaging to determine more pre-cisely the brain circuits and mechanisms that account for the symptoms of this disorder.

In the second selection, Victor D. Sanua objects to simplistic explana-tions of a complex disorder, expressing particular concern about the tendency of contemporary researchers to minimize the effects of environment on the development of schizophrenia. He questions why theorists pay so little atten-tion to the causal role of troubling life experiences, such as poverty, child abuse, family stress, and so on. Sanua objects to an overreliance on the medi-cal model, which he believes pays inordinate attention to organic causes of the multifaceted clinical condition.

POINT

- Researchers are confident that schizo-phrenia is caused by a disruption in brain circuitry.

- The studies of researchers in various biologically based fields continue to support the notion that mental disor-ders are caused by disturbances in the brain.

- An increased understanding of the causes of schizophrenia has emerged from research findings in four fields of study: cognitive psychology, neu-robiology, psychobiology/neurophys-iology, and clinical psychiatry.

- Scientists are using diverse technolo-gies and techniques to define specific biological markers for mental disor-der.

COUNTERPOINT

- Investigators of schizophrenia should consider the possible causal contribu-tions of various life experiences, such as poverty, abuse, and family stress.

- There has never been so much written material that has been published with so few results confirming a biologi-cal cause for mental disorders such as schizophrenia.

- Many psychologists have been inor-dinately drawn to the medical model as an ideology because of their wish to expand their professional role by gaining prescription privileges, which are currently the exclusive domain of physicians.

- Research is being conducted with in-sufficient attention to the human as-pects of patients, such as feelings, in-tellect, expectations, or anxieties.

Nancy C. Andreasen

 **YES**

Linking Mind and Brain in the Study of Mental Illnesses

Fundamental Conceptual Issues

The relationship between mind and brain. Mental illnesses have historically been distinguished from other medical illnesses because they affect the higher cognitive processes that are referred to as "mind." The relationship between mind and brain has been extensively discussed in contemporary philosophy and psychology, without any decisive resolution. One heuristic solution, therefore, is to adopt the position that the mind is the expression of the activity of the brain and that these two are separable for purposes of analysis and discussion but inseparable in actuality. That is, mental phenomena arise from the brain, but mental experience also affects the brain, as is demonstrated by the many examples of environmental influences on brain plasticity. The aberrations of mental illnesses reflect abnormalities in the brain/mind's interaction with its surrounding world; they are diseases of a psyche (or mind) that resides in that region of the soma (or body) that is the brain.

Mind and brain can be studied as if they are separate entities, however, and this is reflected in the multiple and separate disciplines that examine them. Each uses a different language and methodology to study the same quiddity. The challenge in developing a scientific psychopathology in the 1990s is to use the power of multiple disciplines. The study of mind has been the province of cognitive psychology, which has divided mind into component domains of investigation (such as memory, language, and attention), created theoretical systems to explain the workings of those domains (constructs such as memory encoding versus retrieval), and designed experimental paradigms to test the hypotheses in human beings and animals. The study of brain has been the province of several disciplines. Neuropsychology has used the lesion method to determine localization by observing absence of function after injury, whereas neuroanatomy and neurobiology have mapped neural development and connectivity and studied functionality in animal models. The boundaries between all these disciplines have become increasingly less distinct, however, creating

From Nancy C. Andreasen, "Linking Mind and Brain in the Study of Mental Illnesses," *Science*, vol. 275 (March 1997). Copyright © 1997 by The American Association for the Advancement of Science. Reprinted by permission. References omitted.

the broad discipline of cognitive neuroscience. The term "cognitive" has definitions that range from broad to narrow; its usage here is broad and refers to all activities of mind, including emotion, perception, and regulation of behavior.

Contemporary psychiatry studies mental illnesses as diseases that manifest as mind and arise from brain. It is the discipline within cognitive neuroscience that integrates information from all these related disciplines in order to develop models that explain the cognitive dysfunctions of psychiatric patients based on knowledge of normal brain/mind function.

Using the phenomenotype to find the biotype.   There are at present no known biological diagnostic markers for any mental illnesses except dementias such as Alzheimer's disease. The to-be-discovered lesions that define the remainder of mental illnesses are likely to be occurring at complex or small-scale levels that are difficult to visualize and measure, such as the connectivity of neural circuits, neuronal signaling and signal transduction, and abnormalities in genes or gene expression. Despite their lack of a defining objective index such as glucosuria is for diabetes, however, these illnesses are very real. Not only do they produce substantial morbidity and mortality, but advances in psychiatric nosology have produced objective, criterion-based, assessment techniques that produce reliable and precise diagnoses. In the absence of a pathological marker, the current definitions of mental illnesses are syndromal and are based on a convergence of signs, symptoms, outcome, and patterns of familial aggregation.

Finding the neural mechanisms of mental illnesses must be an iterative process; syndromal clinical definitions (or the phenomenotype) are progressively tested, refined, and redefined through the measurement of neurobiological aspects (or the biotype). This process is not fundamentally different from that used to study other diseases. The diagnosis of diabetes, for example, has evolved from the observation of glucosuria to multiple subdivisions based on age of onset, severity of symptoms and complications, degree of islet cell involvement, and genetic factors. For most mental illnesses, the task is simply made more challenging by the absence of an objective criterion that can provide an initial clue to assist in finding mechanisms, as neuritic plaques have done for Alzheimer's disease....

Linking Mind and Brain: The Example... of Schizophrenia...

Advances that have been made in the study of schizophrenia... illustrate the power of developing cognitive models that derive from different perspectives and apply techniques from multiple domains.

Finding the common thread in schizophrenia.   The name "schizophrenia" ("fragmented mind") was coined by Eugen Bleuler, who wished to emphasize that it was a cognitive disorder in which the "fabric of thought and emotion" was torn or fragmented, and normal connections or associations were no longer present. Schizophrenia poses special challenges to the development of cognitive models because of the breadth and diversity of its symptoms. The symptoms include nearly all domains of function: perception (hallucinations), inferential thinking (delusions), fluency of thought and speech (alogia), clarity and organization of thought and speech ("formal thought disorder"), motor activity (catatonia), emotional expression (affective blunting), ability to initiate and complete goal-directed behavior (avolition), and ability to seek out and experience emotional gratification (anhedonia). Not all these symptoms are present in any given patient, however, and none is pathognomonic of the illness. An initial survey of the diversity of symptoms might suggest that multiple brain regions are involved, in a spotty pattern much as once occurred in neurosyphilis. In the absence of visible lesions and known pathogens, however, investigators have turned to the exploration of models that could explain the diversity of symptoms by a single cognitive mechanism. Exemplifying this strategy are four different models that illustrate the melding of cognitive neuroscience and psychiatry, beginning at four different points of departure. The convergent conclusions of these different models are striking.

Cognitive psychology. Approaching schizophrenia from the background of cognitive psychology, C. D. Frith has divided the symptoms of schizophrenia into three broad groups or dimensions: disorders of willed action (which lead to symptoms such as alogia and avolition), disorders of self-monitoring (which lead to symptoms such as auditory hallucinations and delusions of alien control), and disorders in monitoring the intentions of others ("mentalizing") (which lead to symptoms such as "formal thought disorder" and delusions of persecution). Frith believes that all these are special cases of a more general underlying mechanism: a disorder of consciousness or self-awareness that impairs the ability to think with "metarepresentations" (higher order abstract concepts that are representations of mental states). Frith and his collaborators are currently testing this conceptual framework using positron emission tomography (PET)....

Neurobiology. Approaching schizophrenia from a background that blends lesion studies and single-cell recordings in nonhuman primates for the study of cognition, P. Goldman-Rakic has proposed a model suggesting that the fundamental impairment in schizophrenia is an inability to guide behavior by representation, often referred to as a defect in working memory. Working memory, or the ability to hold a representation "online" and perform cognitive operations using it, permits individuals to respond in a flexible manner, to formulate and modify plans, and to base behavior on internally held ideas and thoughts rather than being driven by external stimuli. A defect in this ability can explain a variety of symptoms of schizophrenia. For example, the inability to hold a discourse plan in mind and monitor speech output leads to disorganized speech and thought disorder; the inability to maintain a plan for behavioral activities could lead to negative symptoms such as avolition or alogia; and the inability to reference a specific external or internal experience against associative memories (mediated by cortical and subcortical circuitry involving frontal/parietal/temporal regions and the thalamus) could lead to an altered consciousness of sensory experience and would be expressed as delusions or hallucinations.

The model ... is consistent with the compromised blood flow to the prefrontal cortex seen in these patients. ...

Psychobiology and neurophysiology. Using techniques originally derived from neurophysiology, D. L. Braff and colleagues have developed another complementary model. This model begins from the perspective of techniques used to measure brain electrical activity, particularly various types of evoked potentials, and hypothesizes that the core underlying deficit in schizophrenia involves information processing and attention. This model derives from the empirical clinical observation that patients with schizophrenia frequently complain that they are bombarded with more stimuli than they can interpret. Consequently, they misinterpret (that is, have delusions), confuse internal with external stimuli (hallucinations), or retreat to safety ("negative symptoms" such as alogia, anhedonia, or avolition). Early interpretations of this observation... postulated that patients had problems with early stages in serial order processing that led to downstream effects such as psychotic or negative symptoms. As serial models have been supplanted by distributed models, the deficit may be better conceptualized in terms of resource allocation: Patients cannot mobilize attentional resources and allocate them to relevant tasks. ...

Clinical psychiatry. Our group has used the clinical presentation of schizophrenia as a point of departure, initially attempting to localize the various symptoms in brain regions through the use of structural and functional neuroimaging techniques. This strategy has led to a search for abnormalities in specific brain regions and theories about symptom-region relationships (such as negative symptoms in the frontal cortex or hallucinations in the superior temporal gyrus), which have been examined by a variety of investigators. This approach is oversimplified, however, and we are currently testing an integrated model that explains clinical symptoms as a consequence of disruptions in anatomically identified circuits that mediate a fundamental cognitive process. ...

The common thread. The common thread in all these observations, spun from four different starting points, is that schizophrenia reflects a disruption in a fundamental cognitive process that affects specific circuitry in the brain and that may be improved through medications that affect that circuitry. The various teams use differing terminology and somewhat different concepts— metarepresentations, representationally guided behavior, information processing/attention, cognitive dysmetria—but they convey a common theme. The cognitive dysfunction in schizophrenia is an inefficient temporal and spatial referencing of information and experience as the person attempts to determine boundaries between self and not-self and to formulate effective decisions or plans that will guide him or her through the small-scale (speaking a sentence) or large-scale (finding a job) maneuvers of daily living. This capacity is sometimes referred to as consciousness.

Using diverse technologies and techniques—PET scanning, animal models, lesion methods, single-cell recordings, evoked potentials—the investigators also converge on similar conclusions about the neuroanatomic substrates of the cognitive dysfunction. All concur that it must involve distributed circuits rather than a single specific "localization," and all suggest a key role for interrelationships among the prefrontal cortex, other interconnected cortical regions, and subcortical regions, particularly the thalamus and striatum. Animal and molecular models are being developed that are based on knowledge of this circuitry and the fundamental cognitive process, which can be applied to understanding the mechanism of drug actions and developing new medications. . . .

Summary and Conclusion

Examples of work applying diverse techniques of cognitive neuroscience to the study of . . . schizophrenia indicate that increasingly sophisticated strategies and conceptualizations are emerging as powerful new technologies are being applied. Focal regions have been replaced by circuits and static changes by plasticity and molecular mechanisms. The power of models is enhanced by efforts to design experiments that can be used in nonhuman species, in order to obtain in vivo measures that will illuminate mechanisms. The power of neuroimaging is also permitting in vivo measures of circuits and mechanisms in the human brain. These advances have created an era in which a scientific psychopathology that links mind and brain has become a reality.

NO ↵

Victor D. Sanua

The Myth of the Organicity of Mental Disorders

In 1994, I attended a conference on schizophrenia arranged by the Columbia University College of Physicians and Surgeons (9th Annual Schizophrenia Conference) and the Alliance for the Mentally Ill. Herbert Pardes, Chairman of the Department of Psychiatry and Dean of the Faculty of Medicine, stated in his introductory remarks that Columbia was installing the largest Magnetic Resonance Imaging (MRI) machine in the world, which would enable scientists to see the workings of the brain. His remarks were sprinkled with optimistic adjectives like, "tremendous excitement," "new hope," and so on. The rest of the day was mostly presentations by the Columbia Faculty on the various theories about the causation of schizophrenia and the research on new antipsychotic drugs. The following are some of the areas of research on causation: genetics, immunological systems, nutritional deficiencies, exposure to influenza, obstetrical complications, structural brain changes, season of birth, neurotropic factors, loss of brain tissue, virus infecting the fetal brain, and others. Basically, schizophrenia was seen as a biological disorder whose mystery would be unveiled only by laboratory work. It should be noted that during the conference, there were no formal discussions about the relationship between neurotransmitters and schizophrenia. The hypotheses of the dysfuctions of the neurotransmitters like serotonin, endorphin and dopamine, which have been quite popular in the past, do not seem to be viable at this time.

There was a general enthusiasm that there would soon be a breakthrough with the kind of scientific research being carried out in modern laboratory facilities. However, such optimism does not seem warranted. A well-known German psychiatrist, Hafner stated, "Our knowledge of the etiology of the disease called schizophrenia has not yet made much progress from [Emil] Kraepelin's days" (1987, p. 366). The fact that there are still so many areas of research awaiting investigation at the Columbia University Conference corroborates Hafner's point. In a workshop in the afternoon, devoted to genetics, evidence for the genetic causation was the much higher concordance of schizophrenia among monozygotic twins than among dizygotic twins. When I suggested to the speaker that this could also be attributed to a similar environment for the monozygotic twins, the response of the presenter was that the evidence is further provided by

From Victor D. Sanua, "The Myth of the Organicity of Mental Disorders," *The Humanistic Psychologist*, vol. 24 (Spring 1996). Copyright © 1996 by The American Psychological Association. Reprinted by permission. References omitted.

the adoption studies of Heston (1966), Kety, Rosenthal, Wender and Schulsinger, and Jacobsen, (1975). . . .

A year later, in a similar conference by Columbia University, Malespina, a biopsychiatrist, stated that it is humbling to the profession to realize that Kraepelin had predicted that it must be left to the future to see how far his theories about schizophrenia are confirmed. According to Malespina, it seems that the future is now because of the new scientific technologies.

Thus psychiatry, at the Columbia University Conference maintained the disease model in its purest form, I never heard in the course of the day any reference to poverty, social class, child abuse, family stress, rejection, ethnicity, aggression, divorce, social conflicts, social disintegration, and [so] on which are so much part of life and which could have a major effect on abnormal behavior. The individual was presented as if it were a machine with some "broken" (Andreasen, 1984) parts, mostly in the brain, which needed to be fixed.

In 1987, Van Kammen, the editor of *Biological Psychiatry*, wrote an editorial, "5 HT, a neurotransmitter for all seasons?" about the constant appearance of studies showing how serotonin has been found to be responsible for numerous aberrations. He stated:

> As clinical researchers, we may look for low CSF 5–HIAA, decreased imipramine binding, decreased alpha receptor activity and positive DST (not again!) in patients with borderline personality disorder, alcoholism, in cocaine or marijuana abusers, cigarette smokers, compulsive gamblers, sadists, flashers and nail biters, rapists, aggressive lesbians, shoplifters, and spouse beaters. (1987, p. 1)

A cover story entitled "The Genetic Revolution" in a major periodical reported on the various ailments which result from faulty genes. Since the article did not include any references on the genetic causation of mental disorders often found in the psychiatric and popular media, I wrote a letter to the editor inquiring about the fact that there is no mention of the genetic causation of mental disorders in this otherwise well-documented article on genetic diseases. His response follows:

Dear Mr. Sanua,

Thank you for writing in response to the cover story "The Genetic Revolution." We certainly appreciate your interest in learning more about genetic indicators for medical disorders. It seems logical that there would be particular genes responsible for conditions of schizophrenia, and researchers have indeed been working to identify them. Despite ongoing study, however, *most finds to date require substantial further study, and some have been retracted because of problems with methodology* [italics added]. We hope to be able to report soon on encouraging news about genetic advances for mental disorders, of course, and we are pleased that you took the time to register your thoughts on this matter . . .

In the February 21, 1994 issue of *Time*, Overbye, an essayist for the publication entitled his essay "Born to raise hell?" in which he referred to a study which attributed aggression to genetic causation. To demonstrate, in a ludicrous way, how this ideology of genetic factors is connected to a large number of aberrations, Overbye wrote:

> Some of us, it seems were born to be bad. Scientists say they are on the verge of pinning down genetic and biochemical abnormalities that predispose their bearers to violence. An article in the journal *Science* last summer carried the headline "Evidence found for a possible 'aggression gene.' " Waiting in the wings are child-testing programs, drug manufacturers, insurance companies, civil right advocates, defense attorneys, and anxious citizens for whom the violent criminal has replaced the beady-eyed communist as the bogeyman. Crime thus joins homosexuality, smoking, divorce, schizophrenia, alcoholism, shyness, political liberalism, intelligence, religiosity, cancer and blue eyes among the many aspects of human life for which it is claimed that biology is destiny. Physicists have been pilloried for years for this kind of reductionism, but in biology it makes everybody happy: the scientists and pharmaceutical companies expand their domain; politicians have "progress" to point to; the smoker, divorces and serial killers get to blame their problems on biology, and we get the satisfaction of knowing they are sick—not like us at all. (p. 76)

Weinberger (1991), a well-known investigator on the biology of schizophrenia urged his colleagues to have a more cautious attitude about the usual claims we regularly read. He wrote:

> It would be naive to conclude that current research with its neurobiologic emphasis is totally immune to the pitfalls of prior scientific research. Many of the findings that appear rock solid today will likely turn out to be epiphenomena and trivial. This has been the case throughout this century with schizophrenia, a disorder that is still researched largely at the phenomenological level. (p. 3)

However Weinberger seems rather optimistic and belies his cautiousness when he states, on the same page, that neuroanatomical, neurochemical, and neurophysiologic correlates of schizophrenia have accumulated at a seemingly *geometric rate.* [italics added] (p. 3).

A heavy dosage of headlines on the organicity of mental disorders has had some serious influence on a small but very powerful group of clinical psychologists connected with APA [American Psychological Association] who have adopted the medical model as an ideology for the purpose of espousing "prescription privileges" for the profession. I have documented (Sanua, 1993, 1994a) the pronouncement of these psychologists who have not provided in their articles the rationale and the scientific source for their inspiration. In one case, Fox (1988) supports the need for prescription privileges for psychologists (p. 503) based on an article by Adams (1986) which appeared in the *Georgia Psychologist.* Why do biopsychiatrists continue to attribute mental disorders to organic factors, while ignoring completely social factors which offer a more parsimonious explanation for the development of mental disorders? Kovacs (1987) voiced the possibility that if organic causation is deemphasized, in time biopsychiatrists will have no reason to exist. Szasz (1987) made a very pertinent observation to the effect that books on pathology do not mention anything about schizophrenia or manic-depressive psychosis. It is felt that pathologists ought to know more than anybody else about bodily pathological dysfunctions that explain mental disorders. Thus while psychiatrists have not been able to convince pathologists, they seem to be deluding themselves that mental disorders are organic and, worse, seem to be successful in convincing the general public of their pseudo-scientific findings.

The psychiatric journals are replete with presumably sophisticated articles which basically discuss structural and functional dysfunctions of the brain, genetic inheritance, and the chemistry of the urine and blood. These are being analyzed in order to discover some aberration which could be related to the mental disorders. This is being done without ever dealing with the human aspects of the patients, his feelings, his intellect, his expectations and his anxieties about his condition. Modrow (1992) provides a good example of the organic emphasis in mental disorder. If he puts forth the whimsical theory that schizophrenia is a brain disease caused by an allergy to cats, while there are schizophrenics that have never been near a cat, it can always be said that some form of schizophrenia has been caused by an allergy to cats and some forms are not, and thus the theory cannot be falsified. To me this is not a far-fetched or whimisical theory. In the course of my attendance at the Conference on Schizophrenia at Columbia University, I made the acquaintance of a psychiatrist who told me that he knew what causes schizophrenia and he would mail me an article. The two-page article revealed that schizophrenia results from mosquito bites.

... What is hoped for is that with further development of laboratory equipment, like the imaging techniques, the "truth" about the causation of schizophrenia will soon be revealed because "it is around the corner." The "truth" around the corner has been around for almost 100 years. All I can say in reading [the] extensive literature [provided by the National Institute of Mental Health] is that there has never been so much written material that has been published with such few results.

... My analysis of the tremendous efforts spent on biological research reminds me of a story which when applied to the problem of schizophrenia reflects a tragic analogy. This is the story of a drunken man who was looking for something around the lamp post in the evening. When he was asked what he was looking for, he said that he had lost his keys. When he was asked further whether he had lost them around the lamp post, he stated that he was not sure, but that this was the only place with light and, therefore, he was going to look for his keys there.

CHALLENGE QUESTIONS

Is Schizophrenia a Biological Disorder?

1. In line with the thoughts of Andreasen, many mental health experts view biology as playing a central but not exclusive role in causing schizophrenia. Consider the possibility that a person might be born with a biological vulnerability that is sparked by life stresses. What kinds of life experiences would you regard as especially provocative?
2. Imagine that you are a clinician providing therapy to a person showing the first signs of schizophrenia. What information pertaining to the individual's "biology" and what information pertaining to life experience would you want to know in order to understand and treat this client?
3. Andreasen speaks about the benefits of designing experiments using nonhuman species in order to obtain in vivo measures that will shed light on brain mechanisms involved in mental disorder. How will scientists be able to generalize findings from animal research to human functioning?
4. Sanua expresses alarm about the lack of concern among biological researchers for the human aspects of people with mental disorder, such as their feelings, intellect, expectations, and anxieties. How might researchers incorporate attention to these human characteristics in their study of the causes of mental disorder?

Suggested Readings

Alanen, Y. O. (1997). Vulnerability to schizophrenia and psychotherapeutic treatment of schizophrenic patients: Towards an integrated view. *Psychiatry: Interpersonal and Biological Processes*, 60(2), 142–158.

Andreason, N. C. (1998). Jeff: A difficult case of schizophrenia. In R. P. Halgin, & S. K. Whitbourne (Eds.), *A casebook in abnormal psychology: From the files of experts*. (pp. 198–209). New York, NY: Oxford University Press.

Johnstone, E. C. (1994). *Searching for the causes of schizophrenia*. Oxford, England UK: Oxford University Press.

Peele, S., & DeGrandpre, R. (1995). My genes made me do it. *Psychology Today*, 28(4), 50–58.

Wyatt, R. J., Apud, J. A., & Potkins, S. (1996). New directions in the prevention and treatment of schizophrenia: A biological perspective. *Psychiatry: Interpersonal and Biological Processes*, 59(4), 357–371.

ISSUE 6

Does Post-Abortion Syndrome Exist?

YES: E. Joanne Angelo, from "Post-Abortion Grief," *The Human Life Review* (Fall 1996)

NO: Joyce Arthur, from "Psychological Aftereffects of Abortion: The Rest of the Story," *The Humanist* (March/April 1997)

ISSUE SUMMARY

YES: Psychiatrist E. Joanne Angelo contends that women who have abortions are at risk of developing a lasting, serious syndrome consisting of several emotional and behavioral problems.

NO: Social activist Joyce Arthur asserts that a general consensus has been reached in the medical and scientific communities that most women who have abortions experience little or no psychological harm.

Perhaps no issue in the twentieth century has engendered more debate and acrimony than the issue of abortion. Since the Supreme Court case *Roe v. Wade* nearly 30 years ago, the debate has moved from the courthouse to the streets of America, in many instances reaching a boiling point in which activists have engaged in violent crimes, including murder, to advance a politically charged cause. On one side of the debate are those who insist that a woman's body is her own and that any decision she makes, including the choice of abortion, is extremely personal and beyond the scope of societal restriction. On the other side are those who insist that society has a right and a responsibility to influence certain personal decisions, such as abortion, when these choices relate to morality. For three decades abortion debates have consisted of powerfully charged tirades rooted in politics, religion, philosophy, and psychology. Arguments on each side of the discussion are often extreme, as spokespersons use every possible source of data to support their positions. Within the realm of mental health, the debate has centered around the question of whether or not women who have abortions suffer lasting emotional problems as a result.

In the following selection, E. Joanne Angelo contends that the choice to have an abortion has profound and lasting psychological effects not unlike the emotional experiences of a mother who suffers the death of her own child. She sees a significant difference, however, in that a woman who has undergone an abortion typically hides her grief as she struggles to deal with the emotions associated with the realization that she has lost a child she will never know. According to Angelo, some women rely on the defense of denial of such emotional reactions, thus leading to the conclusions drawn by some researchers that psychological problems are rarely evoked by the experience of abortion. Angelo believes that in time, however, many women develop debilitating psychological problems that affect them for years.

In the second selection, Joyce Arthur argues that the research findings are clear on the issue of post-abortion psychological problems—most women who have abortions experience little or no psychological harm. She asserts that some antiabortion spokespersons cite research conducted between 1950 and 1975 to support the notion of post-abortion syndrome, but she maintains that because these studies were conducted at a time when abortion was illegal or highly restricted, the conclusions were biased. According to Arthur, more recent studies have been biased or methodologically flawed, and many writings on this topic have been penned by antichoice advocates who rely on incorrect or out-of-date pop psychology. Arthur states that not only are serious abortion-related psychological problems rare but the emotions experienced by most women following abortion involve feelings of relief, improved self-esteem, and inner strength.

POINT

- The medical literature has increasingly acknowledged that women who have abortions experience many of the same emotional reactions as mothers who suffer the death of a child.
- Following abortion, many women develop a constellation of psychological symptoms, including feelings of sadness and guilt, with some turning to alcohol, drugs, and maladaptive behaviors in their attempts to cope.

- The research that denies post-abortion syndrome is based on assessments of reactions shortly after abortion; insufficient attention is given to long-term negative experiences.

- The symptoms that many women experience as a result of the abortion experience are often characterized by clinicians under the diagnosis "pathological grief reaction."

COUNTERPOINT

- A general consensus has been reached in the medical and scientific communities that most women who have had abortions experience little or no psychological harm.

- The most frequently reported emotions felt by women following abortion are relief and happiness, with many women experiencing improved self-esteem, inner strength, and a motivation to refocus their lives in a meaningful way.

- Reliable studies have pointed to the conclusion that serious and persistent psychological problems are rare and are usually related to circumstances surrounding the abortion rather than the abortion itself.
- There is little need to posit the notion of a psychological disorder in women who have abortions since abortion is not significantly different from any other stressful life experience.

E. Joanne Angelo  **YES**

Post-Abortion Grief

Every woman who subjects herself to an induced abortion suffers the death of her own child. She is at risk not only for the surgical and medical complications of abortion—uterine rupture, sepsis, infertility, increased incidence of cancer. She is also at high risk for pathological grief which often brings with it severe and long-lasting negative sequelae for herself, her partner, her surviving children and the whole of society. Grief following a death in the family is a universally accepted experience. A period of mourning following the loss of a loved one is a normal expectation in every culture. It is also generally understood that if this mourning process is blocked or impacted, there will be negative consequences. Shakespeare, in his tragedy *Macbeth*, says, "Give sorrow words, the grief that does not speak knits up the o'erwrought heart and bids it break" (Act IV, scene 3). Yet a mother's grief after an induced abortion has heretofore seldom been acknowledged.

The death of a child is perhaps the most difficult loss to mourn—even the death of a premature baby, a stillborn child, or a miscarriage. The medical literature in recent years has increasingly acknowledged the significance of perinatal loss for parents. Obstetrical journals describe "perinatal grief teams" consisting of nurses, doctors, social workers, clergy and volunteers who help parents cope with the loss of children who die in neonatal intensive care units. Parents are encouraged to name and hold their dead baby, and to take photographs. Religious services assist them in their mourning, and they are encouraged to bury the child with their loved ones in a family grave which they can visit as often as they wish.(1)

Abortion, whether spontaneous or induced, is part of the same continuum of perinatal grief. However, grief after elective abortion is uniquely poignant because it is largely hidden. There are no provisions made to assist the post-abortion woman in her grieving—she has no child to hold, no photographs, no wake or funeral, and no grave to visit. After an elective abortion, a woman typically finds herself alone to cope not only with the loss of the child she will never know, but also with her personal responsibility in the child's death with its ensuing guilt and shame. She may have difficulty understanding her ambivalent feelings—on the one hand, relief (often very temporary) that she is no longer pregnant, and, on the other hand, a profound sense of loss and

From E. Joanne Angelo, "Post-Abortion Grief," *The Human Life Review*, vol. 22, no. 4 (Fall 1996). Copyright © 1996 by E. Joanne Angelo. Reprinted by permission of the author.

emptiness. In her book, *Anatomy of Bereavement,* Beverley Raphael explains, "A woman may have required a high level of defensive denial of her tender feelings for the baby to allow her to make the decision for termination. This denial often carries her through the procedure and hours afterward, so that she seems cheerful, accepting but unwilling to talk at the time when supportive counseling may be offered by the clinic."(2) This may explain why research into psychiatric sequelae of abortion in the immediate post-abortion period often yields negative results.

The Emotional Effects

In the weeks and months after the abortion, feelings of sadness and guilt often threaten to overwhelm the post-abortion woman, yet society offers her no assistance in mourning—she is expected to be grateful that "her problem is solved" and to "get on with her life" as though nothing significant had happened. At the same time, pain and bleeding remind her of the assault on her body, the sudden endocrine changes cause her to become emotionally labile or unstable. She is poignantly aware of the date her child would have been born. Reminders threaten her defensive denial and repression all too frequently: anniversaries of her abortion, other children of the age her child would have been, Mother's Day, the omni-present abortion debate in the media, a visit to the gynecologist, the sound of the suction machine at the dentist's office, or the sound of a vacuum cleaner at home, a baby in a television ad, a new pregnancy, a death in the family, a film depicting prenatal development or abortion, or a pro-life homily. Any of these may trigger a sudden flood of grief, guilt, anger and even despair, which in turn, calls forth even more intense defensive responses.

The post-abortion woman's attempts to comply with society's expectations that she proceed with her life as though she had undergone an innocuous procedure are bought at great personal expense. She may turn to alcohol or drugs to get to sleep at night or to deaden the pain of the intrusive thoughts which haunt her day and night, "I killed my baby! I killed my baby! I don't deserve to live!" Flashbacks to the abortion procedure may occur at any time. She may throw herself into intense activity—work, study, or recreation, or attempt to deal with her feelings of loneliness and emptiness by binge eating alternating with purging or anorexia, or by intense efforts to repair intimate relationships or develop new ones inappropriately, becoming sexually promiscuous, risking sexually transmitted diseases, and repeating pregnancy and abortion. Complaints of vague abdominal pain or pain on sexual intercourse may cause her to seek medical treatment from one physician after another unsuccessfully, and the very examinations to which she is subjected may cause flashbacks to the abortion experience. Her life spirals downward as her general health, personal relationships and job performance become more and more impaired. Discouragement, despair, clinical depression and suicide attempts often follow.(3) Typically, in presenting symptoms over a period of many years, she is treated by numerous physicians and mental health professionals without ever receiving help for the root cause of her problems, her abortion or abortions.

Psychiatric textbooks subsume all of the above symptoms under the diagnosis of a Pathological Grief Reaction.

Effects on Marriage and Subsequent Children

Short-term research into the psychiatric sequelae of abortion fails to document its devastating long-term negative effects on women and on their forming and sustaining stable spousal relationships, and of caring appropriately for subsequent children. They may have difficulty bonding with a new baby, or, conversely, become overprotective and inappropriately attached to the next child who bears the burden of replacing the aborted baby. These children are often referred to child psychiatrists because of separation anxiety, or because they are judged to be at risk for physical abuse. Couples may be treated for infertility or dysfunctional marriages which stem from a previous abortion or abortions. Substance abuse, "burnout" on the job, psycho-somatic symptoms, eating disorders, chronic depression and suicide attempts which routinely bring women into psychiatric care can often be traced to an abortion experience several years before through a careful and complete history.

In addition to immediate intervention for the presenting problem, successful treatment of women who have suffered the tragedy of abortion requires that the underlying traumatic loss be acknowledged and appropriately grieved. Psychotherapy involves facilitating the work of mourning which has been so long delayed. Within a therapeutic relationship, the woman is encouraged to share her traumatic loss and to acknowledge her role in it. She is helped to share the mental image she has formed of her child—often one of a baby being torn to pieces or crying out in pain. As the grief work proceeds, her image is transformed into a less disturbing picture of her child at peace. She may name the child and arrange for a religious service to be performed for him or her. She accepts God's forgiveness and may be able to forgive herself and ask forgiveness of her child. Eventually she is able to put the child to rest in her mind. Only then is she free to resume her life productively—to make new relationships or repair old ones, to work, to play, and to be creative once again.(4)

With 30 million abortions in this country since *Roe v. Wade*, and the continuing rate of 1.5 million abortions per year, we can no longer deny the public health significance of their psychological and psychophysical sequelae. Epidemiological studies are urgently needed which are statistically sound and which follow women and men for at least ten years post-abortion. However, it is axiomatic that the best treatment for any epidemic is primary prevention. Abortion is an elective surgical procedure performed on healthy women (pregnancy is not a disease). The immediate abolition of elective abortion would eradicate the iatrogenic epidemic of post-abortion pathology and would serve the best interests of women and society. In *Evangelium Vitae* (no. 99) John Paul II spells out the pastoral approach of the church:

> The wound in your heart may not yet have healed. Certainly what happened was and remains terribly wrong. But do not give in to discouragement and do not lose hope. Try rather to understand what happened and face it honestly. If you have not already done so, give yourself over with humility and trust to

repentance. The Father of mercies is ready to give you his forgiveness and his peace in the Sacrament of Reconciliation. You will come to understand that nothing is definitely lost and you will also be able to ask forgiveness from your child, who is now living in the Lord. With the friendly and expert help and advice of other people, and as a result of your own painful experience, you can be among the most eloquent defenders of everyone's right to life.

Notes

1. Wathen, N.C. "Perinatal Bereavement," *British Journal of Obstetrics and Gynecology* 97 [1990]: 759–760.
2. Basic Books: New York, 1983.
3. Speckhard, A. & Rue, V. "Complicated Mourning: Dynamics of Impacted Post-Abortion Grief," *Journal of Pre- and Perinatal Psychology* 8 [1993]: 6–12.
4. Angelo, E.J. "The Negative Impact of Abortion on Women and Families," in *Post-Abortion Aftermath*, Mannion, M. ed. [Sheed and Ward: Kansas City, MO, 1994].

Joyce Arthur

 **NO**

Psychological Aftereffects of Abortion: The Rest of the Story

Over the last decade, a consensus has been reached in the medical and scientific communities that most women who have an abortion experience little or no psychological harm. Yet, a woman's ability to cope psychologically after an abortion continues to be the subject of heated debates. Vocal anti-abortion advocates claim that most women who have abortions will suffer to some degree from a variant of post-traumatic-stress disorder called *post-abortion syndrome,* characterized by severe and long-lasting guilt, depression, rage, and social and sexual dysfunction. Why is there such a major discrepancy between the scientific consensus and anti-abortion beliefs?

Conflicting studies done over the last thirty years have contributed to this atmosphere of confusion and misinformation. A 1989 review article that evaluated the methodology of seventy-six studies on the psychological aftereffects of abortion noted that both opponents and advocates of abortion could easily prove their case by picking and choosing from a wide range of contradictory evidence. For example, many studies—especially those done between 1950 and 1975—purport to have found significant negative psychological responses to abortion. Such studies, though, often suffer from serious methodological flaws. Some were done when abortion was still illegal or highly restricted, thereby biasing the conclusions in favor of considerable (and understandable) psychological distress. In some cases, research was based on women who were forced to prove a psychiatric disorder in order to obtain the abortion. Further, a large number of studies, both early and recent, consist simply of anecdotal reports of a few women who sought psychiatric help after their abortion. In short, many studies which favor anti-abortion beliefs are flawed because of very small samples, unrepresentative samples, poor data analysis, lack of control groups, and unreliable or invalid research questions.

Researcher bias on the part of scientists and physicians has also been a serious problem. In earlier times, society's views on how women "should" feel after an abortion were heavily skewed toward the traditional model of women as nurturing mothers. In one study done in 1973, postdoctoral psychology students taking psychoanalytic training predicted psychological effects far more severe than those predicted by women themselves before undergoing an abortion. This might be because traditional Freudian theory teaches that a desire to avoid childbearing represents a woman's denial of her basic feminine nature.

Some psychiatric studies, along with much of today's anti-abortion literature, tend to cast women who have abortions into one of two roles: victim or deviant (although these terms are not necessarily used). Victims are coerced into abortion by others around them, in spite of their confusion and ambivalence, and against their basic maternal instincts. Deviants have little difficulty with the abortion decision, which is made casually for convenience sake. Such women have no maternal instinct and are often characterized in a derogatory or pitying fashion as selfish, callous, unfeminine, emotionally stunted, and neurotic.

Books written by anti-abortion advocates that deal with post-abortion effects are, by and large, heavily infected with bias. Not only is contrary evidence unrefuted, it is rarely even mentioned. Incorrect and out-of-date "facts" abound. The authors' pop psychology often seems to be based on little more than their own wishful projections about the nature of women and how they should feel. Here are two typical examples from essays in the anti-abortion book The *Psychological Aspects of Abortion* (1977):

> It is interesting that women who need self-punishment do not abort themselves more often.... Abortion is done "to" the woman, with her as only a passive participant. This is further indication of masochism.
>
> — (Howard W. Fisher, "Abortion: Pain or Pleasure")

> ... sooner or later [after the abortion], the truth will make itself known and felt, and the bitter realization that she was not even unselfish enough to share her life with another human being will take its toll. If she had ever entertained a doubt as to whether her parents and others really considered her unlovable and worthless, she will now be certain that she was indeed never any good in their eyes or her own. A deep depression will be inevitable and her preoccupation with thoughts of suicide that much greater.
>
> — (Conrad W. Baars, "Psychic Causes and Consequences of the Abortion Mentality")

With the advent of safe, legal, routinely performed abortions, a wealth of good evidence has come to light that is quite contrary to common anti-abortion assertions. The typical abortion patient is a normal, mentally stable woman who makes a strongly resolved decision for abortion within a few days after discovery of the pregnancy and comes through the procedure virtually unscathed. Several scientific review articles—published from 1990 to 1992 in highly respected journals such as *Science* and *American Journal of Psychiatry*—support this conclusion. The reviews evaluated hundreds of studies done over the last thirty years, noting the unusually high number of seriously flawed studies and pointing out common methodological problems. Based upon the more reliable studies, all the reviews concluded that, although psychological disturbances do occur after abortion, they are uncommon and generally mild and short-lived. In many cases, these disturbances are simply a continuation of negative feelings caused by the pregnancy itself. Serious or persistant problems are rare and are frequently related to the circumstances surrounding the abortion rather than the abortion itself.

Further, many women who were denied an abortion showed ongoing, long-term resentment, and their resulting children were more likely to have increased emotional, psychological, and social problems in comparison with control groups of wanted children. These differences between children widened throughout adolescence and early adulthood. Finally, many studies show that giving birth is much more likely than abortion to be associated with severe emotional aftereffects, such as post-partum depression.

The review articles largely concluded that the most frequently reported emotions felt by women immediately following an abortion (experienced by about 75 percent of women) are relief or happiness. Feelings of regret, anxiety, guilt, depression, and other negative emotions are reported by about 5 percent to 30 percent of women. These feelings are usually mild and fade rapidly, within a few weeks. Months or years after an abortion, the majority of women do not regret their decision. In fact, for many women, abortion appears to improve their self-esteem, provide inner strength, and motivate them to refocus their lives in a meaningful way.

Studies on abortion are done primarily through self-report measures, however, and it is possible that some women may be reluctant to admit negative feelings after their abortion. To help quantify this, consider these figures: every year since 1977, 1.3 million to 1.6 million abortions are performed in the United States; about 21 percent of all American women between the ages of fifteen and forty-four have had an abortion. These are very large numbers indeed. The American Psychological Association has pointed out that, even if only 10 percent of the millions of women who have had abortions experienced problems, there would be a significant mental health epidemic, clearly evident by large numbers of dysfunctional women requesting help. There is no evidence of any such epidemic, thereby supporting the general reliability of self-report measures.

Some women who are disturbed or unhappy with their abortion decision belong to support groups like Women Exploited by Abortion and Victims of Choice. Several anti-abortion studies and books purporting to demonstrate the overall harmfulness of abortion limit their samples to the membership of such groups. Not only does this introduce an immediate and fatal flaw to their argument, it shows deliberate obfuscation on the part of the authors. This does not mean, however, that post-abortion support groups are valueless to women. The very existence of such groups points to the strong need for health professionals to identify and provide extra help to women who are most at risk for developing psychological problems related to abortion. Many studies have shown that women at greater risk tend to include:

- emotionally immature teenagers
- women with previous psychiatric problems
- women aborting a wanted pregnancy for medical or genetic reasons

- women who encounter opposition from their partner or parents for their abortion decision
- women who have strong philosophical or religious objection to abortion
- women who are highly ambivalent or confused about their abortion decision and had great difficulty making it
- women who are coerced by others into having an abortion
- women undergoing second-trimester abortions

In spite of psychological problems suffered by a few women after abortion, the existence of post-abortion syndrome is doubted by most experts. There is little need to posit a unique disorder in this case, since abortion is not significantly different from any other stressful life experience that might cause trauma in certain people. Former Surgeon General C. Everett Koop, himself anti-abortion, noted this in 1988. Unfortunately, facts, evidence, and common sense rarely get in the way of anti-abortion advocates who are determined to prove that women suffer terribly from post-abortion syndrome. Certainly, if this syndrome were real it would be a lethal weapon in the fight to reverse *Roe* v. *Wade.* This was, in fact, the motivation behind a 1989 surgeon general's report on the health effects of abortion on women, which was called for by former President Ronald Reagan on behalf of anti-abortion leaders. Although the report was duly prepared, the surgeon general chose not to release it, apparently because it did not support the anti-abortion position. Meanwhile, anti-abortion literature continues to churn out the myth that women are severely harmed by abortion.

Because abortion is such a volatile issue, it is probably unrealistic to expect this aspect of the controversy to die down soon, if at all. However, by recognizing that a small subset of women may require increased counseling and support during their abortion decision and afterward, the women's community and health professionals can do much to minimize the damage wrought by the anti-abortion movement's dangerous and irresponsible campaign of misinformation.

CHALLENGE QUESTIONS

Does Post-Abortion Syndrome Exist?

1. Considering the fact that the abortion debate is so politically and emotionally charged, what advice would you give to researchers studying the validity of post-abortion reactions to help them avoid bias in their methods and conclusions?
2. To what extent do you believe that women who experience psychological problems following abortion are affected by the intensity of the national debate on this topic?
3. Arthur acknowledges that the women who experience abortion-related psychological problems are those who were at risk because of factors such as immaturity, religious pressures, interpersonal pressures, and medical problems. To what extent should health professionals assess women for such risk factors and provide specialized mental health interventions designed to reduce the extent of their difficulties?
4. The views of Angelo are based on a religious perspective, in that she suggests that women who have had abortions seek God's forgiveness for their life-ending decisions. How should clinicians formulate interventions for religiously committed post-abortion women?
5. Consider your own stand on abortion, and imagine yourself as a clinician trying to help a woman in therapy whose viewpoint is diametrically opposed to yours. How would you approach your treatment of this client?

Suggested Readings

Adler, N. E., David, H. P., Major, B. N., Roth, S. H., Russo, N. F., & Wyatt, G. E. (1992). Psychological factors in abortion: A review. *American Psychologist, 47*(10), 1194–1204.

Beckman, L. J., & Harvey, S. M. (Eds.) (1998). *The new civil war: The psychology, culture and politics of abortion.* Washington, DC: American Psychological Association.

Lewis, W. J. (1997). Factors associated with post-abortion adjustment problems: Implications for triage. *The Canadian Journal of Human Sexuality, 6*(1), 9–16.

Russo, N. F., & Dabul, A. J. (1997). The relationship of abortion to well-being: Do race and religion make a difference? *Professional Psychology: Research and Practice, 28*(1), 23–31.

Stotland, N. (1992). The myth of the abortion trauma syndrome. *Journal of the American Medical Association, 268*(15), 2078–2079.

ISSUE 7

Are Repressed Memories Valid?

YES: Richard P. Kluft, from "The Argument for the Reality of Delayed Recall of Trauma," in Paul S. Appelbaum, Lisa A. Uyehara, and Mark R. Elin, eds., *Trauma and Memory: Clinical and Legal Controversies* (Oxford University Press, 1997)

NO: Elizabeth F. Loftus, from "Creating False Memories," *Scientific American* (September 1997)

ISSUE SUMMARY

YES: Psychiatrist Richard P. Kluft supports the notion that people can recover memories that have been long unavailable, and he cites several verified examples in which psychotherapy patients recalled previously inaccessible memories of traumatic events.

NO: Psychologist Elizabeth F. Loftus cites extensive laboratory research to support her conclusion that suggestion and imagination can create "memories" of events that never actually occurred.

Experienced psychotherapists know that many psychotherapy patients find it difficult to discuss emotionally charged experiences. For some of these patients, discussion of upsetting life events seems too disturbing, so they intentionally avoid it. For others, however, memories seem to spontaneously arise with regard to events that the patients have not thought about in years. Sometimes these memories are relatively insignificant, and sometimes they involve disturbing images, possibly of traumatic events early in life. Astute clinicians recognize the importance of responding to such recollections with empathy, as well as caution, particularly when the events cannot be verified and might have explosive consequences in the patient's life. During the past two decades numerous stories have appeared in the media about individuals who suddenly retrieved disturbing memories, often within the context of psychotherapy. Some of the well-publicized cases involved individuals accusing parents or grandparents of having engaged in sexual, physical, or ritualistic abuse very early in the person's life. Various lawsuits and court cases captured public attention and in some instances resulted in large financial settlements and even imprisonment. Although many Americans, including prominent clinicians, accepted the validity of the repressed memory phenomenon, skeptics raised the possibility that these cases might actually have resulted from the persuasive power of suggestion.

Based on extensive clinical experience, Richard P. Kluft, in the following selection, describes several clinical cases in which patients recalled past traumatic events that they had pushed out of conscious memory and which were subsequently verified as having actually occurred. He takes issue with those who contest the notion of repressed memories, asserting that these skeptics are basing their conclusions on laboratory exercises that do not adequately mirror the real-life experiences of people who have been traumatized. Questioning both the ethics and the methodological design of some of these experiments, Kluft asserts that much of this research is a study of social persuasion rather than memory functioning.

Elizabeth F. Loftus, in the second selection, cites cases in which psychotherapy patients became convinced that they had been the victims of horrendous early life abuse but subsequently disavowed these experiences and attributed the "memories" to the suggestions of their therapists. Loftus cites extensive research that supports the notion that, under the right circumstances, false memories can be instilled rather easily in some people. Many people are especially suggestible and can be led to "remember" events that never actually occurred, she concludes.

POINT

- Kluft, whose clinical files contain hundreds of examples of confirmed recovered memories, summarizes several cases involving patients who recalled traumatic events that they had repressed.

- The phenomenon in which people recover memories of traumatic experiences differs markedly from research phenomena such as the "lost-in-the-mall" research conducted by Loftus.

- Clinicians who attempt to rigidly conform clinical practice to scientific findings are likely to rely on laboratory science, which is not anchored in common sense.

- Some people who retract their stories about having been traumatized do so in response to strong interpersonal pressures.

- A careful scrutiny of the Loftus research shows that only a small minority of subjects who received misdirection cues actually took the indicated misdirection.

COUNTERPOINT

- Some mental health professionals encourage patients to imagine childhood events as a way of recovering supposedly hidden memories.

- More than 200 experiments indicate that people can be led to remember their past in different ways and can even be coaxed into "remembering" entire events that never happened.

- Mental health professionals must be aware of how greatly they can influence the recollection of events and of the urgent need for maintaining restraint in situations in which imagination is used as an aid in recovering presumably lost memories.

- There are several well-publicized cases in which psychotherapy patients came to realize that their psychotherapists encouraged them to "remember" traumatic events that never occurred.

- Misinformation can invade memories when people talk to other people, are suggestively interrogated, or when they read or view media coverage about some event that they may have experienced.

Richard P. Kluft

 **YES**

The Argument for the Reality of Delayed Recall of Trauma

In any debate over the reality of recovered memory, it is useful to clarify the grounds of the debate, that is, to specify the issue that is being debated. If arguments are being proposed to the effect that there is no such thing as re-covered memory, so that any apparently recovered memory can be discounted a priori, the premise of the debate can be formulated: resolved, that there is no demonstrable instance in which accurate, once unavailable memories have been recovered. I have avoided the use of the terms *recovered memory* and *repressed memory* in the resolution itself because these terms not only have become politicized, but the former term has no correlation to traditional clinical lit-erature, and the latter represents an overgeneralized use of the term *repression,* which is only one of the processes by which the defensive exclusion of auto-biographical experience from available and routinely retrievable memory may occur.

If the affirmative case is proven, then there is no such thing as a recovered memory. Should the negative prevail, such a phenomenon exists. The debate concerns whether there are demonstrable instances of the recovery of repressed, dissociated, or otherwise unavailable memory. Circumspect authorities would observe that since it is impossible to prove a negative, the debate can only be won by the affirmative side's discounting of any and all evidence that repressed and recovered memories exist. This is why vigorous attacks have been launched against virtually every article that appears to document this phenomenon, and efforts have been made to overextend implications that memory not only can be but will be distorted by various forms of suggestion and influence. Another consideration in this debate is that the affirmative side must make its case by advancing falsifiable arguments. Opinions cannot be stated as if they were facts. All recovered memories must be demonstrated to be false by objective data, and by unimpeachable corroborations of their falseness, not simply by allegations or statements of belief. Pope[1] has explored this dilemma very thoughtfully. That is, advancing lines of reasoning that cannot be tested, but permit the infinite, defensive rationalization of one's point of view from a lofty retreat remote from all threat of disconfirmation, falls short of scientific acceptability....

Clinical Experiences Supporting the Recovery of Long-Unavailable Memories

For many years, in addition to conducting a psychiatric practice in Philadelphia, I had the privilege of treating patients in a small city surrounded by farmlands and semirural areas. During that period, that city's population base was stable, with relatively little mobility. For most of that time the area was underserved by mental health professionals and there was relatively little therapist-switching. I had the opportunity to observe the life cycles of many families over a period of 18 years. It was predominantly in this setting that I followed 210 patients with dissociative identity disorder (DID; formerly multiple personality disorder [MPD]) and was able to sketch out the natural history of this disorder.[2] I came to know many patients and their families in a manner that I rarely experienced in my urban practice, and I remained in contact with them over a prolonged period of time. Often information that was unavailable during my patients' treatments came my way a decade later. In this setting I learned that many of the allegations of abuse that were made by my patients (whether always in conscious awareness or recovered in therapy) were in fact true, even allegations that were vehemently denied by their families at the time when I first treated the patients. I also learned that some of the accusations were lies, and that some were based on misperceptions or distorted recall. In 1984 I cautioned that the therapist "must remain aware ... that material influenced by intrusive inquiry or iatrogenic dissociation may be subject to distortion. In a given patient, one may find episodes of photographic recall, confabulation, screen phenomena, confusion between dreams or fantasies and reality, irregular recollection, and willful misrepresentation. One awaits a goodness of fit among several forms of data, and often must be satisfied to remain uncertain."[3] I did not encounter instances in which false accusations were triggered in therapy, but I must acknowledge that the possibility exists.

Here I will focus on several examples of confirmed recovered memories. My files contain hundreds of such confirmations.

In the mid-1970s I was treating a female colleague who seemed unable to sort out her relationships with men. A bright and attractive woman, she had distanced herself from her alcoholic family only after winning her own battles with addiction. As her psychoanalytically oriented psychotherapy proceeded, which was supported by her participation in Alcoholics Anonymous, we both appreciated that she became unable to express herself whenever transference feelings toward me came under exploration. After several months of mutual confusion, we decided to use hypnosis to explore her block. She was an excellent hypnotic subject. While in trance she recovered memories of her first therapy, which was conducted by an addiction counselor. He had encouraged the development of an extremely positive transference and then exploited it to seduce her. Once out of trance she was mortified, but she steeled herself to report that, although she had completely forgotten that particular experience, she had reenacted the same pattern with the leader of a therapy group. She had not felt comfortable enough to admit her growing fears that the same might happen with me. Now her shutting down whenever she began to experience feelings toward me made sense to both of us. Her therapy continued to a successful conclusion, and her relationships with men became satisfactory to her.

A decade later, her former alcoholism counselor came to me for psychotherapy. After several sessions, he revealed what he considered the two worst things he had ever done. While an active alcoholic, he had molested his own daughter. When he became a recovering alcoholic and respected therapist, he had become infatuated with a beautiful young patient and had manipulated her idealization of him to seduce her. "You know her. You treated her. You must think I'm a real bastard." He spoke briefly about his relationship with my other patient, confirming her hypnotically retrieved account in detail. The next day, he left me a message which said that he was too embarrassed to return. He transferred to a therapist who had never known his victim.

In another case, two sisters, who were long estranged, were reunited after twenty years as they attended their dying mother. One sister, who was my patient, had always been aware of sexual abuse by her father and had recovered memories of abuse by a baby-sitter in the course of her therapy. She asked her sister if the sister had any knowledge of such an incident. Her sister not only recalled the event but supplied details that confirmed additional circumstances which my patient had recovered in the course of her treatment but which she had not yet shared with her sister. Each confirmed the other's recollection of father-daughter incest, with reference to several specific instances. Furthermore, their dying mother apologized to my patient for her harsh treatment of her, which my patient had recovered in psychotherapy but had doubted to be true.

Another example of confirmed recovered memories concerns a man who had served in Vietnam as a Marine who maintained in therapy that he and his unit had seen no combat over a particular period. However, also in therapy, he recovered memories of an attack on his base and of his killing several armed Vietnamese attackers. After recovering these memories, he disbelieved them. At a Washington, D.C. commemoration for Vietnam veterans he became irritated when a wartime buddy reminded him of his role in this firefight. He told the friend that he must be wrong, that he had never fired his weapon in combat. The man was shocked, and shook his head, uncomprehending. "You were a . . . hero, man!" The patient's military records reveal that his unit had indeed been in combat and had maintained a defensive perimeter around a supply base that was frequently under attack throughout the period during which the patient maintained that his unit had seen no action. For reasons unrelated to this account, this man had joined the Marines, hoping to be killed. He had repeatedly volunteered for hazardous duty in the effort to bring about his own death. Although he eagerly placed himself at risk, he was passionately opposed to taking another human life. Ultimately, he was able to confront the fact that despite his beliefs and apparent wish to die, when faced with a genuine life-and-death decision, he had methodically and efficiently dispatched several enemy combatants at close range, an act that was witnessed by his buddy. His repugnance and conflict over this action apparently drove it from his memory. It took months to work through his guilt over his having taken the lives of the Vietcong attackers.

A woman with multiple personality disorder underwent hypnosis to access personalities and to explore missing periods of time in her life. During her assessment and treatment, she had denied that she had ever been mistreated by a previous therapist. Fourteen months later, a personality that was contacted through hypnosis indicated that the patient's prior psychiatrist had exploited her sexually. Against my advice, she revealed this information to her prior psychiatrist. When he learned that his former patient was revealing his boundary violations, he telephoned me. He asked me to treat him, he admitted his indiscretions, and he insisted that since he was now my patient, I could not reveal what I knew, due to my duty of confidentiality! He was not pleased when I reminded him that I had never agreed to treat him, and that I was not disposed to accept the constraints he tried to impose. This case was one of several in which alleged therapist abuses, which were often not in patients' conscious awareness at the beginning of the patients' therapy with the author, were later confirmed.[4,5]

A married woman in her late 20s who had been adopted at birth came for a consultation to discuss the pluses and minuses of tracing her birth parents. Now the mother of two toddlers, she was increasingly curious about her own origins. After she located her birth parents, she returned to discuss her reactions. During this interview she spoke at length about the mental illness of her adoptive mother, who ultimately had been institutionalized as a paranoid schizophrenic. While discussing her adoptive mother's suspiciousness and unusual behavior (such as shooting a rifle at aircraft flying over the family farm), she dissociated into an alter personality and began to talk about a psychotic ritual of her mother's, a practice that was repeated over and over again. In it, her mother and she undressed. Her mother made her lie under a blanket on her abdomen and crawl out between her legs to be "born." Then her mother would express delight at her daughter's birth. When the patient switched back to her previous personality, she was amnestic for the above revelations. However, within minutes, she had a flashback of bizarre enematization experiences at her mother's hands.

She decided to enter treatment to explore these phenomena and to better understand herself. Much abuse material emerged under hypnosis. After the third hypnotic session the patient was sure that the recollections were inaccurate, but she appreciated that her long-standing depression was fading. We discussed how to approach the resolution of her uncertainty. Her adoptive parents were deceased. They had raised her on an isolated farm in a wooded rural area with no close neighbors. No close relatives of her parents were available as resources. I asked her to bring in any school and medical records, and any family materials or photo albums in her possession for us to review. I really had no hopes that anything would emerge, but wanted to leave no stone unturned. The next day she called me in tears. Not only had she found albums, she had found her mother's diaries, which described her mother's "experiments on the girl." They included detailed accounts of every abuse the patient had shared with me. Unable to tolerate having this material in her home, she presented me with a box of her mother's diaries and with yearly school pictures of herself, on the backs of which were written her mother's comments and planned experiments (i.e., abuses). When I asked her what she thought I should do with these materials, she paused thoughtfully and replied: "Someday you may find people don't believe child abuse happens, and that people can forget their abuse. If you ever need to prove it happens, you have this box." That conversation occurred in 1978. Upon an 18-year follow-up, she is integrated, symptom-free, and well. Several years after the conclusion of her therapy she went to graduate school in psychology. She currently is a practicing mental health professional. . . .

Perspectives on Discrediting the Possible Recovery of Repressed Memory

Limitations of space preclude the possibility of my making a detailed critique of the arguments against the possibility of the recovery of repressed or otherwise unavailable memory. However, I will comment briefly on a small number of the issues that have been raised in that connection.

Often the argument is made that there are no data to sustain the notion of repression, so that any material alleged to have been repressed and then recovered is a priori suspect. Concepts such as repression and the unconscious mind have proven very elusive subjects of study in the experimental setting. Many laboratory models that have been advanced are far from convincing as paradigms.

The work of Holmes[6] is frequently cited in arguments opposing the existence of repression. It is of historical note that this work appears in an important book[7] containing 18 contributions, 17 of which come to different conclusions than that of Holmes. In this publication, Holmes demonstrates that several experimental constructs of repression were subject to plausible alternative explanations. Unfortunately, he uses motivated skepticism[8] adroitly. His dismissal of the possible relevance of criticism of his paradigms and his disregard of anecdotal clinical information is glib and cavalier.

In his 1970 study he tested the hypothesis that the recall of experiences is determined by the intensity of affect associated with the experiences at the time of recall; that the intensity of the affect associated with given experiences declines over time; and that the affect associated with displeasure will decline more rapidly than that associated with pleasant experiences. He had college students keep a diary of their pleasant and unpleasant experiences for a week. They were to score each experience for pleasantness and unpleasantness on a nine-point scale. A week later they were asked unexpectedly to write down the experiences from their diary cards and to score them again. The results indicated that unpleasant experiences showed greater declines than did pleasant ones and were less likely to be recalled. Holmes concluded that recall of unpleasant experiences was due to reduced affective intensity rather than to repression. He speculated that intensity was reduced because unpleasant experiences, such as failing a French test, were found not to matter that much, or remediative actions could alter the nature of the experience. He also proposed that, with further thought, the attitudes toward the events might become more positive, and therefore the intensity of the negativity would be reduced.

I would like to raise the possibility that the nature of the phenomena that Holmes studied is somewhat different from the materials encountered by clinicians working with traumatized populations. An incestuous experience or a gang-rape might be more traumatic than failing a French test. I do not quarrel with Dr. Holmes' experiment per se, but I do think that trauma-related problems of memory may be managed in a different manner and that this different manner may involve repression and dissociation. I do not think his experimental universe was sufficiently diverse to support his conclusions. Although I consider Holmes's work thought-provoking and ingenious, I seriously doubt that his arguments against the possibility of the recovery of memories[9] deal with the phenomena in question.

When we turn to the famous lost-in-the-mall scenario... of Elizabeth Loftus, who is often regarded as a very influential participant in the debate over recovered memory, we encounter another family of difficulties. In her study, 5 young subjects, "all friends and relatives of our research group"[10,11] were taken through a reflection on early life experiences, most of which were accurate, but one of which—the experimentally suggested one—was not. The subjects were led by siblings and others to believe that they had been lost in a mall, when this had not occurred. Not only was it possible to cause the subjects to report this, but they often confabulated additional details as their stories took on lives of their own. On this basis she argued that it is possible for therapists to implant false memories that will be elaborated further and regarded as credible.[10,11]

I wonder about the generalizability of this experiment, and am troubled by its ethics. Young children were exposed to deliberately mendacious behavior by their siblings and concerned others, and were then told they were duped. I question whether the possible deleterious long-term effects on the relationship of those involved is acceptable. I wonder about the appropriateness of the strategy of teaching children to become involved in systematic deception. I also wonder about the message conveyed about authority figures and the nature of truth that is given to the young subjects. Were I on a human subjects review committee, I would not have passed on this one. When Dr. Loftus has been asked about this, she dismisses such concerns by stating there have been no adverse effects. She offers as proof that when the children understood what had occurred, some of her own subjects took to doing similar deceptions with their friends.[11] To me this is chilling. Perhaps these subjects are only engaging in a benign attempt to achieve mastery, but I would like to raise the possibility that adult authority figures have taught them to think that truth is a malleable commodity that can be distorted at one's convenience or whimsy. These children may be demonstrating the mechanism of identification with the aggressor, a severely pathological defensive adaptation.

I also think the design leaves much to be desired, because it does not narrow the variables in a manner that allows the results to mean anything. It becomes a Rorschach to confirm one's bias. We see a study not of memory but of social persuasion. Whether the implantation of the so-called memory by an older sibling who says he was there as an eye-witness and who has a powerful affective relationship with and position of authority over the child mirrors the position of the therapist is questionable. The therapist was not a first-hand witness to a patient's past, and the therapist is not lying, or trying consciously to systematically direct the patient's perception of the truth, or using techniques verging on the interrogatory. In addition, children are accustomed to the idea of getting lost.[12] It is a normal fear, it is the plot of innumerable fairy tales, and it is the subject of myriad maternal warnings. Children likely have a preexisting schema in mind with regard to getting lost, which can be tapped readily by suggestion because it is already present.[12] With regard to incest, however, the incest fantasies described as universal by Freud are not traumatic in nature, like the ones reported by incest victims. We cannot assume that there is a schema for abrupt anal or oral rape, for example, that is lying dormant and ready to be brought to immediate fruition by a therapist who asks a bland question about whether the patient has had any unwanted sexual experiences.

As a study on social persuasion, however, the lost-in-the-mall scenario demonstrates that when a family has a story about how an event happened, it may drive out the autobiographical memory of those involved. This need not be an instance in which a child is convinced that an event has occurred when it has not. It could just as easily explain how a child is persuaded that an event that did occur has not occurred, a possibility Loftus herself has acknowledged.[11] It is a curious irony that in 1983, a syndrome was described in which the family conspires to deny the reality of a traumatic event, and finally the victim endorses the alternate reality. This, of course, is the child sexual abuse accommodation syndrome, which was explored by Roland Summit—one of the experts frequently attacked by those who believe that recovered memories of childhood sexual abuse should be discredited. Loftus's lost-in-the-mall scenario offers confirmation of Summit's earlier observations: a family determined to distort a child's sense of reality has a good chance of achieving its objectives.

It is possible that insights gained from Loftus's lost-in-the-mall scenario and Summit's child sexual abuse accommodation syndrome may cast some light on a phenomenon that is of great interest in the current false memory controversy. Retractors are individuals who at one time believed that they were abused, but who have come to believe that their memories of abuse are inaccurate. Some retractors change their minds in the context of strong interpersonal pressures that have features in common with those exerted upon individuals in the lost-in-the-mall scenario and the child sexual abuse accommodation syndrome. Could it be that retractors rather than therapy patients demonstrate the forces that Dr. Loftus has studied? This could prove an interesting subject for future research.

Another aspect of the Loftus research that has received little attention is that only a small minority of the subjects who received misdirection cues took the indicated misdirections. Most did not. This research might be cited as evidence that most persons, even those subjected to an intense campaign to distort their memories and induce confabulations, will reject such suggestions.

Since the reader of this [selection] may have heard many an attack on the gullibility and ineptitude of clinicians by speakers representing themselves as guardians of science, it may be useful to consider an analysis from the perspective of a clinician who worries that the perfect can be the enemy of the good, and that taking too literally the warnings of researchers can destroy the capacity to render good therapy.

The progress of science is a parade of paradigms[13] that strut their arrogant hour upon the stage, expressing themselves in allegories called experiments, depreciating, belittling, and berating everything the paradigm of choice does not embrace. Paradigms collapse by virtue of their exclusion of or failure to address data they had deemed unimportant within the worldview of that particular paradigm. In the language of Greek tragedy, every paradigm has a tragic flaw, overstates its applicability (overweening pride), and is humiliated by fate (retribution).

By disregarding information, paradigms embrace the same mechanisms that we find in the more familiar processes of dissociation, repression, denial, splitting, and even more primitive mechanisms. Perhaps the excesses of such uses of science so fascinate me as a clinician because it helps me to appreciate that laboratory science that is unanchored in common sense is a primitive character disorder verging on decompensation into psychosis, a term that indicates that there is a major failure to appreciate reality. We mock the mad scientist in a grade-B movie and enjoy his or her downfall precisely because, like an incestuous Greek king or a Shakespearean regicide, the order of the universe is destroyed by his or her arrogance and false attempts to impose his or her self-deceived facsimile of natural order upon reality, and his or her defeat is necessary in order to preserve the true order of the world. It follows that the attempt to conform clinical practice rigidly to scientific findings is doomed to defeat, because it will introduce borderline and/or psychotic features into the thinking of the clinician.

Additional Remarks on the Recollection and the Nonrecollection of Trauma

... Elizabeth Loftus, Ph.D., is a brilliant researcher and scholar. She has described her own experiences of abuse and reflected upon her incomplete recollection of it. Her words are captured in a deposition cited by Whitfield.[14] She both denies she repressed the memory of the abuse, and speaks of her uncertainty about the number of occurrences, and of her memory having taken and destroyed her recollections of her abuser. In the same account we find both recollection and the absence of recollection. This might be understood as either confusing, or expectable. As Whitfield notes, trauma dissociates and confuses memory, and trying to block traumata out with guilt, shame, and/or threats of harm can drive its mental representation out of awareness.

Loftus's experience can be understood as capturing the essence of the intimately intertwined nature of both the memory and the banishing from memory of traumatization. Rather than polarized opposites, they may be understood by analogy with the intrusive and numbing aspects of the posttraumatic response. While there are some instances in which clear and striking memory is retained, and some in which its abolition is virtually complete, more often, the two processes proceed side by side. An example of this may be that often only the central aspect of a traumatic event is recalled. The details may neither be registered not retrieved.

References

1. Pope KS: Memory, abuse, and science: questioning claims about the false memory epidemic. Am Psychol 1996; 51:957–974.
2. Kluft RP: The natural history of multiple personality disorder. *In* RP Kluft (Ed.), Childhood Antecedents of Multiple Personality. Washington, DC: American Psychiatric Press, 1985, pp. 197–238.
3. Kluft RP: Treatment of multiple personality disorders. Psychiatr Clin North Am 1984; 7:121–134a.
4. Kluft RP: Dissociation and subsequent vulnerability: a preliminary study. Dissociation 1990; 3:167–173.
5. Kluft RP: Incest and subsequent revictimization: the case of therapist-patient sexual exploitation, with a description of the sitting duck syndrome. *In* RP Kluft (Ed.), Incest-related Syndromes of Adult Psychopathology. Washington, DC: American Psychiatric Press, 1990, pp. 263–287.
6. Holmes DS: The evidence for repression. *In* JL Singer (Ed.), Repression and Dissociation. Chicago: University of Chicago Press, 1990, pp. 85–102.
7. Singer JL (Ed.): Repression and Dissociation. Chicago: University of Chicago Press, 1990.
8. Ditto PH, Lopez DF: Motivated skepticism: use of differential decision criteria for preferred and non-preferred conclusions. J Pers Soc Psychol 1992; 63:568–584.
9. Holmes DL: Repression: theory versus evidence. Paper presented at the University of Kansas Medical Center's Conference on Childhood Sexual Abuse and Memories: Current Controversies. Kansas City, Kansas, April 1995.
10. Loftus E: The nature of memory: what we know. Paper presented at the University of Kansas Medical Center's Conference on Childhood Sexual Abuse and Memories: Current Controversies. Kansas City, Kansas, April 1995.
11. Loftus E: Eyewitness memory: implications for the dissociative disorders field. Paper presented at the meeting of the International Society for the Study of Dissociation, International Fall Conference. Orlando, FL, September 1995.
12. Pedzek K, Roe C: Memory for childhood events: how suggestible is it? Consciousness Cogn 1994; 3:374–387.
13. Kuhn TS: The Structure of Scientific Revolutions (2nd ed., enlarged). Chicago: University of Chicago Press, 1971.
14. Whitfield CL: Memory and Abuse: Remembering and Healing the Effects of Trauma. Deerfield Beach FL: Heath Communications, Inc., 1995.

NO ↰

Elizabeth F. Loftus

Creating False Memories

In 1986 Nadean Cool, a nurse's aide in Wisconsin, sought therapy from a psychiatrist to help her cope with her reaction to a traumatic event experienced by her daughter. During therapy, the psychiatrist used hypnosis and other suggestive techniques to dig out buried memories of abuse that Cool herself had allegedly experienced. In the process, Cool became convinced that she had repressed memories of having been in a satanic cult, of eating babies, of being raped, of having sex with animals and of being forced to watch the murder of her eight-year-old friend. She came to believe that she had more than 120 personalities—children, adults, angels and even a duck—all because, Cool was told, she had experienced severe childhood sexual and physical abuse. The psychiatrist also performed exorcisms on her, one of which lasted for five hours and included the sprinkling of holy water and screams for Satan to leave Cool's body.

When Cool finally realized that false memories had been planted, she sued the psychiatrist for malpractice. In March 1997, after five weeks of trial, her case was settled out of court for $2.4 million.

Nadean Cool is not the only patient to develop false memories as a result of questionable therapy. In Missouri in 1992 a church counselor helped Beth Rutherford to remember during therapy that her father, a clergyman, had regularly raped her between the ages of seven and 14 and that her mother sometimes helped him by holding her down. Under her therapist's guidance, Rutherford developed memories of her father twice impregnating her and forcing her to abort the fetus herself with a coat hanger. The father had to resign from his post as a clergyman when the allegations were made public. Later medical examination of the daughter revealed, however, that she was still a virgin at age 22 and had never been pregnant. The daughter sued the therapist and received a $1-million settlement in 1996.

About a year earlier two juries returned verdicts against a Minnesota psychiatrist accused of planting false memories by former patients Vynnette Hamanne and Elizabeth Carlson, who under hypnosis and sodium amytal, and after being fed misinformation about the workings of memory, had come to remember horrific abuse by family members. The juries awarded Hammane $2.67 million and Carlson $2.5 million for their ordeals.

In all four cases, the women developed memories about childhood abuse in therapy and then later denied their authenticity. How can we determine if memories of childhood abuse are true or false? Without corroboration, it is very difficult to differentiate between false memories and true ones. Also, in these cases, some memories were contrary to physical evidence, such as explicit and detailed recollections of rape and abortion when medical examination confirmed virginity. How is it possible for people to acquire elaborate and confident false memories? A growing number of investigations demonstrate that under the right circumstances false memories can be instilled rather easily in some people.

My own research into memory distortion goes back to the early 1970s, when I began studies of the "misinformation effect." These studies show that when people who witness an event are later exposed to new and misleading information about it, their recollections often become distorted. In one example, participants viewed a simulated automobile accident at an intersection with a stop sign. After the viewing, half the participants received a suggestion that the traffic sign was a yield sign. When asked later what traffic sign they remembered seeing at the intersection, those who had been given the suggestion tended to claim that they had seen a yield sign. Those who had not received the phony information were much more accurate in their recollection of the traffic sign.

My students and I have now conducted more than 200 experiments involving over 20,000 individuals that document how exposure to misinformation induces memory distortion. In these studies, people "recalled" a conspicuous barn in a bucolic scene that contained no buildings at all, broken glass and tape recorders that were not in the scenes they viewed, a white instead of a blue vehicle in a crime scene, and Minnie Mouse when they actually saw Mickey Mouse. Taken together, these studies show that misinformation can change an individual's recollection in predictable and sometimes very powerful ways.

Misinformation has the potential for invading our memories when we talk to other people, when we are suggestively interrogated or when we read or view media coverage about some event that we may have experienced ourselves. After more than two decades of exploring the power of misinformation, researchers have learned a great deal about the conditions that make people susceptible to memory modification. Memories are more easily modified, for instance, when the passage of time allows the original memory to fade.

False Childhood Memories

It is one thing to change a detail or two in an otherwise intact memory but quite another to plant a false memory of an event that never happened. To study false memory, my students and I first had to find a way to plant a pseudomemory that would not cause our subjects undue emotional stress, either in the process of creating the false memory or when we revealed that they had been intentionally deceived. Yet we wanted to try to plant a memory that would be at least mildly traumatic, had the experience actually happened.

My research associate, Jacqueline E. Pickrell, and I settled on trying to plant a specific memory of being lost in a shopping mall or large department store at about the age of five. Here's how we did it. We asked our subjects, 24 individuals ranging in age from 18 to 53, to try to remember childhood events that had been recounted to us by a parent, an older sibling or another close relative. We prepared a booklet for each participant containing one-paragraph stories about three events that had actually happened to him or her and one that had not. We constructed the false event using information about a plausible shopping trip provided by a relative, who also verified that the participant had not in fact been lost at about the age of five. The lost-in-the-mall scenario included the following elements: lost for an extended period, crying, aid and comfort by an elderly woman and, finally, reunion with the family.

After reading each story in the booklet, the participants wrote what they remembered about the event. If they did not remember it, they were instructed to write, "I do not remember this." In two follow-up interviews, we told the participants that we were interested in examining how much detail they could remember and how their memories compared with those of their relative. The event paragraphs were not read to them verbatim, but rather parts were provided as retrieval cues. The participants recalled something about 49 of the 72 true events (68 percent) immediately after the initial reading of the booklet and also in each of the two follow-up interviews. After reading the booklet, seven of the 24 participants (29 percent) remembered either partially or fully the false event constructed for them, and in the two follow-up interviews six participants (25 percent) continued to claim that they remembered the fictitious event. Statistically, there were some differences between the true memories and the false ones: participants used more words to describe the true memories, and they rated the true memories as being somewhat more clear. But if an onlooker were to observe many of our participants describe an event, it would be difficult indeed to tell whether the account was of a true or a false memory.

Of course, being lost, however frightening, is not the same as being abused. But the lost-in-the-mall study is not about real experiences of being lost; it is about planting false memories of being lost. The paradigm shows a way of instilling false memories and takes a step toward allowing us to understand how this might happen in real-world settings. Moreover, the study provides evidence that people can be led to remember their past in different ways, and they can even be coaxed into "remembering" entire events that never happened.

Studies in other laboratories using a similar experimental procedure have produced similar results. For instance, Ira Hyman, Troy H. Husband and F. James Billing of Western Washington University asked college students to recall childhood experiences that had been recounted by their parents. The researchers told the students that the study was about how people remember shared experiences differently. In addition to actual events reported by parents, each participant was given one false event—either an overnight hospitalization for a high fever and a possible ear infection, or a birthday party with pizza and a clown—that supposedly happened at about the age of five. The parents confirmed that neither of these events actually took place.

Hyman found that students fully or partially recalled 84 percent of the true events in the first interview and 88 percent in the second interview. None of the participants recalled the false event during the first interview, but 20 percent said they remembered something about the false event in the second interview. One participant who had been exposed to the emergency hospitalization story later remembered a male doctor, a female nurse and a friend from church who came to visit at the hospital.

In another study, along with true events Hyman presented different false events, such as accidentally spilling a bowl of punch on the parents of the bride at a wedding reception or having to evacuate a grocery store when the overhead sprinkler systems erroneously activated. Again, none of the participants recalled the false event during the first interview, but 18 percent remembered something about it in the second interview and 25 percent in the third interview. For example, during the first interview, one participant, when asked about the fictitious wedding event, stated, "I have no clue. I have never heard that one before." In the second interview, the participant said, "It was an outdoor wedding, and I think we were running around and knocked something over like the punch bowl or something and made a big mess and of course got yelled at for it."

Imagination Inflation

The finding that an external suggestion can lead to the construction of false childhood memories helps us understand the process by which false memories arise. It is natural to wonder whether this research is applicable in real situations such as being interrogated by law officers or in psychotherapy. Although strong suggestion may not routinely occur in police questioning or therapy, suggestion in the form of an imagination exercise sometimes does. For instance, when trying to obtain a confession, law officers may ask a suspect to imagine having participated in a criminal act. Some mental health professionals encourage patients to imagine childhood events as a way of recovering supposedly hidden memories.

Surveys of clinical psychologists reveal that 11 percent instruct their clients to "let the imagination run wild," and 22 percent tell their clients to "give free rein to the imagination." Therapist Wendy Maltz, author of a popular book on childhood sexual abuse, advocates telling the patient: "Spend time imagining that you were sexually abused, without worrying about accuracy, proving anything, or having your ideas make sense.... Ask yourself... these questions: What time of day is it? Where are you? Indoors or outdoors? What kind of things are happening? Is there one or more person with you?" Maltz further recommends that therapists continue to ask questions such as "Who would have been likely perpetrators? When were you most vulnerable to sexual abuse in your life?"

The increasing use of such imagination exercises led me and several colleagues to wonder about their consequences. What happens when people imagine childhood experiences that did not happen to them? Does imagining a childhood event increase confidence that it occurred? To explore this, we designed a three-stage procedure. We first asked individuals to indicate the likelihood that certain events happened to them during their childhood. The list contains 40 events, each rated on a scale ranging from "definitely did not happen" to "definitely did happen." Two weeks later we asked the participants to imagine that they had experienced some of these events. Different subjects were asked to imagine different events. Sometime later the participants again were asked to respond to the original list of 40 childhood events, indicating how likely it was that these events actually happened to them.

Consider one of the imagination exercises. Participants are told to imagine playing inside at home after school, hearing a strange noise outside, running toward the window, tripping, falling, reaching out and breaking the window with their hand. In addition, we asked participants questions such as "What did you trip on? How did you feel?"

In one study 24 percent of the participants who imagined the broken-window scenario later reported an increase in confidence that the event had occurred, whereas only 12 percent of those who were not asked to imagine the incident reported an increase in the likelihood that it had taken place. We found this "imagination inflation" effect in each of the eight events that participants were asked to imagine. A number of possible explanations come to mind. An obvious one is that an act of imagination simply makes the event seem more familiar and that familiarity is mistakenly related to childhood memories rather than to the act of imagination. Such source confusion—when a person does not remember the source of information—can be especially acute for the distant experiences of childhood.

Studies by Lyn Goff and Henry L. Roediger III of Washington University of recent rather than childhood experiences more directly connect imagined actions to the construction of false memory. During the initial session, the researchers instructed participants to perform the stated action, imagine doing it or just listen to the statement and do nothing else. The actions were simple ones: knock on the table, lift the stapler, break the toothpick, cross your fingers, roll your eyes. During the second session, the participants were asked to imagine some of the actions that they had not previously performed. During the final session, they answered questions about what actions they actually performed during the initial session. The investigators found that the more times participants imagined an unperformed action, the more likely they were to remember having performed it.

Impossible Memories

It is highly unlikely that an adult can recall genuine episodic memories from the first year of life, in part because the hippocampus, which plays a key role in the creation of memories, has not matured enough to form and store long-lasting memories that can be retrieved in adulthood. A procedure for planting "impossible" memories about experiences that occur shortly after birth has been developed by the late Nicholas Spanos and his collaborators at Carleton University. Individuals are led to believe that they have well-coordinated eye movements and visual exploration skills probably because they were born in hospitals that hung swinging, colored mobiles over infant cribs. To confirm whether they had such an experience, half the participants are hypnotized, age-regressed to the day after birth and asked what they remembered. The other half of the group participates in a "guided mnemonic restructuring" procedure that uses age regression as well as active encouragement to re-create the infant experiences by imagining them.

Spanos and his co-workers found that the vast majority of their subjects were susceptible to these memory-planting procedures. Both the hypnotic and guided participants reported infant memories. Surprisingly, the guided group did so somewhat more (95 versus 70 percent). Both groups remembered the colored mobile at a relatively high rate (56 percent of the guided group and 46 percent of the hypnotic subjects). Many participants who did not remember the mobile did recall other things, such as doctors, nurses, bright lights, cribs and masks. Also, in both groups, of those who reported memories of infancy, 49 percent felt that they were real memories, as opposed to 16 percent who claimed that they were merely fantasies. These findings confirm earlier studies that many individuals can be led to construct complex, vivid and detailed false memories via a rather simple procedure. Hypnosis clearly is not necessary.

How False Memories Form

In the lost-in-the-mall study, implantation of false memory occurred when another person, usually a family member, claimed that the incident happened. Corroboration of an event by another person can be a powerful technique for instilling a false memory. In fact, merely claiming to have seen a person do something can lead that person to make a false confession of wrongdoing.

This effect was demonstrated in a study by Saul M. Kassin and his colleagues at Williams College, who investigated the reactions of individuals falsely accused of damaging a computer by pressing the wrong key. The innocent participants initially denied the charge, but when a confederate said that she had seen them perform the action, many participants signed a confession, internalized guilt for the act and went on to confabulate details that were consistent with that belief. These findings show that false incriminating evidence can induce people to accept guilt for a crime they did not commit and even to develop memories to support their guilty feelings.

Research is beginning to give us an understanding of how false memories of complete, emotional and self-participatory experiences are created in adults. First, there are social demands on individuals to remember; for instance, researchers exert some pressure on participants in a study to come up with memories. Second, memory construction by imagining events can be explicitly encouraged when people are having trouble remembering. And, finally, individuals can be encouraged not to think about whether their constructions are real or not. Creation of false memories is most likely to occur when these external factors are present, whether in an experimental setting, in a therapeutic setting or during everyday activities.

False memories are constructed by combining actual memories with the content of suggestions received from others. During the process, individuals may forget the source of the information. This is a classic example of source confusion, in which the content and the source become dissociated.

Of course, because we can implant false childhood memories in some individuals in no way implies that all memories that arise after suggestion are necessarily false. Put another way, although experimental work on the creation of false memories may raise doubt about the validity of long-buried memories, such as repeated trauma, it in no way disproves them. Without corroboration, there is little that can be done to help even the most experienced evaluator to differentiate true memories from ones that were suggestively planted.

The precise mechanisms by which such false memories are constructed await further research. We still have much to learn about the degree of confidence and the characteristics of false memories created in these ways, and we need to discover what types of individuals are particularly susceptible to these forms of suggestion and who is resistant.

As we continue this work, it is important to heed the cautionary tale in the data we have already obtained: mental health professionals and others must be aware of how greatly they can influence the recollection of events and of the urgent need for maintaining restraint in situations in which imagination is used as an aid in recovering presumably lost memories.

CHALLENGE QUESTIONS

Are Repressed Memories Valid?

1. Kluft suggests that Loftus's research in the laboratory bears little resemblance to the work of the clinician in the context of psychotherapy. What kind of research design could be used to assess the validity of memories that are recovered within the real-life context of psychotherapy?
2. The debate between Loftus and Kluft mirrors many debates between scientists and clinicians. What other issues can you identify in which scientists have been at odds with clinical practitioners?
3. Kluft raises some serious ethical objections with regard to the "lost-in-the-mall" research conducted by Loftus. What arguments can you enumerate on both sides of the debate about the legitimacy of research that involves deception?
4. Imagine that you are a clinician conducting psychotherapy with a woman who seems to remember "out of the blue" some disturbing images involving sexual abuse by her parents when she was three years old. How would you go about dealing with this issue in the therapy?
5. Imagine that you are a member of an ethics committee with the task of writing a set of guidelines for practitioners on the topic of repressed memories. Specify three or four guidelines that you would recommend for clinicians to follow.

Suggested Readings

Baker, R. A. (Ed.) (1998). *Child sexual abuse and false memory syndrome*. Amherst, NY: Prometheus Books.

Loftus, E. F. (1997). Memory for a past that never was. *Current Directions in Psychological Science*, 6(3), 60–65.

Pope, K. S. & Brown, L. S. (Eds.) (1996). *Recovered memories of abuse: Assessment, therapy, forensics*. Washington, DC: American Psychological Association.

Reisner, A. D. (1996). Repressed memories: True and false. *Psychological Record*, 46(4), 563–580.

Williams, L. M. & Banyard, V. L. (Eds.) (1999). *Trauma and memory*. Thousand Oaks, CA: Sage Publications, Inc.

On the Internet . . .   DUSHKIN ONLINE

How Therapy Helps

At this site the American Psychological Association comments on the usefulness of psychotherapy and offers advice on finding a qualified therapist.

http://helping.apa.org/therapy/psychotherapy.html

The American Psychological Society

This is the Web site for the American Psychological Society (APS), an organization that is dedicated to furthering the field of psychology through scientific
research.

http://www.psychologicalscience.org

National Institutes of Health Consensus Statement No. 110

This is the National Institutes of Health (NIH) Consensus Statement on the
Diagnosis and Treatment of Attention Deficit Hyperactivity Disorder.

http://odp.od.nih.gov/consensus/cons/110/
110_statement.htm

Psychosurgery

In this paper, G. Rees Cosgrove and Scott L. Rauch, physicians in the Departments of Neurosurgery and Psychiatry, respectively, of the Massachusetts
General Hospital, review the history of the physiological basis for and current
perspectives on the practice of psychosurgery.

http://neurosurgery.mgh.harvard.edu/psysurg.htm

PART 3

Treatment

*U*nlike the field of medicine, in which treatment for most medical problems is fairly standardized, the field of mental health is characterized by a wide range of interventions, some of which are regarded as quite controversial. Some critics have questioned whether or not psychotherapy in general is effective in reducing emotional problems and facilitating happiness and personal growth. Other commentators have emphasized the importance of limiting the practice of psychotherapy to reliance only on techniques that researchers have demonstrated are effective. Another set of controversies has arisen about somatic interventions that involve recommendations for medication or even psychosurgery.

- Have *Consumer Reports* Researchers Proven That Psychotherapy Helps?

- Has Too Much Emphasis Been Placed on Empirically Supported Therapies?

- Is Ritalin Overprescribed?

- Should Psychosurgery Be Used to Treat Certain Psychological Conditions?

ISSUE 8

Have *Consumer Reports* Researchers Proven That Psychotherapy Helps?

YES: Martin E. P. Seligman, from "The Effectiveness of Psychotherapy: The *Consumer Reports* Study," *American Psychologist* (December 1995)

NO: Neil S. Jacobson and Andrew Christensen, from "Studying the Effectiveness of Psychotherapy," *American Psychologist* (October 1996)

ISSUE SUMMARY

YES: Martin E. P. Seligman, a leading researcher in the field of psychotherapy, praises the study of psychotherapy conducted by researchers at the popular magazine *Consumer Reports*, which he says is the most extensive study on record demonstrating the effectiveness of psychotherapy.

NO: Psychotherapy researchers Neil S. Jacobson and Andrew Christensen criticize the *Consumer Reports* study on methodological grounds, asserting that it adds little to understanding the effectiveness of psychotherapy.

For the past several decades millions of dollars have been spent on research designed to determine whether or not psychotherapy is effective. In countless studies and numerous meta-analyses, psychotherapy researchers have tried to ascertain if mental health interventions actually help people and, if so, which aspects are central to the therapeutic process. The vast amount of psychotherapy research has been conducted under laboratory-like conditions, which often pale in comparison to the complexities of real-life psychotherapy conditions. Many researchers rely on analogue studies that involve artificially constructed research designs in which only a few variables are studied under controlled conditions.

Because of the limitations of many psychotherapy research studies, in recent years some skeptics have wondered whether or not the efforts of mental health professionals make any difference in the lives of people. To answer this question, the editors of *Consumer Reports* (*CR*) decided to ask their many thousands of readers to respond to a survey about psychotherapy, which was included in the publication's annual survey of subscribers' experiences with cars, dishwashers, insurance companies, and the like. The *CR* study sent shock waves through the psychology departments of universities and medical schools, where psychotherapy research has traditionally been conducted. Some researchers were disturbed by the possibility that research by a consumer magazine could trivialize their own efforts and underplay the importance of psychotherapy in general. Others applauded these endeavors in the belief that this effort, the largest ever undertaken in the field of psychotherapy research, could provide valuable information about real-life experiences.

In the following selection, Martin E. P. Seligman confesses that the *CR* study shook his belief about efficacy studies, which had long been regarded by himself and other experts as the "gold standard" of psychotherapy research. In efficacy studies researchers use experimental methods, with control groups and manipulated variables, to evaluate psychotherapy's effectiveness. In the landmark *CR* study, however, investigators studied how real-life patients evaluate their experiences in real-life psychotherapy contexts. The "consumers" who responded to this survey reported a number of benefits associated with psychotherapy and offered some interesting insights into aspects of intervention that they consider especially effective.

In the second selection, Neil S. Jacobson and Andrew Christensen acknowledge that the *CR* findings are very persuasive, but they contend that this study does not add much to the existing data showing that psychotherapy is effective. In fact, they criticize the methodology of the *CR* study and assert that controlled experiments that avoid the pitfalls of the study are far more valuable in leading to valuable conclusions about what makes psychotherapy work.

POINT	COUNTERPOINT
• The *CR* study is superior to efficacy studies because it studied how patients fare under actual conditions of treatment in the field.	• The *CR* findings are highly questionable because of the study's methodological shortcomings.
• Many investigators have naively come to think that an efficacy study is the "gold standard" for measuring whether or not a treatment works rather than relying on more naturalistic studies such as the one conducted by *CR*.	• It would be unfortunate if psychotherapy researchers abandoned controlled experiments; despite limitations, these studies are far superior to the type of design reflected in the *CR* study.
• The *CR* study has particular value because it is the most extensive psychotherapy study on record.	• The *CR* study is little more than a measure of consumer satisfaction.
• The *CR* study is valid and valuable not only for its results and its credible source but for its method.	• The *CR* study is problematic for many of the same reasons that pioneering research, such as that conducted by Hans Eysenck in 1952, was criticized.

Martin E. P. Seligman

YES

The Effectiveness of Psychotherapy: The *Consumer Reports* Study

How do we find out whether psychotherapy works? To answer this, two methods have arisen: the *efficacy study* and the *effectiveness study*. An efficacy study is the more popular method. It contrasts some kind of therapy to a comparison group under well-controlled conditions....

The high praise "empirically validated" is now virtually synonymous with positive results in efficacy studies, and many investigators have come to think that an efficacy study is the "gold standard" for measuring whether a treatment works....

But my belief has changed about what counts as a "gold standard." And it was a study by *Consumer Reports* (1995, November) that singlehandedly shook my belief. I came to see that deciding whether one treatment, under highly controlled conditions, works better than another treatment or a control group is a different question from deciding what works in the field (Muñoz, Hollon, McGrath, Rehm, & VandenBos, 1994). I no longer believe that efficacy studies are the only, or even the best, way of finding out what treatments actually work in the field. I have come to believe that the "effectiveness" study of how patients fare under the actual conditions of treatment in the field, can yield useful and credible "empirical validation" of psychotherapy and medication. This is the method that *Consumer Reports* pioneered....

Consumer Reports Survey

Consumer Reports (CR) included a supplementary survey about psychotherapy and drugs in one version of its 1994 annual questionnaire, along with its customary inquiries about appliances and services. *CR's* 180,000 readers received this version, which included approximately 100 questions about automobiles and about mental health. *CR* asked readers to fill out the mental health section "if at any time over the past three years you experienced stress or other emotional problems for which you sought help from any of the following: friends, relatives, or a member of the clergy; a mental health professional like a

From Martin E. P. Seligman, "The Effectiveness of Psychotherapy: The *Consumer Reports* Study," *American Psychologist*, vol. 50, no. 12 (December 1995). Copyright © 1995 by The American Psychological Association. Reprinted by permission of The American Psychological Association and the author. Notes and references omitted.

psychologist or a psychiatrist; your family doctor; or a support group." Twenty-two thousand readers responded. Of these, approximately 7,000 subscribers responded to the mental health questions. Of these 7,000 about 3,000 had just talked to friends, relatives, or clergy, and 4,100 went to some combination of mental health professionals, family doctors, and support groups. Of these 4,100, 2,900 saw a mental health professional: Psychologists (37%) were the most frequently seen mental health professional, followed by psychiatrists (22%), social workers (14%), and marriage counselors (9%). Other mental health professionals made up 18%. In addition, 1,300 joined self-help groups, and about 1,000 saw family physicians. The respondents as a whole were highly educated, predominantly middle class; about half were women, and the median age was 46. . . .

There were a number of clear-cut results, among them:

- Treatment by a mental health professional usually worked. Most respondents got a lot better. Averaged over all mental health professionals, of the 426 people who were feeling *very poor* when they began therapy, 87% were feeling *very good, good,* or at least *so-so* by the time of the survey. Of the 786 people who were feeling *fairly poor* at the outset, 92% were feeling *very good, good,* or at least *so-so* by the time of the survey. These findings converge with meta-analyses of efficacy (Lipsey & Wilson, 1993; Shapiro & Shapiro, 1982; Smith, Miller, & Glass, 1980).
- Long-term therapy produced more improvement than short-term therapy. This result was very robust, and held up over all statistical models. . . .
- There was no difference between psychotherapy alone and psychotherapy plus medication for any disorder (very few respondents reported that they had medication with no psychotherapy at all).
- While all mental health professionals appeared to help their patients, psychologists, psychiatrists, and social workers did equally well and better than marriage counselors. Their patients' overall improvement scores (0–300 scale) were 220, 226, 225 (not significantly different from each other), and 208 (significantly worse than the first three), respectively.
- Family doctors did just as well as mental health professionals in the short term, but worse in the long term. Some patients saw both family doctors and mental health professionals, and those who saw both had more severe problems. For patients who relied solely on family doctors, their overall improvement scores when treated for up to six months was 213, and it remained at that level (212) for those treated longer than six months. In contrast, the overall improvement scores for patients of mental health professionals was 211 up to six months, but climbed to 232 when treatment went on for more than six months. The advantages of long-term treatment by a mental health professional held not only for the specific problems that led to treatment, but for a variety of general functioning scores as well: ability to relate to others,

coping with everyday stress, enjoying life more, personal growth and understanding, self-esteem and confidence.

- Alcoholics Anonymous (AA) did especially well, with an average improvement score of 251, significantly bettering mental health professionals. People who went to non-AA groups had less severe problems and did not do as well as those who went to AA (average score = 215).

- Active shoppers and active clients did better in treatment than passive recipients (determined by responses to "Was it mostly your idea to seek therapy? When choosing this therapist, did you discuss qualifications, therapist's experience, discuss frequency, duration, and cost, speak to someone who was treated by this therapist, check out other therapists? During therapy, did you try to be as open as possible, ask for explanation of diagnosis and unclear terms, do homework, not cancel sessions often, discuss negative feelings toward therapist?").

- No specific modality of psychotherapy did any better than any other for any problem. These results confirm the "dodo bird" hypothesis, that all forms of psychotherapies do about equally well (Luborsky, Singer, & Luborsky, 1975). They come as a rude shock to efficacy researchers, since the main theme of efficacy studies has been the demonstration of the usefulness of specific techniques for specific disorders.

- Respondents whose choice of therapist or duration of care was limited by their insurance coverage did worse, ... (determined by responses to "Did limitations on your insurance coverage affect any of the following choices you made? Type of therapist I chose; How often I met with my therapist; How long I stayed in therapy").

These findings are obviously important, and some of them could not be included in the original *CR* article because of space limitations. Some of these findings were quite contrary to what I expected, but it is not my intention to discuss their substance here. Rather, I want to explore the methodological adequacy of this survey. My underlying questions are "Should we believe the findings?" and "Can the method be improved to give more authoritative answers?"

Consumer Reports Survey: Methodological Virtues

Sampling   This survey is, as far as I have been able to determine, the most extensive study of psychotherapy effectiveness on record. The sample is not representative of the United States as a whole, but my guess is that it is roughly representative of the middle class and educated population who make up the bulk of psychotherapy patients. It is important that the sample represents people who choose to go to treatment for their problems, not people who do not "believe in" psychotherapy or drugs. The *CR* sample, moreover, is probably weighted toward "problem solvers," people who actively try to do something about what troubles them.

Treatment duration   CR sampled all treatment durations from one month or less through two years or more. Because the study was naturalistic, treatment, it can be supposed, continued until the patient (a) was better, (b) gave up unimproved, or (c) had his or her coverage run out. This, by definition, mirrors what actually happens in the field. In contrast to all efficacy studies, which are of fixed treatment duration regardless of how the patient is progressing, the CR study informs us about treatment effectiveness under the duration constraints of actual therapy.

Self-correction   Because the CR study was naturalistic, it informs us of how treatment works as it is actually performed—without manuals and with self-correction when a technique falters. This also contrasts favorably to efficacy studies, which are manualized and not self-correcting when a given technique or modality fails.

Multiple problems   The large majority of respondents in the CR study had more than one problem. We can also assume that a good-sized fraction were "subclinical" in their problems and would not meet *DSM-IV* [Diagnostic and Statistical Manual of Mental Disorders, 4th Ed.] criteria for any disorder. No patients were discarded because they failed exclusion criteria or because they fell one symptom short of a full-blown "disorder." Thus the sample more closely reflected people who actually seek treatment than the filtered and single-disordered patients of efficacy studies.

General functioning   The CR study measured self-reported changes in productivity at work, interpersonal relations, well-being, insight, and growth, in addition to improvement on the presenting problem.... Importantly, more improvement on the presenting problem occurred for treatments which lasted longer than six months. In addition, more improvement occurred in work, interpersonal relations, enjoyment of life, and personal growth domains in treatments which lasted longer than six months. Since improvements in general functioning, as well as symptom relief, is almost always a goal of actual treatment but rarely of efficacy studies, the CR study adds to our knowledge of how treatment does beyond the mere elimination of symptoms.

Clinical significance   There has been much debate about how to measure the "clinical significance" of a treatment. Efficacy studies are designed to detect statistically significant differences between a treatment and control groups, and an "effect size" can be computed. But what degree of statistical significance is clinical significance? How large an effect size is meaningful? The CR study leaves little doubt about the human significance of its findings, since respondents answered directly about how much therapy helped the problem that led them to treatment—from *made things a lot better* to *made things a lot worse*. Of those who started out feeling *very poor*, 54% answered treatment *made things a lot better,* and another one third answered it made things *somewhat better.*

Unbiased   Finally, it cannot be ignored that *CR* is about as unbiased a scrutinizer of goods and services as exists in the public domain. They have no axe to grind for or against medications, psychotherapy, managed care, insurance companies, family doctors, AA, or long-term treatment. They do not care if psychologists do better or worse than psychiatrists, marriage and family counselors, or social workers. They are not pursuing government grants or drug company favors. They do not accept advertisements. They have a track record of loyalty only to consumers. So this study comes with higher credibility than studies that issue from drug houses, from either APA [American Psychiatric Association], from consensus conferences of the National Institute of Mental Health, or even from the halls of academe. . . .

The Ideal Study

The *CR* study, then, is to be taken seriously—not only for its results and its credible source, but for its method. It is large-scale; it samples treatment as it is actually delivered in the field; it samples without obvious bias those who seek out treatment; it measures multiple outcomes including specific improvement and more global gains such as growth, insight, productivity, mood, enjoyment of life, and interpersonal relations; it is statistically stringent and finds clinically meaningful results. Furthermore, it is highly cost-effective.

Its major advantage over the efficacy method for studying the effectiveness of psychotherapy and medications is that it captures how and to whom treatment is actually delivered and toward what end. At the very least, the *CR* study and its underlying survey method provides a powerful addition to what we know about the effectiveness of psychotherapy and a pioneering way of finding out more.

The study is not without flaws, the chief one being the limited meaning of its answer to the question "Can psychotherapy help?" This question has three possible kinds of answers. The first is that psychotherapy does better than something else, such as talking to friends, going to church, or doing nothing at all. Because it lacks comparison groups, the *CR* study only answers this question indirectly. The second possible answer is that psychotherapy returns people to normality or more liberally to within, say, two standard deviations of the average. The *CR* study, lacking an untroubled group and lacking measures of how people were before they became troubled, does not answer this question. The third answer is "Do people have fewer symptoms and a better life after therapy than they did before?" This is the question that the *CR* study answers with a clear "yes."

NO ⤺

**Neil S. Jacobson and
Andrew Christensen**

Studying the Effectiveness
of Psychotherapy

[T]here is considerable debate about the merits of a recent *Consumer Reports (CR)* survey (1995).... This survey has received a great deal of attention within psychology and has been publicized in the popular press. Seligman (1995) suggested that this is the best study ever conducted on the effectiveness of psychotherapy.

Much like Freud's case studies, the report by *CR* (1995) is very persuasive and will probably have a great deal of influence on the public perception of psychotherapy. However, the purpose of this article is to show that most of what the *CR* study says has already been proven to the satisfaction of both practitioners and psychotherapy researchers. Moreover, those findings from the *CR* study that have not been previously established are highly questionable because of the study's methodological shortcomings. Finally, controlled experiments that avoid the methodological pitfalls of the *CR* study can answer virtually all of the questions considered by Seligman (1995) to be beyond the scope of clinical trials. In fact, it would be unfortunate if the field of psychotherapy research abandoned the controlled experiment when attempting to answer questions regarding the effectiveness of psychotherapy. Although clinical trials have their limitations and may need to be supplemented by other types of methodologies, they are far superior to the type of design reflected in the *CR* study, a design that has already been debated and rejected by both practitioners and researchers....

A Critique of the New Findings from
the *Consumer Reports* Survey

The methodological shortcomings of the *CR* (1995) survey greatly limit their evidentiary value. Seligman (1995) mentioned some of these shortcomings but not others; the ones he did mention tended to be minimized. Here are a sample of these shortcomings.

From Neil S. Jacobson and Andrew Christensen, "Studying the Effectiveness of Psychotherapy," *American Psychologist*, vol. 51, no. 10 (October 1996). Copyright © 1996 by The American Psychological Association. Reprinted by permission of The American Psychological Association and the author. Notes and references omitted.

A Retrospective Survey Is Not an Ideal Prototype for Effectiveness Research

Seligman (1995) suggested that the CR (1995) study is a well-done effectiveness study and was careful to distinguish this study from an efficacy study—a randomized clinical trial. However, in fact, the CR survey is not necessarily a good model for an effectiveness study as that term is typically used. The main virtue of the CR survey, according to Seligman, is its "realism"; that is, it is a report about real therapy, conducted by real therapists, with real clients, in the real world. The retrospective biases that are impossible to rule out are not seen as fatal flaws but simply as aspects of the design that need to be refined.

There are two fundamental problems with retrospective surveys. The first is that, because they are retrospective, there is no opportunity to corroborate respondents' reports. When participants are reporting on their own previous experiences, whether in therapy or otherwise, there is no way of assessing their accuracy. Various biases may contaminate their responses, ranging from demand characteristics to memory distortion. With a prospective study, some of these biases can be minimized, whereas others can be evaluated, using corroborative measures coming from different modalities. For example, self-report data can be supplemented with observational data. With retrospective surveys, such validation is impossible, and thus the responses are hard to interpret.

The second problem with retrospective surveys is the possibility that an unrepresentative subsample of those surveyed returned their questionnaires. Although it cannot be proven that those who benefited from psychotherapy were more likely to complete the survey than were those who did not, neither can that possibility be disproven. With a prospective study, one doesn't have to guess. This additional problem makes the improvement rates reported in the CR (1995) survey hard to interpret.

The most striking example of this selectivity problem is in the findings pertaining to Alcoholics Anonymous (AA), which had the highest mean improvement rate of any treatment category reported by Seligman (1995). In fact, as a treatment, AA significantly outperformed other mental health professionals. This finding can be contrasted with the lack of evidence supporting the efficacy of AA in prospective studies (McCrady & Delaney, 1995). Seligman acknowledged the strong possibility of sampling bias in AA and offered some speculations on why one might expect AA to be particularly susceptible to such biases. However, he then inexplicably minimized the likelihood of similarly extensive biases operating in the sample as a whole, suggesting that

> a similar kind of sampling bias, *to a lesser degree,* [italics added] cannot be overlooked for other kinds of treatment failures. At any rate, it is quite possible that there was a *large* [italics added] oversampling of successful AA cases and a *smaller* [italics added] oversampling of successful treatment for problems other than alcoholism.(p. 971)

Is it not possible that the oversampling of successful cases was as large for other problems as it was for AA? Is there any evidence to the contrary?

In addition to contaminating the overall estimates of treatment gains, sampling bias could easily explain the apparent superiority of long-term therapy reported by the respondents in the CR (1995) study. Unlike Howard et al. (1986), who found a negatively accelerated dose–response relationship, the CR survey found a linear relationship: the more therapy, the better the outcome. This would indeed be an important finding if it were interpretable; unfortunately, it is not interpretable. Seligman (1995) argued against the possibility of sampling bias by focusing on one potential source. He suggested that, if early dropouts are treatment failures and those who remain in treatment are beneficiaries, then earlier dropouts should have lower rates of "problem resolution" than later dropouts. In fact, the rates are uniform: About two thirds of dropouts quit because the problem is resolved, whether they quit therapy one month or two years after they started.

The problem with Seligman's (1995) refutation is that it fails to rule out the primary source of interpretive ambiguity—spontaneous remission. The longer people stay in therapy, the greater the opportunity for factors other than therapy to produce improvement. There is no way of knowing whether the superiority of long-term therapy is due to the treatment itself or simply to increased opportunities for other factors to produce improvements.

Seligman (1995) argued that the main virtue of the CR (1995) study is its realism. If one thinks of realism using the metaphor of a snapshot, the implication is that the CR survey provides a snapshot of what psychotherapy is really like. But, because the study is retrospective, the snapshot may be out of focus. With a prospective study, one can take a snapshot of psychotherapy whose focus is indisputable. But, with a retrospective survey, the negatives are gone forever.

The Absence of Control Groups of Any Kind Constitutes an Additional Fatal Flaw

Seligman (1995) fully acknowledged the problems introduced by the uncontrolled nature of the study but suggested that there are "internal controls" that can be used as surrogates. Unfortunately, none of Seligman's internal controls can be considered adequate substitutes for control groups.

First, he suggested that the inferior performance of marriage counselors allowed them to serve as a reference group because they controlled for various nonspecific factors such as the presence of an attentive listener. However, because marriage counselors may have differed systematically from other professionals in the client population with whom they worked, their performance cannot be compared with that of other mental health professionals who may have treated more mental health problems that were not primarily related to marital distress. In other words, there may have been a systematic confounding between type of problem treated and profession, which rendered marriage counselors useless as an internal control.

Second, Seligman (1995) noted that long-term treatment worked better than short-term treatment, thus allowing the use of the first point in the dose–response curve as a control group. As we have already suggested, this internal control is useless because of the confound with greater opportunity for spontaneous remission in long-term therapy.

Third, according to Seligman (1995), because it is known that drugs outperform placebos, and because psychotherapy did as well as psychotherapy plus drugs in the *CR* (1995) study, one can infer that psychotherapy would have outperformed an adequate placebo if one had been included in the *CR* study. This argument is specious for a number of reasons: It is not known what drugs were used for which problems in the *CR* study; it is not known whether the pharmacotherapy performed was adequate (compliance, dosage, etc.); and most importantly, it is not known whether the sample of patients in the *CR* study was similar to those in which drugs typically outperform placebos.

Fourth, family doctors did not perform as well as mental health professionals when treatment continued beyond six months, thus suggesting family doctors as an internal control. However, family doctors saw clients for a fewer number of sessions than did mental health professionals, creating a confound that Seligman (1995) himself acknowledged.

Seligman (1995) concluded that spontaneous remission is an unlikely explanation for the high improvement rates reported by respondents in the *CR* (1995) study. We come to a different conclusion, because none of the proposed internal controls are adequate. We conclude that factors other than psychotherapy might very well have accounted for the improvement rates reported by the respondents. We come to this conclusion for several reasons. First, there is no adequate control to rule it out, thus no compelling reason to reject the null hypothesis. Second, because the 4,000 respondents in the *CR* study were, to use Seligman's (1995) terminology, "middle class and educated" (p. 969) and "a good-sized fraction were 'subclinical'... and would not meet *DSM-IV* [Diagnostic and Statistical Manual of Mental Disorders, 4th Edition; American Psychiatric Association, 1994] criteria for any disorder" (p. 970), we have the kind of sample that is most likely to spontaneously remit, or to benefit from any treatment, specific or nonspecific (Jacobson & Hollon, 1996). As Seligman noted, in most clinical trials, the single largest basis for exclusion is that the client is not sufficiently distressed or dysfunctional to be included.

For example, in research on depression, by far the most common basis for exclusion is that not enough symptoms are present for the patient to meet criteria for major depressive disorder; even if *DSM-IV* criteria are met, participants are often excluded because the major depressive disorder is not severe enough (Jacobson et al., 1996). In efficacy studies, there is a good reason to exclude these participants: They seem to get better no matter what they receive. Even the less severe patients who make it into these trials tend to respond as well to placebos as they do to active treatments (cf. Jacobson & Hollon, 1996). Thus, it is a fair assumption that many of the respondents to the *CR* (1995) survey who improved would have improved without therapy.

The Measures in the *Consumer Reports* Survey Were Not Only Unreliable but Unrevealing

The *CR* (1995) survey measured little more than consumer satisfaction. Consumer satisfaction is far from trivial. However, consumer satisfaction ratings are uncorrelated with symptomatic outcome and general functioning. In the *CR* survey, three questions were asked in the assessment of improvement, one pertaining to "satisfaction with therapist," a second pertaining to "improvement in the presenting problem," and a third pertaining to "improvement in overall functioning." The latter measure was a change score, derived by subtracting posttest scores from pretest scores (both obtained retrospectively); the other two measures were simply posttest scores. Seligman (1995) seized on these three questions to argue that three different constructs are being measured: consumer satisfaction, symptom relief, and general functioning. However, since all three questions are global and retrospective and have method variance in common, they cannot be considered independent assessments of functioning or to be measuring different constructs. Furthermore, the three questions were combined into a multivariate composite for the calculation of improvement rates, thus making it impossible to separate out consumer satisfaction from the other items.

The Specificity Question Revisited: The *Consumer Reports* Survey Did Not Assess Which Therapies Led to Improvement in Which Problems

Researchers are long past the stage of referring to psychotherapy as if it were uniform, without specifying the nature of the problem being treated or the treatment used. Yet, the *CR* (1995) study failed to inform the public about any particular treatment for any particular problem and thus provides little information that advances knowledge about psychotherapy. The data may be available to answer more specific questions. But even if they were available, and were released, they would be based on respondent reports: Respondents would be reporting what their presenting problem was and the kind of treatment they received (we have already seen some data on this latter question), and they would be defining both the profession and the theoretical orientation of the therapist. How reliable are survey respondents at describing the theoretical orientation of their therapist or at fitting their presenting problem into one of a series of choices on a survey, especially in retrospect? Both of us have small private practices, and a large proportion of our clients are couples. We have heard ourselves referred to as marriage counselors, psychologists, and even, on occasion, psychiatrists. We doubt whether the number of our clients who could correctly identify our theoretical orientation would much exceed chance.

Even Assuming Methodological Adequacy, the Results as Reported by *Consumer Reports* and by Seligman Are Misleading

Although the sound bite coming out of both the *CR* (1995) report and Seligman's (1995) article says that 90% of the respondents found psychotherapy beneficial, it is worth noting that this figure comes from combining those who were helped "a great deal," "a lot," and "somewhat." Only 54% reported that they were helped "a great deal." This is not a very impressive figure from the standpoint of clinical significance, especially when one takes into account the number of subclinical respondents in the sample and the possibility that the respondents may be overrepresented by those who found treatment to be helpful.

The Eysenck Evaluation Revisited

The *CR* (1995) survey bears remarkable resemblance to the controversial evaluation of psychotherapy reported by Eysenck (1952). In this report, Eysenck summarized the results of 24 reports of psychoanalytic and eclectic psychotherapy with more than 7,000 neurotic patients treated in naturalistic settings. Using therapist ratings of improvement, Eysenck reported a 44% improvement rate for psychoanalytic therapy and a 64% improvement rate for eclectic psychotherapy. Unlike the *CR* survey, however, these reports were prospective in that the therapist evaluations occurred at the time of termination. Also unlike the *CR* survey, Eysenck used control groups: One consisted of all improved patients who had been discharged from hospitals in New York between 1917 and 1934 for "neurotic" conditions, receiving nothing but custodial care; the other consisted of 500 disability claimants who were periodically evaluated by general practitioners without receiving psychotherapy, so it could be determined whether they were improved enough to go back to work. Improvement for this latter control group was defined as their ability to return to work, which was decided by the general practitioner. Eysenck reported, on the basis of these two control groups, that the spontaneous remission rate for these minimally treated patients was 72% and that psychotherapy was therefore ineffective.

The merits of these findings and the methodology supporting them were debated vigorously for 20 years. Initially, Luborsky (1954) criticized the study on the grounds that the measures of improvement were flawed, the control groups were inadequate, and the treatments were lacking on both uniformity and representativeness. Similar critiques were registered by Rosenzweig (1954) and De Charrus, Levy, and Wertheimer (1954). These and more recent critiques (e.g., Bergin, 1971) argued, with considerable merit, that Eysenck (1952) had underestimated the success of therapy and overestimated the spontaneous remission rate. As recently as the mid-1970s, Eysenck's study was subject to refutation by more optimistic appraisals and interpretations of psychotherapy's impact (Luborsky et al., 1975; Meltzoff & Kornreich, 1970). Now, the controversy has largely subsided, and Eysenck's study has been rejected by clinical scientists. In fact, in the most recent edition of Bergin and Garfield's (1994) *Handbook of Psychotherapy and Behavioral Change* the study is not even cited.

When it is referenced nowadays, it is primarily for its historical impact and its heuristic value.

What is interesting about examining Eysenck's (1952) study in light of the *CR* (1995) survey is that virtually all of the criticisms leveled at Eysenck's evaluation also apply to the *CR* survey, even though Eysenck's evaluation was more sophisticated from a methodological perspective. Eysenck had a sample that was almost twice as large as the sample reported in the *CR* survey; he did at least include control groups, however inadequate they might have been; the measures of improvement were concurrent rather than retrospective; and the measures were obtained from trained therapists rather than from the clients themselves. Given Seligman's (1995) assumptions that therapists are able to self-correct their therapeutic work and cannily select which clients need drugs and psychotherapy, therapists should also be better judges of when clients have made genuine improvement versus transitory symptom change. However, the field was correct in rejecting Eysenck's evaluation: The control groups and the measures of outcome were inadequate. We don't see any reason to revert to a methodology that was rejected for its methodological inadequacies 20 years ago.

CHALLENGE QUESTIONS

Have *Consumer Reports* Researchers Proven That Psychotherapy Helps?

1. Seligman is impressed by the large number of respondents to the *CR* survey, but he does acknowledge some of the limitations of the sample. Expand on this discussion of sample bias by considering characteristics of the typical *CR* subscriber as well as characteristics of the people who are most likely to respond to this kind of survey.
2. Jacobson and Christensen criticize the retrospective nature of the *CR* survey. What might motivate some respondents to evaluate their experiences in psychotherapy as having been positive and helpful?
3. Managed care insurance companies are committed to reimbursing only for interventions that are helpful to patients. To what extent should a managed care company rely on reports of patients about the effectiveness of their psychotherapy? Why?
4. Imagine that you have just been awarded an extremely large grant to study the effectiveness of psychotherapy. How would you go about conducting such a study?
5. Jacobson and Christensen offer some compelling criticisms of the *CR* study. What factors might motivate university researchers to find fault with a research study conducted by a popular magazine?

Suggested Readings

Crits-Christoph, P. (1997). Limitations of the Dodo bird verdict and the role of clinical trials in psychotherapy research. *Psychological Bulletin, 122,* 221–225.

Dawes, R. (1994). Psychotherapy. The myth of expertise. In R. Dawes, *House of cards.* (pp. 38–74). New York, NY: The Free Press.

Lambert, M., & Bergin, A. (1994). The effectiveness of psychotherapy. In A. Bergin, & S. Garfield (Eds.), *Handbook of psychotherapy and behavior change* (4th ed.). (pp. 143–189). New York, NY: John Wiley & Sons, Inc.

Nathan, P., & Gorman, J. (Eds.) (1998). *A guide to treatments that work.* New York, NY: Oxford University Press.

Wampold, B., Mondin, G., Moody, M., Stich, F., Benson, K., & Ahn, H. (1997). A meta-analysis of outcome studies comparing bonafide psychotherapies: Empirically, "all must have prizes." *Psychological Bulletin, 122,* 203–215.

Has Too Much Emphasis Been Placed on Empirically Supported Therapies?

YES: Sol L. Garfield, from "Some Comments on Empirically Supported Treatments," *Journal of Consulting and Clinical Psychology* (February 1998)

NO: Philip C. Kendall, from "Empirically Supported Psychological Therapies," *Journal of Consulting and Clinical Psychology* (February 1998)

ISSUE SUMMARY

YES: Psychologist and psychotherapy researcher Sol L. Garfield asserts that too much emphasis is being placed on the importance of using empirically supported or validated therapies for treating people with specific psychiatric disorders.

NO: Psychologist and psychotherapy researcher Philip C. Kendall contends that psychotherapists should rely on the knowledge derived from extensive research when they select treatments for clients with particular psychiatric disorders.

T he field of health care has experienced revolutionary changes that most people, providers as well as patients, could never have anticipated 15 years ago. Due to the skyrocketing costs of health care, which became a national concern in the 1980s, third-party payers, such as insurance companies, were forced to scrutinize all expenditures in order to avoid the astronomical insurance premiums that would be needed to cover the costs of medical care. Concerns about health care costs were especially felt within the mental health field, where increasing pressure was being placed on clinicians to document the appropriateness and effectiveness of their interventions. Long-term psychoanalytically informed psychotherapy, which was once so popular, was questioned in terms of effectiveness and cost, particularly by managed care companies, whose mission it was to pay for the best possible treatment at the lowest possible cost. Pressures were placed on clinicians to move beyond idiosyncratic preferences with regard to psychotherapeutic choices and to rely increasingly on focused forms of intervention whose efficacy had been demonstrated by research findings. For example, a woman seeking treatment for her dog phobia would presumably benefit from systematic desensitization, an intervention that researchers and clinicians have demonstrated is especially effective for treating phobias. Although a clinician might opt instead to recommend psychoanalysis to treat this client, managed care insurance companies would not support this approach, nor would most experienced clinicians. What seems on the surface like a straightforward issue, however, is rarely so simple in real clinical situations. What if the woman is also having marital problems and has a history of early-life trauma? How does the clinician decide which approach to use? Complexities such as these form the basis for the intense debate in the field of mental health about the importance of empirically supported treatments.

In the following selection, Sol L. Garfield expresses concern about the overemphasis on empirically supported treatments and the increasing endorsement of briefer forms of therapy. He asserts that attempts to certify and mandate the use of specific therapies for specific psychiatric diagnoses are premature; furthermore, such simplistic efforts minimize the importance of patient variability and therapist skill.

In the second selection, Philip C. Kendall contends that empirical validations of therapy are necessary to provide measures of therapy outcome other than the conclusions drawn by the practitioners themselves about the effectiveness of their interventions. He states that it is important that mental health professionals rely on research findings to make treatment decisions; namely, what treatments, provided by whom, are best applied to what types of clinical problems.

POINT

- The efforts of some clinical psychologists to certify and mandate the use of specific therapies for specific disorders is premature and inappropriate.

- Linking the accreditation of clinical psychology graduate programs and internships to the teaching of empirically supported treatments is unacceptable.

- There is considerable variation in the therapeutic skill and quality of therapy among therapists, even those purporting to practice the same kind of therapy with comparable training.

- Different individuals may share the same diagnosis but may have individual attributes that affect the psychotherapy differently.

COUNTERPOINT

- The goal is not to produce a mandated list of psychiatric treatments but rather to identify those treatments that have been supported by empirical research to date.

- An attempt to require that only therapies identified as empirically supported could be taught or applied is not what is being recommended, because such efforts would impede progress.

- Empirical evaluations of treatment are designed to reduce or eliminate therapist factors and demonstrate what treatments, provided by whom, are best applied to what types of clinical problems.

- Diagnosis does not need to be the basis for determining the type of therapy; rather, other dimensions can be defined as the basis for choosing appropriate treatments.

Sol L. Garfield  **YES**

Some Comments on Empirically Supported Treatments

A number of developments have occurred in the field of psychotherapy in recent years. One pertains to the emphasis on empirically supported or validated therapies for specific psychiatric disorders. Although this emphasis on empirical support is a positive one, the creation of numerous forms of therapy for specific psychiatric categories, and the possible implication that training in such therapies becomes the basis for accreditation of university programs, is viewed critically. A focus on forms of psychotherapy also tends to diminish the importance of patient and therapist characteristics in producing positive outcomes. Future research needs to ascertain the variables that actually produce positive patient change.

The development and expansion of psychological treatment has been one of unanticipated rapid growth, paralleling the growth of clinical psychology since the second World War. During the past 35–40 years, psychologists have also noted a number of important changes (Garfield, 1994b; Garfield & Bergin, 1994). To many people, for example, clinical psychology is essentially synonymous with psychotherapy. The number of different psychotherapies appears limitless, and there are almost as many different forms or types of eclectic and integrative psychotherapies. Where once psychologists spoke of psychotherapy, today one must speak of psychotherapies. Furthermore, with the publication of the various editions of the *Diagnostic and Statistical Manual of Mental Disorders (DSMs;* American Psychiatric Association, 1994), there is today a greater emphasis on mental illness and a more disease-oriented approach to psychotherapy. All of these developments witnessed a greater involvement in research on psychotherapy, particularly by psychologists. These recent developments, accompanied by a greater emphasis on briefer forms of psychotherapy and accountability, have produced what might be viewed as a period of heightened awareness and concern. In this article, I focus on just a few of these developments as they pertain to potential issues related to the recent emphasis on validated or empirically supported psychological treatments.

From Sol L. Garfield, "Some Comments on Empirically Supported Treatments," *Journal of Consulting and Clinical Psychology*, vol. 66, no. 1 (February 1998). Copyright © 1998 by The American Psychological Association. Reprinted by permission of The American Psychological Association and the author. References omitted.

As a number of readers undoubtedly are aware, a task force of the Division of Clinical Psychology published a report on empirically validated psychological treatments (Task Force on Promotion and Dissemination of Psychological Procedures [Task Force], 1995). There were several aspects of the report that I felt were both premature and too strongly stated. As a result, I wrote a critique of these aspects of the report and will just refer briefly to them here (Garfield, 1996).

One of the things to which I reacted was the use of the word, validated, to designate the therapies listed and the criteria used for their selection. Outside of my viewing the adjective *validated* as implying an unrealistically favorable and overfinalized appraisal of these therapies, I need not repeat other related comments. D. L. Chambless (1996), in her commentary on my article, has reformulated this descriptive terminology as empirically supported psychological treatments. This, in my opinion, is a great improvement, and I have no quarrel with this new terminology. The amount and quality of empirical support may vary for particular therapeutic approaches, and therapists and others can make their separate appraisals of the supporting evidence.

Thus, I have no quarrel with attempts to indicate therapies that have received empirical support and, in fact, have supported such attempts. What I have been critical of was what I perceived as an attempt to certify and mandate the use of such therapies prematurely, to link accreditation of graduate training and internships to such designated therapies, also to link every therapy to a specific psychiatric diagnosis, and by emphasizing the name or form of psychotherapy, essentially to minimize the importance of patient variability and therapist skill.

As mentioned, each of the specific validated therapies listed in the Task Force report were for use with a designated psychiatric diagnostic category. With over 260 designated disorders, does it make any difference which validated therapy or therapies are chosen for training and accreditation purposes? Should the training for the treatment of specific disorders be viewed as basic training in psychotherapy or as advanced training that follows more general introductory courses in psychotherapy? To one who has been involved in the training of clinical psychologists in some fashion or other since 1946, such questions posed some potential problems.

One of the inherent issues concerns the matter of training generalists or specialists and basing the decision for the latter on psychiatric nosology. Most psychologists in graduate training have been given some type of brief overview or introduction to some of the well-known schools of psychotherapy, and then in their practicum and internship training they may experiment with some of these approaches or follow the preferences of their supervisors. There may also be some attempt to provide the trainee with some variety of patient problems so that he or she at least gets some range of experience in working with different patients. However, if we psychologists focus to some extent on training students in specified validated or empirically supported treatments as currently listed, we would have to restrict our instruction to a very few disorders. If we should, for example, provide training only in behavioral marital therapy and behavior therapy for headache and for irritable bowel syndrome, would we not be training specialists who would be limited to those designated disorders? Would there be a tendency, therefore, to focus in training on the more frequently occurring disorders such as depression and generalized anxiety disorder? Would psychologists who have received training in just a few disorders be ethically bound to turn away patients with other disorders? As mentioned by Chambless and Hollon (1998), the development of specialized clinics for particular problems might be a way to offer superior treatment.

The tying of forms of psychotherapy to specific psychiatric diagnostic categories, however, appears to me to present real problems, both for training and for practice. In some ways it seems similar to cookbook recipes, with a different form of therapy listed for each disorder in the index. Is each form of therapy completely distinctive and different from all other forms, or are there some common ingredients in most of them? If we tend to secure comparable results from an interpersonal therapy and a cognitive–behavioral therapy for the treatment of depression, should we really regard these as two absolutely different forms of psychotherapy? It is clearly important to demonstrate empirically that over one half of clinically depressed patients who received either of these therapies showed significant improvement at the end of treatment (Elkin, 1994). On the other hand, should we psychologists be content simply to continue to train people in one of these approaches using the official manual, or should we try to understand what are the truly therapeutic variables that make for change? Might we psychologists be able to select and combine aspects of both therapies that might even prove more effective than the individual forms alone? Or, might we increase the efficiency of the therapy by omitting aspects that are unnecessary?

The same kind of questions can be asked with regard to therapies for other problems or disorders. If in clinical practice it seems necessary to see individuals presenting with a variety of disorders, will the clinician have to receive training in N forms of therapy? Are there no common characteristics among these forms of therapy or even among the individuals seeking therapy? Many of the empirically supported therapies listed by the Task Force are cognitive–behavioral therapies. Are there no commonalities among these cognitive–behavioral therapies, or is one forced to learn different cognitive–behavioral therapies for each disorder? Furthermore, is it not possible that an astute and well-trained psychotherapist after some years of experience might decide that some modifications from the manuals can be made and aspects of one therapy added to another in order to improve therapeutic effectiveness? I, personally, believe this is what actually happens as graduates of university programs gain in their experience of working with a diverse group of patients. With the more recent emphasis on briefer forms of psychotherapy in particular, therapists trained in specific approaches to psychotherapy have reported a change to becoming eclectics and becoming more efficient in their therapeutic work (Austad, Sherman, Morgan, & Holstein, 1992).

Patient Variability and Therapist Skill

If one examines any number of books on psychotherapy or clinical psychology, the most likely impression that one will have is that type of psychotherapy is the most important aspect of psychotherapy. Introductory textbooks generally present descriptions of a certain number of well-known schools of psychotherapy, and most advanced books generally deal with one form or theoretical approach to psychotherapy. Most of the research on outcome in psychotherapy has evaluated different forms of psychotherapy, and even research on psychotherapy process is usually performed on one type of psychotherapy. As a result of the emphasis that has been placed on the type of psychotherapy performed, other potential variables have appeared to be of secondary importance, and here I refer specifically to patient and therapist variables.

I will first discuss the issue of patient variability. Conceivably, one may refer to *DSM-III* (American Psychiatric Association, 1988) and its successors, as well as the more recent development of psychotherapies, for a number of the disorders mentioned, as clear examples of sensitivity to patient differences. Patients diagnosed as cases of schizophrenia are certainly different from cases with phobic disorders. However, not all of the individuals given the same diagnosis are actually similar in all personal attributes that may be of some importance for conducting psychotherapy. This concern is particularly true in the nonpsychotic group, in which such variables as expectations about therapy, motivation for psychotherapy, feelings of self-efficacy, socioeconomic status, cultural and ethnic aspects, and environmental factors, among others, may significantly influence duration and outcome in psychotherapy (Garfield, 1994c). Thus, not all individuals given the same diagnosis can be viewed as exact replicas of each other, particularly regarding their preferences and participation in psychotherapy. Some will show positive change, and some will not.

In a similar fashion, not all therapists purporting to practice the same form of psychotherapy, having graduated from the same clinical program, or having been trained with the same psychotherapy manual can be viewed as equal in therapeutic skill and as providing the same quality of therapy (Kendall & Hollon, 1983). Even though most, if not all, psychotherapists would likely agree and even say that I am merely stating the obvious, many of the pronouncements and claims regarding various forms of therapy appear to pay relatively little attention to therapist variability. In emphasizing this point here, I in no way want to claim that the form of psychotherapy is of little consequence or that evidence of empirical support is of no importance. I believe they are all important, including client variables and interaction variables. However, in terms of what I perceived as an overemphasis on the forms of validated therapies in the Task Force (1995) report, these other variables of importance in the psychotherapeutic process seemed to be relatively overlooked.

Part of this limited emphasis on the important role of the therapist in psychotherapy is probably due to the type of research conducted in the past, which tended to focus on separate aspects or features of therapists. Various desirable qualities believed to be features of competent therapists have shown correlations with outcome that have been less than anticipated or hoped for (Beutler, Machado, & Neufeldt, 1994). As commented upon recently by Luborsky, McLellan, Diguer, Woody, and Seligman (1997): "With such mixed success of prediction based on ideas of what the therapist should be and should do, it is no wonder that the therapist's contribution to outcome has been a neglected variable" (p. 53–54).

Recently, however, a few interesting studies of therapist performance with therapists who were trained with manuals developed for specific forms of psychotherapy have been published. In the second Sheffield Psychotherapy Project (Shapiro, Firth-Cozens, & Stiles, 1989), in which four therapists saw at least six patients each in a crossover design, one therapist had much better results than the other three with cognitive-behavioral therapy, even though all three used the same treatment manual.

A more detailed series of studies has been reported and summarized recently by Luborsky et al. (1997). An analysis of the caseloads of 22 therapists with seven different samples of drug addicted and depressed patients revealed some clear differences among the therapists studied. Furthermore, a variety of standard outcomes were used and the different measures showed similar ranks. What was particularly interesting was the fact that the 3 therapists who took part in more than one study and more than one caseload showed similar levels of effectiveness in each caseload. Two were consistently at the top levels and 1 was consistently at the bottom, despite being trained with the same manual. The better therapists also had fewer dropouts as well as less negative treatment effects. Thus, despite the fact that the therapists in these studies were trained and guided by treatment manuals, were treating patients with similar diagnoses that were assigned randomly, and were especially selected for competence in the type of therapy being evaluated, "the range of percentages of improvement for the 22 therapists in the seven samples was from slightly negative change, to slightly more than 80% improvement" (Luborsky et al., 1997). Of course, selecting competent therapists and training them through manuals will tend to reduce outcome variance among therapists (Crits-Christoph, 1996). However, how long such results would continue beyond the end of the research study is uncertain.

I have emphasized patient and therapist variability because they are important factors in influencing psychotherapy outcome and in countering the emphasis currently placed on psychiatric diagnosis and type of psychotherapy. Providing periods of training in therapies that have empirical support for individuals who lack certain personal qualities of empathy and warmth as well as skills in relating to and understanding others will not necessarily lead to positive outcomes. There are times when changes must be made during therapy depending on the particular client and his or her life situation. Instead of trying primarily to reduce therapist variability in research on psychotherapy by adherence to training manuals, we psychologists should instead intensively study those therapists who consistently secure the best results and attempt to discover those therapist variables and therapy interactions that appear to be linked to superior outcomes.

Therapeutic Variables and Related Considerations

As I mentioned previously, despite considerable empirical research support for a variety of psychotherapies, more still needs to be learned about the active ingredients or therapeutic factors in these therapies that lead to positive change before we can really understand the therapeutic process. Instead of emphasizing that there are several different empirically supported forms of psychotherapy for depressive or anxiety disorders, and recommending that these be the therapies taught in accredited programs, we therapists should try to comprehend why roughly comparable outcomes have been secured for, supposedly, very different forms of psychotherapy. To fail to do so, in my view, is to reach a premature closure concerning what really produces positive outcomes in psychotherapy. Also, I do not accept the view that practically all of the research on psychotherapy reviewed by Smith, Glass, and Miller (1980) can be disregarded because the studies antedated the publication of *DSM-III* and training manuals were not used in most of the studies. That is an overly severe pronouncement. Some of the issues raised by such views concern the matter of possible common and unique factors in psychotherapy as well as judgments concerning the relative importance of internal versus external validity. Again, because I have discussed these and related matters more fully elsewhere (Garfield, 1996), only a brief comment will be offered here.

It is not difficult to understand why commonalties among the different forms of psychotherapy is not a view that is very warmly received or accepted by individuals identified with specific forms of psychotherapy. As Frank (1976) has commented, "little glory derives from showing that the . . . method one has mastered with so much effort may be indistinguishable from other methods in its effects" (p. 74). Nevertheless, the existence of common factors to account for the preponderance of similar findings in the research on psychotherapy outcome has been increasingly accepted in recent years (Arkowitz, 1992; Arnkoff & Glass, 1992; Garfield, 1994a; Lambert & Bergin, 1994; van Kalmthout, Schapp, & Wojciechowski, 1985; Weinberger, 1995), and such common variables as the therapeutic relationship, the creation of hope, explanations, perceptual and cognitive change, homework assignments, the opportunity for emotional release, and others are easily identified (Garfield, 1995).

Although many individuals see only what their theoretical views dictate, there are studies on cognitive therapy for depression that emphasize the importance of common factors. Burns and Nolen-Hoeksema (1992), for example, found that therapeutic empathy was very positively correlated with decreases in measures of depression. The findings from the study by Castonguay, Goldfried, Wiser, Raue, and Hayes (1996) were even more interesting. Two common variables, the therapeutic alliance and the client's emotional involvement in therapy, were positively correlated with outcome, whereas the therapist's focus on distorted cognitions, a variable emphasized in cognitive therapy, did not show a positive relationship to outcome (but see De Rubeis & Feeley, 1990). The recent study by Jacobson et al. (1996) on a component analysis of cognitive–

behavioral treatment of depression also raises some interesting and important questions about the therapeutic components of this popular therapy.

Such findings suggest that despite significant advances in research methodology, and despite the results secured on psychotherapy outcome, we therapists have much to learn about the variables that actually produce positive outcomes. As Shapiro (1995) stated, "The central goal of psychotherapy research is to achieve an understanding of the change mechanisms giving rise to client's clinical improvement" (p. 1). In his stimulating article, Shapiro offers one approach toward this goal that I can recommend to interested readers.

Clearly there are psychotherapists, largely from the behavioral and cognitive-behavioral orientations, who are comfortably and positively identified with conducting specified disorder-oriented forms of psychotherapy. This emphasis is viewed by them as another sign of progress in psychotherapy, and it does reflect positively on empirical support for psychotherapy. However, there are also a large number of psychologists who, on the basis of their own clinical experience and knowledge of the research on psychotherapy, have found it essential to broaden their views and go beyond the training they received in graduate school. These individuals, have focused much more on selecting the procedures they have found to be particularly efficacious for individual patients; in their therapy, they tend to combine both common factors and specific emphases from a number of therapies. These individuals have identified themselves as eclectics or integrationists (Garfield, 1994a), and even a number of behaviorists have indicated such leanings (Swan, 1979). As Lambert and Bergin (1994) have concluded,

> Given the growing evidence that there are probably some specific technique effects, as well as large common effects across treatments, the vast majority of therapists have become eclectic in orientation. This appears to reflect a healthy response to empirical evidence and a rejection of previous trends toward rigid allegiances to schools of treatment. (p. 181)

Concluding Comments

At present, therefore, several different emphases and value orientations are evident in the fields of psychology and psychotherapy, and it is not simply a matter of practitioners versus researchers, or professionals versus scientists. The importance of relating forms of psychotherapy primarily to psychiatric diagnoses and then developing more than 260 presumably different forms of psychotherapy represents one emphasis with implications for training, research, and practice. Conceivably, this would mean greater specialization, with individuals selecting a limited number of disorders and forms of therapy in which to specialize. This view pays relatively little attention to the research findings of few differences between the psychotherapies and the importance of potential common factors. The latter emphasis has been more characteristic of generalists and eclectics as well as of individuals who place greater value on the personal characteristics of patients and therapists. There are also researchers in this latter group who feel strongly that more session-by-session process research deserves a high priority. Each of the forms of psychotherapy contains its own theoretical views of what variables produce change. However, without conclusive empirical support for such variables, it is possible that the postulated variables are not the only or even the most critical elements producing change.

With the increased importance of third-party payors and the emphasis on efficiency and accountability in providing psychotherapeutic services, at least two types of programs are possible. One emphasizes the empirically supported forms of psychotherapy for specific psychiatric disorders. The other emphasizes the empirically supported performance of individual therapists. It remains to be seen which route may be favored in the future or what new and unanticipated developments occur. It seems likely, also, that at least some research-oriented clinical psychologists will be attempting to learn more about what variables actually contribute to positive patient change.

What is important is that, regardless of personal preferences, we psychologists maintain an open-minded view of the developments that are currently taking place and retain a reasonable degree of flexibility in reaching conclusions. The article by Chambless and Hollon (1998), I believe, reflects a more balanced view of empirically supported therapies than was presented in the Task Force (1995) report, and this I view as a constructive response to earlier comments.

Philip C. Kendall

 **NO**

Empirically Supported Psychological Therapies

Raising topics of politics or religion at small social gatherings and projective tests among psychologists reliably reveals robust and conflicting opinions. To this list of engaging and provocative topics, one can add the contemporary focus on the identification of *empirically supported psychological therapies*. This special section, like the report of the American Psychological Association Task Force on Promotion and Dissemination of Psychological Procedures ([Task Force] 1995), is likely to do more than invite "business as usual" (Wilson, 1996, p. 243).

The present article introduces a special section of the *Journal of Consulting and Clinical Psychology* that addresses empirically supported psychological therapies. By this label, in general, I refer to those psychological treatments that have been exposed to evaluation using the accepted methods of psychological science. Specific word choices were important. For example, the topic has been discussed (and written about) using terms such as *empirically validated, empirically supported,* and *empirically evaluated.* The first term connotes that the treatments are already validated (Garfield, 1996; see also Chambless, 1996), in an almost closed and finished fashion, and that the treatments have been proven effective. However, validation is never completed and closed, and psychological therapies do not produce complete success (see the no-cure criticism; Kendall, 1989). Moreover, the process of evaluation is not completed even if several studies provide supportive evidence. The second phrase, empirically supported therapies, indicates that the treatment has been supported, with the specification that the support comes from an acceptable empirical study. This phase is akin to that used in Britain (evidence-based therapy) but makes it clear that the evidence in question must be empirical in nature.

The third phrase, empirically evaluated therapies, merely indicates that the treatments have been empirically evaluated, with the connotation that they have been supported; however, this is not explicit.[1] That a treatment has been empirically evaluated connotes support, but this can be misleading; there are therapies that have been evaluated but not found to be supported

From Philip C. Kendall, "Empirically Supported Psychological Therapies," *Journal of Consulting and Clinical Psychology*, vol. 66, no. 1 (February 1998). Copyright © 1998 by The American Psychological Association. Reprinted by permission of The American Psychological Association and the author.

by the evidence. The phrase *empirically supported therapies* was chosen because it emphasizes empirical research, requires positive outcomes from the research, and does not prematurely close the process of evaluation. In addition, the phrase connotes and underscores the notion that the process of empirical evaluation, rather than the polemical talents or charismatic features of an individual promoter, best serves as the cornerstone for the endorsement and dissemination of psychological treatment procedures.

There are also connotations regarding the term *psychotherapy*. This term can unintentionally connote a certain type of therapy (e.g., traditional or psychodynamic) and unwittingly be seen as delimiting. Through the use of the phase *psychological therapies* in place of *psychotherapies*, the topic remains open to all forms of psychological treatment.

"Empirical" evaluation, too, is not without connotations. An empirical evaluation using proper statistical analyses can document that a treatment was found to be better than an alternate condition or to be better than no treatment or chance (see also Borkovec & Castonguay, 1998), but this alone may not be sufficient. Statistical tests do not guarantee or suggest that all participants improved or that the improvements were clinically meaningful. Outcomes from empirical evaluations reveal something about the active features of interventions and that the interventions were statistically more potent than comparison conditions. These same evaluations, however, do not indicate whether the degree of change that was beyond chance was also sufficient to return deviant clients to within nondeviant ranges of scores on the relevant measures (e.g., returning initially severe depression scores to within the normal range). To accomplish this latter aspect of empirical evaluation, reports need to include normative comparisons (Kendall & Grove, 1998) and indicate the degree to which a treatment returned distressed clients to within nondisturbed limits on the measures used to assess outcome. Psychological therapies will be advanced following statistical tests that document that change did not occur on a chance basis; statistical significance is needed prior to clinical significance.

... [T]here are criteria that can be applied to the outcome literature (e.g., Chambless & Hollon, 1998) to make decisions with regard to whether or not a treatment has been found to have efficacy and to be effective. There are treatments, within specified areas, that meet the criteria and can therefore be considered empirically supported (Baucom, Shoham, Mueser, Daiuto, & Stickle, 1998; Compas, Haaga, Keefe, Leitenberg, & Williams, 1998; DeRubeis & Crits-Christoph, 1998; Kazdin & Weisz, 1998; see also Dobson & Craig, in press). But... there are diverse opinions about the merits and demerits of the empirical evaluation of psychological therapy (Beutler, 1998; Borkovec & Castonguay, 1998; Garfield, 1998; Goldfried & Wolfe, 1998; Persons & Silberschatz, 1998). ... [S]ome of the factors buttressing the need for the empirical evaluation of psychological therapy as well as some cautions that should guide the enterprise [follow].

Why Do We Need the Empirical Evaluation of Psychological Therapy?

Therapists are trained professionals; can they not be expected and sought to provide objective evaluations of the effects of their treatments? Are all therapies similar and similarly effective? What would be the probable result if we did not rely on empirical evaluations of therapy? Considering these preliminary questions provides a framework for the larger issues.

Avoiding Therapist Bias

Empirical evaluations of therapy are necessary to provide measurements of the outcomes of therapy that are independent of the views of those providing the therapies. A major objection to the notion of empirically evaluating psychological treatments can come from therapists who argue that "data" are not needed to tell them what works; they "know" on the basis of their experience. But as psychologists, we are human and are open to the standard biases in inference and decision making and to inaccurate perceptions. Practitioners, for example, can be influenced by their years of having interacted with clients from their roles as knowing professionals. Stated differently, what are the effects on the practicing therapist of years of having implemented behavior change procedures with other people? Unwittingly, unwanted effects can appear (Kipnis, 1994). Although internal attributions for positive outcomes are generally healthy, might therapists be misled by taking credit for client improvements in the absence of controls for alternate explanations of the outcomes?

Researchers, too, can be subject to bias. Consider allegiance effects, in which the outcomes of certain therapies are superior when the evaluations are conducted by individuals with an allegiance to the particular form of psychological treatment. It would not be satisfactory, for example, if the evidence supporting the efficacy of a therapy were produced solely by an individual promoting the treatment. To avoid biases, the criteria for empirically supported psychological therapies require that evidence be derived from research clinics other than or in addition to that of the developer of the treatment (for example, federally initiated [e.g., Treatment of Depression Collaborative Research Program; Elkin et al., 1989] or investigator-initiated [e.g., Heimberg et al., 1997] multicenter trials). Empirically evaluating psychological treatments is a first-line operationalization of the scientist–practitioner model.

Too Many Therapies? Too Many Therapists?

Even a cursory scanning of the literature on psychological therapy reveals an alarming diversity of types of treatment. Taken to the extreme, every therapist could describe what he or she does as a separate form of therapy (i.e., total therapist variability). Rather, the field has delimited, via theory and science, several approaches that qualify as distinct forms of treatment. Nevertheless, we are still exposed to an inordinately wide array of types of treatment. What variables within these treatments account for positive outcomes if and when they are found?

Many variables have been proposed as explanations of outcome (e.g., therapist factors and treatment techniques), but it has long been clear that what works for one group may not be optimal for another (Kiesler, 1966). Kiesler's (1966) "uniformity myths" are often described in terms of the following question: What form of treatment works best for what type of client? (see also Paul, 1969). Typically, type of therapy has been operationalized by a guiding theory, whereas type of client has been operationalized in terms of diagnoses. Does treatment X produce beneficial gains for clients with diagnosis Y? Although such questions are of interest, these specific operationalizations are not required for empirical evaluation. For example, there are other ways of determining homogeneity of participants (classification based on dimensional methods as opposed to categorical methods), and there are methods to assess and evaluate issues such as comorbidity (see Kendall & Clarkin, 1992).

Therapist variability (see Beutler, Machado, & Neufeldt, 1994), even when treatment is evaluated favorably, can influence whether the treatment will be adequately provided. Empirical evaluation of therapy is a step in the right direction, but it does not guarantee that empirically evaluated treatments will be effective when applied by different therapists. Garfield (1996) argued that it is not enough to know that specific techniques are effective, because there is substantial variability across therapists. Empirical evaluations are designed to reduce or eliminate therapist factors, and cumulative analyses can assess and evaluate their influence. This latter approach is consistent with the tenor of the empirical evaluation movement: Let scientific evaluation make determinations about what treatments, provided by whom, are best applied to what types of client problems (see also Chambless et al., 1996).

What If We Do Not Seek Empirical Evaluation?

Consider what the mental health field would be like for psychologists if we did not use criteria for making evaluative decisions and if we did not consider scientific research evaluation to be a cornerstone of our clinical applications. To what category would the professional practice of clinical psychology be assigned: to philosophy, psychic reader, advisor? Our empirical basis sets and maintains a preferred high standard for the profession, and our practice of professional psychology benefits from this foundation.

There is also a need for the empirical evaluation of psychological therapies to make them part of the larger health care system (see also Beutler, 1998). As Barlow (1996) stated,

> If we do not promote and disseminate existing evidence for the efficacy of our psychological interventions, then we will put psychotherapy at a severe disadvantage and risk a substantial deemphasis if not elimination of psychological interventions in our health care delivery system. (p. 237)

Researchers with varied allegiances need to study the outcomes of those forms of therapy most likely to be effective, most theoretically sound, and most supported to date. For new or not as yet empirically supported therapies, it falls to the proponents of these interventions to undertake the evaluation of their approaches using the accepted methodologies (e.g., randomized clinical trials).

As you contemplate your position with regard to the empirical evaluation of psychological therapies, consider whether there is an acceptable alternative.

Potential for Use and Abuse

The field of psychological therapy has a nascent yet sound base of evidence that can guide and facilitate treatment decisions. But consider for a moment what it would be like if all of the available data were to be fully ignored. On what basis, then, would a treatment decision be made? In contrast, what if the data mandated that certain treatments be provided?

Are these uses—or abuses—of empirically supported therapies? On what basis, and at what time, would it be ethical to provide an as-yet-unevaluated treatment when there are already data that support an alternate therapy? Who will oversee the deployment of empirically supported versus nonsupported therapies? Clinicians may adopt the label of an empirically supported therapy but continue to provide treatments that have not been examined. Rapid and rabid relabeling of the type of treatment provided might result in a procrustean fit within an endorsed approach, yet do little to change actual practice.

What if the empirical evaluation of psychological therapies is taken too far? What if the identification of empirically supported treatments leads to a restrictive list of treatments, restrictive in the sense that only the identified therapies could be taught in graduate schools, applied in clinics, be reimbursed by third parties, or be subjected to further empirical research? Such an outcome is clearly unwanted and unwarranted, because it would put a dead bolt on the door to progress. The goals of the search for empirically supported interventions, like the goals of the APA Task Force (1995), do not include the creation of a closed list of therapies to be taught, practiced, reimbursed, or studied further. As Chambless (1996) stated, the goal is not to produce a "mandated list of treatments" (p. 230). Fears tied to taking the identification of empirically supported therapies too far, however, do not justify avoiding the need to identify those treatments that have been supported by empirical research to date (see Beutler, 1998).

Efforts are required to take the knowledge that we have and transport it from research-oriented clinics and journals to practice-focused clinics and practitioner training settings (see Sobell, 1996). Interventions found to be efficacious need to be transported to service-providing settings. This transportability process, itself, may require research evaluation. To what extent do treatment manuals facilitate transportability, and to what degree should flexibility play a role in applications using treatment manuals? Adhering to a manual does not guarantee quality therapy, yet quality may be an issue in outcome (Kendall & Hollon, 1983). Learning treatment from a manual may facilitate the acquisition of skills, but it does not require a slavish adherence to the manual. Are treatments found to be efficacious in producing desirable gains in a research clinic transportable to a community service setting? What factors affect the transportability of treatment (Kendall & Clarkin, 1992; Kendall & Southam-Gerow, 1996)? Most of the research to date, as Barlow (1996) and Garfield (1996) have noted, indicates that although efficacy for some treatments for some disorders has been established, effectiveness (or clinical utility) requires more work....

Psychological therapies benefit from the knowledge generated through basic psychological research, as well as evaluations of treatment outcomes, and this affiliation is clear in the promotion of evidence-based treatments. The mental health field, and clinical psychologists in particular, should be proud of the efforts that have been directed toward the empirical evaluation of therapy and the outcomes that have emerged. It is my hope that we avoid being hypercritical and recognize the larger and more important point: We can help to advance the field of psychological therapy by careful evaluation and cautious interpretations of the data.

Note

1. Could it be that someone would talk about an empirically evaluated therapy simply because a study was done, even if the study's outcomes were nonsupportive? I think not.

References

Barlow, D. H. (1996). The effectiveness of psychotherapy: Science and policy. *Clinical Psychology: Science and Practice, 3,* 236–240.

Baucom, D. H., Shoham, V., Mueser, K. T., Daiuto, A. D., & Stickle, T. R. (1998). Empirically supported couple and family interventions for marital distress and adult mental health problems. *Journal of Consulting and Clinical Psychology, 66,* 53–88.

Beutler, L. (1998). Identifying empirically supported treatments: What if we didn't? *Journal of Consulting and Clinical Psychology, 66,* 113–120.

Beutler, L. E., Machado, P., & Neufeldt, S. (1994). Therapist variables. In A. Bergin & S. Garfield (Eds.), *Handbook of psychotherapy and behavior change* (4th ed., pp. 229–269). New York: Wiley.

Borkovec, T. D., & Castonguay, L. G. (1998). What is the scientific meaning of empirically supported therapy? *Journal of Consulting and Clinical Psychology, 66,* 136–142.

Calhoun, K. S., Moras, K., Pilkonis, P. A., & Rehm, L. P. (1998). Empirically supported treatments: Implications for training. *Journal of Consulting and Clinical Psychology, 66,* 151–162.

Chambless, D. L. (1996). In defense of dissemination of empirically supported psychological interventions. *Clinical Psychology: Science and Practice, 3,* 230–235.

Chambless, D. L., & Hollon, S. D. (1998). Defining empirically supported therapies. *Journal of Consulting and Clinical Psychology, 66,* 7–18.

Chambless, D. L., Sanderson, W. C., Shoham, V., Johnson, S. B., Pope, K. S., Crits-Christoph, P., Baker, M., Johnson, B., Woody, S. R., Sue, S., Beutler, L., Williams, D. A., & McCurry, S. (1996). An update on empirically validated therapies. *Clinical Psychologist, 49,* 5–14.

Compas, B. E., Haaga, D. A. F., Keefe, F. J., Leitenberg, H., & Williams, D. A. (1998). Sampling of empirically supported psychological treatments from health psychology: Smoking, chronic pain, cancer, and bulimia nervosa. *Journal of Consulting and Clinical Psychology, 66,* 89–112.

DeRubeis, R. J., & Crits-Christoph, P. (1998). Empirically supported individual and group psychological treatments for adult mental disorders. *Journal of Consulting and Clinical Psychology, 66,* 37–52.

Davison, G. C. (1998). Being bolder with the Boulder model: The challenge of education and training in empirically supported treatments. *Journal of Consulting and Clinical Psychology, 66,* 163–167.

Dobson, K., & Craig, K. (Eds.). (in press). *Best practice: Developing and promoting empirically supported interventions.* Newbury Park, CA: Sage.

Elkin, I., Shea, M. T., Watkins, J., Imber, S., Sotsky, S., Collins, J., Glass, D., Pilkonis, P., Leber, W., Docherty, J., Fiester, S., & Parloff, M. (1989). National Institute of Mental Health Treatment of Depression Collaborative Research Program: General effectiveness of treatments. *Archives of Generally Psychiatry, 46,* 971–982.

Garfield, S. L. (1996). Some problems with "validated" forms of psychotherapy. *Clinical Psychology: Science and Practice, 3,* 218–229.

Garfield, S. L. (1998). Some comments on empirically supported treatments. *Journal of Consulting and Clinical Psychology, 66,* 121–125.

Goldfried, M. R., & Wolfe, B. E. (1998). Toward a more clinically valid approach to therapy research. *Journal of Consulting and Clinical Psychology, 66,* 143–150.

Heimberg, R. G., Liebowitz, M. R., Hope, D. A., Schneier, F. R., Holt, C. S., Welkowitz, L., Juster, H. R., Campeas, R., Bruch, M. A., Cloitre, M., Fallon, B., & Klein, D. (1997). *Cognitive-behavioral group therapy versus phenelzine in the treatment of social phobia: I. Twelve-week outcome.* Manuscript submitted for publication.

Kazdin, A. E., & Weisz, J. R. (1998). Identifying and developing empirically supported child and adolescent treatments. *Journal of Consulting and Clinical Psychology, 66,* 19–36.

Kendall, P. C. (1989). The generalization and maintenance of behavior change: Comments, considerations, and the "no-cure" criticism. *Behavior Therapy, 20,* 357–364.

Kendall, P. C., & Clarkin, J. (Eds.). (1992). Comorbidity and treatment implications [special section]. *Journal of Consulting and Clinical Psychology, 60,* 833–908.

Kendall, P. C., & Grove, W. (1988). Normative comparisons in therapy outcome. *Behavioral Assessment, 10,* 147–158.

Kendall, P. C., & Hollon, S. (1983). Calibrating therapy: Collaborative archiving of tape samples from therapy outcome trials. *Cognitive Therapy and Research, 7,* 199–204.

Kendall, P. C., & Southam-Gerow, M. (1996). Issues in the transportability of treatment. *Journal of Consulting and Clinical Psychology, 63,* 702–708.

Kiesler, D. (1966). Some myths of psychotherapy research and the search for a paradigm. *Psychological Bulletin, 65,* 110–136.

Kipnis, D. (1994). Accounting for the use of behavior technologies in social psychology. *American Psychologist, 49,* 165–172.

Paul, G. (1969). Behavior modification research: Design and tactics. In C. Franks (Ed.), *Behavior therapy: Appraisal and status.* New York: McGraw-Hill.

Persons, J. B., & Silberschatz, G. (1998). Are results of randomized controlled trials useful to psychotherapists? *Journal of Consulting and Clinical Psychology, 66,* 126–135.

Sobell, L. C. (1996). Bridging the gap between scientists and practitioners: The challenge before us. *Behavior Therapy, 27,* 297–320.

Task Force on Promotion and Dissemination of Psychological Procedures, Division of Clinical Psychology. (1995). Training in and dissemination of empirically-validated psychological treatments: Report and recommendations. *Clinical Psychologist, 48,* 3–23.

Wilson, G. T. (1996). Empirically validated treatments: Reality and resistance. *Clinical Psychology: Science and Practice, 3,* 241–244.

CHALLENGE QUESTIONS

Has Too Much Emphasis Been Placed on Empirically Supported Therapies?

1. Garfield expresses alarm about the possible linking of accreditation of clinical psychology graduate programs and internships to the incorporation of training in empirically supported treatments. If you were a member of an accreditation team, how would you assess the extent to which trainees are learning the therapy techniques that they will need in their careers?
2. Based on your reading of the selections, what kinds of questions would you recommend that a prospective psychotherapy client ask a psychotherapist before committing to a course of treatment?
3. Garfield contends that several important variables, such as the importance of the therapeutic relationship, tend to be overlooked by those emphasizing empirically supported treatments. How important do you think the quality of the client's relationship with the therapist is in influencing therapy outcome? Why?
4. Consider a common form of anxiety (e.g., fear of public speaking) and develop a brief "treatment manual" in which you enumerate clinical methods that you believe might help an individual overcome this kind of fear. On what basis would you include the specific recommendations, and how would you evaluate their effectiveness?

Suggested Readings

Beutler, L. E. (1998). Identifying empirically supported treatments: What if we didn't? *Journal of Consulting and Clinical Psychology*, 66(1), 113–120.

Borkovec, T. D., & Castonguay, L. G. (1998) What is the scientific meaning of empirically supported therapy? *Journal of Consulting and Clinical Psychology*, 66(1), 136–142.

Calhoun, K. S., Moras, K., Pilkonis, P. A., & Rehm, L. P. (1998). Empirically supported treatments: Implications for training. *Journal of Consulting and Clinical Psychology*, 66(1), 151–162.

Chambless, D. L., & Holton, S. D. (1998). Defining empirically supported therapies. *Journal of Consulting and Clinical Psychology*, 66(1), 7–18.

Goldfried, M. R., & Wolfe, B. E. (1998). Toward a more clinically valid approach to therapy research. *Journal of Consulting and Clinical Psychology*, 66(1), 143–150.

ISSUE 10

Is Ritalin Overprescribed?

YES: Peter R. Breggin, from "Drugging Our Children Won't Cure the Problems in Schools," *Insight on the News* (August 14, 1995)

NO: Russell Barkley, from "Critics' Claims Are Not Based on Medical Reality," *Insight on the News* (August 14, 1995)

ISSUE SUMMARY

YES: Physician Peter R. Breggin, founder of the International Center for the Study of Psychiatry and Psychology, asserts that behavior-modifying medications such as Ritalin are vastly overused by parents and teachers who have come to view normal childhood behaviors as pathological conditions warranting psychiatric interventions.

NO: Professor of psychiatry Russell Barkley views behavior disorders of childhood, such as attention deficit hyperactivity disorder (ADHD), as serious conditions warranting medical intervention in order to reduce the likelihood of social, academic, and emotional problems.

Concerns about out-of-control children have grown tremendously in recent years, and for good reason. A decade ago it would have been unfathomable to imagine an elementary or secondary school child entering a school and gunning down his or her classmates; yet such images have become indelibly marked in the minds of Americans. Such alarming events have caused educators, parents, and mental health professionals to increasingly focus their attention on the behavior of young people, look for ways to help underachievers reach their potential, and make sure troubled youth get the help they need. Children with attention deficit hyperactivity disorder (ADHD) have been of particular concern not only because of the psychological problems they experience but also because of the disruption they cause at school, at home, and in the community.

ADHD is a disorder involving inattentiveness and hyperactivity-impulsivity, and it is a condition that is usually evident early in life. Even during the toddler years, children with this condition show a range of problematic behaviors, including defiance, resistance, and hostility. Many of them are incessant in their hyperactivity, incapable of paying attention even briefly. Their lives usually involve impaired relationships and serious inner distress. The most common interventions for ADHD involve behavioral techniques and medication, particularly stimulants such as Ritalin (methylphenidate). It is estimated that more than 2 million children currently take such medications. Proponents of medication express relief about the fact that such an effective intervention is available to help young people who need it; opponents are distressed by the increasing tendency to rely on a chemical for controlling active children rather than on methods that have been used for generations.

Peter R. Breggin is appalled by the extensive use of Ritalin-like medications, which he sees as the result of a scientific medical approach to educating and rearing children. In the following selection, he asserts that parents and teachers have come to view many normal childhood behaviors, such as restlessness, as symptoms of a mental disorder that is best treated with medication. Breggin contends that in many cases the "attention deficit" is not in the child but in adults who need to attend better to the child's needs. He urges his psychiatric colleagues to stop blaming the problems of children on some chemical defect but rather to rededicate themselves to meeting the authentic needs of children.

In the second selection, Russell Barkley acknowledges that many children are active, energetic, and exuberant; but he also maintains that there are many children whose behavior is pathologically outside the norm. He asserts that some children are at great risk for developing serious problems socially, academically, and emotionally. Barkley points to biological data that support the notion that ADHD is a genetically linked neurodevelopmental condition and should therefore be treated with an intervention appropriate for treating a condition of the brain.

POINT

- Attributing a child's problematic behaviors to a mental disorder, such as ADHD, tells adults that they have no responsibility for the cause of the problems or the alleviation of the child's difficulties.
- Instead of viewing the misbehaving child's behavior as "bad," such a child's behavior is being viewed as "sick," resulting in a demoralizing stigma that can last into adulthood.

- There is no compelling evidence that children diagnosed with ADHD have anything physically wrong with them.
- Compared to the seemingly frequent diagnosis of ADHD in the United States, the diagnosis is rarely made—and Ritalin-like drugs are rarely prescribed—in Great Britain, Sweden, and Denmark.

COUNTERPOINT

- The actions of parents and teachers have never been shown by themselves to create ADHD in previously normal children, nor have they been shown to cure this condition.

- Without appropriate diagnosis and treatment, many children will experience harsh moral judgment, punishment, and social rejection, and they will be perceived by others as lazy, unmotivated, immature, and willfully irresponsible.

- There is compelling evidence that ADHD is a neurodevelopmental disorder that is genetically linked.

- In virtually every country where studies have evaluated school-age children, 3 to 5 percent have met the diagnostic criteria for ADHD.

Peter R. Breggin

 **YES**

Drugging Our Children Won't Cure the Problems in Schools

Family values are being fiercely debated, yet so far the debate has failed to focus on forces that are radically undermining American family life. Traditionally, adults have held themselves responsible for teaching and rearing children and have felt justifiably proud when those children have done well. Although some children were considered to be incorrigible—resistant to any and all adult intervention—until recently, the incorrigible have been relatively few.

In recent years, the basic principle of adult responsibility for children has been drastically eroded by a scientific medical approach to educating and rearing children. Health professionals began telling many adults—parents as well as teachers—that they have no responsibility for the misconduct or failures of the children under their care. Similarly, these adults are told that they cannot take responsibility for improving the lives of troubled or troublesome children. Instead, parents and teachers are taught to believe that millions of children suffer from exotic psychiatric maladies such as attention-deficit disorder, oppositional-defiant disorder and conduct disorder. These mental disorders supposedly make children unable to adjust to school or family life, regardless of the quality of teaching or parenting. Difficult children thus are labeled incorrigible through the subtle means of psychiatric diagnosis.

Overall, there probably are more than 2 million youngsters in the United States taking the stimulant drug Ritalin. Millions more have been given prescriptions for other psychiatric medication such as Prozac and lithium—that have not even been FDA-approved for children. More ominously, during the last three or four years, there has been an enormous escalation in the prescription for children of Ritalin and similar medications.

The diagnosis most often used to justify this medicating of children is attention-deficit hyperactivity disorder, or ADHD. According to the American Psychiatric Association's *Diagnostic and Statistical Manual of Mental Disorders,* fourth ed., ADHD takes two forms—hyperactivity-impulsivity and inattention. For hyperactivity-impulsivity, the chief diagnostic symptoms in descending order are the following: "Often fidgets with hands or feet or squirms in seat; often leaves seat in classroom; often runs about or climbs excessively in situations in which it is inappropriate; often has difficulty playing or engaging in

From Peter R. Breggin, "Drugging Our Children Won't Cure the Problems in Schools," *Insight on the News*, vol. 11, no. 31 (August 14, 1995). Copyright © 1995 by News World Communications, Inc. Reprinted by permission of *Insight on the News*.

leisure activities quietly." For diagnosing the inattention form of ADHD, the most common symptoms are defined as these: "Fails to give close attention or makes mistakes in schoolwork; often has difficulty sustaining attention; often does not seem to listen when spoken to directly; fails to follow instructions or to finish chores or schoolwork."

Daydreaming by a girl used to be considered a sign of boredom in a bright child; restlessness in class on the part of a spunky boy was considered a disciplinary problem. Now these behaviors are considered symptoms of mental disorder.

Many of us are concerned that ADHD is really a catchall label for children who frustrate or anger adults, especially when the adults are unable or unwilling to give them sufficient attention. Even the diagnostic manual recognizes that the symptoms commonly disappear when the child is "under very strict control, is in a novel setting, is engaged in especially interesting activities, is in a one-to-one situation." In my office, most ADHD children show remarkable capacities for concentration as they sit with their parents to discuss problems in the family or at school. Often the children do fine during vacations or in the care of other adults.

The "symptoms" of ADHD should not be used to red-flag children as suffering from mental disorders. The "attention deficit" is not in the child but in the adults who need to attend better to the child's needs. Children don't become bored, inattentive, undisciplined, resentful or violent in the home or school because of something innately wrong with them. To the contrary, these children usually are more energetic and more spirited than most. To fulfill their special promise, they need a more disciplined, interesting and loving child-oriented environment. When they get it, they often become our most creative, outstanding and responsible members of society.

Blaming the distress and misconduct of children on mental disorders recently reached a boiling point when the federal mental-health establishment claimed that inner-city children suffer from genetic and biochemical defects that predispose them to violence. In 1992 and 1993, proposals were made to focus federal research on finding supposed biological markers for violence with the aim of treating inner-city children with drugs. Ginger Ross Breggin and I sounded an alarm about these plans, creating a national controversy. We described this in our book, *The War Against Children*, resulting in the government withdrawing its overall plan.

While working with parents from the inner city, we found that most of them rejected the medical diagnosis and drugging of their difficult or disturbed children. Unhappily, we discovered a far different attitude among mainstream Americans, including parents and teachers in the affluent suburbs of Washington. Conditioned intellectually to accept the modern psychiatric viewpoint, they often embraced the idea that a large proportion of their children are inherently incorrigible and hence in need of drug treatment.

In any suburban public elementary classroom, several children are likely to be taking prescribed medication to control their behavior. In more specialized public- and private-school classes, half or more may be on Ritalin or other medications. Often the parents and teachers of these students are taking Prozac and therefore assume that Ritalin might be good for the children.

Health professionals frequently tell ADHD children that the reason they must take drugs is that they have "crossed wires" or a "biochemical imbalance" in their heads. Advocates of this approach say that medical explanations relieve children of guilt and shame about their problems or misconduct. Instead of being bad: "the child is encouraged to view himself or herself as sick." But what's better for a child—to think of himself or herself as bad or as mentally ill? It is far more demoralizing for a child to believe that he or she has a defective mind or brain. That makes the child feel deformed, like a freak, cheated of a normal mind. The child is robbed of the concept of self-discipline or self-control, and the future can seem hopelessly limited.

I have treated adults who found their lives stifled by the demoralizing effects of these childhood diagnoses. One 25-year-old man came to me for a second opinion after his psychiatrist wanted him to resume Ritalin. Instead, we worked on learning to deal with the underlying emotional turmoil that disrupted his attention, as well as on how to impose self-discipline. He now has gone on to a successful medication-free college career. It not only is demoralizing to attribute the child's problems to a brain disorder, it also is untrue. There is no compelling evidence that children diagnosed with ADHD have anything physically wrong with them. Since the diagnosis in reality reflects conflict between children and adults, it is unlikely that its "cause" will ever be found to reside in the child's brain.

I have described the medical hazards associated with controlling children through the use of psychotropic drugs in my books, *Toxic Psychiatry* and *The War Against Children*. In both works I argue that there's little scientific justification for the practice. In Great Britain, Sweden and Denmark, these diagnoses rarely are made and the drugs are almost never used.

While the use of Ritalin in the United States at present only affects a relatively small percentage of children, some advocates estimate that up to 10 percent of boys should be on medication. Meanwhile, the philosophy guiding the enthusiasm for medication has changed profoundly how we view children in general. Today, a "difficult child" typically is referred to professionals for medication. Not only are we drugging our most energetic and potentially most creative children, we are intimidating all of them.

In a vicious circle, the medical approach escalates the deterioration of school and family life by blaming inadequacies or failures on disorders in the children; this removes any incentive for the adults to improve the child's family and school life.

Every national commission on education has found that our schools fail to respond to the moral, social and educational needs of youngsters. Meanwhile, it's also apparent that too many families are unable, ill-equipped or unwilling to raise children in a secure, disciplined and loving manner.

But, drugging children is not the remedy for dysfunctional families. This is a cruel and unethical approach to problems that lie with the adults in the child's life. The vulnerable child is not the cause of these problems: We are. The national debate about family values has the potential to promote the well-being of children but, thus far, the debate has overlooked this psychiatrically induced crisis in our values. Millions of parents and teachers are being taught by medical and psychological experts that they cannot and should not take responsibility for the lives of their children.

On the contrary, adults do play the determining role in the lives of children, since adults provide them with nutrition, medical care and shelter, as well as protection from physical, sexual or emotional abuse. All children need adults to offer them unconditional love—to treasure them for themselves. They also need adult guidance in developing self-esteem through the mastery of age-appropriate tasks. Children need grown-ups to discipline them in a rational manner and to teach them personal responsibility and respect for others. They need their teachers and parents to instruct them in academic and social skills in a manner that's consistent with their individual vulnerabilities and strengths.

For reasons that often are beyond their control, teachers and parents commonly feel overwhelmed and in need of relief. The scientific medical approach reassures them: "You are not to blame for the problems of your children." This may temporarily assuage adult guilt. But this approach cannot be taken without undermining the most fundamental family value of all—that adults are responsible for the lives of their children.

As a psychiatrist, I call upon my medical colleagues to stop blaming the problems of children on some chemical defect in the children themselves and to rededicate themselves to meeting children's authentic needs. As a parent, I remind all parents that we cannot take pride in how well our children do in life while disavowing responsibility for their problems.

Russell Barkley

Critics' Claims Are Not Based on Medical Reality

Children, especially preschoolers, are active, energetic and exuberant, flitting from one activity to another. Young children also are notorious for being easily bored, acting without much forethought and responding impulsively to events around them.

But when children persistently display levels of activity that are far in excess of their age group, when they are unable to sustain attention, interest or persistence as well as their peers, and when their impulse control lags far behind expectations for their developmental level, they are no longer simply expressing the joie de vivre that characterizes childhood. Instead, they are at significant risk for a number of problems in their social, intellectual, academic, familial and emotional development.

Many such children currently are diagnosed as having attention-deficit hyperactivity disorder, or ADHD. We should neither be surprised nor alarmed to learn that 1 or even 2 percent of school-age children may be taking medications such as the stimulants Ritalin, Dexedrine and Cylert to help them improve their behavior and school performance. Those being treated constitute barely half of all children who may have this condition. Nor should we see high drama, government scandal, nefarious motives of drug companies or "toxic psychiatry" in the finding that medicating children with stimulants has been increasing rapidly over the past 20 years. Such a rapid increase is to be expected in any area of clinical practice in which new and effective treatments are discovered for the management of a disorder. This trend will level off once a majority of those afflicted are found, diagnosed and treated for their condition.

Without this medication, such children often will experience the harsh moral judgment, censure, punishment and social rejection reserved for those society deems lazy, unmotivated, selfish, thoughtless, immature and willfully irresponsible. Children with this disorder have captured public interest and commentary for at least 130 years and scientific interest for nearly 100. And, while the diagnostic labels for the problem have changed many times over this century, its actual nature has changed little, if at all, from descriptions presented by the British physician George Still in 1902.

In fact, the range of behavioral problems seen in these children may constitute one of the most well-studied childhood disorders of our time, with more than several thousand scientific articles published about them and their treatment. Yet these children remain an enigma to Western societies that now must struggle to cope with the rather heretical notion that some children have a developmental disability of self-control even though nothing physically seems wrong with them.

The problematic behaviors they display arise early, often by 3 to 4 years of age, but certainly by middle childhood in over 95 percent of the cases that are diagnosed. When the diagnostic criteria for ADHD are applied to large populations of children, researchers typically find that approximately 3 to 5 percent of school-age children have ADHD, with boys being nearly three times more likely to have this condition than girls. In virtually every country where studies have evaluated school-age children for this behavior pattern, it has been found to exist to this extent or to be even more prevalent.

These studies consistently have demonstrated that such children carry a high risk for impairment in their school, social and family functioning. The general professional and scientific consensus is that children with ADHD have a disorder of behavioral inhibition and self-control that appears neurological or developmental in origin. Although the precise neurodevelopmental problem has yet to be clearly demonstrated, the weight of the evidence greatly favors this interpretation.

Some critics have objected to the labeling of such children as having a mental disorder. Others charge that this behavioral problem was "medicalized" to justify giving behavior-modifying drugs such as Ritalin to these children. A few critics have gone so far as to say that ADHD is a myth: an attempt by mental-health professionals to gain more money through the labeling and treatment of otherwise normal children. They accuse those who diagnose and treat ADHD children of wanting to label nonconformists—the Huck Finns or Tom Sawyers of this world—as mentally ill so as to medicate them into a stuporous submission or conformity.

Other critics admit that children with ADHD display deviant patterns of behavior, but blame these behavior problems on dysfunctional child-rearing techniques, intolerant or permissive teachers, the failings of our educational system or even sugary foods and too much television. According to these views, medicating such children fails to remedy the real causes of the problem.

If ADHD is truly a myth, we should find no important differences between groups of children diagnosed with ADHD and groups of normal children. This is hardly the case, as numerous scientific studies demonstrate. Researcher Judith Rapoport of the National Institute of Mental Health found children with ADHD to be far more active than normal children of their age, to be significantly less able to maintain persistence and concentration toward lengthy tasks and to be substantially more impulsive or poorly self-controlled in their conduct when compared to normal children of the same age. Their symptoms are no figment of parental or clinical imagination nor is their treatment an effort to conduct a "war against children," as a few critics have proclaimed.

My studies and those of Susan Campbell of the University of Pittsburgh have shown that children with ADHD are well behind other children in early academic skills, self-care habits, social skills and intellectual development even in their preschool years. During the last five years my research team screened more than 5,000 children entering public kindergarten in Worcester, Mass., for the presence of this behavior pattern. Not only did we replicate such findings, we also found these children to cause significantly more stress on their parents, more conflicts with their siblings and peers and more disruption to their classrooms than normal children.

This has been found to be true at whatever age these children have been studied. Compared with normal children, those with ADHD have been documented to receive more punishment, rejections and even physical and emotional abuse by others as a result of their delay in developing self-control. Many follow-up studies confirm that, as children with ADHD progress through formal schooling, most persist in this deviant behavioral pattern.

The academic risks posed to children by ADHD are probably the most serious. By adolescence, 30 percent of those with ADHD in my study were retained in grade, 46 percent were suspended from school and the ADHD group was more than seven times as likely to be expelled or to drop out of school as our normal control group. More than 30 percent were placed in special-education classes for the learning disabled and another 30 percent or more were in classes for students with behavioral problems. Young adults with ADHD had more than three times the number of auto accidents and four times as many speeding citations as our control group. These findings are similar to other such long-term studies of ADHD clients in New York City, Los Angeles, Iowa City, Montreal and London.

Joseph Biederman and his colleagues at Massachusetts General Hospital as well as others during the last decade have done large-scale studies of the biological families of children with ADHD and have shown that the condition of ADHD occurs five to 10 times more often among first-degree biological relatives of such children. These studies confirm what the scientific literature on ADHD hinted at nearly 100 years ago: ADHD runs in families and seems to have a strong hereditary predisposition. The pattern of this transmission across generations suggests that the behavioral trait or condition of ADHD is due to a few genes or even a single dominant gene.

But we do not need to know the gene(s) behind ADHD to know that heredity makes a major contribution to the pattern of deviant behaviors we call ADHD. Many studies have proved that as much as 80 percent of the differences among children in this behavioral pattern are the result of heredity. Five to 20 percent appear to be attributable to environmental or nongenetic factors, including pregnancy troubles and birth complications, exposure to toxins such as alcohol and nicotine during pregnancy, head trauma, disease and other brain injuries suffered during childhood. But this figure also incorporates the unproven causes raised by social critics: poor child-rearing, bad families or poor teaching. Thus, even when all nongenetic causes of ADHD are combined, they explain less than one-fifth of the extent to which people differ in this behavior pattern.

The hereditary nature of ADHD now is "a fact in the bag." It would be a waste of time to regress 40 years to the heyday of psychoanalytic thinking when all childhood problems were attributed to bad parents.

True, a minority of children with ADHD may develop it for reasons other than heredity. ADHD is likely, therefore, to have many possible causes: One can inherit it or one can acquire it, but one is not likely to pick up ADHD and persist in it merely through learning or choice. In many people ADHD is not a pathological condition but an extreme degree of a normal trait. In some cases, however, where it is acquired through some neurological injury, it may be pathological. Viewing a disorder such as ADHD as both trait and pathology is not new. It has been applied fruitfully to scientific efforts to understand other developmental disorders, such as mental retardation, reading disabilities and even schizophrenia.

Granted, family, school and social environments can make the disorder worse. A large body of research, including my own studies, demonstrates that the way parents and teachers react to the behaviors of children with ADHD can exacerbate or diminish their severity and even contribute to other possible secondary problems such as frequent interpersonal conflicts with parents or teachers, low self-esteem, loss of interest in schoolwork or even a drift toward delinquency. But such actions by parents and teachers have never been shown by themselves actually to create ADHD in previously normal children nor to cure it. Parent- and teacher-bashing cannot be justified by scientific knowledge.

CHALLENGE QUESTIONS

Is Ritalin Overprescribed?

1. Breggin is critical of the tendency to minimize the role of parents and teachers in causing and maintaining problematic behaviors in children. Taking his viewpoint, enumerate some dysfunctional styles that might contribute to children's acting out of control.
2. Breggin expresses concern about the stigma and impaired sense of identity that might result from labeling a child with ADHD. How might this kind of diagnostic label result in problems for a child? How might the child benefit from receiving this diagnosis?
3. Some social critics have expressed alarm about the extent to which people are managing problems with medications such as Ritalin and Prozac. Discuss the extent to which medication provides a treatment for the basic problem (neurochemical dysfunction) or serves as a temporary method for alleviating symptoms of a more deeply rooted emotional nature.
4. Imagine that you are a psychiatrist being consulted by the parents of a five-year-old boy who is reportedly "acting up" in kindergarten. They request a prescription of Ritalin for him. What kind of information would you want to have before making your decision about the prescription, and what kind of preliminary steps would you recommend before going along with the parents' request?
5. Imagine that you are a researcher who has been given research support to study different methods of intervening in a class composed of 20 "hyperactive" boys. What research methods would you use to compare the effectiveness of Ritalin to behavioral methods aimed at reducing the activity level of these boys?

Suggested Readings

Breggin, P. R. & Breggin, G. R. (1995). The hazards of treating "attention-deficit/hyperactivity disorder" with methylphenidate (Ritalin). *Journal of College Student Psychotherapy*, 10(2), 55–72.

DeGrandpre, R. J. (1999). *Ritalin nation: Rapid-fire culture and the transformation of human consciousness.* New York, NY: W. W. Norton.

Diller, L. H. (1998). *Running on ritalin: A physician reflects on children, society, and performance in a pill.* New York, NY: Bantam Books.

Goldman, L. S., Genel, M., Bezman, R. J., & Slanetz, P. J. (1998). Diagnosis and treatment of attention-deficit/hyperactivity disorder in children and adolescents. *Journal of the American Medical Association*, 279(14), 1100–1107.

Mash, E. J., & Barkley, R. A. (1998). *Treatment of childhood disorders* (2d ed.). New York, NY: The Guilford Press.

ISSUE 11

Should Psychosurgery Be Used to Treat Certain Psychological Conditions?

YES: Fred Ovsiew and Jonathan Bird, from "The Past and Future of Psychosurgery," *Current Opinion in Psychiatry* (January 1997)

NO: Frank T. Vertosick, Jr., from "Lobotomy's Back," *Discover* (October 1997)

ISSUE SUMMARY

YES: Psychiatrists Fred Ovsiew and Jonathan Bird assert that psychosurgery is an invaluable intervention for certain kinds of seriously disordered patients who have not responded to other forms of treatment, and they insist that failure to provide this intervention to those who need it would be ethically questionable.

NO: Neurosurgeon Frank T. Vertosick, Jr., argues that psychosurgical procedures rest on a shaky scientific foundation and involve procedures that cause irreversible injury to the brain.

$\mathbf{P}$rior to the introduction of antipsychotic medications in the 1950s, psychosurgery was the treatment of choice for several serious mental disorders. In the 1930s psychosurgical techniques involved severing the connections between areas of the brain that were thought to be responsible for symptoms of disorders, such as schizophrenia. These relatively primitive surgical techniques did result in the reduction of some problematic symptoms, but they also caused some disturbing personality changes. Much of the barbarism associated with earlier versions of psychosurgery caused this procedure to fall out of favor, although in recent years there has been a minor resurgence of interest.

Some professionals recommend the use of psychosurgery for patients who do not benefit from psychotherapy or medication and whose symptoms are regarded as so debilitating as to seriously impair living. For example, people with severe cases of obsessive-compulsive disorder have been treated with cingulotomy, a procedure that involves the precise lesioning of the cingulate bundle, an area of the brain implicated in anxiety and compulsive behavior. Small holes, less than two centimeters in diameter, are drilled into the skull, and electrodes are positioned in each cingulate bundle. Then electric current is used to create lesions, which results in the reduction of obsessions and compulsions. This psychosurgical procedure and others like it have produced some compelling case histories of people who report that their lives improved remarkably as a result of the only intervention that had any effect. At the same time, the invasive nature of a surgical procedure in what many consider the most important part of the human body evokes intense anxiety associated with the potentially devastating effects of the slightest of errors.

In the following selection, Fred Ovsiew and Jonathan Bird write about the benefits of psychosurgery for patients who have not responded to other forms of intervention. Although Ovsiew and Bird acknowledge that the deliberate injuring of the brain seems anathema to many clinicians and scientists, they maintain that it is important to recognize that significant improvements in personality have been reported in individuals who have experienced brain hemorrhages and strokes. Such findings about the beneficial effects resulting from alterations of the brain concur with the generally positive reports about patients who have undergone psychosurgery for various debilitating mental disorders. In addressing ethical questions associated with psychosurgery, Ovsiew and Bird argue that an adequate theoretical justification is not necessary for the ethical use of psychosurgery; rather, they argue that withholding psychosurgery becomes ethically questionable for severely ill, treatment-resistant patients.

Frank T. Vertosick, Jr., on the other hand, is appalled by a procedure that attempts to cure mental disorders by "frying holes" in parts of the brain. In the second selection, Vertosick recalls the debates of the 1950s when the rising use of psychosurgery ignited a national debate over the morality of inflicting irreversible brain injuries in the most emotionally vulnerable patients. Although he acknowledges that there have been major advances in the way in which surgeons approach psychosurgery, Vertosick remains profoundly concerned that procedures such as cingulotomy rest on no firmer scientific foundation than the disdained prefrontal lobotomy of decades past.

POINT

- Advances in neurosurgical equipment and techniques allow for new approaches to treating psychiatric problems.
- Researchers have demonstrated that psychosurgery has helped a considerable number of treatment-resistant patients.
- Withholding psychosurgery becomes ethically questionable for severely ill, treatment-resistant patients.
- A theoretical justification is not necessary for the ethical use of psychosurgery, only adequate demonstrations of safety and efficacy.

COUNTERPOINT

- Neurosurgery remains a crude endeavor in which parts of the brain are destroyed in order to treat mental illness.
- Some forms of contemporary psychosurgery, such as cingulotomy, rest on no firmer scientific foundation than lobotomy.
- Too much of the decision about psychosurgery rests on the recommendation of a psychiatrist rather than on the experiences of the patient.
- Only a few major medical centers can muster the psychiatric, bioethical, and surgical resources to perform and evaluate the procedure correctly.

Fred Ovsiew and Jonathan Bird  **YES**

The Past and Future of Psychosurgery

The history of neurosurgical treatment for psychiatric disorders is not a happy one. It comprises misunderstanding of brain function, indifference to complications, and resorting to desperate treatments for lack of better ones. Egaz Moniz, a Portuguese neurologist, was fascinated by the improved behavior of Fulton's and Jacobson's chimpanzee Becky after frontal lobectomy but ignored the opposite effects of the surgery on the simultaneously reported Lucie (1). Moniz's frontal lobotomy procedure was taken up worldwide, notably by Freeman and Watts in the USA, and by the advent of the neuroleptic era tens of thousands of surgical procedures had been performed on psychiatric patients (2). Despite efforts consistent with the methods of the day, adequate studies of surgical interventions were not performed (2).

Today, pharmacological and psychological treatments of proven efficacy and relative safety have replaced psychosurgery. Yet treatment-resistant patients remain, although data recording their prevalence are limited. In a comprehensive review, Fava and Davidson (3) found that nonresponsiveness to antidepressant pharmacotherapy occurred in between 19 and 34% of depressed patients. However, treatment resistance is variably defined and the number of patients still disabled by depression after maximum use of all available modalities of treatment over a prolonged period is unknown. The proportion of patients with obsessive-compulsive disorder (OCD) meeting similar criteria is unstudied; Mindus et al. (4) estimated that 10% of OCD patients have 'malignant' refractory illnesses.

Does psychosurgery have a place in the contemporary management of this extreme group of psychiatric patients? Developments in neurosurgical techniques may allow new approaches to psychiatric problems (5).

Stereotaxis is well established and can be guided by contemporary neuroimaging. Electrical stimulation can reversibly shut down gray matter regions and avert destructive lesioning techniques with a possible reduction in cognitive morbidity (6–8). Gamma irradiation (the gamma knife) produces precisely focused lesions without open procedures and may reduce morbidity, although some results have been disappointing (9) and the dosimetry of the procedure is still under investigation (10). Avoiding the need for burr holes allows the possibility of controlled studies using sham psychosurgical procedures, a desideratum always considered ethically impossible (4). Thalamic and striatal gamma knife lesions have alleviated pain and movement disorders (11,12), even as open procedures continue to be employed successfully for these indications, with electrophysiological recording during open procedures allowing identification of functionally significant areas before lesioning (13–17).

Deliberately injuring the brain is anathema to many clinicians and scientists whose professional activities cannot but lead to nearly religious awe of the complexity and precision of brain function. Yet after subarachnoid hemorrhage, a small group of patients exhibits an improvement in psychiatric state. Storey's careful study of personality change after subarachnoid hemorrhage (18) identified patients who emerged from the neurological catastrophe not just undamaged but better than ever before. Of his 261 patients, 13 (5%) fell into the 'improved personality' group: 'less sarcastic and irritable, less tense and anxious, less fussy and overmeticulous, and more pleasant to live with generally' (p 137) (18). These patients lacked intellectual and, for the most part, motor disability.

Similar findings came from a study by Logue et al. (19). In nine (10%) of 90 patients after subarachnoid hemorrhage, the patient and an informant agreed that the personality had changed for the better. In three, a pre-existing depressive illness had been relieved. A tendency to compulsive checking was reduced in one of the nine; a more severe OCD was relieved in another patient who did not fit into the 'improvement in personality' category. However, eight of the nine patients with improved personality showed memory impairment and for several patients adverse emotional changes were present along with favorable ones.

Improvement in movement disorders after stroke has been reported in at least nine patients (20–26), although for the most part the reports lack information on functional status. The typical patient has parkinsonism and after subthalamic nucleus stroke (a lesion that ordinarily produces hemiballism) experiences contralateral relief of akinesia and rigidity. Indeed, James Parkinson noted relief after a stroke in one of the patients he originally reported (27).

Such curious observations of spontaneously occurring brain lesions notwithstanding, only appropriately controlled studies of psychosurgery patients will answer nagging questions about efficacy and safety. Investigators have recognized this challenge. Hay et al. (28) reported retrospectively 26 Australian OCD patients treated surgically; six had only cingulate lesions, three had only orbitomedial lesions, and 17 had both sets of lesions. 'Obvious' improvement was seen in 10 (38%) and comparison with matched unoperated control individuals confirmed that the improvement was caused by surgery. Four (15%) of these patients had an adverse change in personality traits of initiative and energy (29). Although no general intellectual deterioration was seen, the surgical patients as a group performed more poorly than the control individuals on the Wisconsin Card Sort Test (30). Both personality and cognitive alterations represent just the kind of 'frontal' deterioration feared from psychosurgery. However, the procedures performed in many of these patients were more extensive than is the current practice in other centers.

Hodgkiss et al. (31) reviewed the experience of the Geoffrey Knight National Unit for Affective Disorders, the major psychosurgical program in the UK. Of 249 patients with severe mood disorder or OCD who underwent bilateral lesions of subcaudate white matter, 84 (34%) were judged 'well' at 1-year follow-up. In a prospective study of 23 patients, no adverse cognitive alternations were seen at long-term follow-up, even though 'frontal' tests were transiently impaired in the immediate postoperative period (32). Improvement of depression in these patients, however, was correlated with reduced performance on a number of neuropsychological tasks, including tests of frontal function (33).

Baer et al. (34) in Boston, USA, conducted a prospective but unblinded and uncontrolled study of cingulotomy in OCD. The authors found that five (28%) of 18 patients had responded well; three (17%) others were noted on less solid evidence to have improved. No adverse consequences were seen by careful clinical assessment but neuropsychological data were not available.

Nyman and Mindus (35) studied the effect of anterior capsulotomy on neuropsychological status in Swedish patients treated surgically for anxiety disorders including OCD. One-half of a group of 10 patients showed increased perseverative response on neuropsychological tasks, although the authors commented on the lack of clinical observation of perseveration. They further noted that longer term follow-up of a different group of patients who underwent gamma knife capsulotomy suggested that the abnormalities may be transient. Mindus et al. (4) proposed a controlled trial of gamma knife anterior capsulotomy for OCD. Preliminary data from an open trial by investigators at Brown University and the Massachusetts General Hospital in the USA and the Karolinska Institute in Sweden, meant to establish the safety and optimal size and site of the procedure, showed improvement in about one-third of 25 patients with no adverse acute or longer term consequences for cognition or personality (Rasmussen S, personal communication).

If psychosurgery works, how does it work? An answer to this question presupposes an understanding of the pathophysiology of the disorders for which psychosurgery is performed and such understanding is incomplete to say the least. Increasingly, data implicate a limbic loop involving lateral frontal and orbitofrontal cortex, striatum, cingulate gyrus, and thalamus in depression and OCDs as well as Tourette syndrome (36–40). In particular, cingulate and orbitofrontal hyperactivity have been recognized in OCD and depression. Jeanmonod et al. (41) proposed that spiking in medial thalamic nuclei was the pathophysiological commonality for 'positive symptoms', including central pain, abnormal movements, and certain psychiatric symptoms, and on this basis performed stereotactic thalamotomy with intra-operative electrophysiological recording in 104 patients. Such findings have yet to produce a fully elaborated and confirmed theory. Moreover, abnormal findings, whether by electrophysiology or by functional neuroimaging, may reflect downstream effects of more fundamental disturbances, even compensatory ones, the eradication of which is undesirable. Thus, despite progress, psychosurgical interventions cannot at present be fully rationally grounded on adequate theories of psychiatric disorders.

However, this does not mean that psychosurgery must be held in abeyance. The same reservations could be expressed about many medical treatments, including the pharmacological treatment of psychiatric disorders, which remains largely empirical. Perhaps psychosurgery programs, with careful neuropsychiatric assessment of seriously ill patients including even the possibility of intracranial recording, can yield information helpful in theory formation. An adequate theoretical justification is not necessary for the ethical use of psychosurgery, only adequate demonstrations of safety and efficacy. If such are forthcoming, withholding psychosurgery becomes ethically questionable for the small proportion but substantial number of severely ill, treatment-resistant patients. Depression and OCD are proper indications; aggressive behavior and possible applications, although surgical approaches to Tourette syndrome itself have been disappointing (42). Appropriate evaluation procedures have been outlined for OCD patients (43). At present, no clear choice can be made among the available procedures, although some data suggest that cingulotomy is safest, although least often effective (44,45). Legal and ethical safeguards for informed consent and other issues must be in place (46,47). With such precautions, especially in a research setting, psychosurgical intervention now deserves a respectful hearing.

References

1. Jasper HH, Riggio S, Goldman-Rakic PS: A historical perspective: the rise and fall of prefrontal lobotomy. In Epilepsy and the functional anatomy of the frontal lobe. Edited by Jasper HH, Riggio S, Goldman-Rakic PS. New York: Raven Press; 1995: 97–114.
2. Swayze VW: Frontal leukotomy and related psychosurgical procedures in the era before antipsychotics (1935–1954): a historical overview. Am J Psychiatry 1995, 152: 505–515.
3. Fava M, Davidson KG: Definition and epidemiology of treatment-resistant depression. Psychiatr Clin North Am 1996, 19: 179–200.
4. Mindus P, Rasmussen SA, Lindquist C: Neurosurgical treatment for refractory obsessive-compulsive disorder: implications for understanding frontal lobe function. J Neuropsychiatry Clin Neurosci 1994, 6: 467–477.
5. Yudofsky S, Ovsiew F: Neurosurgical and related interventions for the treatment of patients with psychiatric disorders. J. Neuropsychiatry Clin Neurosci 1990, 2: 253–255.
6. Caparres-Lefebvre D, Blond S, Pecheux N, Pasquier F, Petit H: Neuropsychological evaluation before and after thalamic stimulation in 9 parkinsonian patients [in French]. Rev Neurol (Paris) 1992, 148: 117–122.
7. Benabid AL, Pollak P, Gao D, Hoffmann D, Limousin P, Gay E, Payen I, Benazzouz A: Chronic electrical stimulation of the ventralis intermedius nucleus of the thalamus as a treatment of movement disorders. J Neurosurg 1996, 84: 203–214.
8. Iacono RP, Lonser RR, Mandybur G, Yamada S: Stimulation of the globus pallidus in Parkinson's disease. Br J Neurosurg 1995, 9: 505–510.
9. Friedman JH, Epstein M, Sanes JN, Lieberman P, Cullen K, Lindquist C, Daamen M: Gamma knife pallidotomy in advanced Parkinson's disease. Ann Neurol 1996, 39: 535–538.

10. Kihlstrom L, Guo W-L, Lindquist C, Mindus P: Radiobiology of radio-surgery for refractory anxiety disorders. Neurosurgery 1995, 36: 294–302.
11. Friehs GM, Ojakangas CL, Pachatz P, Schrottner O, Ott E, Pendl G: Thalamotomy and caudatotomy with the gamma knife as a treatment for parkinsonism with a comment on lesion sizes. Stereotact Funct Neurosurg 1994, 64 (suppl 1): 209–221.
12. Young RF, Vermeulen SS, Grimm P, Posewitz AE, Jacques DB, Rand RW, Copcut BG: Gamma knife thalamotomy for the treatment of persistent pain. Stereotact Funct Neurosurg 1994, 64 (suppl 1): 172–181.
13. Baron MS, Vitek JL, Bakay RAE, Green J, Kaneoke Y, Hashimoto T, Turner RS, Woodard JL, Cole SA, McDonald WM, DeLong MR: Treatment of advanced Parkinson's disease by posterior GPi pallidotomy: 1-year results of a pilot study. Ann Neurol 1996, 40: 355–366.
14. Goetz CG, Diederich NJ: There is a renaissance of interest in pallidotomy for Parkinson's disease. Nature Med 1996, 2: 510–514.
15. Bergman H, Wichmann T, DeLong MR: Reversal of experimental parkinsonism by lesions of the subthalamic nucleus. Science 1990, 249: 1436–1438.
16. Jankovic J, Cardoso F, Grossman RG, Hamilton WJ: Outcome after stereotactic thalamotomy for parkinsonian, essential, and other types of tremor. Neurosurgery 1995, 37: 680–687.
17. Cardoso F, Jankovic J. Grossman RG, Hamilton WJ: Outcome after stereotactic thalamotomy for dystonia and hemiballismus. Neurosurgery 1995, 36: 501–508.
18. Storey PB: Brain damage and personality change after subarachnoid hemorrhage. Br J Psychiatry 1970, 117: 129–142.
19. Logue V, Durward M, Pratt RTC, Miercy M, Nixon WLB: The quality of survival after rupture of an anterior cerebral aneurysm. Br J Psychiatry 1968, 114: 137–160.
20. Dubois B, Pillon B, De Saxce H, Lhermitte F, Agid Y: Disappearance of parkinsonian signs after spontaneous vascular 'thalamotomy'. Arch Neurol 1986, 43: 815–817.
21. Hashimoto T, Fujita T, Yanagisawa N: Improvement in hemiballism after transient hypoxia in a case of subthalamic hemorrhage [in Japanese]. Rinsho Shinkeigaku (Clin Neurol) 1990, 30: 877–882.
22. Rivest J, Quinn N, Gibbs J, Marsden CD: Unilateral abolition of extra-pyramidal rigidity after ipsilateral cerebellar infarction. Mov Disord 1990, 5: 328–330.
23. Scoditti U, Rustichelli P, Calzetti S; Spontaneous hemiballism and disappearance of parkinsonism following contralateral lenticular lacunar infarct. Ital J Neurol Sci 1989, 10: 575–577.
24. Sellal F, Hirsch E, Lisovoski F, Mutschler V, Collard M, Marescaux C: Contralateral disappearance of parkinsonian signs after subthalamic hematoma. Neurology 1992, 42: 255–256.
25. Stephenson JW: Disappearance of tremor in a case of paralysis agitans following an attack of hemiplegia with comments on the production of the tremor in paralysis agitans. Arch Neurol Psychiatry 1930, 23: 199–200.
26. Yamada A, Takeuchi H, Miki H: Unilateral abolition of parkinsonian rigidity after subthalamic nucleus hemorrhage [in Japanese]. Rinsho Shinkeigaku (Clin Neurol) 1992, 32: 887–889.
27. Parkinson J: An essay on the shaking palsy. London: Sherwood, Neely and Jones; 1817.
28. Hay P, Sachdev P, Cumming S, Smith JS, Lee T, Kitchener P, Matheson J: Treatment of obsessive-compulsive disorder by psychosurgery. Acta Psychiatr Scand 1993, 87: 197–207.
29. Sachdev P, Hay P: Does neurosurgery for obsessive-compulsive disorder produce personality change? J Nerv Ment Dis 1995, 183: 408–413.
30. Cumming S, Hay P, Lee T, Sachdev P: Neuropsychological outcome from psychosurgery for obsessive-compulsive disorder. Aust NZ J Psychiatry 1995, 29: 293–298.

31. Hodgkiss AD, Malizia AL, Bartlett JR, Bridges PK: Outcome after the psychosurgical operation of stereotactic subcaudate tractotomy, 1979-1991. J Neuropsychiatry Clin Neurosci 1995, 7: 230-234.

32. Kartsounis LD, Poynton A, Bridges PK, Bartlett JR: Neuropsychological correlates of stereotactic subcaudate tractotomy: a prospective study. Brain 1991, 114: 2657-2673.

33. Poynton AM, Kartsounis LD, Bridges PK: A prospective clinical study of stereotactic subcaudate tractotomy. Psychol Med 1995, 25: 763-770.

34. Baer L, Rauch SL, Ballantine HT, Martuza R, Cosgrove R, Cassem E, Giriunas I, Manzo PA, Dimino C, Jenike MA: Cingulotomy for intractable obsessive-compulsive disorder: prospective long-term follow-up of 18 patients. Arch Gen Psychiatry 1995, 52: 384-392.

35. Nyman H, Mindus P: Neuropsychological correlates of intractable anxiety disorder before and after capsulotomy. Acta Psychiatr Scand 1995, 91: 23-31.

36. Ebert D, Ebmeier KP: The role of the cingulate gyrus in depression: from functional anatomy to neurochemistry. Biol Psychiatry 1996, 39: 1044-1050.

37. Weeks RA, Turjanski N, Brooks DJ: Tourette's syndrome: a disorder of cingulate and orbitofrontal function? Quart J Med 1996, 89: 401-408.

38. Zald DH, Kim SW: Anatomy and function of the orbital frontal cortex, II: function and relevance to obsessive-compulsive disorder. J Neuropsychiatry Clin Neurosci 1996, 8: 249-261.

39. Zald DH, Kim SW: Anatomy and function of the orbital frontal cortex, I: anatomy, neurocircuitry, and obsessive-compulsive disorder. J Neuropsychiatry Clin Neurosci 1996, 8: 125-138.

40. Wolf SS, Jones DW, Knable MB, Gorey JG, Lee KS, Hyde TM, Coppola R, Weinberger DR: Tourette syndrome: prediction of phenotypic variation in monozygotic twins by caudate nucleus D2 receptor binding. Science 1996, 273: 1225-1227.

41. Jeanmonod D, Magnin M, Morel A: Low-threshold calcium spike bursts in the human thalamus: common pathophysiology for sensory, motor and limbic positive symptoms. Brain 1996, 119: 363-375.

42. Rauch SL, Baer L, Cosgrove GR, Jenike MA; Neurosurgical treatment of Tourette's syndrome: a critical review. Compr Psychiatry 1995, 36: 141-156.

43. Mindus P, Jenike MA: Neurosurgical treatment of malignant obsessive compulsive disorder. Psychiatr Clin North Am 1992, 15: 921-938.

44. Sachdev P, Hay P: Site and size of lesion and psychosurgical outcome in obsessive-compulsive disorder: a magnetic resonance imaging study. Biol Psychiatry 1996, 39: 739-742.

45. Cosgrove GR, Rauch SL: Psychosurgery. Neurosurg Clin North Am 1995, 6: 167-176.

46. Hundert EM: Autonomy, informed consent, and psychosurgery. J Clin Ethics 1994, 5: 264-266.

47. Stagno SJ, Smith ML, Hassenbusch SJ: Reconsidering 'psychosurgery': issues of informed consent and physician responsibility. J Clin Ethics 1994, 5: 217-223.

Frank T. Vertosick, Jr.　　　　　　　　　　 **NO**

Lobotomy's Back

In 1949 lobotomy was hailed as a medical miracle.

But images of zombielike patients and surgeons with ice picks soon put an end to the practice.

Now, however, the practitioners have refined their tools.

Last year a team of Harvard investigators headed by neurosurgeon G. Rees Cosgrove published a technical report bearing the ponderous title "Magnetic Resonance Image—Guided Stereotactic Cingulotomy for Intractable Psychiatric Disease." Although steeped in medical jargon, the report's central thesis—that psychiatric diseases can be treated by the selective destruction of healthy brain tissue—dates back to a much earlier, less sophisticated age when the search for a surgical cure for mental illness spawned an entire medical specialty known as psychosurgery.

Psychosurgery enjoyed a brief period of global acceptance around the time of World War II but was quickly driven from the medical mainstream with the advent of better, nonsurgical methods of treating the mentally ill. Now, almost half a century after psychosurgery's demise, the Harvard Medical School and a handful of other centers are hoping that new and improved surgical techniques can revive it. Today's neurosurgeons are also trying to rename the field "psychiatric surgery," presumably to avoid the Hitchcockian overtones of the older moniker. But, as rock star Prince discovered, shedding the name that made you famous isn't easy.

In their 1996 paper that appeared in the respected journal *Neurosurgery,* Cosgrove and his co-workers described a brain operation designed to relieve emotional distress and reduce abnormal behavior. Between 1991 and 1995, they performed cingulotomies—which means, essentially, that they burned dime-size holes in the frontal lobes of the brain—on 34 patients suffering from one of the following afflictions: severe depression; bipolar disorder, or manic-depression; obsessive-compulsive disorder (OCD); and generalized anxiety disorder. The target of their operations, the cingulate gyrus, is a thin ribbon of gray matter believed to play a role in human emotional states. The authors used a computer-guided technique known as stereotaxis to advance an electrode into the cingulate gyrus, then cooked the tissue with electric current.

Cingulotomy produced major clinical improvement, as judged by psychiatrists, in a little over a third of the patients; another quarter of them had a "possible response" to surgery. Not stellar results to be sure, but the Harvard patients all had severe disease that had proved resistant to all other available therapies. Any good outcomes in this population might be significant, and the investigators believed that their results were good enough to warrant a larger trial of cingulotomy.

Despite its high-tech approach, however, the Harvard paper still looks anachronistic, to say the least. Finding a paper extolling the virtues of psychosurgery in today's medical literature is rather like finding one advocating blood-letting. Modern neurosurgeons destroying normal brain to treat mental illness? To borrow from Samuel Johnson, this is akin to a dog walking on its hind legs—the question is not how well the act can be done but why it's even attempted.

In spite of its elevated reputation, neurosurgery is a crude business, even— or especially—to a neurosurgeon, and I've been in practice for ten years. When confronted with an exposed brain at the operating table, I feel as if I'm about to repair a computer with a chain saw. The living brain has a surreal fragility; its porcelain surface is laced with delicate arteries that begin as thick cords but quickly branch into finer and finer threads. Looking at the surface of the brain is like looking at a satellite photo of a large city—one immediately senses a function far more complex than what is visible.

The idea that a sophisticated derangement in brain function, like OCD, can be cured by frying holes in the frontal lobe looks as patently absurd as recovering a lost file from a floppy disk by burning it with a curling iron. But experience suggests that such lesions can work, if they are done correctly and on the right patients.

Psychosurgery got its start back in 1890 when Gottlieb Burckhart, a Swiss psychiatrist and surgeon, tried removing portions of the cerebral cortex from schizophrenic brains. His victims, previously agitated and tormented by violent hallucinations, became more "peaceful" after the operation. Burckhart's operation didn't impress his colleagues, though, and an angry outcry from the European medical community prevented its further use.

Psychosurgery surfaced again with a vengeance in Portugal, during the mid-1930s; shortly thereafter, neurologist Walter Freeman enthusiastically imported it to the United States. Psychiatrists started to believe Freeman's proselytizing hype, and desperate families of the mentally ill began seeking surgery for their loved ones. During World War II the United States saw an increased demand for mental health care as thousands of combat-fatigued veterans crowded already overburdened hospitals. In this setting, psychosurgery became established as a standard therapy. Over the 20-odd years that psychosurgery held the attention of the medical mainstream, perhaps as many as 35,000 patients underwent psychiatric operations of one form or another.

But as Burckhart had discovered decades earlier, the medical community could not long ignore the ethical quagmire surrounding psychiatric brain operations. In the 1950s the rising use of psychosurgery ignited a national debate over the morality of inflicting irreversible brain injuries on the most emotionally vulnerable patients. While this debate smoldered among academics right up to the 1970s, the introduction of the tranquilizer chlorpromizine in 1954 rendered many of the concerns about psychosurgery moot.

Armed with effective chemical therapies, psychiatrists soon turned to pills instead of the knife and quit referring their patients for surgery. A few centers continued to use modified forms of psychosurgery on very small numbers of patients, both here and in Europe, well into the 1980s, so psychosurgery as a specialty never died—although psychosurgery as an industry did.

Should psychosurgery be brought back from the realm of the experimental and made a mainstream treatment once again? Should we reopen this ethical can of worms? As Cosgrove's report shows, there are those who think we should. Hundreds of severely incapacitated people fail all other treatments, including drugs, electroshock, and psychotherapy, leaving surgery their only option. The illness most helped by cingulotomy—major depression—can be life-threatening. If psychosurgery works, shouldn't it be used?

The successful resurrection of extinct brain operations has a recent precedent: pallidotomy for parkinsonism. In this procedure, parts of the globus pallidus, a clump of tissue in the core of the brain controlling limb coordination, are surgically destroyed. The operation is technically similar to cingulotomy, and in the past few years it has enjoyed a renaissance. Before the discovery of L-dopa—a chemical substitute for the brain chemical dopamine—surgeons carried out pallidotomies and a number of other destructive procedures to ease the tremor and rigidity of Parkinson's disease. After the introduction of L-dopa, the role of the surgeon in the treatment of Parkinson's lessened, and the operations soon fell into relative disuse.

While L-dopa did revolutionize the treatment of Parkinson's, the drug proved ineffective in a small number of patients. Still others responded to medical therapy only to become resistant to it months or years later. As neurologists accumulated more experience with drug treatments for Parkinson's, they realized that medical therapy alone could not keep the disease at bay. A growing demand for alternative treatments renewed interest in pallidotomy, and several medical centers began trying it again. Since today's image-guided pallidotomy can be done with far greater accuracy than was ever possible before, modern surgical results have been excellent, and pallidotomy is currently available nationwide.

But bringing back pallidotomy, an operation with no historical baggage, was a piece of cake. To achieve a similar comeback in their own field, modern neurosurgeons must overcome psychosurgery's dark past—a considerably more difficult task.

Looking back today, psychosurgery is seen as nothing short of a mental health holocaust perpetrated by mind-stealing hacks in the dimly lit clinics of public psychiatric hospitals. It will always be synonymous with the flagship operation of its heyday, the dreaded prefrontal lobotomy. In the conventional form of the operation, a neurosurgeon poked holes in the patient's skull just above and in front of the ear canals on both sides of the head and plunged a flat knife, called a leucotome, into the frontal lobes to a depth of about two inches.

By sweeping the leucotome up and down within the brain, the surgeon amputated the anterior tips of the frontal lobes, the so-called prefrontal areas, from the rest of the brain. In contrast to the half-inch lesions of pallidotomy and cingulotomy, the lobotomist sliced an area of brain equal to the cross section of an orange.

This technique soon gave way to a quicker, albeit somewhat grislier, version of prefrontal lobe destruction. Before World War II, brain surgeons—not exactly a dime a dozen even today—were quite scarce; this lack of surgical expertise hindered the wider use of psychosurgery. To rid himself of the need for a surgeon, Freeman began tinkering with the transorbital approach invented by Amarro Fiamberti in Italy. (At this point, James Watts, Freeman's surgical colleague in conventional lobotomies, ended their collaboration, saying the transorbital procedure was too risky.)

In Freeman's modification of the procedure, the lobotomist inserted an ice pick (yes, an ice pick) under the upper eyelid and drove it upward into the frontal lobe with a few sharp raps of a mallet. The pick was then twisted and jiggled about, thus scrambling the anterior frontal lobes. The ice-pick lobotomy could be done by anyone with a strong stomach, and, even better, it could be done anywhere. Freeman carried his ice pick in his pocket, using it on one occasion to perform a lobotomy in a motel room. A cheap outpatient procedure, the ice-pick lobotomy became a common psychosurgical choice in state hospitals across the country.

In the late 1950s lobotomy's popularity waned, and no one has done a true lobotomy in this country since Freeman performed his last transorbital operation in 1967. (It ended in the patient's death.) But the mythology surrounding lobotomies still permeates our culture. Just last year the operation surfaced on the television show *Chicago Hope*. Few of us have ever met a lobotomized patient, but we all know what to expect—or at least we think we do. Who can forget the vacant stare of the freshly knifed Jack Nicholson in *One Flew Over the Cuckoo's Nest*? At best, according to the popular conception, the luckier victims recovered enough to wander about like incontinent zombies.

Although some patients ended up this way, or worse, the zombie stereotype derives more from Hollywood fiction than from medical reality. Lobotomy peaked in the 1950s, not during the Middle Ages. While we may have been a little more bioethically challenged back then, we weren't Neanderthals either. Lobotomy could never have survived for 20 years if it yielded a lot of cretins. In fact, intelligence, in those cases where it was measured pre- and postoperatively by formal testing, remained unaffected by a competent lobotomy and in some cases it even improved.

Not surprisingly, the operation did have disturbing side effects. Patients often suffered major personality changes and became apathetic, prone to inappropriate social behavior, and infatuated with their own toilet habits. They told pointless jokes and exhibited poor hygiene. Postoperative deaths, although uncommon, occurred and could be gruesome. But all these problems must be put into the context of the era: in the 1940s brain surgery for any disease was very risky.

It's easy for us to forget that the media first hailed psychosurgery as a medical miracle. Lobotomy's reputation once ran so high that the Nobel committee awarded the prize in Medicine and Physiology to its inventor, the Portuguese neurologist Egas Moniz, in 1949. But less than a decade after this endorsement, lobotomy was dead and its memory vilified.

The operation's descent into disgrace had many causes. For one thing, lobotomy never had a scientific basis. Moniz got the idea for it in a flash after hearing a presentation by Fulton and Jacobsen, two Yale physicians, during a 1935 neurological conference in London. The Americans described two chimpanzees, Becky and Lucy, that had become remarkably calm after frontal lobe ablation.

This single, almost casual observation prompted Moniz to return home and begin human trials immediately. Further animal work would not be useful, he argued, since no animal models of mental illness existed. Why he rejected the thought of further animal experimentation while still viewing Fulton and Jakcobsen's tiny report as a virtual epiphany remains a mystery. Moniz, who had just endured a nasty priority fight concerning his invention of cerebral angiography, may have rushed into human trials in order to stake the earliest claim to lobotomy.

The association of the frontal lobes with emotional and intellectual dysfunction was hardly a radical idea, even in 1935. The frontal lobes of lower mammals are vanishingly tiny; even chimps and apes have fairly small ones. In humans, on the other hand, the frontal lobes make up nearly two-thirds of the cerebrum, or higher brain. Since mental illnesses are uniquely human afflictions, a therapeutic surgical assault on the frontal lobes seemed quite plausible.

Moniz subsequently created a fanciful theory of "abnormally stabilized pathways" in the brain to justify his operation. He reasoned that cutting brain fibers might interrupt the abnormal brain circuitry of psychiatric patients, freeing them from a cycle of endless rumination. Since then, no better rationale for lobotomy has been advanced. Nevertheless, a lack of scientific justification doesn't doom an operation as long as the operation works. Many good operations, pallidotomy included, can trace their origins to pseudoscience or serendipity. But was lobotomy ever a good operation? We've had half a century to study it and we're still not sure.

Unfortunately, lobotomists showed no great talent for comprehensive, long-term analysis of their data. The esteemed Moniz often followed his patients for only a few weeks after their surgery. The peripatetic Freeman drove about the country doing hundreds of ice-pick procedures, but only near the end of his life did he find out how the majority of them fared. Even then, his assessments proved vague and unconvincing.

Only a single certain conclusion emerged from the dozens of lobotomy studies that have appeared over the years: schizophrenics don't get better after surgery. This is ironic, given that they were the first to undergo psychosurgery. We now have an inkling as to why the treatment doesn't work. Unlike depression and mania, which are disorders of mood, schizophrenia is a disorder of thought. And what a lobotomy alters is emotional state, not cognitive abilities.

Most lobotomists had vague and paternalistic ideas of what constituted a "good" result. Results were typically judged by psychiatrists, families, or institutional custodians; detailed surveys of what the patients thought rarely appear in the psychosurgery literature. This seems strange, since a cure, as judged by outsiders, may not be viewed that way by the patient. Is the patient, although inwardly miserable, cured because he no longer assaults the nursing staff, or because he can now sit quietly for hours without screaming? A careful reading of Freeman's more detailed case histories shows that a few patients didn't even see themselves as ill in the first place, although they realized that their behavior disturbed others.

Probably the most important factor in lobotomy's demise was its deep physical and metaphysical ugliness. More than one seasoned professional vomited or passed out while watching Freeman crack through a patient's orbital bone with his ice pick. Moreover, prospective patients often had to be dragged to an operating room or clinic. In *Psychosurgery,* the textbook he coauthored with Watts, Freeman frankly describes his unorthodox methods of obtaining "consent" for lobotomy. Occasionally, forcible sedation was needed to keep the patient from backing out at the last minute.

Freeman's landmark treatise also notes that if the patient was "too disturbed" to sign a consent, a close relative could give permission instead. He didn't elaborate on how disturbed a person needed to be to abdicate his right to refuse lobotomy. Freeman never considered the possibility that relatives might have less than honorable motives for agreeing to the dissection of their loved one's frontal lobes. Tennessee Williams, however, had no trouble envisioning such a nasty scenario. In his play *Suddenly Last Summer,* Mrs. Venable orders her young niece, Catharine, to be lobotomized. Catharine knew a little too much about the deviate practices of Mrs. Venable's late son, Sebastian. Who would believe the poor child after she had the appropriate "therapy" at Lion's View asylum?

It's doubtful that many real families ever had such fanciful motives behind their surrogate assents for lobotomy, although even mundane motives can be illegitimate. Was it right to authorize a lobotomy to make an argumentative person a quiet one? Or to stop behaviors repugnant to everyone—everyone, that is, except the patient?

In retrospect, the real question isn't why lobotomy died, but why it survived for so long. The answer is simple: Walter Freeman. Lobotomy became his career, his crusade, and he spread psychosurgery's gospel with boundless enthusiasm. His elegant bearing and Freudian goatee gave him the look of a world-renowned healer of minds. In the end, his force of will could no longer counter lobotomy's growing ethical opposition and pharmaceutical competition. Freeman did his best to carry on, but it was no use.

Modern psychosurgery has no evangelist equal to Freeman to spread its message, and so it must survive only on its merits. Time will tell whether it can.

There are good reasons to think the field can be revived. For starters, modern procedures like magnetic, resonance-guided cingulotomy bear little resemblance to the ugly lobotomies of the past. Computer-guided electrodes the thickness of pencil lead that can inflict minute injuries with millimeter precision have replaced ice picks and leucotomes. Procedures now take place only in sophisticated operating theaters, not in motel rooms or in the back rooms of county hospitals.

Modern neurosurgeons like Cosgrove approach their operations not as true believers but as skeptical scientists. Freeman's arm-twisting consents are also gone; today multidisciplinary committees review each patient on a rigorous case-by-case basis. And no one but the patient can give consent for cingulotomy—there were no Mrs. Venables involved in the Harvard study. Unlike the itinerant lobotomists of Freeman's time, modern psychosurgeons follow their patients closely for years and test them exhaustively.

But two problems remain. First, Cosgrove's report, like earlier psychosurgery studies, makes no mention of the patients' perception of their operations; it details only what their psychiatrists thought. Patients can't even request this surgery on their own; an operation is offered only if the psychiatrist agrees. In other "quality of life" operations—face-lifts, surgical removal of herniated spinal disks, elective joint replacements—the patient approaches the surgeon directly, requests surgery, and then personally decides if the postoperative outcome is satisfactory. An orthopedic surgeon doesn't ask an internist if a knee replacement has alleviated a patient's pain. So why must we rely on psychiatrists to tell us if a patient no longer feels depressed after cingulotomy?

Second, the cingulotomy rests on no firmer scientific foundation than lobotomy did. First performed in 1952 as a modified version of the lobotomy, cingulotomy was based on Freeman's observations that lobotomy patients seemed to have less "psychological tension" when fibers near the cingulate gyrus were severed. This ribbon of brain tissue is thought to be a conduit between the limbic region, a primitive area involved in emotional behavior, and the frontal lobes, the seat of reason and judgment. But we lack any more detailed understanding of how the cingulate gyrus functions. As such, cingulotomy can trace its intellectual heritage right back to the chimps Becky and Lucy.

Psychosurgery will never become as routine as it was in the 1940s and 1950s. The most refractory of the chronically disabling mental illnesses, schizophrenia, can't be treated surgically. Depression, while quite common, usually responds to one of the many excellent medical therapies that must be tried first, leaving few patients as candidates for surgery. And patients with OCD often respond to nonsurgical treatments. Thus, the pool of patients likely to benefit from cingulotomy will always be fairly small. In addition, few major medical centers can muster the psychiatric, bioethical, and surgical resources to perform and evaluate the procedure correctly.

Then there is that sticky public relations problem. No matter how refined their surgeries, modem psychosurgeons will still be perceived as lobotomists. An unfair label, perhaps, but one that will prove difficult to shed.

A greater concern may be that the public won't care at all. In Freeman's day, society paid to house and care for great numbers of the mentally infirm, making psychiatric disease a public health problem of the first order. This may be why no one bothered to ask the patients what they thought of surgery—the lobotomists weren't treating patients, they were treating a national crisis. Since lobotomy did make patients easier to care for, and even got many out of institutions and off the public dole, psychosurgeons served the national interest well. Freeman acknowledged that the lobotomist often put the needs of society over those of the individual, arguing that it was better for a patient "to have a simplified intellect capable of elementary acts than an intellect where reigns disorder of subtle synthesis. Society can accommodate itself to the humble laborer, but it justifiably mistrusts the mad thinker."

The goal of lobotomy wasn't to control disease but to control patients. Some would argue that our present heavy use of psychotropic drugs is just as flawed, in that we don't make the patients better—we just succeed in preventing them from bothering us.

As a nation, we could seriously question all our recent efforts in the mental health arena. During the last three decades, mental illness has been literally cast into the streets. Asylums have vanished and many private health plans now refuse to pay for psychiatric treatment. Before we judge the lobotomists of old too severely, we should go to the nearest street grate and see how we are dealing with our mental health crisis today. High-profile diseases like AIDS and breast cancer dominate the headlines and the federal research budgets, leaving many victims of mental illness to suffer in silent solitude.

Modern psychosurgeons are thus courageous in seeking to address a difficult problem. By trying to bring the best neurosurgical technologies to a group of patients who have run out of hope, they risk the scorn of those who see only what psychosurgery was and not what it can be. I wish them luck. Given the lessons of history, they'll surely need it.

CHALLENGE QUESTIONS

Should Psychosurgery Be Used to Treat Certain Psychological Conditions?

1. Ovsiew and Bird support the use of psychosurgery for seriously impaired patients who do not respond to psychotherapy or medication. What criteria should be used to determine the appropriateness of psychosurgery as an intervention?
2. Vertosick raises ethical concerns about the use of psychosurgery. In what ways is psychosurgery markedly different from other major elective surgery?
3. A significant concern about extreme interventions such as psychosurgery is the issue of informed consent. What are some of the issues involved for loved ones and clinicians who are trying to make a life-changing surgical decision for an individual who is considered incapable of making the decision?
4. What problems would be involved in designing a research study to compare the efficacy of psychosurgery and medication for the treatment of debilitating obsessive-compulsive disorder?
5. Considering that psychosurgery is still regarded as an experimental procedure, many insurance companies resist reimbursing for this intervention. What are the arguments for and against this?

Suggested Readings

Jenike, M. A. (1998). Neurosurgical treatment of obsessive-compulsive disorder. *British Journal of Psychiatry*, 173(35S), 79–90.

Marino, J. R., & Cosgrove, G. R. (1997). Neurosurgical treatment of neuropsychiatric illness. *Psychiatric Clinics of North America*, 20(4), 933–943.

Pressman, J. D. (1998). *Last resort: Psychosurgery and the limits of medicine*. New York, NY: Cambridge University Press.

Sachdev, P., & Sachdev, J. (1997). Sixty years of psychosurgery: Its present status and its future. *Australian and New Zealand Journal of Psychiatry*, 31(4), 457–464.

Weingarten, S. M. (1999). Psychosurgery. In B. L. Miller, & J. L. Cummings (Eds.), *The human frontal lobes: Functions and disorders. The science and practice of neuropsychology series.* (pp. 446–460). New York, NY: The Guilford Press.

On the Internet ...

Media Psychology: Division 46 of the American Psychological Association

The American Psychological Association's Division of Media Psychology provides information on the impacts and importance of the media.

http://www.apa.org/divisions/div46/

Feminists Against Censorship

This is the Web site of Feminists Against Censorship (FAC), a group of feminists from academia and elsewhere promoting free speech and fighting censorship from a feminist perspective.

http://www.fiawol.demon.co.uk/FAC/

Santa Barbara County—Citizens Against Pornography

This is the Web site of Santa Barbara County—Citizens Against Pornography (SBC-CAP), a coalition that focuses on the reduction of sexual violence and victimization through public awareness of the harms of pornography.

http://www.rain.org/~sbc-cap

Upstream

This site contains a collection of articles defending and attacking the controversial publication *The Bell Curve* by Richard J. Herrnstein and Charles Murray.

http://www.cycad.com/cgi-bin/Upstream/Issues/
bell-curve/index.html

The American Association of Pastoral Counselors

This Web site of the American Association of Pastoral Counselors (AAPC) provides information about pastoral counseling and referrals to certified pastoral counselors.

http://www.aapc.org

Institute on Independent Living

This Web site of the Institute on Independent Living provides information, advocacy, and support for disabled people who are seeking greater autonomy.

http://www.independentliving.org

PART 4

Social Issues

*M*any issues in the field of abnormal psychology interface with social issues, with heated debates emerging about topics with societal impact. Some of the controversies pertain to questions about the extent to which societal forces cause psychological disturbance; for example, some critics have raised concerns about the impact of exposure to media violence or pornography on behavior. Other issues pertain to processes by which people are made to feel peripheral in society either because of race, a history of psychiatric disturbance, or even religious commitment.

- Does Media Violence Promote Violent Behavior in Young People?

- Is Pornography Harmful?

- Is the *Bell Curve* Theory Valid?

- Does Religious Commitment Improve Mental Health?

- Has the Deinstitutionalization of the Mentally Ill Worked?

ISSUE 12

Does Media Violence Promote Violent Behavior in Young People?

YES: L. Rowell Huesmann and Jessica Moise, from "Media Violence: A Demonstrated Public Health Threat to Children," *Harvard Mental Health Letter* (June 1996)

NO: Jonathan L. Freedman, from "Violence in the Mass Media and Violence in Society: The Link Is Unproven," *Harvard Mental Health Letter* (May 1996)

ISSUE SUMMARY

YES: Psychology and communication researchers L. Rowell Huesmann and Jessica Moise assert that there is a clear relationship between aggression and children's viewing of media violence, and they point to several theoretical explanations for this connection.

NO: Psychology professor Jonathan L. Freedman disagrees with the conclusion of researchers that there is a relationship between aggression and children's viewing of media violence, and he argues that many conclusions in this area are based on methodologically flawed studies.

In recent years the attention of American society has been drawn to a number of profoundly troubling events in which young children have engaged in unthinkable forms of violence. Following the massacre at Columbine High School in Littleton, Colorado, in the spring of 1999, Americans were bewildered in their efforts to understand why teenagers would carefully plan out the murder of their classmates and then turn the guns on themselves. In looking for answers, many commentators turned to the proliferation of violent images on television, in the movies, and in video games. To explain why young Americans have turned from traditional pursuits of youth to aggression and violence, critics of media violence have pointed to the explosion of graphic imagery in every medium.

Social learning theorists have provided ample experimental support for the notion that exposure to media violence can significantly influence the behavior of young people. According to social learning theory, people acquire many new responses by imitating the behavior of another person. Social learning theorist Albert Bandura proposed that people receive vicarious reinforcement when they identify with a person whom they observe being reinforced. Thus, if a boy watches a violent man in a movie receive attention and admiration from others, he might be drawn to engage in similar behaviors on the premise that such adulation can also come his way.

In the following selection, L. Rowell Huesmann and Jessica Moise contend that there is a clear relationship between aggression and children's viewing of media violence. They specify five well-validated theoretical explanations for this connection: (1) children imitate what they observe; (2) media violence stimulates aggression by desensitizing children; (3) children watch violent media portrayals in an attempt to justify their own aggression; (4) the observation of aggression results in cognitive priming, or the activation of existing aggressive thoughts; and (5) children become physiologically aroused in response to observing violence.

Jonathan L. Freedman, in the second selection, asserts that research on the relationship between exposure to media violence and aggression has yielded inconsistent results. He points to methodological problems inherent in much of the research; for example, demand characteristics within research studies cause children to respond in ways that they know the experimenter expects. Furthermore, Freedman says, a corresponding set of expectations influences researchers who become involved in such research with the anticipation that they will find a connection between exposure to violence and aggressive behavior.

POINT

- The relationship between aggression and exposure to media violence has been supported by a wide variety of experiments conducted in different countries by researchers with different points of view.

- Despite Freedman's insistence that the correlation between aggression and exposure to violence is statistically small, its impact has real social significance.

- Because media heroes are admired and have special authority, children are likely to imitate their behavior and learn that aggression is an acceptable solution to conflict.

- Children younger than 11 do not make the distinction between fiction and reality very well.

COUNTERPOINT

- Most of the studies of the relationship between aggression and exposure to media violence have serious methodological flaws and have yielded inconsistent results.

- The correlations between aggression and violence exposure are quite small, accounting for only 1 to 10 percent of individual differences in the aggressiveness of children.

- If children are learning anything from the media, it is that the forces of good will overcome evil assailants, who are the first to use violence.

- Children are able to recognize fiction as early as the age of 5; those watching retaliatory violence do not believe they could act successfully by engaging in such behaviors.

L. Rowell Huesmann
and Jessica Moise

 **YES**

Media Violence: A Demonstrated Public Health Threat to Children

Imagine that the Surgeon General is presented with a series of studies on a widely distributed product. For 30 years well-controlled experiments have been showing that use of the product causes symptoms of a particular affliction. Many field surveys have shown that this affliction is always more common among people who use the product regularly. A smaller number of studies have examined the long-term effects of the product in different environments, and most have shown at least some evidence of harm, although it is difficult to disentangle effects of the product itself from the effects of factors that lead people to use it. Over all, the studies suggest that if a person with a 50% risk for the affliction uses the product, the risk rises to 60% or 70%. Furthermore, we have a fairly good understanding of how use of the product contributes to the affliction, which is persistent, difficult to cure, and sometimes lethal. The product is economically important, and its manufacturers spend large sums trying to disparage the scientific research. A few scientists who have never done any empirical work in the field regularly point out supposed flaws in the research and belittle its conclusions. The incidence of the affliction has increased dramatically since the product was first introduced. What should the Surgeon General do?

This description applies to the relationship between lung cancer and cigarettes. It also applies to the relationship between aggression and children's viewing of mass media violence. The Surgeon General has rightly come to the same conclusion in both cases and has issued similar warnings.

Cause and Effect

Dr. Freedman's highly selective reading of the research minimizes overwhelming evidence. First, there are the carefully controlled laboratory studies in which children are exposed to violent film clips and short-term changes in their behavior are observed. More than 100 such studies over the last 40 years have shown that at least some children exposed to visual depictions of dramatic violence behave more aggressively afterward both toward inanimate objects and

From L. Rowell Huesmann and Jessica Moise, "Media Violence: A Demonstrated Public Health Threat to Children," *Harvard Mental Health Letter*, vol. 12, no. 12 (June 1996). Copyright © 1996 by The President and Fellows of Harvard College. Reprinted by permission of The Harvard Medical School Health Publications Group.

toward other children. These results have been found in many countries among boys and girls of all social classes, races, ages, and levels of intelligence.

Freedman claims that these studies use dubious measures of aggression. He cites only one example: asking children whether they would want the researcher to prick a balloon. But this measure is not at all representative. Most studies have used such evidence as physical attacks on other children and dolls. In one typical study Kaj Bjorkqvist exposed five- and six-year-old Finnish children to either violent or non-violent films. Observers who did not know which kind of film each child had seen then watched them play together. Children who had just seen a violent film were more likely to hit other children, scream at them, threaten them, and intentionally destroy their toys.

Freedman claims that these experiments confuse the effects of arousal with the effects of violence. He argues that "anyone who is aroused will display more of almost any behavior." But most studies have shown that pro-social behavior decreases after children view an aggressive film. Finally, Freedman says the experiments are contaminated by demand characteristics. In other words, the children are only doing what they think the researchers want them to do. That conclusion is extremely implausible, considering the wide variety of experiments conducted in different countries by researchers with different points of view.

Large Body of Evidence

More than 50 field studies over the last 20 years have also shown that children who habitually watch more media violence behave more aggressively and accept aggression more readily as a way to solve problems. The relationship usually persists when researchers control for age, sex, social class, and previous level of aggression. Disbelievers often suggest that the correlation is statistically small. According to Freedman, it accounts for "only 1% to 10% of individual differences in children's aggressiveness." But an increase of that size (a more accurate figure would be 2% to 16%) has real social significance. No single factor has been found to explain more than 16% of individual differences in aggression.

Of course, correlations do not prove causality. That is the purpose of laboratory experiments. The two approaches are complementary. Experiments establish causal relationship, and field studies show that the relationship holds in a wide variety of real-world situations. The causal relationship is further confirmed by the finding that children who view TV violence at an early age are more likely to commit aggressive acts at a later age. In 1982 Eron and Huesmann found that boys who spent the most time viewing violent television shows at age eight were most likely to have criminal convictions at age 30. Most other long-term studies have come to similar conclusions, even after controlling for children's initial aggressiveness, social class, and education. A few studies have found no effect on some measures of violence, but almost all have found a significant effect on some measures.

Freedman singles out for criticism a study by Huesmann and his colleagues that was concluded in the late 1970s. He says we found "no statistically significant effect for either sex in Australia, Finland, the Netherlands, Poland, or kibbutz children in Israel." That is not true. We found that the television viewing habits of children as young as six or seven predicted subsequent increases in childhood aggression among boys in Finland and among both sexes in the United States, in Poland, and in Israeli cities. In Australia and on Israeli kibbutzim, television viewing habits were correlated with simultaneous aggression. Freedman also suggests that another study conducted in the Netherlands came to conclusions so different from ours that we banned it from a book we were writing. In fact, the results of that study were remarkably similar to our own, and we did not refuse to publish it. The Dutch researchers themselves chose to publish separately in a different format.

Cultural Differences

Freedman argues that the strongest results reported in the study, such as those for Israeli city children, are so incongruous that they arouse suspicion. He is wrong. Given the influence of culture and social learning on aggressive behavior, different results in different cultures are to be expected. In fact, the similarity of the findings in different countries is remarkable here. One reason we found no connection between television violence viewing and aggression among children on kibbutzim is the strong cultural prohibition against intragroup aggression in those communities. Another reason is that kibbutz children usually watched television in a group and discussed the shows with an adult caretaker afterward.

Two recently published meta-analyses summarize the findings of many studies conducted over the past 30 years. In an analysis of 217 experiments and field studies, Paik and Comstock concluded that the association between exposure to television violence and aggressive behavior is extremely strong, especially in the data accumulated over the last 15 years. In the other meta-analysis, Wood, Wong, and Chachere came to the same conclusion after combined analysis of 23 studies of unstructured social interaction.

We now have well-validated theoretical explanations of these results. Exposure to media violence leads to aggression at least five ways. The first is imitation, or observational learning. Children imitate the actions of their parents, other children, and media heroes, especially when the action is rewarded and the child admires and identifies with the model. When generalized, this process creates what are sometimes called cognitive scripts for complex social problem-solving: internalized programs that guide everyday social behavior in an automatic way and are highly resistant to change.

Turning Off

Second, media violence stimulates aggression by desensitizing children to the effects of violence. The more televised violence a child watches, the more acceptable aggressive behavior becomes for that child. Furthermore, children who watch violent television become suspicious and expect others to act violently—an attributional bias that promotes aggressive behavior.

Justification is a third process by which media violence stimulates aggression. A child who has behaved aggressively watches violent television shows to relieve guilt and justify the aggression. The child then feels less inhibited about aggressing again.

A fourth process is cognitive priming or cueing—the activation of existing aggressive thoughts, feelings, and behavior. This explains why children observe one kind of aggression on television and commit another kind of aggressive act afterward. Even an innocuous object that has been associated with aggression may later stimulate violence. Josephson demonstrated this... in a study of schoolboy hockey players. She subjected the boys to frustration and then showed them either a violent or a non-violent television program. The aggressor in the violent program carried a walkie-talkie. Later, when the referee in a hockey game carried a similar walkie-talkie, the boys who had seen the violent film were more likely to start fights during the game.

A Numbing Effect

The fifth process by which media violence induces aggression is physiological arousal and desensitization. Boys who are heavy television watchers show lower than average physiological arousal in response to new scenes of violence. Similar short-term effects are found in laboratory studies. The arousal stimulated by viewing violence is unpleasant at first, but children who constantly watch violent television become habituated, and their emotional and physiological responses decline. Meanwhile the propensity to aggression is heightened by any pleasurable arousal, such as sexual feeling, that is associated with media violence.

Freedman argues that in violent TV shows, villains "start the fight and are punished" and the heroes "almost always have special legal or moral authority." Therefore, he concludes, children are learning from these programs that the forces of good will overcome evil assailants. On the contrary, it is precisely because media heroes are admired and have special authority that children are likely to imitate their behavior and learn that aggression is an acceptable solution to conflict. Freedman also claims that media violence has little effect because children can distinguish real life from fiction. But children under 11 do not make this distinction very well. Studies have shown that many of them think cartoons and other fantasy shows depict life as it really is.

The studies are conclusive. The evidence leaves no room for doubt that exposure to media violence stimulates aggression. It is time to move on and consider how best to inoculate our children against this insidious threat.

Jonathan L. Freedman

 **NO**

Violence in the Mass Media and Violence in Society

I magine that the Food and Drug Administration (FDA) is presented with a series of studies testing the effectiveness of a new drug. There are some laboratory tests that produce fairly consistent positive effects, but the drug does not always work as expected and no attempt has been made to discover why. Most of the clinical tests are negative; there are also a few weak positive results and a few results suggesting that the drug is less effective than a placebo. Obviously the FDA would reject this application, yet the widely accepted evidence that watching television violence causes aggression is no more adequate.

In laboratory tests of this thesis, some children are shown violent programs, others are shown nonviolent programs, and their aggressiveness is measured immediately afterward. The results, although far from consistent, generally show some increase in aggression after a child watches a violent program. Like most laboratory studies of real-world conditions, however, these findings have limited value. In the first place, most of the studies have used dubious measures of aggression. In one experiment, for example, children were asked, "If I had a balloon, would you want me to prick it?" Other measures have been more plausible, but none is unimpeachable. Second, there is the problem of distinguishing effects of violence from effects of interest and excitement. In general, the violent films in these experiments are more arousing than the neutral films. Anyone who is aroused will display more of almost any behavior; there is nothing special about aggression in this respect. Finally and most important, these experiments are seriously contaminated by what psychologists call demand characteristics of the situation: the familiar fact that people try to do what the experimenter wants. Since the children know the experimenter has chosen the violent film, they may assume that they are being given permission to be aggressive.

Putting It to the Test

The simplest way to conduct a real-world study is to find out whether children who watch more violent television are also more aggressive. They are, but the correlations are small, accounting for only 1% to 10% of individual differences in children's aggressiveness. In any case, correlations do not prove causality. Boys watch more TV football than girls, and they play more football than girls, but no one, so far as I know, believes that television is what makes boys more interested in football. Probably personality characteristics that make children more aggressive also make them prefer violent television programs.

To control for the child's initial aggressiveness, some studies have measured children's TV viewing and their aggression at intervals of several years, using statistical techniques to judge the effect of early television viewing on later aggression. One such study found evidence of an effect, but most have found none.

For practical reasons, there have been only a few truly controlled experiments in which some children in a real-world environment are assigned to watch violent programs for a certain period of time and others are assigned to watch non-violent programs. Two or three of these experiments indicated slight, short-lived effects of TV violence on aggression; one found a strong effect in the opposite of the expected direction, and most found no effect. All the positive results were obtained by a single research group, which conducted studies with very small numbers of children and used inappropriate statistics.

Scrutinizing the Evidence

An account of two studies will give some idea of how weak the research results are and how seriously they have been misinterpreted.

A study published by Lynette Friedrichs and Aletha Stein is often described (for example, in reports by the National Institute of Mental Health and the American Psychological Association) as having found that children who watched violent programs became more aggressive. What the study actually showed was quite different. In a first analysis the authors found that TV violence had no effect on physical aggression, verbal aggression, aggressive fantasy, or object aggression (competition for a toy or other object). Next they computed indexes statistically combining various kinds of aggression, a technique that greatly increases the likelihood of connections appearing purely by chance. Still they found nothing.

They then divided the children into two groups—those who were already aggressive and those who were not. They found that children originally lower in aggression seemed to become more aggressive and children originally higher in aggression seemed to become less aggressive no matter which type of program they watched. This is a well-known statistical artifact called regression toward the mean, and it has no substantive significance. Furthermore, the less aggressive children actually became more aggressive after watching the neutral program than after watching the violent program. The only comfort for the experimenters was that the level of aggression in highly aggressive children fell more when they watched a neutral program than when they watched a violent program. Somehow that was sufficient for the study to be widely cited as strong evidence that TV violence causes aggression.

An ambitious cross-national study was conducted by a team led by Rowell Huesmann and Leonard Eron and reported in 1986. In this widely cited research the effect of watching violent television on aggressiveness at a later age was observed in seven groups of boys and seven groups of girls in six countries. After controlling for initial aggressiveness, the researchers found no statistically significant effect for either sex in Australia, Finland, the Netherlands, Poland, or kibbutz children in Israel. The effect sought by the investigators was found only in the United States and among urban Israeli children, and the latter effect was so large, so far beyond the normal range for this kind of research and so incongruous with the results in other countries, that it must be regarded with suspicion. Nevertheless, the senior authors concluded that the pattern of results supported their position. The Netherlands researchers disagreed; they acknowledged that they had not been able to link TV violence to aggression, and they criticized the methods used by some of the other groups. The senior authors refused to include their chapter in the book that came out of the study, and they had to publish a separate report.

A Second Look

If the evidence is so inadequate, why have so many committees evaluating it concluded that the link exists? In the first place, these committees have been composed largely of people chosen with the expectation of reaching that conclusion. Furthermore, committee members who were not already familiar with the research could not possibly have read it all themselves, and must have relied on what they were told by experts who were often biased. The reports of these committees are often seriously inadequate. The National Institute of Mental Health, for example, conducted a huge study but solicited only one review of the literature, from a strong advocate of the view that television violence causes aggression. The review was sketchy—it left out many important studies— and deeply flawed.

The belief that TV violence causes aggression has seemed plausible because it is intuitively obvious that this powerful medium has effects on children. After all, children imitate and learn from what they see. The question, however, is what they see on television and what they learn. We know that children tend to imitate actions that are rewarded and avoid actions that are punished. In most violent television programs villains start the fight and are punished. The programs also show heroes using violence to fight violence, but the heroes almost always have special legal or moral authority; they are police, other government agents, or protectors of society like Batman and the Power Rangers. If children are learning anything from these programs, it is that the forces of good will overcome evil assailants who are the first to use violence. That may be overoptimistic, but it hardly encourages the children themselves to initiate aggression.

Telling the Difference

Furthermore, these programs are fiction, and children know it as early as the age of five. Children watching Power Rangers do not think they can beam up to the command center, and children watching "Aladdin" do not believe in flying carpets. Similarly, children watching the retaliatory violence of the heroes in these programs do not come to believe they themselves could successfully act in the same way. (Researchers concerned about mass media violence should be more interested in the fights that occur during hockey and football games, which are real and therefore may be imitated by children who play those sports).

Recently I testified before a Senate committee, and one Senator told me he knew TV made children aggressive because his own son had met him at the door with a karate kick after watching the Power Rangers. The Senator was confusing aggression with rough play, and imitation of specific actions with learning to be aggressive. Children do imitate what they see on television; this has strong effects on the way they play, and it may also influence the forms their real-life aggression takes. Children who watch the Ninja Turtles or Power Rangers may practice martial arts, just as years ago they might have been wielding toy guns, and long before that, wrestling or dueling with wooden swords. If there had been no television, the Senator's son might have butted him in the stomach or poked him in the ribs with a gun. The question is not whether the boy learned his karate kick from TV, but whether TV has made him more aggressive than he would have been otherwise.

Television is an easy target for the concern about violence in our society but a misleading one. We should no longer waste time worrying about this subject. Instead let us turn our attention to the obvious major causes of violence, which include poverty, racial conflict, drug abuse, and poor parenting.

CHALLENGE QUESTIONS

Does Media Violence Promote Violent Behavior in Young People?

1. Huesmann and Moise make strong statements to support their argument that children who watch media violence are likely to act aggressively. Assuming that their conclusion is correct, how might parents and educators counteract the negative effects of this kind of exposure?
2. Freedman contends that some misleading conclusions have been drawn from studies involving flawed methodology. If cost were not a concern, what might be the most effective method for studying the relationship between media violence and aggression?
3. What factors influence media executives to produce violent programming?
4. Some might argue that media violence provides a safe outlet for biologically determined fantasies and urges. What arguments can be made for and against this premise?
5. Imagine that you are a clinician who is being asked to consult with a 10-year-old boy whose behavior is excessively aggressive. How would you evaluate the role of media violence? What recommendations would you make if there seemed to be a relationship between the boy's aggressive behavior and his watching violent programs?

Suggested Readings

Freedman, J. L. (1992). Television violence and aggression: What psychologists should tell the public. In P. Suedfeld, & P. E. Tetlock (Eds.), *Psychology and social policy.* (pp. 179–189). New York, NY: Hemisphere Publishing Corp.

Freedman, J. L. (1988). Television violence and aggression: What the evidence shows. In S. Oskamp (Ed.), *Television as a social issue. Applied social psychology annual, vol. 8.* (pp. 144–162). Beverly Hills, CA: Sage Publications, Inc.

Hepburn, M. A. (1997). T.V. violence! A medium's effect under scrutiny. *Social Education, 61*(5), 244–249.

Huesmann, L. R., Moise, J. F., & Podolski, C. (1997). The effects of media violence on the development of antisocial behavior. In D. M. Stoff, & J. Breiling (Eds.), *Handbook of antisocial behavior.* (pp. 181–193). New York, NY: John Wiley & Sons, Inc.

Smith, S. L., & Donnerstein, E. (1998). Harmful effects of exposure to media violence: Learning of aggression, emotional desensitization, and fear. In R. G. Green, & E. Donnerstein (Eds.), *Human aggression: Theories, research, and implications for social policy.* (pp. 167–202). San Diego, CA: Academic Press, Inc.

ISSUE 13

Is Pornography Harmful?

YES: Diana E. H. Russell, from *Dangerous Relationships: Pornography, Misogyny, and Rape* (Sage Publications, 1998)

NO: Nadine Strossen, from *Defending Pornography: Free Speech, Sex, and the Fight for Women's Rights* (Scribner, 1995)

ISSUE SUMMARY

YES: Sociology professor Diana E. H. Russell considers pornography profoundly harmful because it predisposes men to want to rape women and undermines internal and social inhibitions against acting out rape fantasies.

NO: Law professor Nadine Strossen contends that there is no credible research to support the claim that sexist, violent imagery leads to harmful behavior against women.

Social learning theorists have long held that people are prone to engage in behaviors that other people seem to find pleasurable. As exposure to graphic sexual imagery has become mainstream in American society, increasing numbers of people of all ages and both sexes have been stimulated by images that provoke intense, pleasurable biological responses. As the limits in social definitions of what is acceptable have been pushed further and further, the appetites of many people have turned toward images that are increasingly novel and unfamiliar. In the realm of pornography, images that were once unspeakable have become common ingredients on X-rated Internet sites and in adult videos. Debates over pornography have been based on a variety of arguments, including political, religious, psychological, and social. On one side are those who see pornography as an insidious force that undermines individual psychological functioning, interpersonal relationships, and social mores. On the other side are those who view pornography in political terms as involving a very personal choice about what people choose to read or watch.

Diana E. H. Russell considers pornography in the most negative of terms and as the basis for much of the violence that men perpetrate against women. In the following selection, she contends that pornography predisposes some males to want to rape women and undermines some males' internal and social inhibitions against acting out their desire to rape. According to Russell, pornography objectifies and dehumanizes women, perpetuates myths that women enjoy rape, and desensitizes males to rape.

In the second selection, Nadine Strossen contends that there is no credible evidence to support the contention that exposure to sexist, violent imagery leads to sexist, violent behavior. Furthermore, she states that experiments have failed to establish a link between women's exposure to such materials and their development of negative self-images, an assertion that some have made. Strossen argues that the alleged causal relationship is conclusively refuted by the fact that levels of violence and discrimination against women are often inversely related to the availability of sexually explicit materials, including violent sexually explicit materials.

POINT

- Pornography predisposes some males to want to rape women.

- Viewers of pornography can develop arousal patterns to depictions of rape, murder, child sexual abuse, or other assaultive behavior.

- Exposure to pornography is associated with a marked increase in males' acceptance of male dominance in intimate relationships.

- Exposure to pornography increases men's self-reported likelihood of committing rape.
- Exposure to pornography leads to a desensitization, which results in increased violence and sexual exploitation of women.

COUNTERPOINT

- There is no credible evidence to substantiate a clear connection between any type of sexually explicit material and any sexist or violent behavior.
- Levels of violence and discrimination against women are often inversely related to the availability of sexually explicit materials, including violent sexually explicit materials.
- Violence and discrimination against women is common in countries where sexually oriented material is almost completely unavailable (e.g., Saudi Arabia, Iran, and China), yet violence is uncommon in countries where such material is readily available (e.g., Denmark, Germany, and Japan).
- There are no consistent correlations between exposure to pornography and violence against women.
- Research shows that sex offenders had less exposure to sexually explicit materials than most men, that they first saw such materials at a later age than nonoffenders, that they were overwhelmingly more likely to have been punished for looking at these materials as teenagers, and that they often find sexual images more distressing than arousing.

Diana E. H. Russell

 **YES**

Pornography as a Cause of Rape

Sociologist David Finkelhor has developed a very useful multicausal theory to explain the occurrence of child sexual abuse. According to Finkelhor's (1984) model, in order for child sexual abuse to occur, four conditions have to be met. First, someone has to *want* to abuse a child sexually. Second, this person's internal inhibitions against acting out this desire have to be undermined. Third, this person's social inhibitions against acting out this desire (e.g., fear of being caught and punished) have to be undermined. Fourth, the would-be perpetrator has to undermine or overcome his or her chosen victim's capacity to avoid or resist the sexual abuse.

According to my theory, these four conditions also have to be met in order for rape, battery, and other forms of sexual assault on adult women to occur (Russell, 1984). Although my theory can be applied to other forms of sexual abuse and violence against women besides rape, this formulation of it will focus on rape because most of the research relevant to my theory has been limited to this form of sexual assault.

In *Sexual Exploitation* (1984), I suggest many factors that may predispose a large number of males in the United States to want to rape or assault women sexually. Some examples discussed in that book are (a) biological factors, (b) childhood experiences of sexual abuse, (c) male sex-role socialization, (d) exposure to mass media that encourage rape, and (e) exposure to pornography. Here I will discuss only the role of pornography.

Although women have been known to rape both males and females, males are by far the predominant perpetrators of sexual assault as well as the biggest consumers of pornography. Hence, my theory will focus on male perpetrators.

. . . As previously noted, in order for rape to occur, a man must not only be predisposed to rape, but his internal and social inhibitions against acting out his rape desires must be undermined. My theory, in a nutshell, is that pornography (a) predisposes some males to want to rape women and intensifies the predisposition in other males already so predisposed; (b) undermines some males' internal inhibitions against acting out their desire to rape; and (c) undermines some males' social inhibitions against acting out their desire to rape.

The Meaning of "Cause"

Given the intense debate about whether or not pornography plays a causal role in rape, it is surprising that so few of those engaged in it ever state what they mean by "cause." ...

[P]ornography clearly does not cause rape, as it seems safe to assume that some pornography consumers do not rape women and that many rapes are unrelated to pornography. However, the concept of *multiple causation* (defined below) *is* applicable to the relationship between pornography and rape.

> With the conception of MULTIPLE CAUSATION, various possible causes may be seen for a given event, any one of which may be a sufficient but not necessary condition for the occurrence of the effect, or a necessary but not sufficient condition. ...

This section will provide the evidence for the four different ways in which pornography can induce this predisposition.

1. Predisposes by pairing of sexually arousing stimuli with portrayals of rape.   The laws of social learning (e.g., classical conditioning, instrumental conditioning, and social modeling), about which there is now considerable consensus among psychologists, apply to all the mass media, including pornography. As Donnerstein (1983) testified at the hearings in Minneapolis: "If you assume that your child can learn from Sesame Street how to count one, two, three, four, five, believe me, they can learn how to pick up a gun" (p. 11). Presumably, males can learn equally well how to rape, beat, sexually abuse, and degrade females.

A simple application of the laws of social learning suggests that viewers of pornography can develop arousal responses to depictions of rape, murder, child sexual abuse, or other assaultive behavior. Researcher S. Rachman of the Institute of Psychiatry, Maudsley Hospital, London, has demonstrated that male subjects can learn to become sexually aroused by seeing a picture of a woman's boot after repeatedly seeing women's boots in association with sexually arousing slides of nude females (Rachman & Hodgson, 1968). The laws of learning that operated in the acquisition of the boot fetish can also teach males who were not previously aroused by depictions of rape to become so. All it may take is the repeated association of rape with arousing portrayals of female nudity (or clothed females in provocative poses).

Even for males who are not sexually excited during movie portrayals of rape, masturbation following the movie reinforces the association between rape and sexual gratification. This constitutes what R. J. McGuire, J. M. Carlisle, and B. G. Young refer to as "masturbatory conditioning" (Cline, 1974, p. 210). The pleasurable experience of orgasm—an expected and planned-for activity in many pornography parlors—is an exceptionally potent reinforcer. The fact that pornography is widely used by males as ejaculation material is a major factor that differentiates it from other mass media, intensifying the lessons that male consumers learn from it.

2. Predisposes by generating rape fantasies.   Further evidence that exposure to pornography can create in males a predisposition to rape where none existed before is provided by an experiment conducted by Malamuth. Malamuth (1981a) classified 29 male students as sexually force-oriented or non-force-oriented on the basis of their responses to a questionnaire. These students were then randomly assigned to view either a rape version of a slide-audio presentation or a mutually consenting version. The account of rape and the pictures illustrating it were based on a story in a popular pornographic magazine, which Malamuth describes as follows:

> The man in this story finds an attractive woman on a deserted road. When he approaches her, she faints with fear. In the rape version, the man ties her up and forcibly undresses her. The accompanying narrative is as follows: "You take her into the car. Though this experience is new to you, there is a temptation too powerful to resist. When she awakens, you tell her she had better do exactly as you say or she'll be sorry. With terrified eyes she agrees. She is undressed and she is willing to succumb to whatever you want. You kiss her and she returns the kiss." Portrayal of the man and woman in sexual acts follows; intercourse is implied rather than explicit. (p. 38)

In the mutually consenting version of the story the victim was not tied up or threatened. Instead, on her awakening in the car, the man told her that she was safe and "that no one will do her any harm. She seems to like you and you begin to kiss." The rest of the story is identical to the rape version (Malamuth, 1981a, p. 38).

All subjects were then exposed to the same audio description of a rape read by a female. This rape involved threats with a knife, beatings, and physical restraint. The victim was portrayed as pleading, crying, screaming, and fighting against the rapist (Abel, Barlow, Blanchard, & Guild, 1977, p. 898). Malamuth (1981a) reports that measures of penile tumescence as well as self-reported arousal "indicated that relatively high levels of sexual arousal were generated by all the experimental stimuli" (p. 33).

After the 29 male students had been exposed to the rape audio tape, they were asked to try to reach as high a level of sexual arousal as possible by fantasizing about whatever they wanted but without any direct stimulation of the penis (Malamuth, 1981a, p. 40). Self-reported sexual arousal during the fantasy period indicated that those students who had been exposed to the rape version of the first slide-audio presentation created more violent sexual fantasies than those exposed to the mutually consenting version *irrespective of whether they had been [previously] classified as force-oriented or non-force oriented* (p. 33).

As the rape version of the slide-audio presentation is typical of what is seen in pornography, the results of this experiment suggest that similar pornographic depictions are likely to generate rape fantasies even in previously non-force-oriented male consumers. As Edna Einsiedel (1986) points out,

> Current evidence suggests a high correlation between deviant fantasies and deviant behaviors.... Some treatment methods are also predicated on the link between fantasies and behavior by attempting to alter fantasy patterns in order to change the deviant behaviors. (1986, p. 60)

Because so many people resist the idea that a desire to rape may develop as a result of viewing pornography, let us focus for a moment on behavior other than rape. There is abundant testimonial evidence that at least some males decide they would like to perform certain sex acts on women after seeing pornography portraying such sex acts. For example, one of the men who answered Shere Hite's (1981) question on pornography wrote: "It's great for me. *It gives me new ideas to try and see,* and it's always sexually exciting" (p. 780; emphasis added). Of course, there's nothing wrong with getting new ideas from pornography or anywhere else, nor with trying them out, as long as they are not actions that subordinate or violate others. Unfortunately, many of the behaviors modeled in pornography *do* subordinate and violate women, sometimes viciously.

The following statements about men imitating abusive sexual acts that they had seen in pornography were made by women testifying at the pornography hearings in Minneapolis, Minnesota, in 1983 (Russell, Part 1, 1993b). Ms. M testified that

> I agreed to act out in private a lot of the scenarios that my husband read to me. These depicted bondage and different sexual acts that I found very humiliating to do.... He read the pornography like a textbook, like a journal. When he finally convinced me to be bound, he read in the magazine how to tie the knots and bind me in a way that I couldn't escape. Most of the scenes where I had to dress up or go through different fantasies were the exact same scenes that he had read in the magazines.

Ms. O described a case in which a man

> brought pornographic magazines, books, and paraphernalia into the bedroom with him and told her that if she did not perform the sexual acts in the "dirty" books and magazines, he would beat her and kill her.

Ms. S testified about the experiences of a group of women prostitutes who, she said,

> were forced constantly to enact specific scenes that men had witnessed in pornography.... These men... would set up scenarios, usually with more than one woman, to copy scenes that they had seen portrayed in magazines and books.

For example, Ms. S quoted a woman in her group as saying,

> He held up a porn magazine with a picture of a beaten woman and said, "I want you to look like that. I want you to hurt." He then began beating me. When I did not cry fast enough, he lit a cigarette and held it right above my breast for a long time before he burned me.

Ms. S also described what three men did to a nude woman prostitute. They first tied her up while she was seated on a chair, then,

> They burned her with cigarettes and attached nipple clips to her breasts. They had many S and M magazines with them and showed her many pictures of women appearing to consent, enjoy, and encourage this abuse. She was held for twelve hours while she was continuously raped and beaten.

Ms. S also cited the following example of men imitating pornography:

> They [several johns] forced the women to act simultaneously with the movie. In the movie at this point, a group of men were urinating on a naked woman. All the men in the room were able to perform this task, so they all started urinating on the woman who was now naked.

When someone engages in a particularly unusual act previously encountered in pornography, it suggests that the decision to do so was inspired by the pornography. One woman, for example, testified to the *Attorney General's Commission on Pornography* (1986) about the pornography-related death of her son:

> My son, Troy Daniel Dunaway, was murdered on August 6, 1981, by the greed and avarice of the publishers of *Hustler* magazine. My son read the article "Orgasm of Death," set up the sexual experiment depicted therein, followed the explicit instructions of the article, and ended up dead. He would still be alive today were he not enticed and incited into this action by *Hustler* magazine's "How to Do" August 1981 article, an article which was found at his feet and which directly caused his death. (p. 797)...

3. Predisposes by sexualizing dominance and submission. The first two ways in which pornography can predispose some males to desire rape, or intensify this desire..., both relate to the viewing of *violent* pornography. However, both violent *and* nonviolent pornography sexualizes dominance and submission. Hence, nonviolent pornography can also predispose some males to want to rape women.

... Check and Guloien conducted an experiment in which they exposed 436 male Toronto residents and college students to one of the three types of sexual material [sexually violent pornography, nonviolent dehumanizing pornography, and erotica] over three viewing sessions, or to no sexual material. Subjects in the no-exposure condition (the control group) participated in only one session in which they viewed and evaluated a videotape that was devoid of sexual material.

These researchers investigated the impact of exposure to pornography and erotica on many variables, including the subjects' self-reported likelihood of raping and their self-reported sexually aggressive behavior. The latter behavior ranged from having coerced "a woman to engage in sexual intercourse by 'threatening to end the relationship otherwise,'" to actually holding a woman down and physically forcing her to have intercourse" (Check & Guloien, 1989, pp. 165–166). Significantly, in an earlier study by Check and his colleagues, convicted rapists had scored three times higher on sexually aggressive behavior than had a control group of violent non-sex offenders (p. 166).

Following are some of the significant findings that Check and Guloien (1989) reported:

- "More than twice as many men who had been exposed to sexually violent or to nonviolent dehumanizing pornography reported that there was at least some likelihood that they would rape, compared to the men in the no-exposure condition" (p. 177).

- "High-frequency consumers who had been exposed to the nonviolent, dehumanizing pornography subsequently reported a greater likelihood of raping, [and] were more sexually callous... than high-frequency pornography consumers in the no-exposure condition" (p. 176).
- "Exposure to the nonviolent, erotica materials did not have any demonstrated antisocial impact" (p. 178).

... [M]en's self-reported likelihood of raping is not the best measure of *desire* to rape because this variable combines desire with the self-reported probability of acting out that desire. Nevertheless, since rape is clearly an act of dominance that forces submission, as are other coerced sex acts, Check and Guloien's finding that exposure to pornography increases men's self-reported likelihood of rape does offer tentative support for my theoretical model's claim that pornography predisposes some males to desire rape or intensifies this desire by sexualizing dominance and submission. Furthermore, this effect is not confined to violent pornography. It also makes sense theoretically that the sexualizing of dominance and submission would include the eroticization of rape and/or other abusive sexual behavior for some males. . . .

Predisposes by creating an appetite for increasingly stronger material.   Dolf Zillmann and Jennings Bryant (1984) have studied the effects of what they refer to as "massive exposure" to pornography. (In fact, it was not particularly massive: 4 hours and 48 minutes per week over a period of 6 weeks. In later publications, Zillmann and Bryant use the term "prolonged exposure" instead of "massive" exposure.) These researchers, unlike Malamuth and Donnerstein, are interested in ascertaining the effects of nonviolent pornography and, in the study to be described, their sample was drawn from an adult nonstudent population.

Male subjects in the so-called *massive exposure* condition saw 36 nonviolent pornographic films, six per session per week; male subjects in the *intermediate* condition saw 18 such movies, three per session per week. Male subjects in the control group saw 36 nonpornographic movies. Various measures were taken after 1 week, 2 weeks, and 3 weeks of exposure. Information was also obtained about the kind of materials that the subjects were most interested in viewing.

Zillmann and Bryant (1984) report that as a result of massive exposure to pornography, "consumers graduate from common to less common forms" (p. 127), including pornography portraying "some degree of pseudoviolence or violence" (p. 154). These researchers suggest that this change may be "because familiar material becomes unexciting as a result of habituation" (p. 127).

According to Zillmann and Bryant's research, then, pornography can transform a male who was not previously interested in the more abusive types of pornography into one who *is* turned on by such material. This is consistent with Malamuth's findings . . . that males who did not previously find rape sexually arousing generate such fantasies after being exposed to a typical example of violent pornography.

The Role of Pornography in Undermining Some Males' *Internal* Inhibitions Against Acting Out Their Desire to Rape

... Evidence has [shown] that 25% to 30% of males admit that there is some likelihood that they would rape a woman if they could be assured that they would get away with it. It is reasonable to assume that a substantially higher percentage of males would *like* to rape a woman but would refrain from doing so because of their internal inhibitions against these coercive acts. Presumably, the strength of these males' motivation to rape as well as their internal inhibitions against raping range from very weak to very strong, and also fluctuate in the same individual over time.

[There are] seven ways in which pornography can undermine some males' internal inhibitions against acting out rape desires....

1. Objectifying women. Feminists have been emphasizing the role of objectification (treating females as sex objects) in the occurrence of rape for many years (e.g., Medea & Thompson, 1974; Russell, 1975). Males' tendency to objectify females makes it easier for them to rape girls and women. Check and Guloien (1989) note that other psychologists (e.g., Philip Zimbardo, H. C. Kelman) have observed that "dehumanization of victims is an important disinhibitor of cruelty toward others" (p. 161). The rapists quoted in the following passages demonstrate the link between objectification and rape behavior.

> It was difficult for me to admit that I was dealing with a human being when I was talking to a woman, because, if you read men's magazines, you hear about your stereo, your car, your chick. (Russell, 1975, pp. 249–250)

After this rapist had hit his victim several times in the face, she stopped resisting and begged him not to hurt her.

> When she said that, all of a sudden it came into my head, "My God, this is a human being!" I came to my senses and saw that I was hurting this person. (p. 249)

Another rapist said of his victim, "I wanted this beautiful fine *thing* and I got it" (Russell, 1975, p. 245; emphasis added).

Dehumanizing oppressed groups or enemy nations in times of war is an important mechanism for facilitating brutal behavior toward members of those groups. Ms. U, for example, testified that

> A society that sells books, movies, and video games like "Custer's Last Stand [Revenge]" on its street corners, gives white men permission to do what they did to me. Like they [her rapists] said, I'm scum. It is a game to track me down, rape and torture me. (Russell, 1993b)

The dehumanization of women that occurs in pornography is often not recognized because of its sexual guise and its pervasiveness. It is also important to note that the objectification of women is as common in nonviolent pornography as it is in violent pornography.

Doug McKenzie-Mohr and Mark Zanna (1990) conducted an experiment to test whether certain types of males would be more likely to objectify a woman sexually after viewing 15 minutes of nonviolent pornography. They selected 60 male students whom they classified into one of two categories: masculine sex-typed or gender schematic individuals who "encode all cross-sex interactions in sexual terms and all members of the opposite sex in terms of sexual attractiveness" (Bem, 1991, p. 361); and androgynous or gender aschematic males who do not encode cross-sex interactions and women in these ways (McKenzie-Mohr & Zanna, 1990, pp. 297, 299).

McKenzie-Mohr and Zanna (1990) found that after exposure to nonviolent pornography, the masculine sex-typed males "treated our female experimenter who was interacting with them in a professional setting, in a manner that was both cognitively and behaviorally sexist" (p. 305). In comparison with the androgynous males, for example, the masculine sex-typed males positioned themselves closer to the female experimenter and had "greater recall for information about her physical appearance" and less about the survey she was conducting (p. 305). The experimenter also rated these males as more sexually motivated based on her answers to questions such as, "How much did you feel he was looking at your body?" "How sexually motivated did you find the subject?" (p. 301).

This experiment confirmed McKenzie-Mohr and Zanna's hypothesis that exposure to nonviolent pornography causes masculine sex-typed males, in contrast to androgynous males, to view and treat a woman as a sex object.

2. Rape myths.   If males believe that women enjoy rape and find it sexually exciting, this belief is likely to undermine the inhibitions of some of those who would like to rape women. Sociologists Diana Scully (1985) and Martha Burt (1980) have reported that rapists are particularly apt to believe rape myths. Scully, for example, found that 65% of the rapists in her study believed that "women cause their own rape by the way they act and the clothes they wear"; and 69% agreed that "most men accused of rape are really innocent." However, as Scully points out, it is not possible to know if their beliefs preceded their behavior or constitute an attempt to rationalize it. Hence, findings from the experimental data are more telling for our purposes than these interviews with rapists.

Since the myth that women enjoy rape is widely held, the argument that consumers of pornography realize that such portrayals are false is totally unconvincing (Brownmiller, 1975; Burt, 1980; Russell, 1975). Indeed, several studies have shown that portrayals of women enjoying rape and other kinds of sexual violence can lead to increased acceptance of rape myths in both males and females. In an experiment conducted by Neil Malamuth and James Check (1985), for example, one group of college students saw a pornographic depiction in which a woman was portrayed as sexually aroused by sexual violence, and a second group was exposed to control materials. Subsequently, all subjects were shown a second rape portrayal. The students who had been exposed to the pornographic depiction of rape were significantly more likely than the students in the control group:

1. to perceive the second rape victim as suffering less trauma;
2. to believe that she actually enjoyed being raped; and
3. to believe that women in general enjoy rape and forced sexual acts. (Check & Malamuth, 1985, p. 419)

Other examples of the rape myths that male subjects in these studies are more apt to believe after viewing pornography are as follows:

- A woman who goes to the home or the apartment of a man on their first date implies that she is willing to have sex;
- Any healthy woman can successfully resist a rapist if she really wants to;
- Many women have an unconscious wish to be raped, and may then unconsciously set up a situation in which they are likely to be attacked;
- If a girl engages in necking or petting and she lets things get out of hand, it is her own fault if her partner forces sex on her. (Briere, Malamuth, & Check, 1985, p. 400)

In Maxwell and Check's 1992 study of 247 high school students (described above), they found very high rates of what they called "rape supportive beliefs," that is, acceptance of rape myths and violence against women. The boys who were the most frequent consumers of pornography, who reported learning a lot from it, or both, were more accepting of rape supportive beliefs than their peers who were less frequent consumers of pornography and/or who said they had not learned as much from it.

A quarter of girls and 57% of boys expressed the belief that it was at least "maybe okay" for a boy to hold a girl down and force her to have intercourse in one or more of the situations described by the researchers. In addition, only 21% of the boys and 57% of the girls believed that forced intercourse was "definitely not okay" in any of the situations. The situation in which forced intercourse was most accepted was when the girl had sexually excited her date. In this case, 43% of the boys and 16% of the girls stated that it was at least "maybe okay" for the boy to force intercourse on her (Maxwell & Check, 1992).

According to Donnerstein (1983), "After only 10 minutes of exposure to aggressive pornography, particularly material in which women are shown being aggressed against, you find male subjects are much more willing to accept these particular [rape] myths" (p. 6). These males are also more inclined to believe that 25% of the women they know would enjoy being raped (p. 6).

Acceptance of interpersonal violence.   Males' internal inhibitions against acting out their desire to rape can also be undermined if they consider male violence against women to be acceptable behavior. Studies have shown that when male subjects view portrayals of sexual violence that have positive consequences —as they often do in pornography—it increases their acceptance of violence against women. Examples of some of the beliefs used to measure acceptance of interpersonal violence include the following:

- Being roughed up is sexually stimulating to many women;
- Sometimes the only way a man can get a cold woman turned on is to use force;
- Many times a woman will pretend she doesn't want to have intercourse because she doesn't want to seem loose, but she's really hoping the man will force her. (Briere et al., 1985, p. 401)

Malamuth and Check (1981) conducted an experiment of particular interest because the movies shown were part of the regular campus film program. Students were randomly assigned to view either a feature-length film that portrayed violence against women as being justifiable and having positive consequences (*Swept Away* or *The Getaway*) or a film without sexual violence. Malamuth and Check found that exposure to the sexually violent movies increased the male subjects' acceptance of interpersonal violence against women, but not the female subjects' acceptance of this variable. These effects were measured several days after the films had been seen.

Malamuth (1986) suggests several processes by which sexual violence in the media "might lead to attitudes that are more accepting of violence against women" (p. 4). Some of these processes also probably facilitate the undermining of pornography consumers' internal inhibitions against acting out rape desires.

1. Labeling sexual violence more as a sexual rather than a violent act.
2. Adding to perceptions that sexual aggression is normative and culturally acceptable.
3. Changing attributions of responsibility to place more blame on the victim.
4. Elevating the positive value of sexual aggression by associating it with sexual pleasure and a sense of conquest.
5. Reducing negative emotional reactions to sexually aggressive acts. (Malamuth, 1986, p. 5)

Trivializing rape.   According to Donnerstein (1985), in most studies on the effects of pornography, "subjects have been exposed to only a few minutes of pornographic material" (p. 341). In contrast, Zillmann and Bryant (1984) examined the impact on male subjects of what they refer to as "massive exposure" to nonviolent pornography (4 hours and 48 minutes per week over a period of 6 weeks...). After 3 weeks the subjects were told that they were participating in an American Bar Association study that required them to evaluate a trial in which a man was prosecuted for the rape of a female hitchhiker. At the end of this mock trial, various measures were taken of the subjects' opinions about the trial and about rape in general. For example, they were asked to recommend the prison term they thought most fair.

Zillmann and Bryant (1984) found that the male subjects who had been exposed to the massive amounts of pornography considered rape a less serious crime than they had before they were exposed to it; they thought that prison sentences for rape should be shorter; and they perceived sexual aggression and abuse as causing less suffering for the victims, even in the case of an adult male having sexual intercourse with a 12-year-old girl (p. 132). The researchers concluded that "heavy exposure to common nonviolent pornography trivialized rape as a criminal offense" (p. 117).

The more trivialized rape is in the perceptions of males who would like to rape women or girls, the more likely they are to act out their desires. Since the research cited above shows that exposure to pornography increases males' trivialization of rape, it is reasonable to infer that this process contributes to undermining some male consumers' internal inhibitions against acting out their desires to rape.

5. *Sex callousness toward females.*   In the same experiment on massive exposure, Zillmann and Bryant (1984) found that "males' sex callousness toward women was significantly enhanced" by prolonged exposure to pornography (p. 117). These male subjects, for example, became increasingly accepting of statements such as, "A woman doesn't mean 'no' until she slaps you"; "A man should find them, fool them, fuck them, and forget them"; and "If they are old enough to bleed, they are old enough to butcher." However, judging by these statements, it is difficult to distinguish sex callousness from a general hostility toward women.

Check and Guloien (1989) divided their sample of 436 male subjects into high-frequency pornography consumers (once per month or more often) and low-frequency pornography consumers (less than once per month). They found that the high-frequency pornography consumers scored significantly higher than the low-frequency consumers on sex callousness toward women (pp. 175–176). In addition, after high-frequency consumers had been exposed to the nonviolent, dehumanizing pornography, they became significantly more sexually callous toward women than the high-frequency consumers in the control group who had not been exposed to any sexual materials. The low-frequency consumers, on the other hand, were unaffected by exposure to the nonviolent dehumanizing pornography (p. 176).

Rapists as a group score higher than nonrapists on sex callousness and hostility toward women. Since the research cited above shows that exposure to pornography increases males' sex calloused attitudes toward women, it is reasonable to infer that this process contributes to undermining some male consumers' internal inhibitions against acting out their desires to rape.

6. *Acceptance of male dominance in intimate relationships.*   A marked increase in males' acceptance of male dominance in intimate relationships was yet another result of the massive exposure to pornography (Zillmann & Bryant, 1984,

p. 121). The notion that women are, or ought to be, equal in intimate relationships was more likely to be abandoned by these male subjects (p. 122). Finally, their support of the women's liberation movement also declined sharply (p. 134).

These findings demonstrate that pornography increases the acceptability of sexism. As Van White (1984) points out, "by using pornography, by looking at other human beings as a lower form of life, they [the pornographers] are perpetuating the same kind of hatred that brings racism to society" (p. 186).

For example, Ms. O testified about the ex-husband of a woman friend and next-door neighbor: "When he looked at the magazines, he made hateful, obscene, violent remarks about women in general and about me. He told me that because I am female I am here to be used and abused by him, and that because he is a male he is the master and I am his slave" (Russell, 1993b, p. 51).

Rapists as a group reveal a higher acceptance of male dominance in intimate relationships than nonrapists. Since Zillman and Bryant's research shows that exposure to pornography increases males' acceptance of male dominance in intimate relationships, it is reasonable to infer that this process contributes to undermining some male consumers' internal inhibitions against acting out their desires to rape.

7. Desensitizing males to rape.   In an experiment specifically designed to study desensitization, Donnerstein and Linz showed 10 hours of R-rated or X-rated movies over a period of 5 days to male subjects (Donnerstein & Linz, 1985, p. 34A). Some students saw X-rated movies depicting sexual assault; others saw X-rated movies depicting only consenting sex; and a third group saw R-rated sexually violent movies....

Donnerstein and Linz (1985) described the impact of the R-rated movies on their subjects as follows:

> Initially, after the first day of viewing, the men rated themselves as significantly above the norm for depression, anxiety, and annoyance on a mood adjective checklist. After each subsequent day of viewing, these scores dropped until, on the fourth day of viewing, the males' levels of anxiety, depression, and annoyance were indistinguishable from baseline norms. (p. 34F)

By the fifth day, the subjects rated the movies as less graphic and less gory and estimated fewer violent or offensive scenes than after the first day of viewing. They also rated the films as significantly less debasing and degrading to women, more humorous, and more enjoyable, and reported a greater willingness to see this type of film again (Donnerstein & Linz, 1985, p. 34F). Their sexual arousal to this material, however, did not decrease over this 5-day period (Donnerstein, 1983, p. 10).

On the last day, the subjects went to a law school, where they saw a documentary reenactment of a real rape trial. A control group of subjects who had never seen the films also participated in this part of the experiment. Subjects who had seen the R-rated movies: (a) rated the rape victim as significantly more worthless, (b) rated her injury as significantly less severe, and (c) assigned greater blame to her for being raped than did the subjects who had not seen the films. In contrast, these effects were not observed for the X-rated nonviolent films. However, the results were much the same for the violent X-rated films, despite the fact that the R-rated material was "much more graphically violent" (Donnerstein, 1985, pp. 12–13).

Donnerstein and Linz (1985) point out that critics of media violence research believe "that only those who are *already* predisposed toward violence are influenced by exposure to media violence" (p. 34F). This view is contradicted by the fact that Donnerstein and Linz actually preselected their subjects to ensure that they were not psychotic, hostile, or anxious; that is, they were not predisposed toward violence prior to the research.

Donnerstein and Linz's research shows that exposure to woman-slashing films (soft-core snuff pornography) increases males' desensitization to extreme portrayals of violence against women. It seems reasonable to infer that desensitization contributes to undermining some male viewers' internal inhibitions against acting out their desires to rape.

In summary: I have presented only a small portion of the research evidence for seven different effects of pornography, all of which probably contribute to the undermining of some males' internal inhibitions against acting out their rape desires. This list is not intended to be comprehensive.

NO ↩

Nadine Strossen

Why Censoring Pornography Would Not Reduce Discrimination or Violence Against Women

The only thing pornography is known to cause directly is the solitary act of masturbation. As for corruption, the only immediate victim is English prose.

— Gore Vidal, writer

[I have] aimed to illuminate the legal flaws and misconceptions of MacKinnon-Dworkin-style antipornography laws, to show how such law undermines rather than advances important women's rights and human rights causes, and to paint a picture of the suppressed society that this type of law would produce when put in practice. Especially given recently renewed interest in MacDworkinite laws, they—and their chilling consequences—are my immediate concern. I have accordingly exposed the overwhelming problems that are inherent in all such laws. But, for the sake of argument, let's make the purely hypothetical assumption that we could fix those problems: let's pretend we could wave a magic wand that would miraculously make the laws do what they are supposed to without trampling on rights that are vital to everyone, and without stifling speech that serves women.

Even in this "Never-Never Land," where we could neutralize its negative side effects, would censorship "cure"—or at least reduce—the discrimination and violence against women allegedly caused by pornography? That is the assumption that underlies the feminist procensorship position, fueling the argument that we should trade in our free speech rights to promote women's safety and equality rights. In fact, though, the hoped-for benefits of censorship are as hypothetical as our exercise in wishing away the evils of censorship. I will show this by examining the largely unexamined assumption that censorship would reduce sexism and violence against women. This assumption rests, in turn, on three others:

- that exposure to sexist, violent imagery leads to sexist, violent behavior;

- that the effective suppression of pornography would significantly reduce exposure to sexist, violent imagery; and
- that censorship would effectively suppress pornography.

To justify censoring pornography on the rationale that it would reduce violence or discrimination against women, one would have to provide actual support for all three of these assumptions. Each presupposes the others. Yet the only one of them that has received substantial attention is the first—that exposure to sexist, violent imagery leads to sexist, violent behavior—and, as I show later . . . there is no credible evidence to bear it out. Even feminist advocates of censoring pornography have acknowledged that this asserted causal connection cannot be proven, and therefore fall back on the argument that it should be accepted "on faith." Catharine MacKinnon has well captured this fallback position through her defensive double negative . . . : "There is no evidence that pornography does no harm."

Of course, given the impossibility of proving that there is *no* evidence of *no* harm, we would have no free speech, and indeed no freedom of any kind, were such a burden of proof actually to be imposed on those seeking to enjoy their liberties. To appreciate this, just substitute for the word "pornography" in MacKinnon's pronouncement any other type of expression or any other human right. We would have to acknowledge that "there is no evidence" that television does no harm, or that editorials criticizing government officials do no harm, or that religious sermons do no harm, and so forth. There certainly is no evidence that feminist writing in general, or MacKinnon's in particular, does no harm.

In its 1992 *Butler* decision, accepting the antipornography feminist position, the Canadian Supreme Court also accepted this dangerous intuitive approach to limiting sexual expression, stating:

> It might be suggested that proof of actual harm should be required. . . . [I]t is sufficient . . . for Parliament to have a reasonable basis for concluding that harm will result and this requirement does not demand actual proof of harm.

Even if we were willing to follow the Canadian Supreme Court and pro-censorship feminists in believing, without evidence, that exposure to sexist, violent imagery does lead to sexist, violent behavior, we still should not accept their calls for censorship. Even if we assumed that *seeing* pornography leads to committing sexist and violent actions, it still would not follow that *censoring* pornography would reduce sexism or violence, due to flaws in the remaining two assumptions: we still would have to prove that pornography has a corner on the sexism and violence market, and that pornography is in fact entirely suppressible.

Even if pornography could be completely suppressed, the sexist, violent imagery that pervades the mainstream media would remain untouched. Therefore, if exposure to such materials caused violence and sexism, these problems would still remain with us. But no censorship regime could completely suppress pornography. It would continue to exist underground. In this respect, censorship would bring us the worst of both worlds. On one hand, as we have just seen from examining the Canadian situation, suppressive laws make it difficult to obtain a wide range of sexually oriented materials, so that most people would not have access to those materials. On the other hand, though, some such materials would continue to be produced and consumed no matter what. Every governmental effort to prohibit any allegedly harmful material has always caused this kind of "double trouble." Witness the infamous "Prohibition" of alcohol earlier in this century, for example.

Let's now examine in more detail the fallacies in each of the three assumptions underlying the feminist procensorship stance. And let's start with the single assumption that has been the focus of discussion—the alleged causal relationship between exposure to sexist, violent imagery and sexist, violent behavior.

Monkey See, Monkey Do?

Aside from the mere fear that sexual expression might cause discrimination or violence against women, advocates of censorship attempt to rely on four types of evidence concerning this alleged causal link: laboratory research data concerning the attitudinal effects of showing various types of sexually explicit materials to volunteer subjects, who are usually male college students; correlational data concerning availability of sexually oriented materials and anti-female discrimination or violence; anecdotal data consisting of accounts by sex offenders and their victims concerning any role that pornography may have played in the offenses; and studies of sex offenders, assessing factors that may have led to their crimes.

As even some leading procensorship feminists have acknowledged, along with the Canadian Supreme Court in *Butler,* none of these types of "evidence" prove that pornography harms women. Rather than retracing the previous works that have reviewed this evidence and reaffirmed its failure to substantiate the alleged causal connection, I will simply summarize their conclusions.

Laboratory Experiments

The most comprehensive recent review of the social science data is contained in Marcia Pally's 1994 book *Sex and Sensibility: Reflections on Forbidden Mirrors and the Will to Censor.* It exhaustively canvasses laboratory studies that have evaluated the impact of exposing experimental subjects to sexually explicit expression of many varieties, and concludes that no credible evidence substantiates a clear causal connection between any type of sexually explicit material and any sexist or violent behavior. The book also draws the same conclusion from its thorough review of field and correlation studies, as well as sociological surveys, in the U.S., Canada, Europe, and Asia.

Numerous academic and governmental surveys of the social science studies have similarly rejected the purported link between sexual expression and aggression. The National Research Council's Panel on Understanding and Preventing Violence concluded, in 1993: "Demonstrated empirical links between pornography and sex crimes in general are weak or absent."

Given the overwhelming consensus that laboratory studies do not demonstrate a causal tie between exposure to sexually explicit imagery and violent behavior, the Meese Pornography Commission Report's contrary conclusion, not surprisingly, has been the subject of heated criticism, including criticism by dissenting commissioners and by the very social scientists on whose research the report purportedly relied.

The many grounds on which the Commission's report was widely repudiated include that: six of the Commission's eleven members already were committed antipornography crusaders when they were appointed to it; the Commission was poorly funded and undertook no research; its hearings were slanted toward preconceived antipornography conclusions in terms of the witnesses invited to testify and the questions they were asked; and, in assessing the alleged harmful effects of pornography, the Commission's report relied essentially upon morality, expressly noting at several points that its conclusions were based on "common sense," "personal insight," and "intuition."

Two of the Meese Commission's harshest critics were, interestingly, two female members of that very Commission, Judith Becker and Ellen Levine. Becker is a psychiatrist and psychologist whose entire extensive career has been devoted to studying sexual violence and abuse, from both research and clinical perspectives. Levine is a journalist who has focused on women's issues, and who edits a popular women's magazine. In their formal dissent from the Commission's report, they concluded:

> [T]he social science research has not been designed to evaluate the relationship between exposure to pornography and the commission of sexual crimes; therefore efforts to tease the current data into proof of a casual [sic] link between these acts simply cannot be accepted.

Three of the foremost researchers concerned with the alleged causal relationship between sexually explicit materials and sexual violence, Edward Donnerstein, Daniel Linz, and Steven Penrod, also have sharply disputed the Meese Commission's findings about a purported causal relationship.

Since the feminist censorship proposals aim at sexually explicit material that allegedly is "degrading" to women, it is especially noteworthy that research data show no link between exposure to "degrading" sexually explicit material and sexual aggression.

Even two research literature surveys that were conducted for the Meese Commission, one by University of Calgary professor Edna Einseidel and the other by then–Surgeon General C. Everett Koop, also failed to find any link between "degrading" pornography and sex crimes or aggression. Surgeon General Koop's survey concluded that only two reliable generalizations could be made about the impact of exposure to "degrading" sexual material on its viewers: it caused them to think that a variety of sexual practices were more common than they had previously believed, and it caused them to more accurately estimate the prevalence of varied sexual practices.

Experiments also fail to establish any link between women's exposure to such materials and their development of negative self-images. Carol Krafka found that, in comparison with other women, women who were exposed to sexually "degrading" materials did not engage in more sex-role stereotyping; nor did they experience lower self-esteem, have less satisfaction with their body image, accept more anti-woman myths about rape, or show greater acceptance of violence against women. Similar conclusions have been reached by Donnerstein, Linz, and Penrod.

Correlational Data

Both the Meese Commission and procensorship feminists have attempted to rely on studies that allegedly show a correlation between the availability of sexually explicit materials and sexual offense rates. Of course, though, a positive correlation between two phenomena does not prove that one causes the other. Accordingly, even if the studies did consistently show a positive correlation between the prevalence of sexual materials and sexual offenses—which they do not—they still would not establish that exposure to the materials *caused* the rise in offenses. The same correlation could also reflect the opposite causal chain— if, for example, rapists relived their violent acts by purchasing sexually violent magazines or videotapes.

Any correlation between the availability of sexual materials and the rate of sex offenses could also reflect an independent factor that causes increases in both. Cynthia Gentry's correlational studies have identified just such an independent variable in geographical areas that have high rates of both the circulation of sexually explicit magazines and sexual violence: namely, a high population of men between the ages of eighteen and thirty-four. Similarly, Larry Baron and Murray Straus have noted that areas where both sexual materials and sexual aggression are prevalent are characterized by a "hypermasculated or macho culture pattern," which may well be the underlying causal agent. Accordingly, Joseph Scott and Loretta Schwalm found that communities with higher rape rates experienced stronger sales not only of porn magazines, but also of *all* male-oriented magazines, including *Field and Stream.*

Even more damning to the attempt to rest the "porn-causes-rape-or-discrimination" theory on alleged correlations is that there simply are no consistent correlations. While the asserted correlation would not be *sufficient* to prove the claimed causal connection, it is *necessary* to prove that connection. Therefore, the existence of the alleged causal relationship is conclusively refuted by the fact that levels of violence and discrimination against women are often *inversely* related to the availability of sexually explicit materials, including violent sexually explicit materials. This inverse relationship appears in various kinds of comparisons: between different states within the United States; between different countries; and between different periods within the same country.

Within the United States, the Baron and Straus research has shown no consistent pattern between the availability of sexual materials and the number of rapes from state to state. Utah is the lowest-ranking state in the availability of sexual materials but twenty-fifth in the number of rapes, whereas New Hampshire ranks ninth highest in the availability of sexual materials but only forty-fourth in the number of rapes.

The lack of a consistent correlation between pornography consumption and violence against women is underscored by one claim of the procensorship feminists themselves: they maintain that the availability and consumption of pornography, including violent pornography, have been increasing throughout the United States. At the same time, though, the rates of sex crimes have been decreasing or remaining steady. The Bureau of Justice Statistics reports that between 1973 and 1987, the national rape rate remained steady and the attempted rape rate decreased. Since these data were gathered from household surveys rather than from police records, they are considered to be the most accurate measures of the incidence of crimes. These data also cover the period during which feminists helped to create a social, political, and legal climate that should have encouraged higher percentages of rape victims to report their assaults. Thus, the fact that rapes reported to the Bureau of Justice Statistics have not increased provokes serious questions about the procensorship feminists' theories of pornography-induced harm. Similar questions are raised by data showing a decrease in wife battery between 1975 and 1985, again despite changes that should have encouraged the increased reporting of this chronically underreported crime.

Noting that "[t]he mass-market pornography... industr[y] took off after World War II," Marcia Pally has commented:

> In the decades since the 1950s, with the marketing of sexual material..., the country has seen the greatest advances in sensitivity to violence against women and children. Before the... mass publication of sexual images, no rape or incest hot lines and battered women's shelters existed; date and marital rape were not yet phrases in the language. Should one conclude that the presence of pornography... has inspired public outrage at sexual crimes?

Pally's rhetorical question underscores the illogicality of presuming that just because two phenomena happen to coexist, they therefore are causally linked. I have already shown that any correlation that might exist between the increased availability of pornography and *increased* misogynistic discrimination or violence could well be explained by other factors. The same is true for any correlation that might exist between the increased availability of pornography and *decreased* misogynistic discrimination or violence.

In a comparative state-by-state analysis, Larry Baron and Murray Straus have found a positive correlation between the circulation of pornographic magazines and the state's "index of gender equality," a composite of twenty-four indicators of economic, political, and legal equality. As the researchers have observed, these findings may suggest that both sexually explicit material and gender equality flourish in tolerant climates with fewer restrictions on speech.

The absence of any consistent correlation between the availability of sexual materials and sexual violence is also clear in international comparisons. On the one hand, violence and discrimination against women are common in countries where sexually oriented material is almost completely unavailable, including Saudi Arabia, Iran, and China (where the sale and distribution of erotica is now a capital offense). On the other hand, violence against women is uncommon in countries where such material is readily available, including Denmark, Germany, and Japan.

Furthermore, patterns in other countries over time show no correlation between the increased availability of sexually explicit materials and increased violence against women. The 1991 analysis by University of Copenhagen professor Berl Kutchinsky revealed that, while nonsexual violent crime had increased up to 300 percent in Denmark, Sweden, and West Germany from 1964 to 1984, all three countries' rape rates either declined or remained constant during this same period, despite their lifting of restrictions on sexual materials. Kutchinsky's studies further show that sex crimes against girls dropped from 30 per 100,000 to 5 per 100,000 between 1965, when Denmark liberalized its obscenity laws, and 1982.

In the decade 1964–1974, there was a much greater increase in rape rates in Singapore, which tightly restricts sexually oriented expression, than in Sweden, which had liberalized its obscenity laws during that period. In Japan, where sexually explicit materials are easily accessible and stress themes of bondage, rape, and violence, rape rates decreased 45 percent during the same decade. Moreover, Japan reports a rape rate of 2.4 per 100,000 people, compared with 34.5 in the United States, although violent erotica is more prevalent in Japan.

Anecdotes and Suspicions

As Seventh Circuit Court of Appeals Judge Richard Posner observed about MacKinnon's book *Only Words*:

> MacKinnon's treatment of the central issue of pornography as she herself poses it—the harm that pornography does to women—is shockingly casual. Much of her evidence is anecdotal, and in a nation of 260 million people, anecdotes are a weak form of evidence.

Many procensorship advocates attempt to rest their case on self-serving "porn-made-me-do-it" claims by sexual offenders, as well as on statements by victims or police officers that sexual offenders had sexually explicit materials in their possession at the time they committed their crimes. .

The logical fallacy of relying on anecdotes to establish a general causal connection between exposure to sexual materials and violence against women was aptly noted by journalist Ellen Willis: "Anti-porn activists cite cases of sexual killers who were also users of pornography, but this is no more logical than arguing that marriage causes rape because some rapists are married."

Even assuming that sexual materials really were the triggering factors behind some specific crimes, that could not justify restrictions on such materials. As former Supreme Court justice William O. Douglas wrote: "The First Amendment demands more than a horrible example or two of the perpetrator of a crime of sexual violence, in whose pocket is found a pornographic book, before it allows the Nation to be saddled with a regime of censorship." If we attempted to ban all words or images that had ever been blamed for inspiring or instigating particular crimes by some aberrant or antisocial individual, we would end up with little left to read or view. Throughout history and around the world, criminals have regularly blamed their conduct on a sweeping array of words and images in books, movies, and television.

As noted by the 1979 report of the British Committee on Obscenity and Film Censorship, "For those who are susceptible to them, the stimuli to aggressive behavior are all around us." To illustrate the innumerable crimes that have been incited by words or images, the Committee cited a young man who attempted to kill his parents with a meat cleaver after watching a dramatized version of Dostoyevsky's *The Brothers Karamazov*, and a Jamaican man of African descent in London who raped a white woman, saying that the televised showing of Alex Haley's *Roots* had "inspired" him to treat her as white men had treated black women. Additional examples cited by Ohio State University law professor Earl Finbar Murphy underscore that word blaming and image blaming extend to many religious works, too:

> Heinrich Pommerenke, who was a rapist, abuser, and mass slayer of women in Germany, was prompted to his series of ghastly deeds by Cecil B. De-Mille's *The Ten Commandments*. During the scene of the Jewish women dancing about the Golden Calf, all the doubts of his life became clear: Women were the source of the world's troubles and it was his mission to both punish them for this and to execute them. Leaving the theater, he slew the first victim in a park nearby. John George Haigh, the British vampire who sucked his victims' blood through soda straws and dissolved their drained bodies in acid baths, first had his murder-inciting dreams and vampire longings from watching the "voluptuous" procedure of—an Anglican High Church Service.

Were we to ban words or images on the grounds that they had incited some susceptible individuals to commit crimes, the Bible would be in great jeopardy. No other work has more often been blamed for more heinous crimes by the perpetrators of such crimes. The Bible has been named as the instigating or justifying factor for many individual and mass crimes, ranging from the religious wars, inquisitions, witch burnings, and pogroms of earlier eras to systematic child abuse and ritual murders today.

Marcia Pally's *Sex and Sensibility* contains a lengthy litany of some of the multitudinous, horrific bad acts that have been blamed on the "Good Book." She also cites some of the many passages depicting the "graphic, sexually explicit subordination of women" that would allow the entire Bible to be banned under the procensorship feminists' antipornography law. Pally writes:

> [T]he Bible has unbeatable worldwide sales and includes detailed justification of child abuse, wife battery, rape, and the daily humiliation of women. Short stories running through the text serve as models for sexual assault and the mauling of children. The entire set of books is available to children, who are encouraged or required to read it. It is printed and distributed by some of the world's most powerful organizations....
>
> With refreshing frankness, the Bible tells men it is their rightful place to rule women.... [It] specifies exactly how many shekels less than men women are worth. Genesis 19:1–8 tells one of many tales about fathers setting up their daughters to be gang raped. Even more prevalent are... glamorized war stories in which the fruits of victory are the local girls....

[P]erhaps most gruesome is the snuff story about the guy who set his maid up to be gang raped and, after her death from the assault, cut her body up into little pieces.... Unlike movies and television programs, these tales are generally taken to be true, not simulated, accounts.

In 1992, Gene Kasmar petitioned the Brooklyn Center, Minnesota, school board to ban the Bible from school classrooms and libraries on the ground that it is lewd, indecent, obscene, offensive, violent, and dangerous to women and children. He specifically complained about biblical references to concubines, explicit sex, child abuse, incest, nakedness, and mistreatment of women —all subjects, significantly, that would trigger the feminist-style antipornography laws.

In response, the chief counsel of Pat Robertson's American Center for Law and Justice in Virginia, Jay Sekulow, flew to Minnesota and argued that the Bible "is worthy of study for its literary and historic qualities." While the Brooklyn Center School Board apparently agreed with this assessment, voting unanimously to reject Kasmar's petition, it must be recalled that Sekulow's argument would be unavailing under Dworkin-MacKinnon-type antipornography laws. Under the MacDworkin model law, any work could be banned on the basis of even one isolated passage that meets the definition of pornography, and the work could not be saved by any serious literary, historic, or other value it might offer. Consequently, the feminist antipornography law could be used by Kasmar and others to ban the Bible not only from public schools, but also from public libraries, bookstores, and all other venues.

The countless expressive works that have been blamed for crimes include many that convey profeminist messages. Therefore, an anecdotal, image-blaming rationale for censorship would condemn many feminist works. For example, the television movie *The Burning Bed*, which told the true story of a battered wife who set fire to her sleeping husband, was blamed for some "copycat" crimes, as well as for some acts of violence by men against women. The argument that such incidents would justify suppression would mark the end of any films or other works depicting—and deploring—the real violence that plagues the lives of too many actual women.

Under a censorship regime that permits anecdotal, book-blaming "evidence," all other feminist materials would be equally endangered, not "just" works that depict the violence that has been inflicted on women. That is because, as feminist writings themselves have observed, some sexual assaults are committed by men who feel threatened by the women's movement. Should feminist works therefore be banned on the theory that they might well motivate a man to act out his misogynistic aggression?

Studies of Sex Offenders

The scientists who have investigated the impact of exposure to sexual materials in real life have not found that either sexual materials or attitudes toward women play any significant role in prompting actual violence. In general, these studies show that sex offenders had less exposure to sexually explicit materials than most men, that they first saw such materials at a later age than nonoffenders, that they were overwhelmingly more likely to have been punished for looking at them as teenagers, and that they often find sexual images more distressing than arousing.

While no evidence substantiates that viewing pornography leads to violence and discrimination against women, some evidence indicates that, if anything, there may well be an inverse causal relationship between exposure to sexually explicit materials and misogynistic violence or discrimination. One of the leading researchers in this area, Edward Donnerstein of the University of California at Santa Barbara, has written: "A good amount of research strongly supports the position that exposure to erotica can reduce aggressive responses in people who are predisposed to aggress." Similarly, John Money, of Johns Hopkins Medical School, a leading expert on sexual violence, has noted that most people with criminal sexualities were raised with strict, antisexual, repressive attitudes. He predicts that the "current repressive attitudes toward sex will breed an ever-widening epidemic of aberrant sexual behavior."

In one 1989 experiment, males who had been exposed to pornography were more willing to come to the aid of a female subject who appeared to be hurt than were men who had been exposed to other stimuli. Laboratory studies further indicate that there may well be an inverse causal relationship between exposure to violent sexually explicit material and sexual arousal. For example, in 1991, Howard Barbaree and William Marshall, of Queen's College in Ontario, found:

> For most men, hearing a description of an encounter where the man is forcing the woman to have sex, and the woman is in distress or pain, dampens the arousal by about 50 percent compared to arousal levels using a scene of consenting lovemaking.... Ordinarily violence inhibits sexual arousal in men. A blood flow loss of 50 percent means a man would not be able to penetrate a woman.

The foregoing research findings are certainly more consistent with what feminist scholars have been writing about rape than is the procensorship feminists' pornocentric analysis: namely, rape is not a crime about sex, but rather, about violence.

See No Pornography, See No Sexist and Violent Imagery?

Pornography constitutes only a small subset of the sexist or violent imagery that pervades our culture and media. New York Law School professor Carlin Meyer recently conducted a comprehensive survey of the views of women's sexuality, status, and gender roles that are purveyed in nonpornographic media:

> Today, mainstream television, film, advertising, music, art, and popular (including religious) literature are the primary propagators of Western views of sexuality and sex roles. Not only do we read, see and experience their language and imagery more often and at earlier ages than we do most explicit sexual representation, but precisely because mainstream imagery is ordinary

and everyday, it more powerfully convinces us that it depicts the world as it is or ought to be.

Other cultural and media analysts have likewise concluded that more-damaging sexist imagery is more broadly purveyed through mainstream, nonsexual representations. Thelma McCormack, director of York University's Feminist Studies Centre, has concluded that "the enemy of women's equality is our mainstream culture with its images of women as family-centered," rather than imagery of women as sexual. According to McCormack:

> Surveys and public opinion studies confirm the connection between gender-role traditionalism and an acceptance or belief in the normality of a stratified social system. The more traditional a person's views are about women, the more likely he or she is to accept inequality as inevitable, functional, natural, desirable and immutable. In short, if any image of woman can be said to influence our thinking about gender equality, it is the domestic woman not the Dionysian one.

Social science researchers have found that acceptance of the rape myth and other misogynistic attitudes concerning women and violence are just as likely to result from exposure to many types of mass media—from soap operas to popular commercial films—as from even intense exposure to violent, misogynistic sexually explicit materials. Accordingly, if we really wanted to purge all sexist, violent representations from our culture, we would have to cast the net far beyond pornography, notwithstanding how comprehensive and elastic that category is. Would even procensorship feminists want to deal such a deathblow to First Amendment freedoms?

Censor Pornography, See No Pornography?

Procensorship feminists themselves have acknowledged that censorship would probably just drive pornography underground. Indeed, as recently as 1987, Catharine MacKinnon recognized that "pornography cannot be reformed or suppressed or banned."

The assumption that censorship would substantially reduce the availability or impact of pornography also overlooks evidence that censorship makes some viewers more desirous of pornography and more receptive to its imagery. This "forbidden fruits" effect has been corroborated by historical experience and social science research. All recent studies of the suppression of sexual expression, including Walter Kendrick's 1987 book *The Secret Museum: Pornography in Modern Culture* and Edward de Grazia's 1992 book *Girls Lean Back Everywhere: The Law of Obscenity and the Assault on Genius*, demonstrate that any censorship effort simply increases the attention that a targeted work receives. Social scientific studies that were included in the report of the 1970 President's Commission on Obscenity and Pornography suggested that censorship of sexually explicit materials may increase their desirability and impact, and also that a viewer's awareness that sexually oriented parts of a film have been censored may lead to frustration and subsequent aggressive behavior.

The foregoing data about the impact of censoring pornography are consistent with broader research findings: the evidence suggests that censorship of *any* material increases an audience's desire to obtain the material and disposes the audience to be more receptive to it. Critical viewing skills, and the ability to regard media images skeptically and analytically, atrophy under a censorial regime. A public that learns to question everything it sees or hears is better equipped to reject culturally propagated values than is one that assumes the media have been purged of all "incorrect" perspectives.

Even assuming for the sake of argument that there were a causal link between pornography and anti-female discrimination and violence, the insignificant contribution that censorship might make to reducing them would not outweigh the substantial damage that censorship would do to feminist goals. From the lack of actual evidence to substantiate the alleged causal link, the conclusion follows even more inescapably: *Censoring pornography would do women more harm than good.*

CHALLENGE QUESTIONS

Is Pornography Harmful?

1. Readers of Russell's vehement criticism of pornography might conclude that pornography should be banned. Assuming that this position is correct, how would you determine what constitutes pornography?
2. Although many people would concur with Strossen's stand against censorship, most would recognize the importance of prohibiting certain images, such as those involving sexual acts with children. Explain why such images are considered unacceptable in our society.
3. Since the advent of the Internet, there has been increasing concern about the ease with which children can access pornography. Why is the viewing of pornography by children or adolescents worrisome?
4. Imagine that you are a researcher studying the relationship between sexual aggression and exposure to violent pornography. What ethical challenges would you face in conducting this kind of research?
5. Imagine that you are a clinician treating a couple in psychotherapy who are seeking help because the man insists that his wife participate in the sexual activities he has watched in sexually explicit videos. How would you go about treating this couple?

Suggested Readings

Carse, A. L. (1995). Pornography: An uncivil liberty? *Hypatia,* 10(1), 155–182.

Concepcion, C. M. (1999). On pornography, representation and sexual agency. *Hypatia,* 14(1), 97–100.

Donnerstein, E., & Malamuth, N. (1997). Pornography: Its consequences on the observer. In L. B. Schlesinger, & E. Revitch (Eds.), *Sexual dynamics of anti-social behavior.* (pp. 30–49). Springfield, IL: Charles C. Thomas Publisher.

Stock, W. E. (1997). Sex as commodity: Men and the sex industry. In R. F. Levant, & G. R. Brooks (Eds.), *Men and sex: New psychological perspectives.* (pp. 100–132). New York, NY: John Wiley & Sons, Inc.

Strossen, N. (1995). The perils of pornophobia. *The Humanist,* 55(3), 7–10.

ISSUE 14

Is the *Bell Curve* Theory Valid?

YES: Jeffery P. Braden, from "For Whom 'The Bell' Tolls: Why *The Bell Curve* Is Important for School Psychologists," *School Psychology Review* (vol. 24, no. 1, 1995)

NO: Robert J. Sternberg, from "The School Bell and *The Bell Curve*: Why They Don't Mix," *NASSP Bulletin* (February 1996)

ISSUE SUMMARY

YES: Educational psychology professor Jeffery P. Braden supports the *Bell Curve* theory, stating that educators can use its conclusions and recommendations to improve educational opportunities for students.

NO: Psychology professor Robert J. Sternberg dismisses the *Bell Curve* theory as being "bad science" that is theoretically and methodologically flawed and that plays into the societal tendency to blame social problems on things over which we have no control.

The field of abnormal psychology involves the study of various human characteristics that fall along a continuum from normal to abnormal. For some characteristics, such as IQ, the concept of what is "abnormal" is defined in statistical terms. In the case of IQ, an artificially determined mean score of 100 represents average intelligence. People whose IQ falls significantly below 100 are regarded as having certain cognitive deficits in areas such as information, concentration, abstract reasoning, and processing speed. Embedded in many discussions about IQ is the question about the extent to which IQ is determined by genetic makeup versus environmental influences. This thorny question engenders heated debate when the issue of race is brought into the discussion.

When Richard J. Herrnstein and Charles Murray published *The Bell Curve: Intelligence and Class Structure in American Life* (Free Press, 1994), they set off raging arguments by proposing that intelligence is largely, though not completely, an inherited trait that predicts a person's capacity for social success or failure. Their most controversial assertion was that there is an innate difference in intelligence between people of different races. Herrnstein and Murray contended that on the Wechsler scales of intelligence, the IQ of blacks is a standard deviation below that of whites (15 points), and they attributed most of this gap to differences in genetic endowment, which results in subsequent social maladjustment. Critics of Herrnstein and Murray's viewpoint expressed outrage, asserting that IQ is environmentally determined and that most IQ tests are culturally biased.

Recognizing the intense controversy emanating from the publication of *The Bell Curve,* Jeffery P. Braden urged his colleagues in the field of education, particularly school psychologists, to read this book and to use the conclusions and recommendations of Herrnstein and Murray in their efforts to improve educational opportunities for all students, especially those from disadvantaged backgrounds. In the following selection, Braden concurs with the authors' conclusion that the black-white IQ gap is significantly influenced by genetics. Building upon this notion, he challenges educators to make a vigorous commitment to social justice by developing educational initiatives that do more to enhance the potential of all students.

In the second selection, Robert J. Sternberg unabashedly criticizes *The Bell Curve,* which he summarily dismisses as "bad science." He points to theoretical and methodological flaws inherent in the work of Herrnstein and Murray, and he asserts that their conclusions about the nature of intelligence are erroneous. On the issue of race, Sternberg contends that research has failed to support the notion that intelligence is primarily determined by genetic influences. He blasts *The Bell Curve* for playing into the societal tendency to blame the ills of society in general, and of schools in particular, on things over which we have no control.

POINT

- *The Bell Curve* raises some very important points and recommendations about IQ and education that educators, particularly school psychologists, should carefully consider.

- Intelligence tests provide information about tendencies in people's behavior that can be of great value in predicting the behavior of groups.

- People tend to reject the genetics hypothesis because they believe that it supports racism and discourages the education and integration of blacks.

- America has a rich and varied history that consistently shows that test bias has a negligible influence on black-white differences.

- Programs to enhance general cognitive abilities are not successful in producing meaningful long-term gains.

COUNTERPOINT

- *The Bell Curve* is bad science and, hence, bad policy, and it leads educators to blame the ills of society, and of schools in particular, on things over which we have no control.

- When people are tested in real-world contexts, as opposed to paper-and-pencil classroom contexts, they often show skills that IQ tests do not show.

- Those who do not test well either lose access to opportunities or are effectively blocked from access to those opportunities.

- There is no explanation for why there are racial differences in IQ test scores; moreover, it is important to remember that IQ is not tantamount to intelligence.

- Arguments about the degree to which intelligence is genetic should not get in the way of attempts to help students maximize their intellectual potentials.

Jeffery P. Braden

 **YES**

For Whom "The Bell" Tolls

T *he Bell Curve: Intelligence and Class Structure in American Life* (Herrnstein & Murray, 1994) precipitated an incredible media storm during October 1994. Editorials in all major papers, cover stories in *Newsweek, The New Republic, The New York Times Book Review,* and a barrage of "prime time" interviews with the book's surviving author (Charles Murray) called public attention to issues long discussed in school psychology. Editors, media pundits, and reporters asserted that intelligence tests are biased and argued childhood socio-economic status (SES), ethnicity, or gender are more important for social attainment than IQ. The critics claimed that intelligence is irrelevant to occupational success and that individual differences are caused by environmental, not biogenetic, influences. These assertions, although popular within the editorial media, have been refuted by consensus positions among scholars in genetics and psychology (Snyderman & Rothman, 1987) and school psychology.

Many school psychologists, however, would prefer not to be reminded of these facts. Most of us know these things to be true, but we wish they weren't, so we'd rather not remember. Some of us were never exposed to knowledge about individual differences, because our professors preferred to stress other, more educationally acceptable, knowledge. Those of us who study intelligence often devalue our knowledge of its causes and effects and remain silent in the face of critics who offer—or demand—a more appealing message. Many school psychologists even question the motives of Herrnstein and Murray—rather than read the book. This is a huge mistake and an injustice to the teachers, administrators, and parents who look to us as local experts in understanding tests and intelligence.

Because psychologists have an obligation to know, what follows is a frame of reference for those who want to read, understand, and perhaps even explain the book to others. This frame of reference will address four issues: (a) Is IQ really helpful?, (b) Could the black–white IQ gap be genetic?, (c) Could it help to know that the gap is genetic?, and (d) What should educators do about all this?

Is IQ Really Helpful?

Recently, some school psychologists have turned away from intelligence tests and embraced behavioral methods. Ironically, the move to embrace behavioral approaches in school psychology comes as behaviorism is declining in popularity relative to cognitive approaches in general psychology (Robins & Craik, 1994; Robins, Craik, & Gosling, 1994). However, behaviorism offers a powerful idiographic perspective (i.e., focusing on a specific situation and child) for addressing individual cases. Nomothetic perspectives (e.g., knowing how groups with a certain IQ do "in general") are less helpful for planning individualized interventions. Critics of intelligence tests typically adopt an idiographic orientation (i.e., What should be done with this specific child/situation?) and then condemn intelligence tests as irrelevant—or worse—for failing to provide an answer. Most people have firsthand knowledge of a case where a test failed to predict an accurate outcome (e.g., the low-IQ child who earned distinction; the high-IQ failure). Thus is it not reasonable to reject IQ tests as useless?

The short answer is "No." Intelligence tests provide information about *tendencies* in people's behavior. Although this information may be of limited value in a specific case, it can be of great value in predicting the behavior of large groups. For example, latitude provides little specific guidance to a farmer on how to maximize crop yield on a particular plot of land (i.e., it is not especially useful from an idiographic perspective). However, latitude has a substantial impact on crop yield. To ignore the impact of latitude on national agricultural policy would be foolish (despite the fact it tells individual farmers little about how to respond to a crop infestation). Similarly, ignoring the impact of intelligence on national educational and social policy is foolish (despite the fact IQ tells individual teachers little about how to solve a particular problem in a specific classroom). *The Bell Curve* is essentially a compilation of data supporting the use of IQ as a predictor—*on the average*—of the degree to which children succeed or fail as adults in society. Herrnstein and Murray acknowledge that IQ cannot predict whether a specific child will obtain high SES as an adult, go on welfare, have a baby out of wedlock, or be incarcerated. But they show IQ is better than the child's race, gender, SES, and years of schooling for predicting these (and other) behaviors across many children. Although critics may trivialize their argument by creating a straw person (e.g., If IQ can't tell us what to do for an individual, it is useless), school psychologists should know better. Both idiographic and nomothetic perspectives are necessary, and neither is sufficient. Herrnstein and Murray dispel the myth that IQ is unrelated to important social outcomes and thus remind us to include a nomothetic perspective in planning and delivering services to children.

Could the Black–White IQ Gap Be Genetic?

If Herrnstein and Murray had stopped there, *The Bell Curve* would probably be just one more volume driven by library subscriptions. Instead, they propose that the difference in IQ distributions between African-Americans (i.e., blacks) and Euro-Americans (i.e., whites) is (a) real; that is, not due to test bias, (b) intractable; that is, it is not easily nor reliably modifiable, and (c) genetic; that is, it is not due to environmental differences between blacks and whites. The first two assumptions may surprise the media and the public at large, but they should come as no surprise to school psychologists. We have a rich and varied literature that consistently shows test bias has a negligible influence on black-white differences (and to the degree tests are biased, they favor low-scoring minority groups; Berk, 1982; Jensen, 1980; Reynolds & Brown, 1984). Similarly, we know that programs to enhance general cognitive abilities are not successful in producing meaningful, long-term gains (e.g., Spitz, 1986). But attributing the black-white IQ gap to genetics is far more contentious and consequently demands additional discussion.

Although some individuals and isolated studies might dispute that individual differences in intelligence *within* whites and blacks are influenced by genetics, the evidence estimates heritability *within* each group to be between .40 and .80 (i.e., 40–80% of the variability in IQ is due to genetic differences between people; e.g., Bouchard, Lykken, McGue, Segal, & Tellegen, 1990). These estimates are widely shared by experts in psychology and behavior genetics (Snyderman & Rothman, 1987).

However, *within group* heritability is completely unrelated to *between group* heritability. For example, two handfuls of seed scooped from the same bin will have different yields if one handful is raised with water, sun, and nutrients, and the other handful receives less of these essentials. Because plants within each plot share the same environment, genetics causes the differences in plant yields *within* plots. In contrast, environment causes the differences in yield *between* plots.

Following this argument, if blacks and whites had the same genetic endowment, but were raised in radically different environments, they would show high heritability *within groups*, but the difference *between groups* would be solely due to environment. Because racial groups confound genetic and environmental differences, it is not possible to know whether *between group* differences are caused by genetics or environment. If there was a group of people who share environmental hardships associated with minority status, yet whose genotype is from the majority gene pool, it would be possible to separate genetic and environmental effects. There is such a group: people who are deaf.

The case for deafness   As argued elsewhere (Braden, 1987; 1994), deafness represents a drastic form of environmental deprivation. Children who are deaf, and who have normal-hearing parents endure auditory deprivation, profound delays in language exposure, inconsistent and nonstandard language models in home and school, high rates of medical trauma, greater prevalence of abnormal genetic conditions, dysfunctional family/parent dynamics, and social prejudice (e.g., job/housing discrimination, pejorative stereotypes such as "deaf and dumb"). Despite the myriad of environmental disadvantages, their intelligence (as measured by nonverbal tests of intelligence) is the same as the normal-hearing norm (e.g., their average Performance IQ = 99.97). The same tests show blacks score about 0.67–1 SD below the same mean (e.g., the average

Performance IQ for blacks ranges from 85–90). This finding suggests that the environmental hardships experienced by children with deafness have little or no impact on fluid reasoning ability. Consequently, these environmental variables are an unlikely account for black-white IQ differences.

However, studies of children with deafness show that environment unquestionably influences learned, culturally specific (i.e., crystallized) cognitive abilities. Despite their average Performance IQs, their verbal IQs are far below average (Braden, 1992, 1994). More important, most adults with deafness who complete high school are functionally illiterate (i.e., read at less than a fifth grade level) and score far below normal-hearing ethnic minorities on tests of academic achievement (see Allen, 1986). Thus, research on children with deafness suggests that environment little affects intelligence, but it profoundly affects academic achievement.

Of course, environmental disadvantages that children with deafness do not experience could account for between-group differences in IQ. Popular alternatives include SES, years of schooling, prenatal health, and nutrition, to name but a few. My research does not address these—but other research does (including Herrnstein and Murray, who consistently compare or remove the relative effects of IQ, SES, and schooling when describing relationships). The chances are that if a lay person can think of a plausible rival hypothesis (e.g., tests sampling verbal knowledge discriminate against blacks), a scientist also has thought of it—and has researched it (e.g., blacks also score low on nonverbal tests). The upshot of this discussion is not to conclude that the black-white IQ gap is genetic—such a conclusion is not possible without gene mapping or controlled experiments (which are unfeasible for technical or moral reasons). Rather, the purpose of this discussion is to show that a genetic hypothesis is scientifically plausible and is arguably the most parsimonious account of black-white IQ differences currently available. Herrnstein and Murray are on the fringe of public acceptability in suggesting a genetic account, but they are well within the bounds of scientific plausibility.

Could It Help to Know That the Gap Is Genetic?

Readers who might concede that a genetic hypothesis is plausible often reject it because they believe it would support racism, blame the victim, and otherwise discourage the education and integration of blacks. Critics of genetic theories can provide ample evidence of terrible social and moral injustices committed under the guise of eugenics. They often imply that proponents of genetic accounts wittingly or unwittingly advocate fascism, racism, and apartheid. No doubt, racists and fascists embrace genetic accounts of the black-white IQ gap (while ignoring evidence showing Asian-Americans and Jews have average IQs above whites). But there are other morally and scientifically defensible responses to genetic accounts of between-group differences. I believe feminism provides the best illustration.

Feminists have shown how society can successfully accept and accommodate between-group differences that are genetic in origin without reverting to discrimination, blaming the victim, or discouraging integration and equal opportunities for the disadvantaged group. The differences to which I refer are differences in physical ability between males and females. As is true for IQ distributions, physical ability distributions for males and females overlap substantially (e.g., there are strong women and weak men). However, these distributions have different centers, yielding a "gap" between genders that is genetic in origin.

In the past, society stereotyped women because of this difference (e.g., women were the "weaker sex"). Women were denied opportunities to develop and express their physical abilities (e.g., girls did not take physical education, women were banned from construction sites). Contemporary feminists attack sexist stereotypes (e.g., one can be strong and feminine) and sexist practices (e.g., it is illegal to ban females from physical education, sports, or occupations). Although some teams and classes are segregated by gender, it is done out of a sense of fairness (and out of fears of coed nakedness). Things are not perfect; as the father of a daughter, I believe society has more strides to make in promoting athleticism among females (and in eliminating stereotypes equating femininity with weakness).

It is essential to note one major distinction between feminist approaches to gender differences and contemporary approaches to ethnic group differences; namely, outcome. Nobody has seriously proposed equal gender membership for National Football League (NFL) players; athletic departments in colleges are not required to insure equal gender representation on their varsity teams. It would be wrong for a college athletic department, the NFL, or other entities to deny a qualified women the right to play. It would be equally wrong to demand that these entities guarantee proportionate gender representation on teams.

The morals of this example for the black-white IQ controversy are: (a) That individuals, no matter group membership (e.g., gender, ethnicity) should be provided opportunities to develop their talents through education and other social opportunities and (b) Society can tolerate *differences in outcomes* between groups, but it cannot—and must not—tolerate *differences in opportunity* between groups. Just as society must vigilantly avoid sexist stereotypes by demanding the best from children (no matter their gender), it also must avoid racist stereotypes by demanding the best from children (whatever their ethnicity). Society has not eradicated sexism nor racism (i.e., there are strong girls who lack encouragement; there are gifted blacks who lack educational opportunities), but it can strive toward their eradication. This is a socially, morally, and scientifically acceptable framework for dealing with between-groups differences in ability that are genetic in origin.

What Should Educators Do About All This?

There are three general responses to intellectual differences between individuals and groups. They are: (a) the egalitarian approach (i.e., demand equal outcomes among all children and between groups), (b) the individualist approach (i.e., demand equal opportunities among all children without respect to group membership or outcomes), and (c) the elitist approach (i.e., promote unequal outcomes by helping the smartest children or the most promising group).

The elitist approach requires no further discussion, because it has no advocates in K–12 education. Even Herrnstein and Murray do not advocate elitism (although their critics suggest that they do). The crux of the debate is between egalitarian and individualist responses to differences among individuals and groups.

Egalitarian response   Egalitarians believe that all groups are equal, and thus all groups should achieve equal educational outcomes. Demanding equal outcomes guarantees accountability, because it forces schools to continually monitor their practices to insure all groups are equally represented in all levels of achievement. Egalitarians demand outcome conformity while embracing process diversity (i.e., all groups must have the same outcomes, but some groups may need more resources to achieve them). Egalitarians either assume that groups are created identically, or that any differences between groups can be eliminated through schooling. Otherwise, it makes no sense to hold school accountable for differences in outcomes between groups.

Individualist response   Individualists assume that individuals vary widely with respect to abilities. However, individualists make no assumptions about the degree nor malleability of between-group differences. Consequently, individualists hold schools accountable for providing individuals with equal educational opportunities, yet they do not expect identical educational outcomes. In other words, individualists expect outcome diversity while embracing process conformity (i.e., individuals will—and groups might—have different outcomes, but all individuals and groups should get equal resources). Thus, individualists expect that education will exacerbate, rather than eliminate, differences among individuals (e.g., Thomas Jefferson advocated education as the "leavening" of America).

Egalitarianism versus individualism   Both responses are commendable (e.g., fairness suggests those with fewer social advantages deserve more educational resources, and every child should have equal opportunity to develop her talents to the best of her ability.) However, they have different implications for schooling. Most educators accept an individualist philosophy of education—while also fervently believing that groups, and to a lesser extent, individuals, do not differ in ability. Thus, educators are comfortable with individualism, but only if it achieves egalitarian outcomes. That this is a logical tautology (e.g., it would lead to the conclusion that athletic differences between boys and girls exist because we haven't tried hard enough, not because there are differences of ability) is rarely questioned. Indeed, Herrnstein and Murray are criticized because they draw attention to this tautology, and because they argue against it as a basis for educational and social policy.

Herrnstein and Murray's solutions   With these distinctions in mind, I will return to *The Bell Curve*. Herrnstein and Murray clearly and unapologetically place themselves in the individualist camp. In Chapter 18, they propose one general reform, and three explicit policy changes, for PreK–12 education. The general reform is that educators should rededicate themselves to *"restoring the concept of the educated man* [sic]" (p. 422; italics in the original). This reform exhorts educators to demand that (bright) students meet high standards for thoughtful integration of knowledge across academic disciplines. This goal may not be achievable in a world of increasing specialization (Drucker, 1994). But this reform is driven by values, not by data, and must be debated on its philosophical merits.

Herrnstein and Murray recommend three specific policy reforms (note italics are in the original): (a) *"The Federal government should actively support programs that enable all parents, not just affluent ones, to choose the school that their children attend"* (p. 440); (b) Create *"a federal prize scholarship program"* (p. 441) of about $500 million; and (c) *"Reallocate some portion of existing elementary and secondary school federal aid away from programs for the disadvantaged to programs for the gifted"* (pp. 441–442). The first recommendation is a "school choice" initiative. The rationale that Herrnstein and Murray provide for this recommendation is not data-driven. Rather, they justify school choice with political arguments (i.e., every power that reasonably can be should be given back to individuals) and by noting that educators disagree on how best to deal with children's intellectual heterogeneity. Given these two conditions, they advocate parental school choice.

Herrnstein and Murray's dismissal of educational research as a guide for educating a wide range of intellectual abilities is strikingly at odds with their assiduous use of research in support of other points. They simply ignore educational research—perhaps because it does not directly support (nor dispute) school choice. Their support for school choice has more to do with their political agenda than their understanding of educational research. This is not to say that the "choice" movement lacks merit. Sadly Herrnstein and Murray emphasize IQ's effects on what happens *after* school, leading them to ignore much of the literature that could guide them about how IQ influences what happens *during* school.

The second recommendation for a federal prize program based solely on merit, rather than on "need," is more in keeping with their data. They argue that the decline in aptitude and achievement among top high school seniors occurs because there is little demand, nor reward, for these students to excel. Their interpretation is congruent with Scholastic Aptitude Test score changes over the past 50 years (see Chapter 18, pp. 427–435), and so the modest federal prize program is a logical proposal.

Their third recommendation (to reallocate some federal dollars from compensatory education to gifted education) is, at first glance, compelling. Herrnstein and Murray note that, for every dollar spent on gifted and talented education, the 1992 federal education budget spent $922 on "disadvantaged" children, $56 on programs benefitting all children, and $21 on administration costs (p. 434). The 922:1 ratio favoring "disadvantaged" children (which includes special education) over gifted children is shocking—until one considers the role of the federal government in education. Because education is left to the states, local funds constitute most of the education dollars in the United States. The focus on the federal budget overlooks local funds, which partly serve gifted children. This disparity in per-pupil spending between local school districts can be huge (Kozol, 1992) and is in part what spurred the federal government to establish programs for disadvantaged youth (i.e., because disadvantaged children are concentrated in poor areas, their limited local funding base is supplemented with federal aid).

Although Herrnstein and Murray's use of federal data may exaggerate their point, it is still valid. As a personal example, my daughter attends an elementary school in a middle- to upper-class neighborhood. The school staff includes 5 half-time support people (e.g., school psychologist, social worker), 4 full-time teachers, and 4 full-time aides whose efforts focus primarily or exclusively on serving disadvantaged children. In contrast, the school has one half-time coordinator (up from 20% time last year) for gifted programs. Because of the SES distribution of the neighborhood, there are more gifted children in the school than disadvantaged children. Yet, the school targets at least 10 times more funds to serve disadvantaged children than it does to serve gifted children. The 10:1 ratio (which reflects combined federal, state, and local funding) is far less than the 922:1 ratio implied by Herrnstein and Murray, but it is still significant.

Herrnstein and Murray argue that, because the welfare of the country is driven by the economy, and the welfare of the economy is driven disproportionately by the innovations of smart people, it is in the best interests of all (including disadvantaged people) to do more to cultivate the talents of gifted people. Although this argument may offend the egalitarian instincts of most educators, it should not be dismissed. The recommendation to reallocate some federal funds toward gifted children is not a wholesale call to abandon social justice and efforts to characterize it as such should be condemned.

What Herrnstein and Murray Could Have Said

Given the data that exist on the relationship between IQ and academic achievement, there is much that Herrnstein and Murray might have recommended to improve education. An obvious step is grouping by ability or achievement (aka "tracking"). Although tracking is anathema to contemporary educators, carefully controlled research shows students in lower tracks are unaffected, whereas the academic achievement and self-esteem of students in higher tracks are improved (Slavin, 1987). Tracking consistently improves outcomes at the secondary and middle school levels (Kulik & Kulik, 1982).

A related recommendation is to institute "search and find" programs to identify intellectually gifted students in impoverished environments. Even if low SES children have lower average IQs than high SES children, their sheer numbers suggest many gifted children are trapped within settings that diminish their cognitive talents. The U.S. is the only major industrialized country without a clearly defined, nationally supported program for identifying and educating gifted children (Cropley, 1989). Research consistently shows academic acceleration benefits gifted children, yet U.S. educators remain emotionally committed to academic enrichment—and maintain their opposition to acceleration.

These educational policy changes, and others, would be possible if we were to truly embrace an individualist philosophy of education—without insisting that it lead to egalitarian outcomes. Instead, we exhort teachers to individualize education, while we require them to homogenize outcomes. What are the consequences of insisting that schools produce equal outcomes among groups? Basically, schools have two choices: (a) give more to lower scoring groups (and less to higher scoring groups) and (b) change performance measures.

To illustrate this point, let us suppose that schools were required to eliminate gender differences in athletic performance. First, they might reallocate resources to spend more on women's athletics—and less on male athletics (i.e., the easiest way to close the gap is by raising females—and lowering males). Next, schools also might change athletic performance standards by choosing measures that show smaller male/female differences. Some changes might include: (a) replacing high-performance standards (e.g., running a mile in under 4 minutes) with minimum competencies (e.g., being able to walk/run a mile); (b) adopting intraindividual measures (e.g., gains in weight lifting) instead of absolute measures (e.g., amount of weight lifted); (c) implementing heterogeneous grouping (e.g., talented athletes "coach" less talented peers) rather than homogeneous grouping (e.g., talented athletes work together to hone high-level skills); (d) increasing subjective measures (e.g., amount of effort) and decreasing objective measures (e.g., distance one puts the shot); or (e) "feminizing" athletic outcomes by including measures showing smaller differences between genders (e.g., balancing on a beam).

Psychologists can judge the degree to which their schools have adopted similar strategies to reduce academic differences between groups. Granted, some of these changes are positive in other ways (e.g., richer measures of academic performance are worthy in their own right). My purpose is to suggest how education might become skewed when schools are told to eradicate intractable differences between groups. On one hand, holding schools accountable for closing the gap between groups is like holding poor children accountable for coming to school hungry. Both blame the victim, not the culprit, for circumstances over which they have little control. On the other hand, if schooling could eliminate differences between groups, mandating equal opportunities will close the gap slowly—if at all. Herrnstein and Murray offer a compelling case for the intractable difference scenario. Without an equally compelling rebuttal, it behooves policy makers to reconsider individualism (i.e., emphasize equal educational opportunities—not equal educational outcomes).

Epilogue

A careful reading of *The Bell Curve* will challenge psychologists to refine and reconcile what they know with what they believe. For many, the challenge will be to improve their understanding of educational research (e.g., Is IQ really supported in the literature?). Others will be challenged to refine their philosophies and assumptions, and make them congruent with their knowledge base. Too many will prefer the comfort of denial and outright rejection or repudiation (e.g., "Herrnstein and Murray are racist"). I strongly suspect *The Bell Curve* is destined to be a classic in the same way that Arthur Jensen's (1969) "How Much Can We Boost IQ and Achievement?" is a classic: It will have far more critics than readers. Cognitive growth requires disequilibrium, and most will simply avoid the pain and effort required for careful study and cognitive restructuring. However, school psychologists, the resident experts on intelligence and assessment, have an ethical imperative to educate themselves about the book and the issues within it. One need not agree with Herrnstein and Murray, but one ought not to judge their book without first carefully considering their arguments and their data. Psychologists must not be satisfied with second-hand reviews written by critics (or cheerleaders) who know little about psychology, intelligence, and assessment. To paraphrase John Donne: "Never send to know for whom 'The Bell' tolls; it tolls for thee."

References

Allen, T. E. (1986). Patterns of academic achievement among hearing impaired students: 1974 and 1983. In A. N. Schildroth & M. A. Karchmer (Eds.) *Deaf children in America* (pp. 161–206). San Diego, CA: College Hill Press.

Berk, A. (Ed.). (1982). *Handbook of methods for detecting test bias.* Baltimore, MD: Johns Hopkins University Press.

Bouchard, T. J., Lykken, D. T., McGue, M., Segal, N. L., & Tellegen, A. (1990). Sources of human psychological differences: The Minnesota Study of Twins Reared Apart. *Science, 250,* 223–228.

Cropley, A. J. (1989). Gifted and talented: Provision of education. In J. Husen & T. N. Postlethwaite (Eds.), *The international encyclopedia of education: Research and studies* (vol. 1; pp. 377–384). New York: Pergamon.

Drucker, P. F. (1994). The age of social transformation. *The Atlantic Monthly, 274*(5), 53–80.

Herrnstein, R. J., & Murray, C. (1994). *The bell curve: Intelligence and class structure in American life.* New York: Free Press.

Jensen, A. R. (1969). How much can we boost IQ and scholastic achievement? *Harvard Educational Review, 39,* 1–123.

Jensen, A. R. (1980). *Bias in mental testing.* New York: Free Press.

Kozol, J. (1992). *Savage inequalities: Children in America's schools.* New York: Harper-Collins.

Kulik, C. C., & Kulik, J. A. (1982). Effects of ability grouping on secondary school students: A meta-analysis of evaluation findings. *American Educational Research Journal, 19,* 415–428.

Reynolds, C. R., & Brown, R. T. (Ed.). (1984). *Perspectives on Bias in Mental Testing.* New York: Plenum.

Robins, R. W., & Craik, K. H. (1994). A more appropriate test of the Kuhnian displacement thesis. *American Psychologist, 49*(9), 815–816.

Robins, R. W., Craik, K. H., & Gosling, S. (1994). *The rise and fall of scientific paradigms: Citation trends as tests of a Kuhnian displacement thesis.* Berkeley: Department of Psychology, University of California, Berkeley.

Slavin, R. E. (1987). Ability grouping and student achievement in elementary schools: A best-evidence synthesis. *Review of Educational Research, 57,* 293–336.

Snyderman, M., & Rothman, S. (1987). Survey of expert opinion on intelligence and aptitude testing. *American Psychologist, 42*(2), 137–144.

Spitz, H. H. (1987). *The raising of intelligence: A selected history of attempts to raise retarded intelligence.* Hillsdale, NJ: Erlbaum.

Robert J. Sternberg

NO

The School Bell and *The Bell Curve*

As educators, we are constantly faced with the temptation of blaming the ills of society in general, and of our schools in particular, on things over which we have no control. *The Bell Curve* plays right into this temptation.

The Bell Curve (Herrnstein and Murray, 1994) has attracted enormous popular attention in part because it seems to ring a bell: We've heard it before. But it was wrong before; and it's still wrong.

My goal here is not to make yet another ideological statement. There are enough of these statements (see Fraser, 1995; Jacoby and Glauberman, 1995) and, ultimately, they get down to one person's strongly held opinions versus another's. Rather, I will summarize some of the main claims of the book, discuss the scientific arguments regarding these claims, and present the educational implications of the current state of our scientific knowledge. My focus here is on scientific facts and conclusions, not on one or another person's personal, political, or educational ideology. Page numbers of quotations refer to pages in *The Bell Curve*.

Claim #1. "There is such a thing as a general factor of cognitive ability on which human beings differ." (p. 22)

Herrnstein and Murray claim that IQ is a single generalized cognitive ability that captures the important differences among people in intelligence. When you analyze scores from intelligence tests via the technique testing psychologists typically use (called "factor analysis"), you do, in fact, get a single general, IQ-like factor (Carroll, 1993). But the scientific evidence now suggests that the single general factor that results from these analyses cannot be accepted at face value.

First, the statistical technique of factor analysis always yields a general factor by its very nature (Harman, 1967) if the data are not further processed. It is in the nature of the technique. Thus, the existence of a general factor tells more about the statistical technique than it does about the mind.

Second, our own studies show that when you test high school students via a test of intelligence based on a broader theory of intelligence than the one underlying conventional psychometric tests—my own triarchic theory (Sternberg, 1985a, 1988), which posits analytical, creative, and practical aspects of intelligence—and when you fully analyze the data (subjecting the factors to a procedure called "varimax rotation," which will leave a general IQ factor only if there really is one), you do *not* get a general factor.

In our study of high school students from around the country (Sternberg, Ferrari et al., in press)—where we looked at analytical, creative, and practical aspects of intelligence via verbal, quantitative, figural, and essay items—we found that the analytical, creative, and practical aspects of intelligence are only minimally related. In other words, creatively and practically intelligent people excel in a way that is distinct from the analytic way measured by conventional intelligence tests. Incidentally, the creatively and practically intelligent showed more socioeconomic and ethnic diversity than did the analytically intelligent (high-IQ) people.

Third, a number of studies have now shown that when people are tested in real-world, as opposed to paper-and-pencil classroom contexts, they often show skills that the IQ tests just don't show. For example, Carraher, Carraher, and Schiemann (1985) found that Brazilian street children who were failing mathematics could ably carry out the complex computations needed to run their street businesses. Ceci and Liker (1986) found that men who consistently won in betting at the race track by constructing complex intuitive mathematical models had an average IQ of just 97. Lave, Murtaugh, and de la Roche (1984) showed that housewives who could ably do the mental computations to make supermarket price comparisons were unable to do the same computations when tested in a classroom via abstract problems presented on a paper-and-pencil test.

In sum, there may or may not be a single, higher order general factor of intelligence for the limited range of problems presented on conventional intelligence and scholastic aptitude tests. But the evidence is against a general factor when we look at a broader range of important abilities beyond those tested by conventional assessments. *Thus, we cannot assume that IQ scores, or scores on related tests such as the SAT or ACT, tell us all or even most of what is important about students' abilities.* For example, such scores tell us virtually nothing about students' creative and practical abilities.

Claim #2. "IQ scores match, to a first degree, whatever it is that people mean when they use the word intelligent or smart in ordinary language." (p. 22)

The claim that when people use the term intelligent they mean IQ is unsubstantiated by Herrnstein and Murray (1994), and turns out empirically to be false. Neisser (1976) found that people distinguish between academic and practical aspects of intelligence. Sternberg et al. (1981) found even further distinctions. They did a series of studies to find out what lay people mean when they refer to someone as intelligent. Three factors emerged: verbal ability, practical problem-solving ability, and social competence. Conventional tests measure hardly any of these abilities.

One receptive component of verbal ability is measured by conventional ability tests—reading. The other receptive component (listening) as well as the two expressive components (writing and speaking) are typically not measured, or measured only superficially. Although academic problem solving is measured, practical problem solving is not. And social competence is not measured at all.

It turns out that conceptions of intelligence are much more variegated than Herrnstein and Murray realize. If one looks beyond lay people to specialists in various fields, one discovers more differentiated conceptions of intelligence, which are even less well-tapped by conventional ability tests (Sternberg, 1985b).

Perhaps more important, different cultural groups have different conceptions of intelligence. Okagaki and Sternberg (1993) studied conceptions of intelligence among different U.S. ethnic groups. They found that some groups emphasized the cognitive aspect more, and others emphasized the social aspect of intelligence.

The more the group's conception corresponded to the cognitive conception emphasized by the schools, the "smarter" their children were perceived to be. In other words, children are rewarded in school if their sociocultural group's conception of intelligence matches that of the school (see also Heath, 1983).

Outside the United States, conceptions of intelligence become even more diverse (Berry, 1984). For example, our culture emphasizes the importance of speed with which problems are solved as a function of intelligence (Sternberg, 1985a). If you don't work fast, you don't do well on conventional IQ tests, SATs, ACTs, and the like. In other cultures, careful, in-depth, and multifaceted consideration of a problem may be associated with intelligence. Even in our own culture, serious problems—such as decisions about jobs, spouses, children, and the like—are not considered to be "intelligently solved" if they are solved in the seconds usually allotted for ability-test problems.

IQ does *not* adequately sum up people's views of intelligence, and it certainly should not sum up educators' views of intelligence. Most lay people and many psychologists believe there is a lot more to intelligence than IQ (Gardner, 1983; Sternberg, 1985a; Ceci, 1990). If we fail to recognize the diverse and often considerable abilities of our students who do not necessarily have high IQs, we are setting things up to waste our nation's most precious natural resource—its human talent.

Claim #3. "Another line of evidence pointing toward a genetic factor in cognitive ethnic differences is that blacks and whites differ most on the tests that are the best measures of g, or general intelligence." (p. 270)

Herrnstein and Murray believe that all or most of the difference between whites and blacks, and between racial and ethnic groups in general, is due to genetic factors. This claim is surprising, given the scientific evidence.

Seven studies directly investigate the genetic versus environmental bases of black-white differences in intelligence (see Nisbett, 1995). Of the seven, six fail to support a genetic interpretation, and one is equivocal. Herrnstein and Murray seriously discuss only one of the seven studies—predictably, the one that is equivocal. Moreover, although they interpret this study as supporting their genetic argument, the authors of that one study do not: "Results from the Minnesota Transracial Adoption Study provide little or no conclusive evidence of genetic influences underlying racial differences in intelligence and achievement" (Waldman, Weinberg, and Scarr, 1994, p. 29).

In sum, Herrnstein and Murray's argument is inconsistent with the empirical literature on the origin of measured racial differences in IQ. The truth is that we do not know why we get racial differences on IQ tests; moreover, it is important to remember that IQ is not tantamount to intelligence.

Claim #4. "One message of this chapter is that such differences [in cognitive ability across human populations] are real and have consequences." (p. 269)

Herrnstein and Murray try to attribute differences in societal outcomes for various racial and ethnic groups to differences in cognitive ability as measured by IQ tests. Thus, if blacks fare worse in our society than do whites, it is a consequence of their lower IQ. But Herrnstein and Murray's own data are inconsistent with their claim.

Specifically, Herrnstein and Murray do a set of analyses where blacks and whites are equated for average IQ. The authors find that when the two groups are equated, blacks are twice as likely to be in poverty (p. 326), five times more likely to be born out of wedlock (p. 331), three times more likely to be on welfare (p. 332), more than twice as likely to have lived in poverty during the first three years of their life (p. 335), and twice as likely to have low birth weight (p. 334). These differences in societal outcomes could not be due to IQ, because Herrnstein and Murray equated for IQ!

There's one other important thing to remember about the claims of Herrnstein and Murray. Although Herrnstein and Murray repeatedly refer to cognitive ability as measured by IQ in terms of how it "explains" certain things, all the data Herrnstein and Murray present are correlational. Correlations don't explain anything: They merely indicate the presence of a statistical association. Moreover, the associations of which Herrnstein and Murray make so much are weak. Even from their "explanatory" point of view, Herrnstein and Murray admit that "cognitive ability... almost always explains less than 20 percent of the variance, to use the statistician's term, usually less than 10 percent and often less than 5 percent" (p. 117).

In other words, all this fuss is about correlations that usually account for less than 10 percent of the variation in the data, leaving more than 90 percent unexplained. Thus, all those 845 pages and countless graphs are about statistics expressing what by any standard are weak relationships between variables.

Using Herrnstein and Murray's own data, we can see that societal differences in outcomes for different groups, such as blacks and whites, cannot be due solely to IQ, and the magnitude of the differences when IQ is equated suggest that they are not due even largely to IQ. We cannot just write off societal inequalities to alleged just desserts as a result of IQ differences. The relation of IQ to societal differences is weak, in any case.

Claim #5. "Taken together, the story of attempts to raise intelligence is one of high hopes, flamboyant claims, and disappointing results. For the foreseeable future, the problems of low cognitive ability are not going to be solved by outside interventions to make children smarter." (p. 389)

Herrnstein and Murray here claim that attempts to improve intelligence have failed. Their reading of the data is puzzling, to say the least. For one thing, one of the most successful interventions for increasing intellectual abilities was described in an article published in a high-quality peer-reviewed journal and senior authored by none other than Herrnstein himself (Herrnstein et al., 1986)! Studies by Ramey (1994) and his colleagues have also shown that interventions can be quite successful. In our own work, we have demonstrated impressive gains in analytical (Sternberg, 1987), creative (Davidson and Sternberg, 1984), and practical abilities (Sternberg, Okagaki, and Jackson, 1990; Gardner et al., 1994). A number of programs based on Gardner's theory of multiple intelligence have also had considerable success (Gardner, 1993).

One other thing should be kept in mind. The modifiability of intelligence has nothing to do with its heritability. In other words, we can argue until we are blue in the face about whether intelligence is heritable to this degree or that: These arguments are irrelevant to the question of whether we can attain meaningful increases in our students' intellectual abilities.

For example, height is highly heritable, yet it has undergone substantial increases during the past several generations. Phenylketonuria is completely heritable, but the mental retardation it can cause can be completely eliminated by an environmental intervention—withholding of phenylalanine from the diet of the afflicted infant. Thus, we should not let arguments about the degree to which intelligence is genetic get in the way of attempts to help our students maximize their intellectual potentials.

Although we cannot turn mentally retarded individuals into intellectual geniuses, we can achieve meaningful increases in intellectual abilities. Any conclusion to the contrary can result only from failing to cite or take seriously the full range of the relevant data. These increases can be achieved, whatever the heritability of intelligence may be.

Claim #6. "No one decreed that occupations should sort us out by our cognitive abilities and no one enforces the process. It goes on beneath the surface, guided by its own invisible hand." (p. 52)

Herrnstein and Murray claim that the forces of nature lead people in higher-prestige occupations to have higher IQs, and people in lower-prestige occupations to have lower IQs. It is true, as Herrnstein and Murray (1994) point out, that people in higher prestige occupations, such as lawyers, doctors, professors, and business managers, tend to have higher IQs and ability test scores in general than do people in lower prestige occupations, such as assembly-line workers, house-cleaning people, car mechanics, and waiters. Herrnstein and Murray would have us believe that this fact reflects a natural sorting by cognitive abilities, yielding what they call a *cognitive elite*. Nonsense.

To be admitted to a selective college, students must take the SAT or the ACT. To be admitted to a selective law school, medical school, graduate school, or business school, students must take the LSAT, MCAT, GRE, or GMAT, respectively. These various tests correlate highly with each other and with IQ. For practical purposes, they are essentially interchangeable.

Thus, those who do not test well lose the access routes to higher prestige occupations, no matter what their nontest qualifications might be. They can't get into the educational institutions that will prepare them for these occupations. We have created an educational testing system that channels good ability-test takers into higher prestige occupations, and that effectively blocks those who do not test well from these occupations.

Consider an analogy. Suppose we admitted people to selective colleges, and later to selective graduate and professional schools, on the basis of height. To be admitted to Harvard College, for example, one might need to be 6'4", and to be admitted to Harvard Law or Medical School, perhaps as tall as 6'7". Thirty years after the institution of this policy, we look at the heights of people in the legal and medical professions, and compare them to the heights of people in lower-prestige occupations. Certainly, we will find those in the higher prestige occupations to be quite a bit taller. There was no "invisible hand" of nature at work here: We created the system.

We can and have used a variety of systems. Before the admissions revolution of the 1960s, the average SATs at places like Harvard were 100 points lower than they were in the late 1960s. In those days, social class and parental wealth accounted for a lot more in the admissions decisions than they did later. The people in higher-prestige occupations tend to be distinguished in large part by parental social class and wealth.

Any society can create whatever system it wants to filter students into higher or lower prestige occupations. We happen to use ability tests. Other societies in the present, and our own society in the past, have used criteria other than multiple-choice ability tests for entrance into the fast track. These criteria may or may not have been ability related. In any case, it is important to remember that societies can look for abilities beyond those that our tests test, such as the entrepreneurial abilities that have become so important for advancement in modern-day Russia.

Claim #7. "Job training and job performance in many common occupations are well predicted by any broadly based test of intelligence, as compared to narrower tests more specifically targeted to the routines of the job. As a corollary: Narrower tests that predict well do so largely because they happen themselves to be correlated with tests of general ability." (p. 70)

Here, Herrnstein and Murray claim that tests of general ability, such as IQ tests, are the only tests that have any serious predictive value for job performance; if other tests work at all, it is only because they measure the same things that IQ tests measure. On this view, if you want to hire good teachers, the only test you need to give them is an IQ test!

The problem is that the data don't support Herrnstein and Murray's claims. My colleagues and I, for example, have done a number of studies investigating an aspect of practical intelligence for job performance (Sternberg and Wagner 1993; Sternberg, Wagner, and Okagaki, 1993; Sternberg, Wagner et al., in press). In study after study, we have found that performance in responsible positions, such as managerial, sales, and teaching positions, is better accounted for by practical than by academic intelligence. Moreover, measures of academic and practical intelligence show virtually no relationship.

Summary

Factors way beyond IQ matter to the prediction of successful job performance. If we want to develop children to succeed in their jobs, we have to develop all our children. We cannot predict who will be successful merely on the basis of IQ, and then think that the high-IQ children are the only ones to whom it is worth paying attention. Not only aspects of intelligence beyond IQ, but other factors altogether, such as motivation, initiative, and personality will contribute in large part to who succeeds and who does not in the world of work.

As educators, we are constantly faced with the temptation of blaming the ills of society in general, and of our schools in particular, on things over which we have no control. *The Bell Curve* plays right into this temptation.

How easy it would be to explain certain children's failures to thrive in school and in the world to their low-IQs. How easy it would be to wash our hands of the whole mess, saying we can't do anything about it. We could just put the losers together, look after them, and not expect much.

That's the temptation of *The Bell Curve*. Don't succumb. *The Bell Curve* is bad science and, hence, bad policy. Don't ring the school bell and the bell curve together. They just don't mix, and they never will, because *The Bell Curve* rings false.

References

Berry, J. W. "Towards a Universal Psychology of Cognitive Competence." In *Chancing Conceptions of Intelligence and Intellectual Functioning*, edited by P. S. Fry. Amsterdam: North-Holland, 1984.

Carraher, T. N.; Carraher, D.; and Schiemann, A. D. "Mathematics in the Streets and in Schools." *British Journal of Developmental Psychology* 3(1985): 21–29.

Carroll, J. B. *Human Cognitive Abilities.* New York: Cambridge University Press, 1993.

Ceci, S. J. *On Intelligence... More or Less: A Bio-Ecological Treatise on Intellectual Development.* Englewood Cliffs, N.J.: Prentice-Hall, 1990.

Ceci, S. J., and Liker, J. "Academic and Nonacademic Intelligence: An Experimental Separation." In *Practical Intelligence: Nature and Origins of Competence in the Everyday World*, edited by R. J. Sternberg and R. K. Wagner. New York: Cambridge University Press, 1986.

Davidson, J. E., and Sternberg, R. J. "The Role of Insight in Intellectual Giftedness." *Gifted Child Quarterly* 28(1984): 58–64.

Fraser, S., ed. *The Bell Curve Wars: Race, Intelligence and the Future of America.* New York: Basic Books, 1995.

Gardner, Howard. *Frames of Mind: The Theory of Multiple Intelligences.* New York: Basic Books, 1983.

_____. *Multiple Intelligences: The Theory in Practice.* New York: Basic Books. 1993.

Gardner, H.; Krechevsky, M.; Sternberg, R. J.; and Okagaki, L. "Intelligence in Context: Enhancing Students' Practical Intelligence for School." In *Classroom Lessons: Integrating Cognitive Theory and Classroom Practice,* edited by K. McGilly. Cambridge, Mass.: Bradford Books, 1994.

Harman, H. H. *Modern Factor Analysis,* 2d ed. Chicago, Ill.: University of Chicago Press, 1967.

Heath, S. B. *Ways with Words.* New York: Cambridge University Press, 1983.

Herrnstein, R., and Murray, C. *The Bell Curve.* New York: Free Press, 1994.

Herrnstein, R.; Nickerson, R. S.; De Sanchez, M.; and Swets, J. A. "Teaching Thinking Skills." *American Psychologist* 41(1986): 1,279–89.

Jacoby, R., and Glauberman, N., eds. *The Bell Curve Debate.* New York: Times Books, 1995.

Lave, J.; Murtaugh, M.; and de la Roche, O. "The Dialectic of Arithmetic in Grocery Shopping." In *Everyday Cognition: Its Development in Social Context,* edited by B. Rogoff and J. Lace. Cambridge, Mass.: Harvard University Press, 1984.

Neisser, U. "General, Academic, and Artificial Intelligence." In *Human Intelligence: Perspectives on Its Theory and Measurement,* edited by L. Resnick. Norwood, N.J.: Ablex, 1976.

Nisbett, R. "Race, IQ, and Scientism." In *The Bell Curve Wars: Race, Intelligence and the Future of America,* edited by S. Fraser. New York: Basic Books, 1995.

Okagaki, L., and Sternberg, R. J. "Putting the Distance into Students' Hands: Practical Intelligence for School." In *The Development and Meaning of Psychological Distance,* edited by R. R. Cocking and K. A. Renninger. Hillsdale, N.J.: Lawrence Erlbaum, 1993.

Ramey, C. "Abecedarian Project." In *Encyclopedia of Human Intelligence,* Vol. 1, edited by R. J. Sternberg. New York: Macmillan, 1994.

Sternberg, R. J. *Beyond IQ: A Triarchic Theory of Human Intelligence.* New York: Cambridge University Press, 1985a.

_____. "Implicit Theories of Intelligence, Creativity, and Wisdom." *Journal of Personality and Social Psychology* 49(1985b): 607–27.

_____. "Most Vocabulary Is Learned from Context." In *The Nature of Vocabulary Acquisition,* edited by M. G. McKeown and M. E. Curtis. Hillsdale, N.J.: Lawrence Erlbaum, 1987.

_____. *The Triarchic Mind: A New Theory of Human Intelligence.* New York: Viking, 1988.

Sternberg, R. J., and Wagner, R. K. "The *g*-ocentric View of Intelligence and Job Performance Is Wrong." *Current Directions in Psychological Science* 1(1993): 1–4.

Sternberg, R. J.; Conway, B. E.; Ketron, J. L.; and Bernstein, M. "People's Conception of Intelligence." *Journal of Personality and Social Psychology* 41(1981): 37–55.

Sternberg, R. J.; Ferrari, M.; Grigorenko, E. L.; and Clinkenbeard, P. "Is There More to Intelligence Than *g*? Toward a Construct Validation of a Triarchic Theory and Test of Human Intelligence," in press.

Sternberg, R. J.; Okagaki, L.; and Jackson, A. "Practical Intelligence for Success in School." *Educational Leadership* 48(1990): 35–39.

Sternberg, R. J.; Wagner, R. K.; and Okagaki, L. "Practical Intelligence: The Nature and Role of Tacit Knowledge in Work and at School." In *Advances in Lifespan Development,* edited by H. Reese and J. Puckett. Hillsdale, N.J.: Erlbaum, 1993.

Sternberg, R. J.; Wagner, R. K.; Williams, W. M.; and Horvath, J. A. "Testing Common Sense." *American Psychologist,* in press.

Waldman, I. D.; Weinberg, R. A.; and Scarr S. "Racial Group Differences in IQ in the Minnesota Transracial Adoption Study: A Reply to Levin and Lynn." *Intelligence* 1(1994): 29–44.

CHALLENGE QUESTIONS

Is the *Bell Curve* Theory Valid?

1. Braden urges his colleagues in the field of education to take the message of *The Bell Curve* to heart and to use the findings of Herrnstein and Murray as the basis for initiating educational reform. Assuming educators concur with Braden, what steps might they take to compensate for genetically determined deficiencies in any student, irrespective of race?
2. Sternberg speaks about the "bad science" inherent in *The Bell Curve*. What points can be made on both sides of the argument about whether or not research should be conducted on the question of cognitive differences associated with race?
3. Imagine that you are a school psychologist working with a racially diverse elementary school population. How would you go about assessing the cognitive abilities of students from different ethnic backgrounds, cultures, and geographic regions?
4. If you were given the task of developing a new definition for the construct of intelligence, how would you go about the task, and what traits would you measure?
5. Testing has become a prominent gate-keeping aspect of American life, and it is part of the process by which people gain access to college, jobs, awards, and various other opportunities. What are some of the emotional costs to individuals who fare poorly on tests, and how might psychologists respond to these issues?

Suggested Readings

Fischer, C. S., Hout, M., Sanchez Jankowski, M., Lucas, S. R., Swidler, A., & Voss, K. (1996). *Inequality by design: Cracking the Bell Curve myth*. Princeton, NJ: Princeton University Press.

Jensen, A. R. (1997). Psychometric g and the race question. In J. Kingma, & W. Tomic (Eds.), *Advances in cognition and educational practice: Reflections on the concept of intelligence*. (pp. 1–23). Greenwich, CT: Jai Press, Inc.

Kincheloe, J. L., Steinberg, S. R., & Gresson, A. D. (1996). *Measured lies: The Bell Curve examined*. New York, NY: St. Martin's Press.

Nisbett, R. E. (1998). Race, genetics, and IQ. In C. Jencks, & M. Phillips (Eds.), *The Black-White test score gap*. (pp. 86–102). Washington, DC: Brookings Institution.

Samuda, R. J. (1998). *Psychological testing of American minorities: Issues and consequences*. Thousand Oaks, CA: Sage Publications, Inc.

ISSUE 15

Does Religious Commitment Improve Mental Health?

YES: David B. Larson, from "Have Faith: Religion Can Heal Mental Ills," *Insight on the News* (March 6, 1995)

NO: Albert Ellis, from "Dogmatic Devotion Doesn't Help, It Hurts," *Insight on the News* (March 6, 1995)

ISSUE SUMMARY

YES: David B. Larson, president of the National Institute for Healthcare, maintains that religion can heal many ills, both physical and psychological, and that religiously committed people fare better psychologically in many facets of life than nonreligious people.

NO: Albert Ellis, president of the Institute for Rational-Emotive Therapy, expresses concern about religious commitment, particularly fanaticism, and he criticizes the research in this area as being biased.

The journey through life involves travel along a path on which many obstacles are encountered. Pain, both physical and psychological, is an inevitable part of human experience. To alleviate physical pain, people turn to a range of prescribed medical remedies, most of which have been well established in terms of efficacy. Remedies for psychological pain, on the other hand, are much more diverse. Although some people prefer to deal with emotional distress within their own thoughts and feelings, many people are inclined to turn outward. They may seek help from a relative, a friend, or a therapist. Some turn to their religion for solace, perhaps seeking support from a cleric or simply from the sense of serenity they derive from spiritual commitment.

The relationship between religious commitment and mental health is controversial for a number of reasons. Some critics of religion see religious commitment as antithetical to healthy psychological functioning in that many religious people espouse beliefs that are unprovable and feel compelled to adhere to rules of behavior that limit personal freedom and choice. Supporters of religious commitment, on the other hand, see turning to religion as an effort to find serenity in an otherwise chaotic world; the choice to adhere to rules of behavior is seen not as a restriction on personal choice but as an opportunity to acquire a sense of inner peace by adhering to the moral standards that one values.

In the following selection, David B. Larson contends that religion can heal many ills, both physical and psychological. According to Larson, religiously committed people are less likely to abuse drugs or alcohol, have higher rates of marital satisfaction, have fewer mental health problems, and have better rates of recovery from medical problems than nonreligious people. Larson expresses dismay at the fact that many mental health professionals have low regard for religious commitment despite research findings that support the beneficial psychological impact of religious involvement.

In the second selection, Albert Ellis expresses concern about religious commitment, particularly religious fanaticism. He is also critical of the research that supports a connection between mental health and religious commitment, stating that the researchers in this field tend to be biased investigators who set out to prove that religionists are healthier than nonreligionists. Ellis's greatest concerns are about those people at the extreme end of the continuum, who become obsessed with religious ideas to the point of psychosis, and those whose fanaticism is so extreme that they resort to violence to advance their causes.

POINT

- Research findings show a clear connection between religious commitment and improved mental health.

- Religiously committed research respondents report a number of positive experiences, including happier marriages, better sex lives, and improved recovery rates from medical problems.

- Research shows that religious individuals who are more committed experience fewer mental health problems than do the less committed.

- Some antireligion clinicians have perpetuated the misconception that religion is associated with psychopathology by labeling spiritual experiences "psychotic."

- Although the vast majority of research studies show that religion has a positive influence on mental health, religious commitment remains at best ignored or at worst maligned by the professional community.

COUNTERPOINT

- Research on religious commitment and mental health is flawed by the bias of investigators who are motivated to prove that religionists are healthier than nonreligionists.

- Religiously committed research respondents overemphasize their "good" and de-emphasize their "poor" behaviors on questionnaires; they contend that they are happier, less stressed, and less addicted than they really are.

- Researchers have demonstrated that people who rigidly and dogmatically maintain religious views are more disturbed than religious followers who are less rigid.

- People diagnosed as psychotic are frequently obsessed with religious ideas and practices, and they often compulsively and scrupulously follow religious teachings.

- Being a philosophical system of psychotherapy, rational-emotive behavior therapy has much to learn from theological and secular religions.

David B. Larson

 **YES**

Have Faith: Religion Can Heal Mental Ills

If a new health treatment were discovered that helped to reduce the rate of teenage suicide, prevent drug and alcohol abuse, improve treatment for depression, reduce recovery time from surgery, lower divorce rates and enhance a sense of well-being, one would think that every physician in the country would be scrambling to try it. Yet, what if critics denounced this treatment as harmful, despite research findings that showed it to be effective more than 80 percent of the time? Which would you be more ready to believe—the assertions of the critics based on their opinions or the results of the clinical trials based upon research?

As a research epidemiologist and board-certified psychiatrist, I have encountered this situation time and again during the last 15 years of my practice. The hypothetical medical treatment really does exist, but it is not a new drug: It is spirituality. While medical professionals have been privately assuming and publicly stating for years that religion is detrimental to mental health, when I actually looked at the available empirical research on the relationship between religion and health, the findings were overwhelmingly positive.

Just what are the correlations that exist between religion and mental health? First, religion has been found to be associated with a decrease in destructive behavior such as suicide. A 1991 review of the published research on the relationship between religious commitment and suicide rates conducted by my colleagues and I found that religious commitment produced lower rates of suicide in nearly every published study located. In fact, Stephen Stack, now of Wayne State University, showed that non-church attenders were four times more likely to kill themselves than were frequent attenders and that church attendance predicted suicide rates more effectively than any other factor including unemployment.

What scientific findings could explain these lower rates of suicide? First, several researchers have noted that the religiously committed report experiencing fewer suicidal impulses and have a more negative attitude toward suicidal behavior than do the nonreligious. In addition, suicide is a less-acceptable alternative for the religiously committed because of their belief in a moral accountability to God, thus making them less susceptible than the nonreligious to this life-ending alternative. Finally, the foundational religious beliefs in an afterlife, divine justice and the possibility of eternal condemnation all help to reduce the appeal of potentially self-destructive behavior.

If religion can reduce the appeal of potentially self-destructive behavior such as suicide, could it also play a role in decreasing other self-destructive behavior such as drug abuse? When this question has been examined empirically, the overwhelming response is yes. When Richard Gorsuch conducted a review of the relationship between religious commitment and drug abuse nearly 20 years ago, he noted that religious commitment "predicts those who have not used an illicit drug regardless of whether the religious variable is defined in terms of membership, active participation, religious upbringing or the meaningfulness of religion as viewed by the person himself."

More recent reviews have substantiated the earlier findings of Gorsuch, demonstrating that even when employing varying measures of religion, religious commitment predicted curtailed drug abuse. Interestingly, a national survey of 14,000 adolescents found the lowest rates of adolescent drug abuse in the most "politically incorrect" religious group—theologically conservative teens. The drug-abuse rates of teens from more liberal religious groups rose a little higher but still sank below rates of drug abuse among nonreligious teens. The correlations between the six measures of religion employed in the survey and the eight measures of substance abuse all were consistently negative. These findings lead the authors of the study to conclude that the amount of importance individuals place on religion in their lives is the best predictor of a lack of substance abuse, implying that "the (internal) controls operating here are a result of deeply internalized norms and values rather than fear ... or peer pressure." For teens living in a society in which drug rates continue to spiral, religion may not be so bad after all.

Just as religious commitment seems to be negatively correlated with drug abuse, similar results are found when examining the relationship between religious commitment and alcohol abuse. When I investigated this area myself, I found that those who abuse alcohol rarely have a strong religious commitment. Indeed, when my colleagues and I surveyed a group of alcoholics, we found that almost 90 percent had lost interest in religion during their teenage years, whereas among the general population, nearly that same percentage reported no change or even a slight increase in their religious practices during adolescence. Furthermore, a relationship between religious commitment and the nonuse or moderate use of alcohol has been extensively documented in the research literature. Some of the most intriguing results have been obtained by Acheampong Amoateng and Stephen Bahr of Brigham Young University, who found that whether or not a religion specifically proscribed alcohol use, those who were active in a religious group consumed substantially less than those who were not active.

Not only does religion protect against clinical problems such as suicide and drug and alcohol abuse, but religious commitment also has been shown to enhance positive life experiences such as marital satisfaction and personal well-being. When I reviewed the published studies on divorce and religious commitment, I found a negative relationship between church attendance and divorce in nearly every study that I located.

To what can these lower rates of divorce be attributed? Some critics argue that the religiously committed stay in unsatisfactory marriages due to religious prohibitions against divorce. However research has found little if any support for this view. In my review I found that, as a group, the religiously committed report a higher rate of marital satisfaction than the nonreligious. In fact, people from long-lasting marriages rank religion as one of the most important components of a happy marriage, with church attendance being strongly associated with the hypothetical willingness to remarry a spouse—a very strong indicator of marital satisfaction. Could these findings be skewed because, as is believed by some in the mental-health field, religious people falsify their response to such questions to make themselves look better? When the studies were controlled for such a factor the researchers found that the religiously committed were not falsifying their responses or answering in a socially acceptable manner and truly were more satisfied in their marriages.

Although the religiously committed are satisfied with their marriages, is this level of satisfaction also found in the sexual fulfillment of married couples? Though the prevailing public opinion is that religious individuals are prudish or even sexually repressed, empirical evidence has shown otherwise. Using data from *Redbook* magazine's survey of 100,000 women in 1975, Carole Tavris and Susan Sadd contradicted the longstanding assumption that religious commitment fosters sexual dysfunction. Tavris and Sadd found that it is the most religious women who report the greatest happiness and satisfaction with marital sex—more so than either moderately religious or nonreligious women. Religious women also report reaching orgasm more frequently than nonreligious women and are more satisfied with the frequency of their sexual activity than the less pious. Thus, while surprising to many, research suggests that religious commitment may play a role in improving rather than hindering sexual expression and satisfaction in marriage.

Not only has religious commitment been found to enhance sexual satisfaction, but overall life satisfaction as well. For example, David Myers of Hope College reviewed well-being literature and found that the religiously committed have a greater sense of overall life satisfaction than the nonreligious. Religion not only seems to foster a sense of well-being and life satisfaction but also may play a role in protecting against stress, with religiously committed respondents reporting much lower stress levels than the less committed. Even when the religiously committed have stress levels that are similar to the nonreligious, the more committed report experiencing fewer mental-illness problems than do the less committed.

Mental-health status has been found to improve for those attending religious services on a regular basis. Indeed, several studies have found a significant reduction in diverse psychiatric symptomatology following increased religious involvement. Chung-Chou Chu and colleagues at the Nebraska Psychiatric Institute in Omaha found lower rates of rehospitalization among schizophrenics who attended church or were given supportive aftercare by religious homemakers and ministers. One of my own studies confirmed that religious commitment can improve recovery rates as well. When my colleagues and I examined elderly women recovering from hip fractures, we found that those women with stronger religious beliefs suffered less from depression and thus were more likely to walk sooner and farther than their nonreligious counterparts.

⟦≈⊙⟧

Yet, despite the abundance of studies demonstrating the beneficial effects of religious commitment on physical and mental health, many members of the medical community seem immune to this evidence. This resistance to empirical findings on the mental-health benefits of religious commitment may stem from the anti-religious views espoused by significant mental-health theorists. For example, Sigmund Freud called religion a "universal obsessional neurosis" and regarded mystical experience as "infantile helplessness" and a "regression to primary narcissism." More recently, Albert Ellis, the originator of rational-emotive therapy, has argued that "unbelief, humanism, skepticism and even thoroughgoing atheism not only abet but are practically synonymous with mental health; and that devout belief, dogmatism and religiosity distinctly contribute to, and in some ways are equal to, mental or emotional disturbance." Other clinicians have continued to perpetuate the misconception that religion is associated with psychopathology by labeling spiritual experiences as, among other things, borderline psychosis, a psychotic episode or the result of temporal-lobe dysfunction. Even the consensus report, "Mysticism: Spiritual Quest or Psychological Disturbance," by the Group for the Advancement of Psychiatry supported the long-standing view of religion as psychopathology; calling religious and mystical experiences "a regression, an escape, a projection upon the world of a primitive infantile state."

What is perhaps most surprising about these negative opinions of religion's effect on mental health is the startling absence of empirical evidence to support these views. Indeed, the same scientists who were trained to accept or reject a hypothesis based on hard data seem to rely solely on their own opinions and biases when assessing the effect of religion on health. When I conducted a systematic review of all articles published in the two leading journals of psychiatry, the *American Journal of Psychiatry* and the *Archives of General Psychiatry,* which assessed the association between religious commitment and mental health, I found that more than 80 percent of the religious-mental health associations located were clinically beneficial while only 15 percent of the associations were harmful—findings that run counter to the heavily publicized opinion of mental-health professionals. Thus, even though the vast majority of published research studies show religion as having a positive influence on mental health, religious commitment remains at best ignored or at worst, maligned by the professional community.

The question then begs to be asked: Why do medical professionals seem to ignore such positive evidence about religion's beneficial effect on mental health? One possible source of this tension could lie in clinicians' unfamiliarity with or rejection of traditional religious expression. For example, not only do mental-health professionals generally hold levels of religious commitment that diverge significantly from the general population, but they have much higher rates of atheism and agnosticism as well. The most recent survey of the belief systems of mental-health professionals found that less than 45 percent of the members of the American Psychiatric Association and the American Psychological Association believed in God—a percentage less than half that of the general population. When asked whether they agreed with the statement, "My whole approach to life is based on my religion," only one-third of clinical psychologists and two-fifths of psychiatrists agreed with that statement—again, a percentage that is nearly half that of the U.S. population. Indeed, more than 25 percent of psychiatrists and clinical psychologists and more than 40 percent of psychoanalysts claimed that they had abandoned a theistic belief system, compared with just less than 5 percent of the general population reporting the same feelings.

Science is assumed to be a domain that progresses through the gradual accumulation of new data or study findings, yet the mental-health community seems to be stalled in its understanding of the interface between religion and mental health. If a field is to progress in its knowledge and understanding of a controversial issue such as religion, empirical data and research must be relied upon more than personal opinions and biases. At a time when the rising cost of health care is causing so much discussion in our country, no factor that may be so beneficial to health can be ignored. The continuing neglect of published research on religion prevents clinicians and policymakers from fully understanding the important role of religion in health care and deprives patients as well as themselves of improved skills and methods in clinical prevention, coping with illness and quality of care. The mental health establishment needs to begin to recognize that it is treating a whole person—mind, body and, yes, even spirit.

NO ↵

Albert Ellis

Dogmatic Devotion Doesn't Help, It Hurts

According to the psychological studies cited by David Larson, religious believers have more satisfying marriages, more enjoyable sex lives, less psychological stress, less depression and less drug and alcohol abuse than nonreligious people. Do these studies present a "true" picture of the mental health benefits of being religious? Probably not, for several reasons. First, the scientific method itself has been shown by many postmodernists to be far from "objective" and unassailable because it is created and used by highly subjective, often biased individuals. Scientists are never purely dispassionate observers of "reality" but frequently bring their own biases to their experiments and conclusions.

Second, practically all the studies that Larson cites were conducted by religious believers; some were published in religious journals. Many of the researchers were motivated to structure studies to "prove" that religionists are "healthier" than nonreligionists and only to publish studies that "proved" this.

None of the studies cited—as I noted when I read many of them myself—eliminated the almost inevitable bias of the subjects they used. I showed, in two comprehensive reviews of personality questionnaires that were published in the *Psychological Bulletin* in 1946 and 1948 and in several other psychological papers, that people often can figure out the "right" and "wrong" answers to these questionnaires and consequently "show" that they are "healthy" when they actually are not. I also showed, in an article in the *American Sociological Review* in 1948, that conservative and religious subjects probably more often were claiming falsely to have "happier" marriages on the Burgess-Locke Marriage Prediction Test than were liberal and nonreligious subjects.

This tendency of conservative, religious, job-seeking and otherwise motivated individuals to overemphasize their "good" and deemphasize their "poor" behavior on questionnaires has been pointed out by a number of other reviewers of psychological studies. Because all these studies included a number of strongly religious subjects, I would guess that many of these religionists had a distinct tendency to claim to be happier, less stressful and less addictive personalities than a good clinician would find them to be. I believe that this is a common finding of psychologists and was confirmed by my reviews mentioned previously.

Although Larson has spent a number of years locating studies that demonstrated that religious believers are healthier than nonreligious subjects, a large number of researchers have demonstrated the opposite. Several other studies have found that people who rigidly and dogmatically maintain religious views are more disturbed than less-rigid religious followers. But all these studies, once again, are suspect because none of them seem to have eliminated the problem of the biased answers of some of their subjects who consciously or unconsciously want to show how healthy they are.

Larson points out that many psychologists are sure that religionists are more disturbed than nonreligionists in spite of their having no real scientific evidence to substantiate their opinions. He is largely right about this, in view of what I have already said. Nonetheless, some reasonably good data back up the views of these psychologists that devout religionists often are disturbed.

Antiabortion killers such as Paul Hill have demonstrated that fanatical beliefs can have deadly consequences. But lesser-known fanatical religious believers have used ruthless tactics to oppose such "enlightened" views as birth control, women's liberation and even separation of church and state. Some religious zealots have jailed, maimed or even killed liberal proponents of their own religions. Nobel laureate Naguib Mahfouz is still recovering from stab wounds inflicted by Muslim extremists last October near his home in Cairo. (Mahfouz, considered by many to be a devout Muslim, frequently has ridiculed religious hypocrisy in his work.) Indian-born author Salman Rushdie has lived for seven years under a death sentence pronounced by the late Ayatollah Khomeini. Rushdie explained to the *New York Times* that dissidents within the Muslim world become "persons whose blood is unclean and therefore deserves to be spilled."

Religious persecution and wars against members of other religions have involved millions of casualties throughout human history Islamic fundamentalists from North Africa to Pakistan have established, or done their best to establish, state religions that force all the citizens of a country or other political group to strictly obey the rules of a specific religious group.

People diagnosed as being psychotic and of having severe personality disorders frequently have been obsessed with religious ideas and practices and compulsively and scrupulously follow religious teachings.

The tragic, multiple suicides of members of the Switzerland-based Order of the Solar Temple last October is only the most recent illustration of an extremist religious cult which manipulated its adherents and induced some of them to harm and kill themselves.

Do these manifestations of religious-oriented fanaticism, despotism, cultism and psychosis prove that religious-minded people generally are more disturbed than nonreligious individuals? Of course not. Many—probably most—religionists oppose the extreme views and practices I have just listed, and some actually make efforts to counteract them. One should not conclude, then, that pious religiosity in and of itself equals emotional disturbance.

However, as a psychotherapist and the founder of a school of psychotherapy called rational emotive behavior therapy, I have for many years distinguished between people who hold moderate religious views and those who espouse devout, dogmatic, rigid religious attitudes. In my judgment, most intelligent and educated people are in the former group and temperately believe God (such as Jehovah) exists, that He or She created the universe and the creatures in it, and that we preferably should follow religious, ethical laws but that a Supreme Being forgives us fallible humans when we do not follow His or Her rules. These "moderate" religionists prefer to be "religious" but do not insist that the rest of us absolutely and completely always must obey God's and the church's precepts. Therefore, they still mainly run their own lives and rarely damn themselves (and others) for religious nonobservance. In regard to God and His or Her Commandments, they live and let live.

The second kind of religious adherents—those who are devout, absolutistic and dogmatic—are decidedly different. They differ among themselves but most of them tend to believe that there absolutely has to be a Supreme Being, that He or She specifically runs the universe, must be completely obeyed and will eternally damn all believers and nonbelievers who deviate from His or Her sacred commands.

Another devout and absolutistic group of people do not believe in anything supernatural, but do rigidly subscribe to a dogmatic, secular belief system —such as Nazism, Fascism or Communism—which vests complete authority in the state or in some other organization and which insists that nonallegiance or opposition to this Great Power must be ruthlessly fought, overthrown, punished and annihilated.

As an advocate of mental and emotional health, I have always seen "moderate" religious believers as reasonably sound individuals who usually are no more neurotic (or otherwise disturbed) than are skeptical, nonreligious people. Like nonbelievers, they are relatively open-minded, democratic and unbigoted. They allow themselves to follow and experience "religious" and "secular" values, enjoyment and commitments. Therefore, they infrequently get into serious emotional trouble with themselves or with others because of their religious beliefs and actions.

This is not the case with fanatical, pietistic religionists. Whether they are righteously devoted to God and the church or to secular organizations and cults (some of which may be atheistic) these extreme religionists are not open-minded, tolerant and undamning. Like nonreligious neurotics and individuals with severe personality disorders, they do not merely wish that other religionists and nonbelievers agree with them and worship their own Supreme Being and their churchly values. They insist, demand and command that their God's and their church's will be done.

Since the age of 12, I have been skeptical of anything supernatural or god-like. But I always have believed that undogmatic religionists can get along well in the world and be helpful to others, and I relate nicely to them. Many, if not most, of the mental-health professionals with whom I have worked in the field of rational emotive behavior therapy are religious. A surprisingly large number of them have been ordained as Protestant ministers, Catholic priests or nuns or Jewish rabbis. A few have even been fundamentalists! So some forms of psychotherapy and moderate religious belief hardly are incompatible.

The important question remains: Is there a high degree of correlation between devout, one-sided, dogmatic religiosity and neurosis (and other personality disorders)? My experience as a clinical psychologist leads me to conclude that there well may be. Some of the disturbed traits and behaviors that pietistic religionists tend to have (but, of course, not always have) include these:

A dearth of enlightened self-interest and self-direction. Pietistic religionists tend to be overdevoted, instead, to unduly sacrificing themselves for God, the church (or the state) and to ritualistic self-deprivation that they feel "bound" to follow for "sacred" reasons. They often give masochistic and self-abasing allegiance to ecclesiastical (and/or secular) lords and leaders. Instead of largely planning and directing their own lives, they often are mindlessly overdependent on religious-directed (or state-directed) creeds, rules and commandments.

Reduced social and human interest. Dogmatic religionists are overly focused on godly, spiritual and monastic interests. They often give greater service to God than to humanity and frequently start holy wars against dissidents to their deity and their church. Witness the recent murders by allegedly devout antiabortionists!

Refusal to accept ambiguity and uncertainty. In an obsessive-compulsive fashion, they hold to absolute necessity and complete certainty, even though our universe only seems to include probability and chance. They deny pliancy, alternative-seeking and pluralism in their own and other people's lives. They negate the scientific view that no hypothesis is proved indisputably "true" under all conditions at all times.

Allergy to unconditional self-acceptance. Emotionally healthy people accept themselves (and other humans) unconditionally—that is, whether they achieve success and whether all significant others approve of them. Dogmatic religionists unhealthily and conditionally accept themselves (and others) only when their God, their church (or state) and similar religionists approve of their thoughts, feelings and behaviors. Therefore, they steadily remain prone to, and often are in the throes of, severe anxiety, guilt and self-condemnation.

In rational-emotive therapy we show people that they "get" emotionally disturbed not only by early or later traumas in their lives but mainly by choosing goals and values that they strongly prefer and by unrealistically, illogically and defeatingly making them into one, two or three grandiose demands: (1) "I absolutely must succeed at important projects or I am an utterly worthless person"; (2) "Other people must treat me nicely or they are totally damnable"; (3) "Life conditions are utterly obligated to give me everything that I think I need or my existence is valueless."

When people clearly see that they are largely upsetting themselves with these godlike commandments, and when they convert them to reasonable—but often still compulsive—desires, they are able to reconstruct their disturbed thoughts, feelings and actions and make themselves much less anxious, depressed, enraged and self-hating and much more self-actualizing and happy.

Being a philosophical system of psychotherapy, rational emotive behavior therapy has much to learn from theological and secular religions. But individuals who choose to be religious also may learn something important from it, namely: Believe whatever you wish about God, the church, people and the universe. But see if you can choose a moderate instead of a fanatical form of religion. Try to avoid a doctrinal system through which you are dogmatically convinced that you absolutely must devote yourself to the one, only, right and unerring deity and to the one, true and infallible church. And try to avoid the certitude that you are God. Otherwise, in my view as a psychotherapist, you most probably are headed for emotional trouble.

CHALLENGE QUESTIONS

Does Religious Commitment Improve Mental Health?

1. Larson's emphasis on the relationship between religious commitment and mental health raises a "chicken and egg" question. How would researchers study the extent to which people who are drawn to religion are psychologically healthier than other people to begin with?
2. Ellis criticizes the research conducted on religious commitment and mental health as being biased by investigators who are trying to confirm their own beliefs. How might this kind of bias be removed from this research?
3. Imagine that you are a clinician treating a client with extremely different religious beliefs from your own. How would you approach this treatment?
4. Ellis speaks about the dangers of religious fanaticism. What factors should be considered in defining the demarcation point between religious commitment and religious fanaticism?
5. Some social commentators criticize some religious segments as being too political. Discuss the complex relationship between political agendas and religious values.

Suggested Readings

Argyle, M. (1999). *Psychology and religion: An introduction.* New York, NY: Routledge.

Koenig, H. G. (1998). *Handbook of religion and mental health.* San Diego, CA: Academic Press, Inc.

Spiegelman, J. M. (Ed). (1998). *Psychology and religion.* Tempe, AZ: New Falcon.

Spilka, B., & McIntosh, D. N. (Eds.). (1997). *The psychology of religion: Theoretical approaches.* Boulder, CO: Westview Press.

Wulff, D. M. (1997). *Psychology of religion: Classic and contemporary.* New York, NY: John Wiley & Sons, Inc.

ISSUE 16

Has the Deinstitutionalization of the Mentally Ill Worked?

YES: Howard H. Goldman, from "Deinstitutionalization and Community Care: Social Welfare Policy as Mental Health Policy," *Harvard Review of Psychiatry* (November/December 1998)

NO: E. Fuller Torrey, from "The Release of the Mentally Ill from Institutions: A Well-Intentioned Disaster," *The Chronicle of Higher Education* (June 13, 1997)

ISSUE SUMMARY

YES: Professor of psychiatry Howard H. Goldman discusses the benefits resulting from deinstitutionalization, a process that he believes has emerged from sound public policy.

NO: Psychiatrist E. Fuller Torrey calls the deinstitutionalization movement a disaster that has resulted in widespread homelessness among the mentally ill. He attributes this failed policy to social errors within the legal and academic realms.

During the middle part of the twentieth century, treatment of the mentally ill involved warehousing hundreds of thousands of people in state psychiatric hospitals in the most barbaric and inhumane conditions. Recognizing the tragedy of the American mental health system, aggressive public deinstitutionalization policies were enacted, with the aim of moving mentally ill people out of psychiatric hospitals and into the community. Although the intentions of the deinstitutionalization movement were admirable, some critics contend that the process has resulted in a national crisis in which countless numbers of people who would have been institutionalized a few decades earlier now roam the streets of America homeless and neglected. The situation is blatantly inhumane.

In tackling the controversy about the effectiveness of deinstitutionalization in the following selection, Howard H. Goldman acknowledges that there have been failures in implementing deinstitutionalization and community care, but he maintains that the basic policies continue to be sound. He contends that the problem is not deinstitutionalization per se but society's general attitude about mental illness, social welfare, and criminal justice that leaves people with severe mental illness at a disadvantage. Goldman advocates an attitude change, with hope and recovery being emphasized rather than expectations being lowered for mentally ill people. He also urges improvements in the social welfare system that will result in improvements in community care of the mentally ill.

In the second selection, E. Fuller Torrey speaks about the "disaster of deinstitutionalization" in which a well-intentioned public policy went wrong, resulting in the troubling phenomenon of widespread homelessness among mentally ill Americans. He contends that the deinstitutionalization process moved too rapidly and was influenced by financial pressures in which states were eager to move the expense of care to the federal government. According to Torrey, the problem was compounded by social errors within the legal and academic realms, where the nature of mental illness was misunderstood. He calls for a focusing of attention on the mistakes of what has been done so that Americans can learn what went wrong and why and can avoid such well-meaning disasters in the future.

POINT

- Although there have been failures in implementing deinstitutionalization and community care, the basic policies continue to be sound.
- Most individuals with severe mental illness have benefited from community care and deinstitutionalization, and so has society.

- Researchers have discovered how to deliver mental health services to individuals with severe mental disorders, particularly those with schizophrenia.

- Outcomes are better when hope and recovery are emphasized rather than limitations and lowered expectations.

- Although new standards of care and treatment have not yet been met, ample information is now available about how to provide effective community-based care.

COUNTERPOINT

- Deinstitutionalization is a perfect example of a well-intentioned public policy gone wrong and resulting in disaster.
- Approximately 150,000 mentally ill Americans are homeless; another 150,000 are in jail due to illness-related crimes; and many others are confined to bleak nursing homes.
- Severe mental illnesses are not merely one end of a spectrum of mental health; it is absurd to think that counseling and psychotherapy are sufficient interventions for people with diseases of the brain.
- Severe psychiatric disorders, such as schizophrenia, are neurological diseases; proper treatment demands expertise in brain physiology and pharmacology rather than in human relationships.
- It is imperative to focus attention on the mistakes that have been made with regard to the severely mentally ill in order to learn what went wrong and why and to avoid such well-meaning disasters in the future.

Howard H. Goldman

 **YES**

Deinstitutionalization and Community Care

H as deinstitutionalization failed, and if so, is it a failure of mental health policy—or of something else? Numerous articles[1-5] in the news media and professional literature in the United States and the United Kingdom seem to reflect a public conclusion that the dual mental health policies of deinstitutionalization and community care are inadequate. The evidence offered includes high rates of homelessness among persons with mental illness and incidents of violence attributable to individuals having a history of contact with the mental health service system. Also cited are the confinement of disproportionate numbers of mentally ill persons in jails and nursing homes, the failure of individuals with a history of mental illness to participate in the work force, and the specter of discharged patients "smoking and rocking away their days" in quiet desperation in board-and-care homes or their own apartments.

Are these observations accurate? If so, are they evidence of the failure of deinstitutionalization and community mental health policies, or do they represent the failure of a broader set of social welfare policies—policies by which individuals with severe and persistent mental illnesses are particularly disadvantaged? By "mental health policy" I mean the set of specific policies regulating the care and treatment of individuals with mental illness. These policies are under the direct control of state and local governmental mental health authorities and various private sector mental health decision-makers, such as providers and corporate benefits managers. By "social welfare policy" I mean the set of general policies regulating the provision of basic welfare benefits and services, such as income supports and rental subsidies, for the general population.

I would contend that although there have been failures in implementing deinstitutionalization and community care, the basic policies continue to be sound. To blame the mental health policies themselves is akin to blaming the victim. I would argue that deinstitutionalization and community care were (and continue to be) the appropriate overarching policies for mental health services, but that society's general attitudes about mental illness, social welfare, and criminal justice leave individuals with severe mental illness at a disadvantage.[6] As a result, some such persons have fallen deep into poverty and homelessness and have been exposed to conditions (for example, in homeless shelters and jails) similar to those that led to the reforms in the past. Nevertheless, I believe that despite limited implementation of the reforms of the 1950s and 1960s most individuals with severe mental illness have benefited from community care and deinstitutionalization—and so has society.

Although the principles of reform were untested when they were initiated during the post–World War II era,[7] we have since discovered how to deliver effective mental health services to individuals with severe mental disorders, particularly those with schizophrenia.[8] Evidence-based treatment recommendations and algorithms are available to guide practice, and research increasingly points out effective strategies to organize and finance care.[9] Service demonstrations, large-scale efforts intended to evaluate innovative approaches to service delivery, have taught us lessons about the design of the mental health services system and about the need to improve the content and quality of care and treatment within that system.[10–12] Although we have not yet succeeded in meeting these standards of care and treatment, we now have ample information about what we need to do to provide effective community-based care and about how to do it.[13]

Is there evidence, however, that more-widespread implementation of practice guidelines and treatment recommendations would solve the problems associated with the failure of current policies? And what do we know about the successes of deinstitutionalization and community care? Would increased prescription of the newer antipsychotics and the appropriate utilization of older agents eliminate homelessness among individuals with mental disorders? Would widespread use of family-supportive interventions prevent inappropriate confinement in jails?

Although more-effective treatment will be necessary to improve outcomes for individuals with severe mental illness, it is not sufficient. The problems of homelessness and misuse of the criminal justice system are not likely to be entirely solved by better treatment and the implementation of service innovations. Likewise, we have learned that improvements in the system of care may also be necessary but are not sufficient to attain improved outcomes.[10,11] It is time to appreciate the insufficiency of either strategy—the clinical or the systemic—alone while endorsing the necessity of both to realize better outcomes from deinstitutionalization and community care.

Patients repeatedly tell us that they prefer the community to the institution. They would rather be free and able to choose than involuntarily committed and ordered into treatment. They wish to live in independent housing, not supervised settings, and to participate in the labor market, not sheltered workshops. They prefer a philosophy guided by principles of recovery and rehabilitation rather than by resignation and lowered expectations.[14–17] Such preferences and choices seem reasonable.

Critics counter that individuals with a serious mental disorder are incapable of making informed choices because of their illness[3] and that innovative interventions are not effective.[1] The failure of patients to adhere to recommended treatment is a problem, undeniably resulting in poorer outcomes.[18] Some patients need supervision; some may require long-term hospitalization.

Involuntary detention for evaluation and longer-term care is a reasonable societal response to the threat of danger to oneself or others or even to grave disability or impaired self-care. Some persons with mental illness may become violent, especially under the influence of alcohol or other drugs.[19] These situations, however, are the exception rather than the rule. The majority of individuals with mental illness have demonstrated that they can live in community settings, most of them without on-site supervision.[20] Some have worked in competitive employment, occasionally requiring specialized support services.[8,21] Although the claims of universal success for supported housing[14] and employment have not been sustained and were probably unrealistic, these approaches to improved community integration have been demonstrated to be effective for substantial numbers of people with severe mental illness.[9] In addition numerous multisite outcomes studies[20,22,23] have demonstrated the effectiveness of other service interventions and benefit programs, such as Section 8 housing certificates for rental subsidy and outreach programs to engage homeless individuals in treatment and obtain disability benefits (such as Supplemental Security Income) for them.

Mainstream social welfare resources can be used effectively and responsibly by persons with severe mental illness. Are failures to implement these lessons evidence of a failed mental health policy, or of failed political will to allocate the resources, especially the social welfare resources, to realize the goals of deinstitutionalization and community care? Do we have the will to make these mental health policies a success by applying social welfare policy fairly to people disabled by mental illness? In my view this is the central problem of deinstitutionalization and community care.[6,13]

Another barrier to realizing the preferences of individuals with severe mental illness is scarcity of resources. Some critics[4,5] argue that the living conditions of people in the community are so poor that many would be better off in the hospital. Self-reported data on quality of life routinely indicate a preference for independent housing, even in impoverished accommodations.[24] Observers[5] have pointed out that individuals with severe mental illness living in poor accommodations in unwelcoming neighborhoods have achieved no more meaning in their lives and no more social integration than they had when living in institutions. This may be true (despite patient self-reports to the contrary[25]), but is it evidence of a failed mental health policy? Would people with serious mental illness be better off in institutions because they have not achieved a sense of greater meaning or purpose while living in the community?

The basic goals of deinstitutionalization and community care have been realized, as is reflected in decreased use of the mental hospitals, dramatically reduced lengths of stay, and increased time spent living in community settings.[26] For most individuals the civil liberties goals of "due process" and freedom from unnecessary or overly long institutional care have also been realized.[27] The cost-containment and distributive objectives have been fulfilled, too, since money that once went toward hospital budgets is increasingly being shifted to fund community resources.[28] Even the clinical goals of reducing the long-term effects of institutionalization[29,30] seem to have been accomplished, based on longer-term follow-up studies of individuals with schizophrenia.[31-33]

The hope that deinstitutionalization and community care would result in better community integration and improved qualify of life has yet to be fulfilled. A recent report from the Group for the Advancement of Psychiatry[34] has suggested that improving the long-term outcomes of individuals with severe mental illness hinges largely on avoidance of social ills (e.g., poverty, homelessness) and preventable behavior (e.g., suicide, misuse of substances). Some aspects of these objectives have been realized for a substantial portion of individuals with severe mental disorders. Some aspects, however, require further work: what we know about treatment and services needs to be implemented, and social welfare entitlements and opportunities shown to be effective in this population need to be instituted rather than denied.

Outcomes are more likely to be superior when we emphasize hope and recovery rather than limitations and lowered expectations. More has probably been gained by higher expectations than by lower ones. The service system and the social welfare system must be prepared to provide supports enabling individuals who can succeed to do so, and intensive care for persons who cannot benefit from the newer treatments. Novel antipsychotics, family interventions, assertive community treatment, supportive housing, crisis intervention, and individualized vocational placement will not help everyone.[8] No one will gain from these interventions, however, if patients are sent back to long-stay hospitals for detention and care. Similarly, not everyone will benefit from local mental health authorities[10] and other forms of services and systems integration,[35] or from jail diversion,[36] aggressive outreach in the streets,[22] centralized financing strategies that let the dollars follow the patient,[12] the Social Security representative payee program,[23] or Section 8 certificates and other rental subsidies.[20,37] But no one will benefit from these proven strategies if we reverse a half-century of deinstitutionalization and community mental health policy, as seems to be recommended by some critics of these policies.[1,3]

Mental health policy makers may be faulted for initiating policies 40 years ago without the tools for successful implementation (i.e., an effective treatment technology and the social welfare system and community support necessary to enable "community care"). The mental health field can be faulted for not doing more to apply what we now know about effective interventions.[9] On the other hand, it is extremely rewarding to visit the demonstration sites in the Center for Mental Health Services ACCESS Program and see mental health teams providing state-of-the-art outreach and treatment services for the most disabled homeless mentally ill individuals—denizens of the street previously thought "unreachable," who were ignored by the mental health system and society. Many of these people had given up on themselves and on the possibilities of housing and improved physical and mental health. Substantial numbers are now better clinically and socially. Some are competitively employed. Few of the 1800 clients enrolled in ACCESS services each year remain homeless, and more than 40% are independently housed.[35] It is frustrating, however, to realize the difficulty of getting mainstream mental health, housing, and social welfare services systems to absorb these once-homeless individuals into their community support systems.

Supportive social welfare policies and initiatives must be coupled with specialized mental health interventions, such as assertive community treatment, if initiatives fashioned after the ACCESS program are to succeed in communities across the nation. At the system level, social welfare agencies must communicate with mental health authorities and engage in joint policy development. Working agreements among agencies should focus on the responsibility that each will accept for meeting the social welfare needs of individuals who receive mental health services. These efforts are particularly critical in this era of cost-containment in health care and retrenchment in welfare and public housing support.

Access to rental subsidies, such as Section 8 certificates, needs to continue to expand—not contract. At the same time as mainstream housing resources are made available, housing policy must remain sensitive to special needs for support services and accommodations for individuals who have a mental disorder. Jail diversion programs should expand, and the criminal justice system should provide appropriate mental health services, as needed, for individuals who are not diverted. Income support programs, especially those for persons disabled by mental impairments, need to provide adequate benefits and be made more accessible if poor individuals with mental illness are to be able to live in the community. Welfare-reform policies, particularly return-to-work programs, should be coordinated with supportive employment interventions being developed in the mental health system, to provide opportunities for competitive employment. Outreach techniques can be applied effectively in each of these instances to increase the likelihood that individuals with mental impairments will be able to gain access to the mainstream benefits to which they are entitled.

Without the political will to implement the technical know-how and the lessons learned—and without a dedicated social welfare system to provide the entitlements and essential support services—the benefits of deinstitutionalization and community care will continue to be unrealized, and the hopes of people with severe mental disorders will go unfulfilled.

References

1. MacDonald H. The homeless don't need "outreach." Wall Street Journal 1997 Nov 17: 26–27.
2. Rose D. Television, madness, and community care. J Community Appl Soc Psychol [In press].
3. Torrey EF. Out of the shadows: confronting America's mental illness crisis. New York: Wiley, 1997.
4. Lamb HR, Weinberger LE. Persons with severe mental illness in jails and prisons: a review. Psychiatr Serv 1998; 49: 483–92.
5. Geller JL. At the margins of human rights and psychiatric care in North America. Acta Psychiatr Scand [In press].
6. Goldman HH, Morrissey JP. The alchemy of mental health policy: homelessness and the fourth cycle of reform. Am J Publ Health 1985; 75: 727–31.
7. Grob G. From asylum to community. Princeton, New Jersey: Princeton University Press, 1991.
8. Schizophrenia: treatment outcomes research. Schizophr Bull 1995; 21 (4).

9. Lehman AF, Steinwachs DM. Translating research into practice: the Schizophrenia Patient Outcomes Research Team (PORT) treatment recommendations. Schizophr Bull 1998; 24: 1–10.

10. Goldman HH, Morrissey JP, Ridgely MS. Evaluating the Robert Wood Johnson Foundation program on chronic mental illness. Millbank Q 1994; 72: 37–47.

11. Bickman L. A continuum of care: more is not always better. Am Psychol 1996; 51: 689–701.

12. Frank R, Morlock L. Managing fragmented public mental health services. New York: Millbank Memorial Fund, 1997.

13. Goldman HH. Implementing the lessons from services demonstrations: human rights issues. Acta Psychiatr Scand [In press].

14. Carling P. Housing, community support, and homelessness: emerging policy in mental health systems. N Engl J Public Policy 1992; 8: 281–95.

15. Ridgway P, Carling P, Chamberlain J. Coming home: ex-patients view housing options and needs. Presented at a National Conference on Housing and Support, Burlington, Vermont, 1988.

16. Rose D. Living in the community. London, England: Sainsbury Centre for Mental Health, 1996.

17. Fisher D. Self-managed care: meaningful participation of consumers/survivors in managed care. In: Minkoff K, Pollack D, eds. Managed mental health care in the public sector: a survival manual. Singapore: Harwood, 1997: 283–93.

18. Weiden P, Olfson M, Essock S. Medication noncompliance in schizophrenia: effects on mental health service policy. In: Blackwell B, ed. Treatment compliance and the therapeutic alliance. Singapore: Harwood, 1997: 35–60.

19. Monahan J, Steadman HJ, eds. Violence and mental disorder: developments in risk assessment. Chicago: University of Chicago Press, 1994.

20. Newman SJ, Reschovsky JD, Kaneda K, Hendrick AM. The effects of independent living on persons with chronic mental illness: an assessment of the Section 8 certificate program. Milbank Q 1994; 72: 171–98.

21. Mueser KT, Bond GR, Drake RE, Resnick SG. Models of community care for severe mental illness: a review of research on case management. Schizophr Bull 1998; 24: 37–74.

22. Barrow SM, Hellman F, Lovell AM, Plapinger JD, Struening EL, Eval2ating outreach services: lessons from a study of five programs. New Dir Ment Health Serv 1991; 52: 29–45.

23. Rosenheck R, Lam J, Randolph F. Impact of representative payees on substance use by homeless persons with serious mental illness. Psychiatr Serv 1997; 48: 800–6.

24. Lehman AF, Slaughter JG, Myers CP. The quality of life in alternative residential settings. Psychiatr Q 1991; 62: 35–49.

25. Drake RE, Wallach MA. Mental patients' attitudes toward hospitalization: a neglected aspect of hospital tenure. Am J Psychiatry 1988; 145: 29–34.

26. Redick R, Witkin M, Atay J, Manderscheid R. Highlights of organized mental health services in 1992 and major national and state trends. In: Manderscheid R, Sonnenschein M, eds. Mental Health, United States, 1996. Washington, DC: US Government Printing Office, 1996: 90–137; DHHS publication no (SMA) 96–3098.

27. Petrila J, Levin B. Impact of mental disability law on mental health policies and services. In: Petrila J, Levin B, eds. Mental health services. New York; Oxford University Press, 1996: 38–62.

28. National Association of State Mental Health Program Directors (NASMHPD) Research Institute. Closing and reorganizing state psychiatric hospitals: 1996. Alexandria, Virginia: NASMHPD Research Institute, 1997; State Mental Health Agency Profile System Highlights no 1.

29. Gruenberg E. The social breakdown syndrome and its prevention. In: Arieti S, ed. American handbook of psychiatry. 2nd ed. New York: Basic, 1974: 697–711.

30. Wing J. Institutionalism in mental hospitals. Br J Soc Clin Psychol 1962; 1: 38–51.

31. Ciompi L. The natural history of schizophrenia in the long term. Br J Psychiatry 1980; 136: 413–20.
32. Harding CM, Brooks GW, Ashikaga T, Strauss JS, Breier A.The Vermont longitudinal study of persons with severe mental illness, I: Methodology, study sample, and overall status 32 years later. Am J Psychiatry 1987; 144: 718–26.
33. Harding CM, Brooks GW, Ashikaga T, Strauss JS, Breier A. The Vermont longitudinal study of persons with severe mental illness, II: Long-term outcome of subjects who retrospectively met DSM-III criteria for schizophrenia. Am J Psychiatry 1987; 144: 727–35.
34. Adler D, Pajer K, Ellison JM, Dorwart R, Siris S, Goldman H, et al. Schizophrenia and the life cycle. Community Ment Health J 1995; 31: 249–62.
35. Rosenheck R, Morrissey J, Lam J, Calloway M, Johnsen M, Goldman H, et al. Service system integration, access to services, and housing outcomes in a program for homeless persons with severe mental illness. Am J Publ Health [In press].
36. Steadman HJ, Barbera SS, Dennis DL. A national survey of jail diversion programs for mentally ill detainees. Hosp Community Psychiatry 1994; 45: 1109–13.
37. Shern DL, Felton CJ, Hough R, Lehman AF, Goldfinger S, Valencia E, et al. Housing outcomes for homeless adults with mental illness: results from the second-round McKinney program. Psychiatr Serv 1997; 48: 239–41.

NO

E. Fuller Torrey

The Release of the Mentally Ill from Institutions

T he practice, over the past four decades, of releasing people with severe mental illnesses from institutions has been one of the largest social experiments in 20th-century America. Research shows that if state psychiatric hospitals today housed the same proportion of the population as they did in 1955, almost 900,000 people would be in such institutions now. Instead, such facilities house fewer than 70,000 patients. Thus, more than 800,000 people are living outside of hospitals who would have been hospitalized 40 years ago.

Where are these people? Approximately half of them are living with their families, in group homes or boarding houses, or on their own. Many of these people are doing well. Among the other half, however, approximately 150,000 are homeless on any given day, and another 150,000 are in jails and prisons, most charged with crimes directly attributable to their mental illnesses. The remainder are confined to nursing homes, many of which—because they lack recreational programs designed for mentally ill residents or are located in urban areas where it is unsafe for residents to walk outside—are substantially bleaker and more restrictive than the state psychiatric hospitals used to be.

What price has the average American citizen paid for this experiment? One cannot go into any city without confronting severely mentally ill people living in parks or on the street. Many public libraries and bus and train stations have become de facto psychiatric shelters. Police officers routinely spend more time responding to psychiatric crises than to robberies or burglaries. And a small number of the severely mentally ill who are not receiving treatment become violent, leading to crimes that include an estimated 1,000 homicides a year—or approximately 4 per cent of all homicides.

The disaster of "deinstitutionalization" is, in fact, a perfect case study of a well-intentioned public policy gone wrong. The policy originated as a reaction against public exposés of state psychiatric hospitals as "snake pits" in the 1940s and 1950s; it was reinforced by the introduction of the first effective medications for treating psychoses in the mid-to-late 1950s. At the time the movement got under way in the late 1950s, we had no pilot programs and virtually no data with which to predict what would happen.

From E. Fuller Torrey, "The Release of the Mentally Ill from Institutions: A Well-Intentioned Disaster," *The Chronicle of Higher Education*, vol. 43, no. 40 (June 13, 1997). Copyright © 1997 by E. Fuller Torrey. Reprinted by permission of the author.

Rather than starting to release patients in a few locales and measuring the outcome, officials implemented the policy in cities and counties across the United States virtually simultaneously, based on the widespread hope that the new drugs would cure people and the widespread belief in state legislatures that the policy would save taxpayers money. In addition, with the publication of Thomas Szasz's *The Myth of Mental Illness* in 1961 and Ken Kesey's *One Flew Over the Cuckoo's Nest* the following year, the idea gained currency that there really wasn't much wrong with those folks in the psychiatric hospitals. Deinstitutionalization quickly became the "humane" thing to do. Without adequate follow-up of the discharged patients, however, it was doomed to failure.

Changes in who paid for the treatment of mentally ill people also guaranteed that deinstitutionalization would fail. Until the early 1960s, almost all of the costs of programs for the mentally ill were borne by the states. However, in the early 1960s, Congress realized that the people who were being discharged would need financial support. It made seriously mentally ill people eligible for such federal programs as Supplemental Security Income, food stamps, and certain housing and Medicaid and Medicare programs. States thus could shift the cost of care for the mentally ill to the federal government simply by discharging patients from state hospitals or transferring them to nursing homes. The states reaped all their savings right away; they had no financial incentive to insure that patients received adequate follow-up care.

The result was a giant fiscal carrot, which the states eagerly devoured. The federal share of total costs for care of the mentally ill climbed to 62 per cent by 1994 from 2 per cent in 1963. With no fiscal incentive to do so, the states provided little, if any, care for the discharged patients, and any student in Public Policy 101 could have successfully predicted the result.

The legal profession and law schools compounded the failure of deinstitutionalization. The 1960s was the decade of civil rights, and many legal activists categorized the mentally ill with blacks, Hispanics, and other ethnic groups as legitimate targets for liberation. The American Civil Liberties Union, the privately supported Mental Health Law Project, and some law schools devoted significant resources to establishing legal precedents to force states to discharge psychiatric patients from hospitals and to make it increasingly difficult to rehospitalize them involuntarily. The lawyers' efforts were abetted by the Citizens Commission on Human Rights, an arm of the Church of Scientology, which has opposed involuntary hospitalization and the use of medications for the mentally ill.

Lawyers made fundamental errors in categorizing severely mentally ill people with blacks and other minority groups and in opposing all involuntary treatment. They assumed that severely mentally ill people, like those who are not mentally ill, are able to think logically about their own needs and to seek help voluntarily if and when they need it. In fact, studies by Xavier Amador, a psychologist at the New York State Psychiatric Institute, and other researchers have shown that approximately half of those with severe mental illnesses have markedly impaired insight into their illnesses and personal needs. This impaired insight is part of the brain dysfunction causing their illnesses. About half of the severely mentally ill people who were "liberated" from psychiatric hospitals never sought treatment, because they did not—and do not—believe there is anything wrong with them.

The lawyers involved would have become aware of this problem if they had asked what was happening to the people being released from institutions. As early as 1972, Marc Abramson, a psychiatrist with the San Mateo County Department of Mental Health in California, noted that "mentally disordered persons are being increasingly subjected to arrest and criminal prosecution" as a result of leaving institutions. By the early 1980s, psychiatrists and other experts had published studies showing that one-third of discharged psychiatric patients were homeless within six months. But the lawyers and the law schools did not ask such questions, for they were driving on the automatic pilot of ideology.

Academic departments of psychiatry, psychology, and social work also share some blame for the disaster. Beginning with the "mental-hygiene movement" of the 1920s, these departments promoted the idea that severe mental illnesses are merely one end of the spectrum of mental health, different in degree but not in kind from the panoply of normal reactions to life's disappointments and vicissitudes. The corollary of this was that one could nip mental illness in the bud by providing counseling and psychotherapy to the "worried well," so that today's unhappiness would not become tomorrow's schizophrenia.

❧

Over the past decade, it has become clear that this view of mental illness is profoundly wrong. Severe psychiatric disorders are no more linked to minor mental perturbations than are multiple sclerosis, Parkinson's disease, or Alzheimer's disease. The severe psychiatric disorders—including schizophrenia, bipolar disorder, severe depression, and obsessive-compulsive disorder—have been, like other neurologically caused diseases such as Parkinson's and Alzheimer's, clearly proved to be diseases of the brain. Their proper treatment demands expertise in brain physiology and pharmacology, rather than in human relationships. We have trained literally hundreds of thousands of mental-health professionals—psychiatrists, psychologists, and psychiatric social workers—to provide counseling when what we really need are a few thousand professionals such as neurologists, who are trained to treat diseases of the brain.

What should be done now? First, a formal divorce of "mental health" from mental illness is overdue. What this would mean is that existing psychologists, social workers, and counselors would continue to focus on helping people to deal with the problems of everyday life. Psychiatry, on the other hand, would merge with neurology to produce researchers and clinicians who possess expertise on the full spectrum of brain diseases. This would place neuropsychiatry as a single entity exactly where it was 100 years ago, before the Freudian revolution and the mental-hygiene movement led it to focus on general mental health rather than the most severe mental disorders.

Second, it is incumbent on the legal profession and law schools to revisit the consequences of their well-meaning but misguided efforts, which have made it extremely difficult to involuntarily hospitalize or treat people with severe mental illnesses. Lawyers and public-interest-law projects should take the lead in trying to modify state laws so that mentally ill people who lack insight into their condition can be treated.

Finally, schools of public policy should study how to structure government programs to include financial incentives to provide services for the mentally ill—rather than incentives not to provide them, as is now the case. For example, states could offer bonuses to local governments that reduced the number of severely mentally ill people in local jails, or that increased the number of such people who hold jobs. Given the major changes under way in the delivery of medical services in this country, this is a propitious time to set up small pilot programs with different incentive systems and to examine a variety of ways to measure their success, including the quality of life of the people being served.

In his *Collected Essays,* Aldous Huxley wrote: "That men do not learn very much from the lessons of history is the most important of all the lessons that history has to teach." It is imperative that we focus attention on the disaster of what we have done to the severely mentally ill so that we may learn what went wrong and why—and avoid such well-meaning disasters in the future. The exercise is not merely academic, however; it directly affects the lives of hundreds of thousands of individuals and their families.

CHALLENGE QUESTIONS

Has the Deinstitutionalization of the Mentally Ill Worked?

1. Goldman takes a fairly positive view with regard to the social impact of deinstitutionalization. Based on your own observations of the mentally ill, how would you respond to his premise that community care of these individuals is adequate?
2. Torrey urges a split in professional responsibilities such that psychologists, social workers, and counselors limit their focus to helping people with the problems of everyday life; psychiatry would merge with neurology to focus on brain diseases. What advantages and disadvantages do you see with this proposal?
3. Imagine that you have the responsibility of ensuring adequate care for 10 mentally ill individuals in your community. How would you design a program to ensure their comprehensive care?
4. Some critics have argued that any person, whether mentally ill or not, has the constitutional right to live a homeless life. What arguments can you generate on both sides of this issue?
5. The legal establishment often faces the difficult choice about what to do with a severely mentally ill person who has committed a serious crime. What factors should be considered in determining the extent to which a mentally ill person should be held responsible for criminal behavior?

Suggested Readings

Dowdall, G. W. (1999). Mental hospitals and deinstitutionalization. In C. S. Anehensel, & J. C. Phelan (Eds.), *Handbook of sociology of mental health. Handbook of sociology and social research.* (pp. 519–537). New York, NY: Kluwer Academic/Plenum Publishers.

Lamb, H. R. (1998). Deinstitutionalization at the beginning of the new millenium. *Harvard Review of Psychiatry*, 6(1), 1–10.

Lamb, H. R. (1993). Lessons learned from deinstitutionalization in the United States. *British Journal of Psychiatry*, 162, 587–592.

Okin, R. L. (1995). Testing the limits of deinstitutionalization. *Psychiatric Services*, 46(6), 569–574.

Torrey, E. F. (1997). *Out of the shadows: Confronting America's mental illness crisis.* New York, NY: John Wiley & Sons, Inc.

On the Internet . . . DUSHKIN ONLINE

Oregon's Death with Dignity Act

This site of the Oregon Health Division of the Oregon Department of Human Resources contains an overview of the 1997 Oregon Death with Dignity Act, which allows physician-assisted suicide for the terminally ill.

http://www.ohd.hr.state.or.us/cdpe/chs/pas/pas.htm

Society for the Psychological Study of Lesbian, Gay, and Bisexual Issues: Division 44 of the American Psychological Association

This division of the American Psychological Association focuses on gaining an understanding for and promoting the education of gay, lesbian, and bisexual issues in psychology.

http://www.apa.org/divisions/div44/

Association for Gay, Lesbian, and Bisexual Issues in Counseling

This is the Web site of the Association for Gay, Lesbian, and Bisexual Issues in Counseling, a division of the American Counseling Association that works toward educating mental health service providers about issues faced by gay, lesbian, bisexual, and transgendered individuals.

http://www.aglbic.org

Institute for Psychological Therapies

This is the Web site of the Institute for Psychological Therapies (IPT), a private practice of clinical psychology whose primary work is related to allegations of child sexual abuse.

http://www.ipt-forensics.com

National Mental Health Association: Electroconvulsive Therapy (ECT)

This factsheet of the National Mental Health Association (NMHA) on electroconvulsive therapy (ECT) outlines the nature, the surrounding controversy, and the usage of ECT.

http://www.nmha.org/infoctr/factsheets/62.cfm

PART 5

Ethical and Legal Issues

*B*ecause *mental health professionals have a potentially tremendous impact on the lives of the clients with whom they work, there are many important ethical and legal issues about which they must be aware. A comprehensive study of abnormal psychology must include consideration of the ethical and legal issues that impact the field. Some of these issues pertain to personal client choices that have profound implications, such as the choice to hasten death, to pursue sexual orientation conversion therapy, or to undergo electroconvulsive therapy. Other controversies have legal implications, such as those involving the arguments of some clients that their criminal behavior should be excused because it resulted from some traumatic life experience.*

- Should Mental Health Professionals Serve as Gatekeepers for Physician-Assisted Suicide?

- Is Sexual Orientation Conversion Therapy Ethical?

- Is the Abuse Excuse Overused?

- Is Electroconvulsive Therapy Ethical?

ISSUE 17

Should Mental Health Professionals Serve as Gatekeepers for Physician-Assisted Suicide?

YES: Rhea K. Farberman, from "Terminal Illness and Hastened Death Requests: The Important Role of the Mental Health Professional," *Professional Psychology: Research and Practice* (vol. 28, no. 6, 1997)

NO: Mark D. Sullivan, Linda Ganzini, and Stuart J. Youngner, from "Should Psychiatrists Serve as Gatekeepers for Physician-Assisted Suicide?" *The Hastings Center Report* (July–August 1998)

ISSUE SUMMARY

YES: Rhea K. Farberman, director of public communications for the American Psychological Association, makes the case that mental health professionals should be called upon to assess terminally ill persons requesting hastened death in order to ensure that decision making is rational and free of coercion.

NO: Psychiatrists Mark D. Sullivan, Linda Ganzini, and Stuart J. Youngner argue that the reliance on mental health professionals to be suicide gatekeepers involves an inappropriate use of clinical procedures to disguise society's ambivalence about suicide itself.

$\mathbf{M}$ost mental health professionals are drawn to their careers out of a desire to help people live happier and healthier lives. Few ever give a thought to the possibility that they might be called upon to help people take their own lives. In recent decades, however, increasing attention has been given to the legal and ethical right of an individual to choose suicide, particularly in cases in which the person has a terminal disease. Michigan physician Jack Kevorkian has brought the issue into public awareness because he has facilitated the deaths of dozens of seriously ill individuals.

The professional assessment of seriously ill individuals wanting to commit suicide is complex primarily because it is difficult to determine the extent to which profound depression about being sick propels these individuals to make impulsive decisions. As Americans have grown increasingly accepting of the right of seriously ill people to take their own lives, they have also turned more and more to mental health professionals to play a role in this process. Mental health professionals have been called upon to help protect the sick person's rights, provide support to loved ones, and evaluate whether or not the sick person has the capacity to make a rational decision.

In the following selection, Rhea K. Farberman argues that a mental health assessment by a qualified mental health professional is imperative for any ill person requesting a hastened death. She contends that the professional should first work to separate clinical depression from the patient's grief, fear of dying, fear of the unknown, and fear of pain. Farberman urges professionals to put aside their personal beliefs on the issue and to strive to ensure that the patient's decision-making process is rational, well reasoned, and free of coercion.

Taking a much more cautious stand on the issue, Mark D. Sullivan, Linda Ganzini, and Stuart J. Youngner argue in the second selection that the reliance on mental health professionals to be suicide gatekeepers is associated with an inappropriate use of clinical procedures to disguise society's ambivalence about suicide itself. They assert that society is shifting responsibility for a troubling moral decision to an outside specialist, rather than relying on shared decision making involving the patient, family, and physician. Sullivan, Ganzini, and Youngner offer several points of caution about using mental health professionals in this context.

POINT

- A mental health assessment by a qualified mental health professional is imperative for any ill person requesting a hastened death.

- A mental health professional helps to evaluate if the patient has the capacity to make a rational decision about dying.

- In light of extensive clinical and research experience, psychologists and other mental health professionals are an underused resource when patients and their significant others are forced to deal with end-of-life care issues.

- Competent mental health professionals recognize the importance of basing recommendations on data derived from several sources, including the involvement of significant others and family members.

COUNTERPOINT

- Mental health professionals should not have the social authority to use themselves as the measure of when it is the right time for a person to die.

- The determination of adequate decision-making capacity is difficult because competence is a complex social, rather than scientific, construct.

- The relevant expertise in this area is limited in light of the fact that so few mental health professionals regularly work with seriously ill and dying patients in hospital, nursing home, and hospice settings.

- There is a risk that, in the absence of robust independent standards, mental health professionals may resolve the ethical dilemmas concerning physician-assisted suicide in an ad hoc fashion, using themselves as the "reasonable person" standard by which to judge the patient's decision to die.

Rhea K. Farberman

 **YES**

Terminal Illness and Hastened Death Requests

Do terminally ill individuals have the right to decide the timing of their death and to have assistance in a hastened death? This article is based on an American Psychological Association briefing paper prepared for the media regarding the June 1997 Supreme Court decision on physician-assisted suicide. The Court's decision clarified the role medical doctors can play in caring for the terminally ill, but the role of mental health professionals is still evolving. It is clear, however, that on the basis of behavioral research and clinical experience, a mental health assessment by a qualified mental health professional is imperative for any ill person requesting a hastened death.

Becoming ill is unfortunately a part of living. The number of terminally ill persons who decide to hasten their death is difficult to define and estimate, but several recent studies have found a fairly large number of requests for assistance in dying as well as a high rate of acquiescence to these requests by physicians. In addition, public opinion polls consistently show that at least 60% of those surveyed are in favor of physician-assisted suicide for terminally ill patients.

New technologies have given health care professionals more effective ways to treat and retard serious illness and therefore sustain life. We can all agree that this medical progress has lengthened life and changed the end-of-life process. However, there is disagreement as to whether this progress is beneficial for the patient. Has the end-of-life process been changed in a way that is harmful to human dignity and self-determination? Or, is every day worth living regardless of the quality of that existence? These are complex questions that involve our fundamental values about life and liberty. They elude easy answers.

In June 1997, the U.S. Supreme Court ruled that terminally ill people do *not* have a constitutional right to doctor-assisted suicide, but the Court gave states the option of enacting their own assistance-in-dying statutes (*Vacco v. Quill*, 96-10, 1997; *Washington v. Glucksberg*, 95-1858, 1997). The Court's decision lent some greater clarity to the role that medical doctors can play in providing care and comfort to the terminally ill; still evolving, however, is the role of the mental health professional in working with terminally ill people. What is clear is that there is still much controversy and difference of opinion

From Rhea K. Farberman, "Terminal Illness and Hastened Death Requests: The Important Role of the Mental Health Professional," *Professional Psychology: Research and Practice*, vol. 28, no. 6 (February 1997). Copyright © 1997 by The American Psychological Association. Reprinted by permission of The American Psychological Association and the author.

about the end-of-life process and, therefore, end-of-life care. Further court challenges about the right of dying people are likely. Because of this uncertainty, it is altogether likely that medical teams and families will still have to deal with hastened death requests from dying patients.

There are several concerns about such a request for a hastened death from a terminally ill person. One such concern is that depression and suicidal thoughts in seriously ill people are common. A 1994 study found that the prevalence rates for both major and minor depression among terminally ill cancer patients receiving palliative (relief of pain and discomfort) care ranged from 13% to 26%. At the same time, the capacity of physicians untrained in psychiatry to diagnose depression is alarmingly low. On the basis of numerous studies, it is estimated that depression is correctly diagnosed by physicians in only 20% to 60% of the cases presented. It is important to remember that the reasoning on which a terminally ill person (whose judgments are not impaired by mental disorders) bases a decision to end his or her life is fundamentally different from the reasoning a clinically depressed person uses to justify suicide.

Depression in Seriously Ill People

Although many people consider depression normal in a seriously ill person, depression is a diagnoseable illness and is highly treatable. The first task of a mental health professional when dealing with a terminally ill person is to separate the patient's prospective grief, fear of dying, fear of the unknown, and fear of pain from clinical depression.

It is often assumed, but not correctly so, that the most pain-ridden, physically distressed terminally ill patients are more likely to become depressed or suicidal when compared to other less afflicted patients. In reality, a person's lifelong values, temperament, and behavior are often better indicators of who is at risk for suicide thoughts when ill. In fact, the importance of terminal illness, physical decline, or chronic pain as a reason for suicide has been seriously questioned by the behavioral science research on end-of-life decisions.

Ill people and elderly people are often concerned about becoming a burden to their families. Some research has in fact shown that control, quality of life, and loss of independence are weightier issues for terminally ill patients than is actual pain. However, pain lessens the patient's ability to do things for him or herself, which in turn adds to the patient's concern about the loss of independence and about burdening loved ones.

In short, there is no simple formula explaining what motivates an ill person to want to end his or her life. Most research points to multiple causes, including anxiety, fear, desire for control and dignity, a lack of information or an inability to get questions answered, depression, and cognitive losses. Although pain management is at times a problem for terminally ill patients (research shows that terminal cancer patients are particularly at risk for insufficient pain control), pain, in and of itself, is not the single most important factor in suicide ideation. Much of this research suggests that what is needed for the terminally ill patient is improved palliative care and more psychosocial support at the end of his or her life.

The Role of Mental Health Professionals in End-of-Life Decisions

In the absence of mental illness, a terminally ill person can be capable of rational thinking and an informed choice. However, separating sadness brought on by the loss of ability and the loss of the persona the patient once was from clinical depression brought on by a mental disorder is a complex clinical judgment. One critical factor is the patient's self-esteem. The self-esteem of a person who is grieving or is terminally ill is not affected by the illness; however, the self-esteem of a clinically depressed person is.

Attempting to determine to what degree, if any, a terminally ill person is experiencing depression or other cognitive impairments is extremely difficult. The mental health professional who is called on to make such an evaluation should have specific training and clinical experience working with that population group, be it elderly persons, cancer patients, AIDS patients, and so forth.

Today, psychologists and other mental health professionals are an underused resource when patients and their significant others are forced to deal with end-of-life care issues. Psychologists not only have clinical experience on this issue, but also have conducted much of the research from which we have learned a great deal about depression, the diagnosis of depressive illness, patients' coping with end of life, and support of significant others during the end-of-life process.

Some health professionals who work in hospitals and hospice settings say that in reality, hastened death is already a relatively common occurrence—the opening of the morphine drip to allow for a lethal dose of the pain killer, for example. The role of the psychologist working with a terminally ill patient who wishes to end his or her life is not to control the patient's decision but to attempt to ensure that the patient's decision-making process is rational, well-reasoned, and free of coercion.

Mental health professionals who work in this area must approach their work in a neutral manner. Their personal beliefs on the issue should not influence the process. The role of the mental health professional is (a) to attempt to ensure that the end-of-life decision-making process includes a complete assessment of the patient's ability to make a rational judgment and (b) to help protect the patient's right to self-determination. The mental health professional attempts to bring the pertinent issues to the patient and his or her family and significant others and to assist the patient and significant others in understanding and working through those issues.

The American Psychological Association (APA) does not advocate for or against assisted suicide. What psychologists do support is high-quality end-of-life care and informed end-of-life decisions that are based on the correct assessment of the patient's mental capacity, social support systems, and degree of self-determination.

Surveys of mental health professionals have found that most (as high as 81% in the case of a survey of members of APA's Division of Psychotherapy) believe that assisted suicide *can be* a rational choice within the following parameters: (a) The patient is acting under his or her own free will, (b) the patient is competent to make an informed and reasonable judgment, (c) the patient's physical condition is hopeless, and (d) the patient is under no outside pressure (financial pressure, pressure from family, and so forth) to make the choice.

The Psychologist's Role

In helping terminally ill patients make end-of-life decisions, psychologists should do the following:

1. Protect the client's rights.
2. Support the family.
3. Don't allow physicians to affix a mental illness diagnosis if it is inappropriate.
4. Help evaluate if the patient has the capacity to make a rational decision, that is, does not have a mental disorder that significantly impairs his or her ability to reason, is fully informed of all treatment options, understands all treatment options, is not being coerced, and is using a rational, reasoned process to reach his or her decision.

Early referral of a terminally ill patient to a mental health professional can help prevent premature deterioration in the quality of life for the patient and allows for the teaching of coping skills to both the patient and his or her family. In addition, research has shown that psychological interventions with both cardiac and cancer patients can help in the recovery process by strengthening medical compliance and by helping the patient make healthful lifestyle choices. Another reason for having a mental health professional available to a person who has been diagnosed with a serious illness is that research has shown that a person with such an illness is at greatest risk for suicide when he or she first learns of the diagnosis.

The analysis of end-of-life care by a psychologist or other competent mental health professional would typically include the assessment of data from multiple interviews with the patient as well as multiple contacts with the family or significant others, a full review of the patient history, and a full cognitive and depression assessment. The psychologist should bring to this work a thorough understanding of the pertinent psychological literature and data on end-of-life issues.

Furthermore, because end-of-life decisions have family and social consequences, significant others and family members should be involved in the decision-making process if at all possible. In fact, there is research that shows that survivors who are involved in end-of-life decisions do better after the death than those who were not part of the decision-making process.

In determining whether a person is competent to make a reasoned end-of-life decision, most psychologists like to see convergent validity across a number of different measures of the patient's mental health and capacity (i.e., multiple assessments that point to the same conclusion). If significant symptoms of a mood disorder or depression are present, treatment should be attempted before any request for assistance in dying is considered. With resolution of the depression, the patient's capacity to weigh the available options may improve and his or her attitude toward death may change.

The Dilemma for Physicians

Adequate pain control is critical for terminally ill patients, but it is often problematic for physicians. Fear of the patient's addiction affects the physician's willingness to prescribe the strong pain drugs required and also interferes with the patient's willingness to take the prescribed medications. Physicians also worry about how state and federal regulatory agencies will interpret their writing such prescriptions.

In addition, as discussed before, most primary care and internal medicine doctors are not trained in the assessment and treatment of psychiatric illness. They cannot be expected to accurately diagnose a depressive disorder.

Public Policy Questions

Additional public discourse and legislative action on the question of end-of-life care are expected. Already some state legislatures are looking at proposed legislation that would mandate certain pain control procedures for terminally ill people.

What continues to be critical for the courts, legislatures, and the public to recognize is the importance of ensuring that an appropriately trained and licensed mental health professional is involved in the end-of-life decision process. Having a terminal illness is a stressful, sad, and painful experience for any human being. However, terminal illness, in and of itself, is not typically the cause of suicide ideation. The important clinical assessment is whether the patient is fearful, is not receiving the correct treatment for pain, and is concerned about the emotional or financial stress he or she feels is being inflicted on the family or whether the patient is suffering from a clinical depression or a cognitive deficit.

Concern does exist within the psychological community that if some states do move to legalize assisted suicide, this could present a slippery slope equation for our society. That is, if hastened death becomes an option for the terminally ill, will society's attitude toward those people with other types of health or physical challenges be affected? How will legalized assisted suicide affect the position within our society of elderly people, people with chronic debilitating illness, or people with disabilities? In short, every American has a stake in whatever course this country takes vis-à-vis end-of-life issues, because the direction taken will affect whole communities. Psychological research has proven without question that behavior is often modeled.

An added caution: At a time when the population is aging (elderly people are disproportionately represented in the national suicide statistics), where there exist extreme financial pressures on the provision of medical care, and when the social safety net is at risk, many mental health professionals worry that physician-assisted suicide may become legal *without* the added requirement of a mental health assessment by a qualified mental health professional.

More Research Needed

Suicidal thoughts are complex and difficult to study. More research about what motivates a person with a terminal illness to want to hasten his or her death is needed. For example, answers are needed to the following questions:

1. What effect do improved social–psychological supports have on the hastened death ideation of terminally ill patients?
2. What effect does improved palliative care have on the hastened death ideation of terminally ill patients?
3. How do the issues of race, age, ageism, disabilities, religious beliefs, and gender play into the risk factors of an individual for end-of-life decisions?

Complicating the issue is the fact that no definitive data exist on the prevalence (with terminally ill patients) of suicide ideation caused by a depressive illness. Studies have shown that about 5% of the total U.S. population will at any one time suffer from a major depression with some level of suicidal thinking. From this figure, it may be assumed that some fraction of terminally ill patients will suffer from clinical depression that coincides with their illness but did not arise from it.

Conclusion

Any discussion about the ending of a life is controversial and highly charged because it involves our most personal value systems. In the final analysis, we may be called on, both individually and as a society, to balance the important and yet competing interests of preserving human life versus the desire to die peacefully and with dignity. This is a vexing equation for all health care professionals, for the ill and their families, for religious institutions, and for society as a whole. What the state-of-the-art behavioral research and clinical experience of mental health professionals can tell us to date is that a mental health assessment of any ill person who is requesting assistance in hastening his or her death is imperative.

Mark D. Sullivan, Linda Ganzini, and
Stuart J. Youngner

 **NO**

Should Psychiatrists Serve as Gatekeepers for Physician-Assisted Suicide?

As our society debates the legalization of physician-assisted suicide for terminally ill persons, mandatory psychiatric evaluation has been suggested as a safeguard against abuse. This is to guarantee that the patient choosing physician-assisted death is mentally competent to do so. As psychiatrists who have provided both psychiatric and ethics consultation for dying patients, we believe there are serious unacknowledged problems with this "safeguard."

Our arguments do not depend on a moral position for or against physician-assisted suicide. Nor do we deny that psychiatry has a great deal to offer in the evaluation and treatment of patients who request assistance in dying. Rather, we argue that due to the lack of applicable objective standards of decisionmaking capacity and the inevitable distortion of the mental health professional's role as a clinician, we should think carefully before requiring psychiatric certification of competence in every case. We are concerned that this "safeguard" inappropriately uses a technical clinical procedure to disguise our society's ambivalence about suicide itself. By making every patient who requests physician-assisted suicide jump the hurdle of psychiatric evaluation, we shift responsibility for a troubling moral decision from the therapeutically directed and socially embedded context of shared decisionmaking of patient, family, and primary physician to an outside specialist. As this specialist, the consultant psychiatrist becomes a secular priest dressed in the clothes of a medical expert.

The Question of Safeguards

Health professionals who believe assisted suicide may sometimes be appropriate have called for safeguards to ensure that suffering patients who are assisted to die are choosing suicide freely and autonomously. To address these concerns, recent initiatives for the legalization of assisted suicide have incorporated specific restrictions to assure autonomous decisionmaking. Some initiatives have included the requirement that the request be expressed consistently over a specified period of time in order to prevent impulsive decisions and allow time for

From Mark D. Sullivan, Linda Ganzini, and Stuart J. Youngner, "Should Psychiatrists Serve as Gatekeepers for Physician-Assisted Suicide?" *The Hastings Center Report*, vol. 28, no. 4 (July–August 1998). Copyright © 1998 by The Hastings Center. Reprinted by permission of The Hastings Center and the authors.

ambivalence to be manifested. A delay of fifteen days in Oregon and nine days in Northern Australia (the only other region in which physician-assisted suicide was legal, until overturned by the Australian Parliament in March 1997) is required between a request for assisted suicide and its implementation.[1]

The most important safeguard of autonomous choice is the restriction of access to physician-assisted suicide to those whose decisionmaking capacity is above a threshold that qualifies them as "competent" to make the choice of suicide. Expert discussion of safeguards in the implementation of physician-assisted suicide frequently includes a call for mandatory psychiatric consultation.[2] The Oregon initiative requires that a psychiatric consultation be completed in just those cases where the primary physician believes that the patient has a mental disorder affecting his or her judgment, but the injunction mentioned this safeguard as inadequate.[3] The Northern Australia statute required psychiatric consultation in all cases, and a "Model State Act to Authorize and Regulate Physician-Assisted Suicide" recently published in the United States mandates that "a professional mental health provider (psychiatrist, psychologist, or psychiatric social worker) evaluate the patient to determine that his or her decision is fully informed, free of undue influence, and not distorted by depression or any other form of mental illness."[4] There is thus widespread support for mandatory psychiatric evaluation to verify the competence of all those who request physician-assisted suicide.

How Our Society Understands and Copes With Suicide

Psychiatrists who have cared for suicidal patients can describe how deeply ambivalent these patients can be about suicide. What is not as apparent from the clinical perspective is the ambivalence of psychiatrists and our culture about the morality of suicide. Talcott Parsons described how societies inevitably institutionalize expectations for their members and how "deviance" from these roles is considered a threat to the social fabric.[5] Suicide is a wonderful object for Parsonian analysis because societies have employed a variety of models, sometimes conflicting and sometimes complementary, to understand and manage suicide. Traditionally, suicide has been viewed as a choice. Reflecting this, for many years our society used the legal model to manage suicide. Suicide was a crime, punishable by the criminal justice system. It was considered not simply an assault on the self, but an assault on the community as well. While suicide is no longer a criminal offense in any state, assisting the suicide of another is in many. The religious/moral model also viewed suicide as a choice, but emphasized an individual's violation of core human values rather than laws that protect the social fabric. The Catholic Church and Orthodox Judaism, for example, are adamantly opposed to all suicide, even if it appears rationally chosen.[6] While Protestant fundamentalists are generally opposed to suicide, some Protestant denominations take a more tolerant stance.[7] Many nonreligious persons also find suicide immoral.

The modern medical model considers suicide to be, not the choice of a rational agent, but a symptom of mental illness. Epidemiological studies have overwhelmingly linked suicide to treatable psychiatric disorders. "Psychological autopsy" studies have documented that up to 90 percent of completed suicides had some psychiatric disorder at the time of death.[8] Treatment studies have shown that identification and treatment of psychiatric disorders can result in a substantial decrease in risk of suicide. Depression, and to a lesser extent medical illness, have been identified as the primary risk factors for suicide in the elderly.[9] This fact has been codified into diagnostic systems (e.g., DSM-IV, ICD-10) that consider suicidal ideas as one of the diagnostic criteria of mental disorder. It has also been codified into law, where danger to self is justification for involuntary mental health treatment.

On balance, this medicalization of suicide has substantially benefited the mentally ill by removing legal and moral sanctions and promoting effective treatment. Over the past few years, however, the hegemony of this medical/ psychiatric view has been challenged. Many in our society now see some suicides among those who are terminally ill as the product of rational choice while continuing to see most suicides in other contexts as the product of mental illness.[10] However, a valid method for determining which suicides are rational and which are not has never been developed by psychiatrists, psychologists, or any other profession.

In summary, our society currently uses all three models—legal, religious/ moral, and medical—to cope with physician-assisted suicide. Different jurisdictions, communities, institutions, and individuals may rely on different models. Acceptance of the conclusions of one model does not necessarily imply agreement with the conclusions of another. One person might believe that suicide is rational in some situations, but always morally unacceptable. Another might believe truly rational suicide would be morally acceptable, but that suicide is nearly always the irrational product of a diagnosable and treatable psychiatric condition. It is likely that many persons, including psychiatrists and other mental health professionals, are not always aware of which model they are employing to analyze a particular case. For example, a recent survey of Oregon psychologists revealed that those who objected to physician-assisted suicide for religious reasons were also more concerned about the mental health and social consequences of the legalization of physician-assisted suicide.[11] Although the concept of competence is intended to sort out rational from irrational decisions, it may blur the lines between the moral and medical models for a highly contentious issue such as assisted suicide.

Competence in the Clinical Setting

Clinical assessment of decisionmaking capacity is ethically important because of the central role that "adequate decisionmaking capacity" or competence plays in valid consent, the cornerstone in the protection of patient autonomy. This makes it inevitable that adequate decisionmaking capacity becomes a key issue in evaluating patients' requests for physician-assisted death. However, requiring that a psychiatrist control access to physician-assisted suicide is problematic for the following reasons. First, competence is a complex social, rather than scientific construct. In fact, psychiatrists use a sliding scale to determine when decisionmaking capacity is adequate, and the scale slides according to the values of the psychiatrists themselves. Second, the relationship of mental illness and decisionmaking capacity in dying patients is not as clear as is implied by some initiatives, statutes, and court decisions. Third, although psychiatrists have a great deal to offer in the assessment and enhancement of patient decisionmaking, casting them in the role of gatekeeper poses risks for patients, society, and the psychiatric profession itself. These risks should not be overlooked in shaping public policy.

Competence as a social construct   A "scientific" or purely objective definition of competence is unattainable because thresholds for adequate decisionmaking capacity are in fact socially established. Indeed, competence is not well measured by standardized instruments, but "is a malleable entity that is inevitably molded to fit the particular interpersonal, emotional, clinical, and cultural context."[12] "Competence" is used clinically to resolve situations in which two extremely important social goals come into conflict—that is, the promotion of self-determination (autonomy) and the promotion of patient welfare (beneficence or nonmaleficence).[13] As the consequences of physician-patient disagreement grow more serious, the tension between the principles of autonomy and beneficence also grows. It is important to recognize that this tension originates beyond the bounds of the physician-patient relationship. The growing visibility of patient requests for physician-assisted suicide has inspired calls for mandatory psychiatric evaluations of competence precisely because many citizens believe that suicide and assisting suicide are often great harms.

Tests of decisionmaking capacity have been traditionally ranked on a continuum of increasing stringency, with more stringent standards used for treatment refusals with more serious consequences. Simply making a choice or agreeing with the physician's recommendation are examples of more lenient standards. More stringent standards demand an examination of the process of reasoning underlying the patient's decision, such as the ability to understand, appreciate, or reason about one's clinical situation.[14] For example, when a patient refuses an invasive intervention with little chance of success, the physician rarely challenges his or her reasoning process. However, when the patient makes a choice that appears to be harmful, more rigorous tests of decisionmaking capacity are brought to bear. By employing this sliding scale, physicians gain flexibility to balance concerns about patient autonomy and patient welfare.

The malleability of competence is a two-edged sword. It allows competence to be used as a socially viable compromise between the conflicting values of respect for autonomy and prevention of harm, but it vests tremendous power in the expert who assesses decisionmaking capacity. The employment of a sliding scale for the determination of adequate decisionmaking capacity blurs the line between the process and product of decisionmaking. Without a truly independent standard for decisionmaking capacity, psychiatrists may apply standards derived from their own opinion of the harms associated with decisions such as requests for assisted suicide.

In the absence of robust independent standards, psychiatrists may resolve the ethical dilemmas concerning physician-assisted suicide in an ad hoc fashion, using themselves as the "reasonable person" standard by which to judge the patient's decision. Do I agree that this patient has an intolerable quality of life? Would I consider such a quality of life intolerable for myself? Would I consider suicide morally acceptable in this situation? Too often, to ask what a competent person would do in such a dire situation comes down to asking ourselves what we would do. In one survey psychiatrists' support for legalized physician-assisted suicide was highly correlated to desire for physician-assisted suicide for themselves in the case of terminal illness.[15] A survey of Oregon psychologists revealed that the conditions under which respondents would consider assisted suicide for themselves are highly correlated to conditions under which they believe it should be allowed for other people.[16]

While psychiatrists have skills relevant to the understanding and evaluation of patients' decisions, they should not have the social authority to use themselves as the measure of when it is right to die. In a society that is as confused and conflicted about physician-assisted death as ours is, allowing such individual discretion will result in arbitrary and unfair practices. Society is unsure about how to honor patients' choices to die, as are individual physicians. Deep disagreement exists about what constitutes an intolerable quality of life and whether suicide is ever an acceptable alternative to suffering. We question whether the clinical apparatus of competence assessment can resolve this tension.

Competence and psychiatric disorders   One reason psychiatrists have been selected to perform competence evaluations in the terminally ill is that the prevalence of psychiatric disorders in this population is high, and diagnosing these disorders is difficult. While there is validity to these concerns, we do not believe they justify universal psychiatric verification of competence in patients requesting assisted suicide.

Psychiatric disorders are common in the terminally ill. Delirium has been noted in 25 to 40 percent of hospitalized cancer patients; in the final stages, up to 85 percent of cancer patients may suffer from delirium.[17] Depression has also been diagnosed in approximately 5 to 58 percent of hospitalized cancer patients, with up to 77 percent of advanced cancer patients having severe depressive symptoms.[18] High rates of psychiatric disorders and interest in physician-assisted suicide have been noted in patients with HIV infection and AIDS.[19] Although the rates of psychiatric disorder climb as medical severity increases, accuracy of diagnosis by primary care physicians diminishes.[20] Not only is depression often missed, but delirium is often misdiagnosed as depression.[21] Psychiatrists may thus offer expertise in diagnosing a mental disorder that primary care physicians lack.

Psychiatric disorders are the commonest cause of impaired capacity to make medical decisions. Yet even the most serious mental disorders may not critically disrupt decisionmaking capacity. It is now widely accepted, for example, that some psychotic patients can provide valid consent to participate in research from which they personally derive no benefit. Meeting criteria for commitment to involuntary treatment no longer implies incompetence to refuse antipsychotic medication.[22] Clinical and legal consensus now demands that a mental disorder be demonstrated to seriously disrupt the relevant decisionmaking capacity before a patient is declared incompetent and forfeits the right to make those specific decisions him- or herself. Making a psychiatric diagnosis may assist in directing the clinician's attention to where decisionmaking might be impaired, but does not itself prove that decisionmaking capacity has been compromised.

Psychiatrists have raised concerns that depression may cause medically ill persons to choose to hasten their deaths, but the available data indicate variable effects of depression on treatment preference. In one study using hypothetical illness scenarios, elderly depressed patients did choose aggressive medical treatment less often than nondepressed patients in the good prognosis scenarios. However, among these mildly to moderately depressed patients, current depression severity was not as strongly linked to treatment preference as were their estimates of their quality of life in these hypothetical situations.[23] Except in a minority who were severely depressed, successful treatment of depression did not significantly alter treatment preferences.[24] Another study of twenty-two depressed elderly patients revealed that moderate to severe major depression was associated with a high rate of treatment refusal in good prognosis hypothetical scenarios, which showed reversal with depression treatment.[25] A study of 2,536 elderly patients found that scoring in the depressed range on a depression scale predicted a desire for more, rather than less life-saving treatment.[26] Therefore, depression may or may not alter decisions about end-of-life treatment by elderly patients. We have argued elsewhere that depression diagnosis and clinical assessment of the capacity to make medical decisions are distinct tasks.[27]

Studies that examine the psychiatric correlates of terminally ill persons' desire for hastened death are few. For example, James Henderson Brown and colleagues queried patients on an inpatient hospital palliative care service regarding their desire for hastened death.[28] Patients were eligible to participate in the study if they had a terminal illness and either pain or severe disfigurement and severe disability, but were not too sick to consent. Of 331 potential participants, only forty-four were eligible using these inclusion criteria. Ten of forty-four (24 percent) patients desired to die, and all were found to have a "clinical depression." The authors concluded that the desire for death in terminally ill persons does not occur in the absence of psychopathology. However, the criteria for participation, which excluded 287 hospice patients, may have limited the generalizability of their findings. Harvey Max Chochinov and colleagues interviewed cancer patients on a hospice inpatient service and found that 8.5 percent acknowledged a desire for death that was serious and pervasive. Although these patients had higher depression scores than patients who did not persistently desire death, 41 percent did not meet criteria for major depressive disorder.[29] Studies led by William Breitbart[30] and Ezekiel Emanuel[31] also demonstrate that terminally ill persons who express an interest in physician-assisted suicide have higher depression scores, but these researchers did not measure the percentage who met criteria for major depression. Nor did major depression indicate those who would and those who would not be interested in assisted suicide in a future state of severe pain among forty-eight patients with painful metastatic cancer.[32] In total, these studies suggest that though depression is common among persons desiring assisted suicide, it clearly does not account for all of the variance in decisionmaking.

Moreover, many psychiatrists do not regularly work with seriously ill and dying patients in hospital, nursing home, and hospice settings. In a survey of over 700 Oregon psychiatrists and psychologists, only three respondents reported working with hospice patients in the past year. Only 6 percent of psychiatrists were very confident that they could, within the context of a single evaluation, assess whether a psychiatric disorder was impairing the judgment of a patient desiring assisted suicide.[33]

Psychiatrists' treatment options for the terminally ill are limited by the limited time available for the treatment to be effective and by the severity of the patient's medical illness. Data suggest that psychiatric treatment may or may not affect treatment preferences. Some patients asking for assisted suicide will be willing to try psychiatric treatment and some will not. Even for patients who actively participate in treatment, it will be difficult to determine when enough treatment has been administered—psychiatrists' values as well as their clinical expertise will inevitably determine when the point of "enough" treatment has been reached. For example, how many trials of antidepressant medication are needed before the psychiatrist concludes that the depression is intractable or that the patient is not really depressed?

These observations point to a useful and important role for trained and experienced psychiatrists in the assessment and treatment of seriously ill patients who wish to hasten their deaths. They also argue for more research and better training for psychiatrists in this critical area. They do not, however, make a convincing case for mandatory involvement and a gatekeeping role for the psychiatrist in all cases....

Counterarguments

There are two remaining arguments for psychiatry's role in determining competence to participate in physician-assisted suicide to which we would like to respond. First, some might argue that the problems in assessing competence for suicide are no different from other situations in which competence is addressed. Why do we specifically object to competence evaluation for those requesting physician-assisted suicide? What makes it different from the psychiatrist's role in evaluating competence to stand trial, to make a will, or even more relevant here, to refuse life-sustaining medical treatment? Do not the same problems of subjectivity and potential for bias exist?

There are a couple of critical differences. The evaluation of competence to stand trial, make a will, or refuse medical treatment is not mandatory for every person who is about to undertake these acts. In each of these cases, patient competence is assumed. The psychiatrist is called in only when competence is challenged or questioned by one of the persons naturally involved in the process, such as a lawyer, judge, or relative. We know of no other clinical situation in which psychiatric evaluation for competence is universally required; the presumption for persons standing trial or making medical decisions (even patients who refuse life-sustaining treatment) is that they are competent. Mandating a mental health evaluation for all patients requesting assisted suicide implies a presumption of incompetence. It makes the request for assisted suicide, although legal, adequate grounds for challenging the competence of the person making the request.

In addition, these other decisions or acts for which competence may be called into question are not in themselves morally controversial. No one argues that standing trial or making a will is morally wrong. Quite the contrary, both are viewed as necessary social functions. Thus, it is highly unlikely that a psychiatrist's opinion about competence will be influenced by his view that standing trial or making a will is harmful per se. Refusal of life-sustaining treatment may be considered to be a harm by a minority of our citizens. However, the legal system clearly recognizes this right and the vast majority of health professionals (including psychiatrists) and citizens accept it as a moral right as well. To argue that because psychiatrists are called in to evaluate competence in some cases of treatment refusal, they should be called in on all requests for physician-assisted suicide is illogical. The view that death through assisted suicide is a greater harm to patients than death through treatment refusal reflects social ambivalence about suicide rather than clearly distinct clinical situations. Since the same psychosocial factors—for example, depression, delirium, and anxiety —that affect requests for physician-assisted suicide also affect treatment refusal, a more consistent argument for those advocating the gatekeeper role would be that psychiatrists should be the gatekeepers for all refusals of life-saving treatment as well.

A second counterargument to our position asserts that psychiatrists, despite their shortcomings, are the professionals best qualified to evaluate decisionmaking capacity and no more biased than other physicians. We do not deny that involvement of psychiatrists in the evaluation and treatment of persons who request physician-assisted suicide can be extremely helpful. The psychiatrist can assist the patient in exploring the often multiple meanings of the request to die. Susan Block and Andrew Billings write, "Most patients, in saying that they want to die are asking for assistance in living—for help in dealing with depression, anxiety about the future, grief, lack of control, dependence, and spiritual despair."[34] The efficacy of psychiatric treatment in the medically ill elderly has been repeatedly demonstrated in recent years.[35] Suffering may be diminished with both psychotherapy and psychotropic medications. The psychiatrist may intervene to improve the patient's relationships with physician and family. Indeed, there are many cases in which psychiatric involvement is absolutely essential.

However, institutionalizing or bureaucratizing such involvement could be problematic. This would imply a greater expertise than is warranted and would shift responsibility from the traditional seat of shared decisionmaking—the patient, the family, and the physician or health care team—to an outside expert who may not have a primary commitment to patient welfare. A required evaluation of competence puts the patient in a "one down" position in which his or her sanity is judged by an outside expert. This intrinsically adversarial position is likely to prevent the development of a therapeutic alliance necessary for the psychiatrist to function in the traditional role as healer. Forcing evaluations in cases where they are neither wanted nor necessary could trivialize the process or turn it into an activity that serves neither patients, society, nor our profession. By making psychiatric involvement optional, a complicated social decision can be kept woven as deeply as possible into the social fabric, allowing society to appreciate rather than avoid its own ambivalence about death, dying, and suicide.

Healers, Not Gatekeepers

We believe that psychiatrists' primary involvement with patients requesting assisted suicide should be in the role of healer rather than gatekeeper. Psychiatric evaluation of the dying patient should always be done for the benefit of the patient. If psychiatric diagnosis is done primarily for social control rather than individual welfare, psychiatrists function as priests or police rather than as physicians. The primary duty of psychiatrists to the dying is not to man the gate to assisted dying, but to nurture autonomous choice and diminish the anguish of the dying process.

We encourage our medical colleagues to involve psychiatrists in the evaluation and care of the dying. Psychotropic medication, supportive therapy, and family intervention can ease suffering and promote autonomous choice. Psychiatric consultation to assess and promote autonomous decisionmaking should be an option initiated by patient, family, or primary physician, not mandated by law. Psychiatrists, on the other hand, must improve their expertise in caring for dying patients and make themselves more available to patients and medical colleagues. An emphasis must be placed on improving the research basis for carrying out psychiatric assessments of dying patients who desire physician-assisted suicide. Legal mandates that require psychiatric certification of competence prior to all cases of euthanasia or physician-assisted suicide hold risks for both the psychiatric profession and the patients it should serve. This practice could distort the role of the psychiatrist as a physician whose first responsibility is the welfare of her patient. It runs the risk of overselling the independence and impartiality of the clinical procedure by which decision-making capacity is assessed. It shifts the accountability for value judgments from the traditional context of patient-family-physician.

There is a price to be paid for not making psychiatric consultation mandatory. Some treatable psychiatric disorders will be missed in those opting for assisted suicide. But the benefit for these individuals must be balanced against the serious problems, the arbitrary evaluations and social obfuscation, that would accompany universal mandatory psychiatric consultation. And it may be more difficult politically to endorse or legalize physician-assisted suicide without the psychiatric safeguard. But the societal debate about assisted suicide will be more honest and revealing.

In our culture's current state of ambivalence and confusion about suicide, the moral and medical models run hopelessly together. Using a technical clinical determination of competence to judge the moral acceptability of suicide obscures important value judgments we are making about when life is worth living and when it is not. To foster the most honest debate possible about assisted suicide and to promote truly patient-centered end-of-life care, we should avoid making psychiatrists gatekeepers for assisted suicide.

References

1. Christopher J. Ryan and Miranda Kaye, "Euthanasia in Australia: the Northern Territory Rights of the Terminally Ill Act," *NEJM* 334 (1996): 326–28.
2. W. F. Baile, J. R. Dimaggio, D. V. Schapira, and J. S. Janofsky, "The Request for Assistance in Dying: The Need for Psychiatric Consultation," *Cancer* 72 (1993): 2786–91; Guy I. Benrubi, "Euthanasia: The Need for Procedural Safeguards," *NEJM* 326 (1992): 197–98.
3. Ballot Measure 16. In Oregon voters' pamphlet. Portland, Ore.: Multnomah County Elections Division, 1994.
4. Charles H. Baron, Clyde Bergstresser, Dan W. Brock, Gabrielle F. Cole et al., "A Model State Act to Authorize and Regulate Physician-Assisted Suicide," *Harvard Journal on Legislation* 33 (1996): 1–34.
5. Talcott Parsons, "Definitions of Health and Disease in Light of American Values and Social Structures." In *Patients, Physicians, and Illness,* ed. E. Gartly Jaco (New York: Free Press, 1979), pp. 120–44.
6. Fred Rosner, "Suicide in Biblical, Talmudic, and Rabbinic Writings," *Tradition: A Journal of Orthodox Thought* 11 (1970): 25–40.
7. Presbyterian Senior Services, The Presbytery of New York, "Pastoral Letter on Euthanasia and Suicide," 9 March 1976, p. 3.
8. Gabrielle A. Carlson, Charles L. Rich, Patricia Grayson, and Richard C. Fowler, "Secular Trends in Psychiatric Diagnoses of Suicide Victims," *Journal of Affective Disorders* 21 (1991): 127–32.
9. Robert L. Frierson, "Suicide Attempts by the Old and the Very Old," *Archives of Internal Medicine* 151 (1991): 141–44; Thomas B. Mackenzie and Michael K. Popkin, "Medical Illness and Suicide." In *Suicide Over the Life Cycle: Risk Factors, Assessment, and Treatment of Suicidal Patients,* ed. Susan J. Blumenthal and David J. Kupfer (Washington D.C.: American Psychiatric Press, 1990), pp. 205–32.
10. Robert J. Blendon, Ulrike S. Szalay, Richard A. Knox, "Should Physicians Aid Their Patients in Dying? The Public Perspective," *JAMA* 269 (1993): 590–91.
11. Darien S. Fenn and Linda Ganzini, personal communication.
12. Stuart J. Youngner, "Competency to Refuse Life-Sustaining Treatment." In *End-of-Life Decisions: A Psychosocial Perspective,* ed. Maurice D. Steinberg and Stuart J. Youngner (Washington, D.C.: American Psychiatric Press, 1998).
13. Loren H. Roth, Alan Meisel, and Charles W. Lidz, "Tests of Competency to Consent to Treatment," *American Journal of Psychiatry* 134 (1977): 279–84; Allen E. Buchanan and Dan W. Brock, *Deciding for Others* (Cambridge: Cambridge University Press, 1989), p. 77.
14. Youngner, "Competency to Refuse Life-Sustaining Treatment."
15. Linda Ganzini, Darien S. Fenn, Melinda A. Lee et al., "Attitudes of Oregon Psychiatrists Toward Physician Assisted Suicide," *American Journal of Psychiatry* 153 (1996): 1469–75.
16. Fenn and Ganzini, personal communication.
17. Mary Jane Massie, Jimmie Holland, and Ellen Glass, "Delirium in Terminal Cancer Patients," *American Journal of Psychiatry* 140 (1983): 1048–50.
18. Judith B. Bukberg, Doris T. Penman, and Jimmie C. Holland, "Depression in Hospitalized Cancer Patients," *Psychosomatic Medicine* 46 (1984): 199–212.
19. William Breitbart, Barry D. Rosenfeld, and Steven D. Passik, "Interest in Physician-Assisted Suicide among Ambulatory HIV-Infected Patients," *American Journal of Psychiatry* 153 (1996): 238–42.

20. H. C. Schulberg, M. Saul, and M. N. McClelland, "Assessing Depression in Primary Medical and Psychiatric Practices," *Archives of General Psychiatry* 42 (1985): 1164–70.

21. Kathleen R. Farrell and Linda Ganzini, "Misdiagnosing Delirium as Depression in Medically Ill Elderly Patients," *Archives of Internal Medicine* 155 (1995): 2459–64.

22. *Rogers v. Okin,* 478 F Supp 1342 (D Mass, 1979).

23. Melinda A. Lee and Linda Ganzini, "Depression in the Elderly: Effect on Patient Attitudes toward Life-Sustaining Therapy," *Journal of the American Geriatric Society* 40 (1992): 983–88.

24. Linda Ganzini, Melinda A. Lee, Ronald T. Heintz et al., "The Effect of Depression Treatment on Elderly Patients' Preferences for Life-Sustaining Medical Therapy," *American Journal of Psychiatry* 151 (1994): 1631–36.

25. S. C. Hooper, K. J. Vaughan, C. C. Tennant, and J. M. Perz, "Major Depression and Refusal of Life-Sustaining Treatment in the Elderly," *Medical Journal of Australia* 165 (1996): 416–19.

26. Joanne M. Garrett, Russell P. Harris, Jean K. Norburn et al., "Life-Sustaining Treatments During Terminal Illness: Who Wants What?" *Journal of General Internal Medicine* 9 (1993): 361–68.

27. Mark D. Sullivan and Stuart J. Youngner, "Depression, Competence, and the Right to Refuse Life-Saving Medical Treatment," *American Journal of Psychiatry* 151 (1994): 971–78.

28. James Henderson Brown, Paul Henteleff, Samia Barakat, and Cheryl June Rowe, "Is It Normal for Terminally Ill Patients to Desire Death?" *American Journal of Psychiatry* 143 (1986): 208–11.

29. Harvey Max Chochinov, Keith G. Wilson, Murray Enns et al., "Desire for Death in the Terminally Ill," *American Journal of Psychiatry* 152 (1995): 1185–91.

30. Mark D. Sullivan, Suzanne A. Rapp, Dermot Fitzgibbon, and C. Richard Chapman, "Pain and the Choice to Hasten Death Among Patients with Painful Metastatic Cancer," *Journal of Palliative Care,* in press.

31. Ezekiel J. Emanuel, "Empirical Studies on Euthanasia and Assisted Suicide," *Journal of Clinical Ethics* 6 (1995): 158–60.

32. Sullivan et al., "Pain and the Choice to Hasten Death."

33. Ganzini et al., "Attitudes of Oregon Psychiatrists."

34. Susan D. Block and J. Andrew Billings, "Patient Requests for Euthanasia and Assisted Suicide: The Role of the Psychiatrist," *Psychosomatics* 36 (1995): 445–57.

35. J. Stephen McDaniel, Dominque L. Musselman, Maryfrances R. Porter et al., "Depression in Patients with Cancer: Diagnosis, Biology, and Treatment," *Archives of General Psychiatry* 52 (1995): 89–99.

CHALLENGE QUESTIONS

Should Mental Health Professionals Serve as Gatekeepers for Physician-Assisted Suicide?

1. Farberman makes some strong arguments with regard to the importance of involving mental health professionals in cases of physician-assisted suicide. What criteria should be specified in order to determine the competence of the mental health professional to play this role?
2. Sullivan, Ganzini, and Youngner do not believe that there is a convincing case for mandatory involvement of mental health professionals in cases of physician-assisted suicide in general. For what kinds of specific cases could a strong argument be made for requiring such involvement?
3. In 1997 the U.S. Supreme Court ruled that terminally ill people do not have a constitutional right to doctor-assisted suicide, but it also declared that states have the option of enacting assistance-in-dying statutes. What arguments can be made for and against the constitutionality of the right to physician-assisted suicide?
4. What kinds of emotional burdens might be experienced by mental health professionals who become involved in the assessment of terminally ill patients?

Suggested Readings

Block, S. D., & Billings, J. A. (1998). Evaluating patient requests for euthanasia and assisted suicide in terminal illness: The role of the psychiatrist. In M. D. Steinberg, & S. J. Youngner (Eds.), *End-of-life decisions: A psychosocial perspective.* (pp. 205–233). Washington, DC: American Psychiatric Press, Inc.

Ganzini, L., Fenn, D. S., Lee, M. A., Heintz, R. T., & Bloom, J. D. (1996). Attitudes of Oregon psychiatrists toward physician-assisted suicide. *American Journal of Psychiatry, 153,* 1469–1475.

Peruzzi, N., Canapary, A., & Bongar, B. (1996). Physician-assisted suicide: The role of mental health professionals. *Ethics & Behavior, 6*(4), 353–366.

ISSUE 18

Is Sexual Orientation Conversion Therapy Ethical?

YES: Mark A. Yarhouse, from "When Clients Seek Treatment for Same-Sex Attraction: Ethical Issues in the 'Right to Choose' Debate," *Psychotherapy: Theory/Research/Practice/Training* (Summer 1998)

NO: Douglas C. Haldeman, from "The Practice and Ethics of Sexual Orientation Conversion Therapy," *Journal of Consulting and Clinical Psychology* (April 1994)

ISSUE SUMMARY

YES: Psychologist Mark A. Yarhouse asserts that mental health professionals have an ethical responsibility to allow individuals to pursue treatment aimed at curbing same-sex attraction, stating that doing so affirms the client's dignity and autonomy.

NO: Psychologist Douglas C. Haldeman criticizes therapy involving sexual reorientation, insisting that there is no evidence that such treatments are effective and that they run the risk of further stigmatizing homosexuality.

It has only been in the last few decades that the American Psychiatric Association (APA) has come to terms with the notion that it was inappropriate to include "homosexuality" in its official listing of mental disorders. This decision followed years of debate, which culminated in the realization that pathologizing people because of sexual orientation is unwarranted. Letting go of homosexuality as a diagnosable mental disorder did not come easily for psychiatry; in fact, for several years the official list of diagnoses included the label "ego-dystonic homosexuality" to refer to individuals who suffered a range of emotional symptoms associated with being gay or lesbian. Eventually, even this diagnostic label was deleted in response to criticisms that it perpetuated the tendency of the mental health establishment to pathologize homosexuality.

Even though homosexuality was removed from the list of diagnostic labels, troubling experiences with discrimination, social exclusion, and inner turmoil continue to haunt millions of men and women in the process of coming to terms with their homosexual orientation. As these individuals have turned to mental health professionals for help through critical times, they have found a range of responses. Many mental health professionals strive to help these clients develop healthy ways of thinking about themselves in which they accept their sexuality and their capacity for living happy and fulfilling lives in intimate and loving relationships with same-sex partners. Other mental health professionals view sexual orientation as a malleable characteristic that can be changed in those who wish to reorient themselves. Rather than focusing on self-acceptance, these clinicians work with the client to change sexual orientation. Debates between these two camps have been intense.

In the following selection, Mark A. Yarhouse contends that psychologists—and, by extension, other mental health professionals—have an ethical responsibility to allow individuals to pursue treatment aimed at curbing experiences of same-sex attraction. He asserts that in this approach to treatment, the clinician affirms the client's rights to dignity and autonomy, and respects the client as an individual capable of choosing among available treatment modalities. Yarhouse contends that, rather than being discriminatory, this approach to clients actually demonstrates respect for diversity.

In the second selection, Douglas C. Haldeman criticizes therapy approaches that involve sexual reorientation and insists that there is no evidence that such treatments are effective. Asserting that conversion therapies are unethical because they are predicated on a devaluation of homosexual identity and behavior, Haldeman maintains that the appropriate focus of the profession should be on what reverses prejudice, not what reverses sexual orientation.

POINT

- When clients feel distressed about their experiences of same-sex attraction and express interest in treatment based on personal, religious, or moral grounds, clinicians have an ethical responsibility to direct them to appropriate services.

- Clients should be seen as having the right to choose treatment for their experiences of same-sex attraction.

- Clinicians should presume that people are autonomous agents, particularly with respect to their decisions concerning their work in therapy.

- Some clients may choose to pursue change of sexual orientation due to religious and cultural values concerning the purpose and design of human sexuality and sexual behavior.

COUNTERPOINT

- It is unethical for clinicians to recommend treatments that are not empirically supported; furthermore, conversion therapies are unethical because they are predicated on a devaluation of homosexual identity and behavior.

- Given the extensive societal devaluation of homosexuality, it is not surprising that many gay people seek to become heterosexual; clinicians should be combating stigma with a vigorous avowal of empirical truth.

- The concept that individuals seek to change their sexual orientation of their own free will is fallacious.

- Many gay males and lesbians consider sexual orientation conversion because of the severe conflict they experience between their homoerotic feelings and their need for acceptance by a homophobic religious community.

Mark A. Yarhouse  **YES**

When Clients Seek Treatment
for Same-Sex Attraction

The focus of this article is the examination of ethical issues related to psychologists providing treatment to clients who experience same-sex attraction and seek change. Of particular concern are the ethical issues of psychologists who work with clients who are distressed as a result of the conflict they experience between same-sex attraction and behavior and their own valuative framework. Obviously, many gay and lesbian clients enter therapy and do not have as their goal a change of orientation or behavior. Rather, they enter therapy for concerns related to mood disorders, anxiety disorders, sexual dysfunctions, relationship problems, and so on. Still others enter therapy concerned about their sexual orientation and want to integrate their impulses into a gay identity and are pursuing "gay-affirmative" therapy. The question of the psychologist's responsibility to assist homosexual persons in these areas is beyond the scope of this article and has been addressed elsewhere (Browning, Reynolds, & Dworkin, 1991; Shannon & Woods, 1991).

There are a number of ethical considerations for psychologists who provide treatment to clients who experience same-sex attraction and are seeking change of behavior or orientation. The purpose of this article is to develop and elaborate on an ethical principle of particular importance in the treatment care of homosexual persons: *Ethical Principle D: Respect for Rights and Dignity* (APA, 1992). Ethical Principle D, which is an aspirational ethical principle for psychologists, provides a foundation for the ethical care of those who report distress concerning their experience of same-sex attraction. This care receives further support from several Ethical Standards that are enforceable standards for the professional conduct of psychologists.

Respect for People's Rights and Dignity

... According to Ethical Principle D, psychologists are to "accord appropriate respect to the fundamental rights, dignity, and worth of all people" (APA, 1992, p. 1599). Perhaps what is most relevant to this discussion of same-sex attraction is that psychologists are called to respect their clients' rights to "privacy, confidentiality, self-determination, and autonomy" (p. 1600), and they are to

From Mark A. Yarhouse, "When Clients Seek Treatment for Same-Sex Attraction: Ethical Issues in the 'Right to Choose' Debate," *Psychotherapy: Theory/Research/Practice/Training*, vol. 35, no. 2 (Summer 1998). Copyright © 1998 by The Division of Psychotherapy (29) of The American Psychological Association. Reprinted by permission.

be aware of difference, including differences related to sexual orientation and religion.

In the space that follows, two points will be developed related to this ethical principle. First, clients should be seen as having the right to choose treatment for their experience of same-sex attraction. It will be argued that this right to choose is grounded in (a) the autonomy and self-respect of persons, and (b) the multicultural dimension of the work of psychologists, which includes respect for normative religious values and cultural differences. Second, in light of a respectful stance toward those who report distress concerning their experience of same-sex attraction, psychologists should provide a form of advanced informed consent to treatment, so that their clients have as much information as possible concerning the state of scientific research pertaining to this controversial topic.

Autonomy and Self-Determination

Psychologists view people as agents capable of comprehending principles related to behavior that they should engage in, as well as behaviors from which they should refrain. The capacity to choose between alternatives is referred to as "agency," which has been defined as "the capacity for an organism to behave in compliance with, in addition to, in opposition to, or without regard for biological or sociological stimulations" (Rychlak, 1988, p. 84). Agency and *autonomy* are related concepts. Sobocinski (1990) discusses what it means to respect a person's antonomy. He argues that respecting others as autonomous individuals involves recognizing them as essentially self-governing agents, capable of exercising competent, self-determination in the selection of choices and actions" (p. 241). In fact, the Ethics Code of the APA (1992) presupposes that under most circumstances clients have the right to choose treatment and to be informed of various treatment modalities and alternatives to treatment. "Psychologists obtain appropriate informed consent to therapy or related procedures, using language that is reasonably understandable to participants" (APA, 1992, p. 1605). In other words, psychologists are ethically obligated to use informed consent precisely because people are capable of agency.

Psychologists generally agree that clients are self-determining agents insofar as they have the ability and right to make decisions regarding therapy. At the same time, some psychologists argue that homosexual clients are unique in that their ability to choose freely between alternatives is diminished (and sometimes eradicated) by negative societal messages about same-sex attraction and behavior. Initial attempts to validate both the existence of negative social stigma and the autonomy and self-determination of the individual were relatively balanced. For example, Pillard (1982, p. 94) quotes Silverstein (1972, p. 4) as arguing that various environmental stressors constrain a person's ability to choose freely: "To suggest that a person comes voluntarily to change his sexual orientation is to ignore the powerful environmental stress, oppression if you will, that has been telling him for years that he should change." Silverstein goes on in his address to argue that after processing the guilt and shame associated with their experience of same-sex attraction (as well as ways in which they have been injured by various social structures), therapists can have a discussion with clients about their desire to pursue change: "After [dissolving the shame about their desires], let them choose, but not before. I don't know any more than you what would happen, but I think their choice would be more voluntary and free than it is at present" (p. 4).

This approach is balanced insofar as psychologists are called upon to recognize powerful societal forces and the impact of those forces on their clients, yet protect the autonomy and self-determination of individuals pursuing treatment. Unfortunately, this approach has been challenged in recent years by a perspective that seems to view any desire to change as a result of internalized homophobia. Some argue that homosexuals never freely make the choice to change their orientation (Davison, 1982; Halderman, 1991, 1994; Murphy, 1992). They argue that people do not have the "right to choose" such treatment, and some appear to favor gay-affirmative therapy to the exclusion of any other kind of treatment....

Psychologists must be cautious about this kind of claim. The perspective that keeps in balance the influences of societal messages, while at the same time respects the autonomy of the individual, is at risk of being replaced by a view based upon a generalization lacking any empirical support. Psychologists cannot verify that homosexuals who choose treatment "almost always" do so because of internalized familial hostility and societal intolerance. Certainly many homosexual clients seek treatment because of the pressure they feel in a predominantly heterosexual society (and psychologists should be sensitive to this as a very real concern for many gay men and lesbians). However, the decision to pursue change of behavior, desires, and even orientation is a complicated one. A more accurate representation is that some homosexuals pursue change because of societal pressure, and so on, while others pursue change for a variety of reasons, including values they hold concerning purpose and design of sexual behavior. These values come from a number of sources, including family, culture, and religion. And while some of these sources may at times reject same-sex behavior or attraction based on prejudices or stereotypes, these sources may also hold normative beliefs or values that are legitimate points of disagreement in a diverse and pluralistic society.

A related argument is whether or not treatment should be provided to a "nondisorder." Some who oppose providing professional services to clients who experience same-sex attraction and seek change note that in 1974 the American Psychiatric Association removed homosexuality as a pathological condition per se from the *Diagnostic and Statistical Manual (DSM)*. However, what often goes unnoticed is that the *DSM* contains relevant diagnostic codes which are appropriate, for example, "when the focus of clinical attention is uncertainty about multiple issues related to identity such as ... sexual orientation and behavior, moral values," and so on (diagnostic code 313.82; American Psychiatric Association, 1994, p. 300). The *DSM* certainly presumes a rationale for providing services when concerns arise surrounding sexual identity and behavior....

Religious Belief and Multiculturalism

In the past 20 years perhaps no change in psychology has been as dramatic as the shift away from treating homosexual clients for their experience of same-sex attraction towards helping them to accept and integrate these impulses as part of a gay or lesbian identity (Browning et al., 1991; Coleman, 1982; Morin, 1991; Shannon & Woods, 1991). As was mentioned above, this new approach is referred to as "gay-affirmative therapy," and can include emphasis on identity development and management, interpersonal concerns, and specific issues such as antigay violence and AIDS (Shannon & Wood, 1991, pp. 197–210), as well as substance abuse, sexual abuse, and domestic violence, which Browning et al. (1991, pp. 189–191) identify as specific concerns for lesbian clients.

An additional concern in gay-affirmative therapy, according to Shannon and Woods (1991) and Browning et al. (1991), is that therapists discuss spiritual and existential issues in their work with homosexual clients. Shannon and Woods argue that "psychotherapy that does not address the existential/spiritual dimension is seriously lacking" (p. 211). Unfortunately, these authors limit their discussion of religious and spiritual themes to the harm religion may cause someone who experiences same-sex attraction, arguing that religion can lead to feelings of "isolation and alienation" (p. 212). Similarly, Browning et al. argue that "traditionally, people have met their spiritual needs through caring for others and through religion. The Western Judeo-Christian tradition has not been kind to lesbian women, with scriptural interpretations, customs, and religious doctrines used to create shame" (p. 192). They suggest that therapists help homosexuals "recognize and validate needs for spiritual community and discover ways to fulfill them" through "alternatives to traditional religion" (p. 192). Shannon and Woods offer a similar solution: they encourage therapists to distinguish between spirituality and religiosity, so that their clients can "find meaning in life without participating in an organized religion that is antithetical to the individual's personhood" (p. 212).

From an organized religious perspective, this understanding of religion is truncated and myopic. Despite efforts in recent years within the APA to incorporate an understanding of genuine religious experience into the clinical practice of psychology (Jones, 1994; Shafranske, 1996), recent literature on the relationship between homosexuality and religion completely ignores the normative or prescriptive dimension of religious experience in many faith communities and erroneously assumes that one view of those who experience same-sex attraction is exhaustive and complete (i.e., to integrate same-sex impulses into a gay identity). One important exception to this prescription of the homosexual community is the silenced minority of those who experience same-sex attraction and seek to change their behavior, impulses, or orientation, or who seek to live rich and fulfilling lives and remain celibate. Those who desire change may have personal convictions informed by religious or cultural values concerning the purpose and design of human sexuality and sexual expression.[1] People may appeal to religious, moral, or cultural values and convictions that serve as valuative frameworks within which they aspire to live. Clearly psychologists must be sensitive to the fact that many homosexual persons disagree with the perspective on human sexuality articulated in the Jewish faith, various Protestant denominations, and the Roman Catholic Church, for example; many homosexuals report anger and frustration in response to the official teachings of these religious communities. At the same time, many homosexual persons are committed to these institutions, agree with the historical teachings concerning the moral status of same-sex behavior, and seek to live in conformity with the teachings of their religious community. This is clearly evidenced in the formation of Courage, a support group for Catholics who experience same-sex attraction and are attempting to live celibate lives in accord with the official teachings of the Roman Catholic Church. Others who report distress concerning their experience of same-sex attraction become involved in various support groups and 12-step groups (some of which have as their goal changing sexual orientation); still others come to psychologists for help.

Multicultural diversity, which is valued in various APA publications, challenges psychologists to respect the cultural, moral, and religious values and convictions of their clients: "In their work-related activities, psychologists respect the rights of others to hold values, attitudes, and opinions that differ from their own" (Ethical Standard 1.09; APA, 1992, p. 1601). Principle D clearly states that psychologists are to be "aware of cultural, individual, and role differences, including those due to... religion" (p. 1600). If psychologists override the values of their clients, are they saying that psychologists can respect and be tolerant of religious diversity so long as clients do not make choices that actually reflect the normative teaching of their religion? Or does one way of understanding diversity (related to sexual orientation) take precedence over other expressions of diversity (religious or cultural diversity)? From an ethical standpoint, when clients present for therapy distressed about their experience of same-sex attraction and express interest in pursuing treatment for their inclinations on personal religious, or moral grounds, psychologists have an ethical responsibility to assess this expressed interest and do all they can to provide and direct them to appropriate services in a responsible manner....

Advanced Informed Consent

Informed consent helps psychologists insure a client's sense of autonomy and self-determination. Informed consent will vary from case to case, but it generally includes an assessment of the capacity of the person to consent, adequate knowledge of the intervention in question, and some written documentation of consent (APA, 1992, p. 1605; Corey, Corey, & Callahan, 1993; Keith-Spiegel & Koocher, 1985).

Clients who enter therapy reporting distress about their experience of same-sex attraction should be in an informed position as to the benefits and drawbacks of pursuing treatment. Considering the present state of knowledge in the areas of human sexuality and same-sex attraction, and in light of the degree of controversy surrounding this research, a comprehensive presentation is important for clients to make a truly informed decision. This raises the topic of *advanced informed consent.* In the case of clients who report distress concerning their experience of same-sex attraction, advanced informed consent to treatment should include the following content areas:

1. Hypotheses as to what is causing their problems (including etiology of same-sex attraction and the subjective experience of distress reported by a particular client)
2. Professional treatments available, including success rates and definitions and methodologies used to report "success"
3. Alternatives to professional treatment, including reported success rates and the relative lack of empirical support for claims of success
4. Possible benefits and risks of pursuing treatment at this time
5. Possible outcomes with or without treatment (and alternative explanations for possible outcomes)

Cause of Difficulties

Psychologists have an ethical obligation to discuss with clients hypotheses as to what may be causing their difficulties. In the case of persons distressed by their experience of same-sex attraction, this can be understood in at least three ways: (a) whether sexual orientation is a stable, enduring, universal reality or whether it is a social construction; (b) the etiology of same-sex attraction; and (c) what makes a particular person feel distress in relation to his or her experience of same-sex attraction. The following subsections provide an introduction only to the kinds of issues that may come up when persons seek treatment for their experience of same-sex attraction.

What is homosexuality? There is significant debate today as to what homosexuality actually is. This debate is generally characterized as being between essentialists and constructivists. Essentialists argue that homosexuality and sexual orientation more generally is a stable, enduring, universal reality, which is accurately described by the taxonomy of our contemporary understanding. Proponents of this view often reference research implicating physiological antecedents related to the experience of same-sex attraction. Some (but not all) essentialists argue that this essence is tied to the core of one's self as a human being, and because this real essence is a part of what properly defines the core of the person, homosexual behavior is naturally occurring, morally blameless behavior that should find expression (Sullivan, 1995).

Constructivists, in contrast, view homosexuality as a social construct, so that the term "homosexuality" does not refer to something real but is a linguistic construct fashioned by a society for discussing sexual preferences. In support of this position, constructivists note that sexual conduct and attitudes toward it vary throughout history and across cultures, and that human homosexual orientation per se has no true parallel in subhuman species (Carrier, 1980; Greenberg, 1988). There are a variety of expressions of constructivism, some of which implicate early childhood development in the construction of a homosexual identity (Troiden, 1993). In any case, what unites the various schools of constructivism is the contention that it is shared cultural meanings and understandings of the organization of sexual behavior that determine the forms through which people experience their sexuality, rather than that experience being determined by an enduring, stable, universal reality.

Etiology.   Researchers also disagree about what causes experiences of same-sex attraction. Psychologists should discuss with clients various competing theories as to the etiology of same-sex attraction. Proponents of gay-affirmative therapy tend to view same-sex behavior as an expression of sexual diversity and often see homosexuality as following a specific developmental course. Troiden (1993), for example, views the development of a homosexual identity as occurring in four stages: (a) sensitization (a person is sensitized by feeling marginalized), (b) identity confusion (often during adolescence, when feeling "different" is associated with same-sex attraction), (c) identity assumption (acceptance of a homosexual identity and association with others who identify themselves as gay), and (d) commitment (marked by increased commitment to and disclosure of homosexual identity).

In contrast, several psychoanalytic and psychodynamic theorists have discussed the etiology of homosexuality from a depth psychology perspective (Bieber et al., 1962; Moberly, 1983; Nicolosi, 1991, 1993; van den Aardweg, 1986). For example, van den Aardweg (1986) draws upon insights from Adler, who stressed the inferiority complex as well as the interpersonal and social dimensions of the person. According to van den Aardweg, homosexuality is symptomatic of a self-pitying neurosis that centers on feeling inferior with respect to one's masculinity. His therapy is referred to "anticomplaining" therapy, in which he develops the concept of the inner child in the adult who experiences same-sex attraction. In contrast, Moberly (1983) developed her theory for the etiology of homosexuality from a psychodynamic perspective. She views homosexuality as signaling a relational deficit with the same-sex parent: "Needs for love from, dependency on, and identification with, the parent of the same sex are met through the child's attachment to the parent" (p. 5). Failure to meet these legitimate developmental needs leads to a "defensive detachment" and a relational "ambivalence," which "marks the abiding defect in the person's actual relational capacity" (p. 6).

Proponents of this view reference empirical studies to support the hypothesis that problems in the parent–child relationship may be in some way related to some experiences of same-sex attraction. These include reports of distant relationships with the same-sex parent, including loss of a father or mother through divorce or death (Saghir & Robins, 1973), as well as studies reporting higher incidence rates of childhood sexual abuse among homosexuals as compared to their heterosexual peers (Doll et al., 1992; Laumann, Gagnon, Michael, & Michaels, 1994; Peters & Cantrell, 1991).

Psychological theories for the etiology of same-sex attraction have been criticized but not refuted. Most recently, researchers have focused on biological explanations for the etiology of homosexuality. These studies have included research on differences in brain structure and function (LeVay, 1991; Swaab & Hofman, 1990), prenatal hormonal mechanisms (Ellis & Ames, 1987), and genetic factors, as evidenced by twin studies (Bailey & Pillard, 1991) and markers on chromosomes that may be associated with homosexuality (Hamer, Hu, Magnuson, Hu, & Pattatucci, 1993; Hu et al., 1995; for a detailed review of this literature, see Byne & Parsons, 1993).

Psychologists should discuss with clients the various theories for the etiology of same-sex attraction and acknowledge that most experts in the field agree that there is no one explanation of homosexuality that accounts for every person's experience of same-sex attraction. Rather, the etiology of homosexuality may be related to a host of interrelated factors—shifting ratios of antecedents to same-sex attraction that vary from person to person and across cultures —some of which may be biological in origin and may provide a "push" in the direction of homosexuality. Other influences may take the form of psychosocial and environmental factors (e.g., parent-child relational deficits or experiences of childhood sexual abuse), as well as decisions made at key times in an individual's life.

Distress. Psychologists should also seek to understand why a particular client is reporting distress with respect to his or her experience of same-sex attraction. A number of concerns may bring a homosexual client into treatment. For example, clients may come into therapy distressed about the social stigma attached to homosexuality. They may feel completely content with their experience of same-sex attraction but may struggle with whether or not to identify themselves as "gay" in a culture that is heterosexual in majority. A related concern has to do with internalized homophobia, which many proponents of gay-affirmative therapy view as the root cause of most concerns among distressed homosexuals (Halderman, 1991; cf., O'Donohue & Caselles, 1993). Along these lines, McConaghy notes that it is important "to establish that [clients] are in their customary state of mental health and are not suffering a psychiatric disorder... any decision about treatment in relation to their sexual orientation should be postponed until they have returned to their normal emotional state" (1993, p. 134).

Other clients may not know what they think about their experiences of same-sex attraction, but they may be asking for a safe place to articulate— perhaps for the first time—their ambivalent feelings toward their impulses and inclinations. Still others may report that their difficulties stem from genuine religious convictions about the proper intention for sexual expression and may be combined to some extent with cultural/ethnic values concerning human sexuality, gender roles, and the propagation of one's race (Greene, 1994). Psychologists should be prepared to respect the values of clients even if they differ from their own, and they should be prepared to discuss a range of options in light of the current research on homosexuality.

Professional Treatments Available

A discussion of available treatments should follow a thorough discussion of the client's goals. Some clients seek change of orientation; others report interest in reducing anxiety about heterosexual behavior or decreasing homosexual thoughts or behavior; still others seek help in living a celibate life.

Change of orientation techniques have included behavioral sex therapy (Masters & Johnson, 1979), individual psychoanalytic therapy (Bieber et al., 1962), individual reparative therapy based on psychodynamic theory (Nicolosi, 1993) and group therapies offered from a psychoanalytic perspective (Hadden, 1958), psychodynamic/reparative therapy perspective (Nicolosi, 1991, 1993), social learning perspective (Birk, 1974, 1980), and a variety of other theoretical perspectives (Beukenkamp, 1960; Mintz, 1966). Success rates have ranged from between 25–50% at best, although success was often measured by self-report and therapist-report, which are susceptible to over reporting of positive outcomes and under reporting of negative outcomes. Only a few studies utilized control groups. It should be noted, however, that the dearth of controlled outcome studies and more stringent methodologies does not disprove the success of treatment. Sometimes it is presumed that improved methodologies would automatically discredit reports of success.

Unfortunately, few researchers today publish studies on therapy for homosexuals who seek change. Those who do report on such interventions are often criticized. For example, a controversial intervention is reparative therapy, which is based on dynamic theory and assumes that some homosexuals experience a same-sex relational deficit. Nicolosi (1991, 1993) offers a detailed description of reparative therapy, which he states "proceeds from the assumption that some childhood developmental tasks were not completed" (p. 211). . . . Because of the assumption that people "eroticize" what they "are not identified with," therapy focuses on "the full development of the client's masculine gender identity" (1993, pp. 199, 211–212).

In any case, those who are asking to change orientation should be informed that a variety of interventions exist. They should also be told that definitions of "success" vary significantly. Early studies defined a "heterosexual shift" as choosing "to change and to give up homosexual contacts" (Pittman & DeYoung, 1971, p. 66). Similar definitions of success have been criticized as superficial. At the other extreme, critics of reorientation programs often define success so strictly as to negate the value of any change whatsoever. For example, Haldeman (1991) argues that any lustful thoughts or same-sex impulses experienced by clients refute the claim of a "cure." At issue here is how to interpret continuing experiences of same-sex attraction and arousal. This may indicate that treatment was ineffective. However, continued struggles with same-sex arousal may be expected residual effects from years of homosexual fantasy and behavior. Psychologists certainly refrain from decrying chemical dependency programs simply because someone experiences cravings following treatment. In any case, this is certainly an area where clarity of definitions and expectations is needed.

Those who seek to change behavior rather than orientation should be aware of research that utilizes rigorous methodology and supports efforts to change, including the use of imaginal desensitization/alternative behavioral completion, covert modeling, behavioral rehearsal, assertiveness training, and aversion therapy. For example, McConaghy (1969, 1970, 1976) reports on the use of behavioral and aversion therapies and the use of penile plethysmograph responses as means of measuring change of homosexual impulses. In one study McConaghy (1970) notes that of 35 patients contracted at one-year follow-up (of a total of 40 in the original study), 7 reported change of orientation from predominantly homosexual to predominantly heterosexual (although McConaghy is conservative in his interpretation of their reported change of orientation). A total of 10 patients showed marked improvement and 15 additional patients showed some improvement. Of these, many reported greater emotional stability and decreased preoccupation with homosexual thoughts; still others were reportedly able to control compulsions to anonymous homosexual encounters. Elsewhere McConaghy (1993, pp. 134–138) discusses a range of cognitive and behavioral interventions for those who seek change and reports that homosexual clients can learn "to control homosexual feelings or behaviors they experience as compulsive and to reduce anxiety concerning heterosexual activity" (1990, p. 576).

Murphy (1992) offers a critical review of a number of other professional interventions to diminish sexual desire, including surgery (which Murphy states have been abandoned as of the early 1980s) and drug and hormone therapy. McConaghy also reviews the use of medroxyprogesterone acetate "to cease unacceptable sexual behaviors while not altering their enjoyment of acceptable behaviors" (1993, p. 134; cf., Silverstein, 1991). Both Murphy and McConaghy also note that interventions are often combined so that, for example, drug treatments are provided in conjunction with behavior therapy.

Alternatives to Professional Treatment

In addition to the professional interventions mentioned above, increasing numbers of paraprofessional religious groups are offering services to persons distressed by their experience of same-sex attraction. A plausible hypothesis is that these groups have emerged in part because of the decrease in professional services provided to homosexuals who seek change. However, while most of these groups do make claims for change of orientation, there are no published controlled outcome studies to support the numerous anecdotal reports of change. Although these groups receive appropriate criticism for not providing empirical support for claims of success, it should be noted that the lack of empirical support does not disprove the effectiveness of these groups. As with professional interventions, it is often presumed that more stringent methodology would automatically discredit these groups. Paraprofessional groups remain attractive to some psychologists and clients because they offer services at little or no charge and are often used as an adjunct to professional therapy, similar to how therapists encourage alcoholics to attend Alcoholics Anonymous (AA) meetings while they continue to receive professional care.

There are several examples of religion-based support groups, including Exodus International-affiliated ministries and Homosexuals Anonymous. These organizations tend to view homosexuality as a learned behavior that can be changed, and proponents give the impression that change of orientation can be expected (Consiglio, 1989, 1993; Dallas, 1991). Other religion-based support groups, such as Courage, emphasize celibacy and behavior change (Harvey, 1987). Although Courage does not discourage those who have the desire and the financial resources to attempt change of orientation from doing so. Courage does take a more conservative approach in general as it cautions people to not be disheartened if, after attempts at change, they are unable to experience a heterosexual orientation. Unfortunately, as with most of the other religion-based groups, Courage publishes no outcome data on those who attend group meetings....

Benefits and Risks of Treatment

Clients should also be made aware of the benefits and risks of treatment. Risks of treatment include the financial and emotional investment for those who pursue change. Professional interventions such as reparative therapy can last for 2 or more years (with no guarantee of "success"), and the financial cost can be tremendous. The financial investment may pale in comparison to the emotional investment, especially depending upon the expectations of the client. For example, those who have as their goal complete change of sexual orientation and who view failure to achieve a "complete heterosexual shift" as evidence of lack of faith, lack of spiritual maturity, or as a sign of moral degradation may be in a far worse state than those who attempt change but recognize the potential limitations of change techniques. A related concern is that lack of success in treatment may lead to anger and resentment. These feelings may be directed inward (taking the form of depression or suicidality), or they may be directed at the therapist, family members, society, God, the church, support groups, and so on. One arguable but plausible hypothesis is that some of those who are truly disillusioned by attempts to change may become the most ardent supporters of gay-affirmative therapy, in part because they held such high hopes for treatment, and the dichotomy between the psychological sense of "success" and "failure" may have been too great a strain to bear. Clearly the risk of failure and what that means to a client is an important part of informed consent.

In addition, some have criticized the use of aversion therapy and some behavioral therapies as potentially harmful to the person seeking change (i.e., may cause depression, anxiety, or decreased self-esteem). Critics of these interventions question their ethical status (Coleman, 1982; Wilson & Davison, 1974) and some note that change away from treating homosexuality as a pathology toward treating it as a moral concern (Murphy, 1992). Moral concerns, however, can still direct the focus of treatment, and psychologists have an ethical responsibility to respect the moral values of clients (Ethical Standards 1.09, APA, 1992).

The benefits of treatment my include change of sexual orientation, although this claim is precisely what is debated among mental health professionals. Some of those who report change of sexual orientation also report satisfying heterosexual relationships, including marriage (although most mental health professionals agree that heterosexual marriage should not be held out as the goal of treatment as such). Other benefits of treatment appear to be greater emotional stability, decreased preoccupation with homosexual thoughts, and decreased compulsive sexual behavior (McConaghy, 1970, reports these gains among several clients at one-year follow up).

Possible Outcomes With and Without Treatment

Possible outcome with treatment has been discussed. Some may experience change of behavior or impulses. It is possible that some may experience change of orientation. Others will not experience change that is satisfying in light of their goals for treatment. Outcome without treatment may be difficult to predict. Some may choose to live a celibate life, having had as their goal change of orientation. Others may choose to limit their sexual relationships to an exclusive or monogamous sexual relationship, having had anonymous sexual encounters or having engaged in compulsive sexual activities in the past. However, the research on rates of nonmonogamy among homosexuals as compared to heterosexuals suggests this may be unlikely. For example, Laumann et al. (1994) published findings that homosexual males on average reported 42.8 lifetime sexual partners as compared to 16.5 lifetime sexual partners among heterosexual males, 9.4 lifetime sexual partners among lesbians, and 4.6 lifetime sexual partners among heterosexual females.

It should be noted, however, that some researchers argue that it is difficult to compare rates of nonmonogamy between homosexuals and heterosexuals. For example, McWhirter and Mattison (1984) contend that homosexual partners may not make promises to each other that they intend to remain monogamous. At least one study has attempted to account for this possibility. Blumstein and Schwartz (1990) created a category for "close-coupled" homosexual partners to distinguish committed male homosexual relationships. Blumstein and Schwartz (1990) found that 79% of close-coupled male homosexuals reported at least one experience of nonmonogamy in the previous year, as compared to 19% of lesbians, 10% of married heterosexuals, and 23% of cohabiting heterosexuals. Even in this study, question remain concerning the relationship between emotional fidelity and sexual exclusivity, as 36% of gay men and 71% of lesbians surveyed valued sexual monogamy.

In any case, those who seek treatment for their experience of same-sex attraction may also choose to integrate their experience of same-sex attraction into a gay identity. These individuals should be aware of concerns identified as relevant to clinical work with gay men and lesbians. This is actually an area where there is some agreement even between otherwise polarized gay-affirmative therapists and reparative therapists, for example. These concerns include increased rates of depressive symptomatology, alcohol and drug use, and suicidal ideation, as well as common sexual practices that increase the risk of physical harm and disease (Laumann et al., 1994; McWhirter & Mattison, 1984). Of course, numerous contradictory theories have been advanced to account for the differences reported in these studies. Some researchers argue that coming out of the closet (as measured by degree of communication about sexual preference and degree of comfort with being gay) and relationship involvement correlate with lower scores on measures of anxiety and depression as compared to those who remain distressed by their experience of same-sex attraction (Schmitt & Kurdek, 1987). For others, being out of the closet may not guarantee lower levels of depression, anxiety, and so on, especially if they experience discrimination (McKirman & Peterson, 1988; Mosbacher, 1993). What complicates our understanding is that most of the major national surveys do not make the distinction between "closeted" and "out" homosexuals, so there is less information from nationally representative samples than is desirable. The largest nationally representative samples include relatively small subpopulations of homosexual individuals, and the survey protocols are often designed for a generic (usually heterosexual) sample rather than a homosexual population (Laumann et al., 1994). The smaller and more famous surveys of homosexual individuals have much smaller sample sizes and tend to be of convenience samples (Bell & Weinberg, 1978).

In any case, clients should have the opportunity to make informed decisions about their treatment, and these findings, though difficult to interpret, may be deemed important by clients making decisions about their health and well-being. Obviously, many people who choose not to pursue treatment do not report these concerns, and there is retrospective research that supports the claim that those who identify themselves as homosexual may feel better about themselves than they did prior to that decision (Bell & Weinberg, 1978). The professional ethical issue here is that, as suggested by Ethical Principle D and in light of the benefit of advanced informed consent to treatment, those who come to therapy reporting distress concerning their experience of same-sex attraction should at some point in treatment have a frank discussion of possible outcomes with or without treatment.

Conclusion

Psychologists take seriously autonomy and agency of the individual. The human capacity to choose is relevant to therapeutic conceptualizations and interventions, and some clients choose to make moral concerns a focus of treatment, or they seek to change their behavior precisely because of an overarching moral evaluative framework. Individuals have the right to seek treatment aimed at curbing homosexual inclinations or modifying homosexual behaviors, not only because it affirms their right to dignity, autonomy, and agency, as persons presumed capable of freely choosing among treatment modalities and behavior, but also because it demonstrates a high regard for cultural and religious differences.

Psychologists who work with clients distressed by their experience of same-sex attraction should only do so with advanced informed consent. A comprehensive presentation of relevant findings should precede any decision for or against treatment, as the use of informed consent respects the autonomy and agency of clients and demonstrates multicultural sensitivity to normative religious values.

Note

1. Beverly Greene (1994) reports on the relationship between cultural and sexual identity among ethnic minority groups. Interestingly, according to Greene, in contrast to other minorities, "African American gay men and lesbians claim a strong attachment to their cultural heritage and to their communities and cite their identities as African American as primary" (p. 246).

References

American Psychiatric Association. (1994). *Diagnostic and statistical manual of mental disorders* (4th ed.). Washington, DC: Author.

American Psychological Association. (1992). Ethical principles of psychologists and code of conduct. *American Psychologist, 47*(12), 1597–1611.

Bailey, J. M., & Pillard, R. C. (1991). A genetic study of male sexual orientation. *Archives of General Psychiatry, 48*, 1089–1096.

Beukenkamp, C. (1960). Phantom patricide. *Archives of General Psychiatry, 3*, 282–288.

Bell, A. P., & Weinberg, M. S. (1978). *Homosexualities: A study of diversity among men and women.* New York: Simon and Schuster.

Bieber, I., Dain, H. J., Dince, P. R., Drellich, M. G., Grand, H. G., Gundlach, R. H., Kremer, M. W., Rifkin, A. H., Wilbur, C. B., & Bieber, T. B. (1962). *Homosexuality: A psychoanalytic study of male homosexuality.* New York: Basic.

Birk, L. (1974). Group psychotherapy for men who are homosexual. *Journal of Sex and Marital Therapy, 1*, 29–52.

Birk, L. (1980). The myth of classical homosexuality: Views of a behavioral psychotherapist. In J. Marmor (Ed.), *Homosexual behavior: A modern reappraisal* (pp. 376–390). New York Basic.

Blumstein, P., & Schwartz, P. (1990). Intimate relationships and the creation of sexuality. In S. A. Sanders & J. M. Reinisch (Eds.), *Homosexuality/heterosexuality: Concepts of sexual orientation* (pp. 307–320). New York: Oxford University Press.

Browning, C., Reynolds, A. L., & Dworkin, S. H. (1991). Affirmative psychotherapy for lesbian women. *The Counseling Psychologist, 19*(2), 177–196.

Byne, W., & Parsons, B. (1993). Human sexual orientation: The biologic theories reappraised. *Archives of General Psychiatry, 50*, 228–239.

Carrier, J. (1980). Homosexual behavior in cross-cultural perspective. In J. Marmor (Ed.), *Homosexual behavior: A modern reappraisal* (pp. 100–122). New York: Basic.

Coleman, E. (1982). Changing approaches to the treatment of homosexuality. In W. Paul, J. D. Weinrich, J. C. Gonsiorek, & M. E. Hotvedt (Eds.), *Homosexuality: Social, psychological, and biological issues* (pp. 81–88). Beverly Hills: Sage.

Consiglio, W. (1989). *Homosexual no more: Practical strategies for Christians overcoming homosexuality.* Wheaton, IL: Victor.

Consiglio, W. (1993). Doing therapy in an alien culture with Christians overcoming homosexuality. *Journal of Pastoral Counseling, 28*, 66–95.

Corey, G., Corey, M. S., & Callahan, P. (1993). *Issues and ethics in the helping professions* (4th ed.). Pacific Grove, CA: Brooks/Cole.

Dallas, J. (1991). *Desires in conflict: Answering the struggle for sexual identity.* Eugene, OR: Harvest House.

Davison, G. C. (1982). Politics, ethics, and therapy for homosexuality. In W. Paul, J. D. Weinrich, J. C. Gonsiorek, & M. E. Hotvedt (Eds.), *Homosexuality: Social, psychological, and biological issues* (pp. 89–98). Beverly Hills: Sage.

Doll, L. S., Joy, D., Bartholow, B. N., Harrison, J. S., Bolan, G., Douglas, J. M., Saltzman, L. E., Moss, P. M., & Delgado, W. (1992). Self-reported childhood and adolescent sexual abuse among adult homosexual and bisexual men. *Child Abuse and Neglect, 16*, 855–864.

Ellis, L., & Ames, A. (1987). Neurohormonal functioning and sexual orientation: A theory of homosexuality-heterosexuality. *Psychological Bulletin, 101,* 233–258.

Greenberg, D. (1988). *The construction of homosexuality.* Chicago: University of Chicago Press.

Greene, B. (1994). Ethnic-minority lesbians and gay men: Mental health and treatment issues. *Journal of Consulting and Clinical Psychology, 62*(2), 243–251.

Hadden, S. B. (1958). Treatment of homosexuality in individual and group psychotherapy. *American Journal of Psychiatry, 114,* 810–815.

Haldeman, D. C. (1991). Sexual orientation conversion therapy: A scientific examination. In J. Gonsiorek & J. Weinrich (Eds.), *Homosexuality: Research implications for public policy* (pp. 149–160). Newbury Park, CA: Sage.

Haldeman, D. C. (1994). The practice and ethics of sexual orientation conversion therapy. *Journal of Consulting and Clinical Psychology, 62*(2), 221–227.

Hamer, D. H., Hu, S., Magnuson, V. L., Hu, N., & Pattatuci, A. M. (1993). A linkage between DNA markers on the X chromosome and male sexual orientation, *Science, 261,* 321–327.

Harvey, J. F. (1987). *The homosexual person: New thinking in pastoral care.* San Francisco: Ignatius.

Hu, S., Pattatucci, A. M., Patterson, C., Li, L., Fulker, D. W., Cherny, S. S., Kruglyak, L., & Hamer, D. H. (1995). Linkage between sexual orientation and chromosome Xq28 in males but not in females. *Nature Genetics, 11,* 248–256.

Jones, S. L. (1994). A constructive relationship for religion with the science and profession of psychology: Perhaps the boldest model yet. *American Psychologist, 49*(3), 184–199.

Keith-Spiegel, P., & Koocher, G. P. (1985). *Ethics in psychology: Professional standards and cases.* New York: Random House.

Laumann, E. O., Gagnon, J. H., Michael, R. T., & Michaels, S. (1994). *The Social organization of sexuality.* Chicago: University of Chicago Press.

LeVay, S. (1991). A difference in the hypothalamic structure between heterosexual and homosexual men. *Science, 253,* 1034–1037.

Masters, W., & Johnson, V. (1979). *Homosexuality in perspective.* Boston: Little, Brown, & Co.

McConaghy, N. (1969). Subjective and penile plethysmograph responses following aversion-relief and apomorphine aversion therapy for homosexual impulses. *British Journal of Psychiatry, 115,* 723–730.

McConaghy, N. (1970). Subjective and penile plethysmograph responses to aversion therapy for homosexuality: A follow-up study. *British Journal of Psychiatry, 117,* 555–560.

McConaghy, N. (1976). Is a homosexual orientation irreversible? *British Journal of Psychiatry, 129,* 556–563.

McConaghy, N. (1990). Sexual deviation. In A. S. Bellack, M. Hersen, & A. E. Kazdin (Eds.), *International handbook of behavior modification and therapy* (2nd ed., pp. 565–580). New York: Plenum.

McConaghy, N. (1993). *Sexual behavior: Problems and management.* New York: Plenum.

McKirman, D. J., & Peterson, P. L. (1988). Stress, expectancies, and vulnerability to substance abuse: A test of a model among homosexual men. *Journal of Abnormal Psychology, 97*(4), 461–466.

McWhirter, D. P., & Mattison, A. M. (1984). *The male couple.* New York: Prentice-Hall.

Mintz, E. E. (1966). Overt male homosexuals in combined group and individual treatment. *Journal of Consulting Psychology, 30*(3), 193–198.

Moberly, E. (1983). *Homosexuality: A new Christian ethic.* Cambridge: James Clarke & Co.

Morin, S. F. (1991). Removing the stigma: Lesbian and gay affirmative counseling. *The Counseling Psychologist, 19*(2), 245–247.

Mosbacher, D. (1993). Alcohol and other drug use in female medical students: A comparison of lesbians and heterosexuals. *Journal of Gay & Lesbian Psychotherapy, 2,* 37–48.

Murphy, T. F. (1992). Redirecting sexual orientation: Techniques and justifications. *The Journal of Sex Research, 29*(4), 501–523.

Nicolosi, J. (1991). *Reparative therapy of male homosexuality: A new clinical approach.* Northvale, NJ: Jason Aronson.

Nicolosi, J. (1993). *Healing homosexuality: Case stories of reparative therapy,* Northvale, NJ: Jason Aronson.

O'Donohue, W., & Caselles, C. E. (1993). Homophobia: Conceptual, definitional, and value issues. *Journal of Psychopathology and Behavioral Assessment, 15*(3), 177–195.

Peters, D. K., & Cantrell, P. J. (1991). Factors distinguishing samples of lesbian and heterosexual women. *Journal of Homosexuality, 21*(4), 1–15.

Pillard, R. C. (1982). Psychotherapeutic treatment for the invisible minority. In W. Paul, J. D. Weinrich, J. C. Gonsiorek, & M. E. Hotvedt (Eds.), *Homosexuality: Social, psychological, and biological issues* (pp. 99–114). Beverly Hills: Sage.

Pittman, F. S., & DeYoung, C. D. (1971). The treatment of homosexuals in heterogeneous groups. *International Journal of Group Psychotherapy, 21,* 62–73.

Rychlak, J. F. (1988). Explaining helping relationships through learning theories and the question of human agency. *Counseling and Values, 32,* 83–92.

Saghir, M. T., & Robins, E. (1973). *Male and female homosexuality: A comprehensive investigation.* Baltimore, MD: Williams and Wilkins.

Schmitt, J. P., & Kurdek, L. A. (1987). Personality correlates of positive identity and relationship involvement in gay men. *Journal of Homosexuality, 13*(4), 101–109.

Shafranske, E. P. (Ed.). (1996). *Religion and the clinical practice of psychology.* Washington, DC: American Psychological Association.

Shannon, J. W., & Woods, W. J. (1991). Affirmative psychotherapy for gay men. *The Counseling Psychologist, 19*(2), 197–215.

Silverstein, C. (1972, October). *Behavior modification and the gay community.* Paper presented at the annual convention of the Association for Advancement of Behavioral Therapy. New York, NY.

Silverstein, C. (1991). Psychological and medical treatments of homosexuality. In J. C. Gonsiorek & J. D. Weinrich (Eds.), *Homosexuality: Research implications for public policy* (pp. 101–114). Newbury Park, CA: Sage.

Sobocinski, M. R. (1990). Ethical principles in the counseling of gay and lesbian adolescents: Issues of autonomy, competence, and confidentiality. *Professional Psychology: Research and Practice, 21*(4), 240–247.

Sullivan, A. (1995). *Virtually normal: An argument about homosexuality.* New York: Alfred A. Knopf.

Swaab, D. F., & Hofman, M. A. (1990). An enlarged suprachiasmatic nucleus in homosexual men. *Brain Research, 537,* 141–148.

Troiden, R. (1993). The formation of homosexual identities. In L. D. Garnets & D. C. Kimmel (Eds.), *Psychological perspectives on lesbian and gay male experiences* (pp. 191–217). NY: Columbia University Press.

Van Den Aardweg, G. J. M. (1986). *On the origins and treatment of homosexuality.* New York: Prager.

Wilson, G. T., & Davison, G. C. (1974). Behavior therapy and homosexuality: A critical perspective. *Behavior Therapy, 5,* 16–28.

Douglas C. Haldeman

The Practice and Ethics of Sexual Orientation Conversion Therapy

The question of how to change sexual orientation has been discussed as long as homoeroticism itself has been described in the literature. For over a century, medical, psychotherapeutic, and religious practitioners have sought to reverse unwanted homosexual orientation through various methods: These include psychoanalytic therapy, prayer and spiritual interventions, electric shock, nausea-inducing drugs, hormone therapy, surgery, and various adjunctive behavioral treatments, including masturbatory reconditioning, rest, visits to prostitutes, and excessive bicycle riding (Murphy, 1992). Early attempts to reverse sexual orientation were founded on the unquestioned assumption that homosexuality is an unwanted, unhealthy condition. Although homosexuality has long been absent from the taxonomy of mental disorders, efforts to reorient gay men and lesbians persist. Recently, for example, a coalition of mental health practitioners formed an organization dedicated to the "rehabilitation" of gay men and lesbians. Many practitioners still adhere to the officially debunked "illness" model of homosexuality, and many base their treatments on religious proscriptions against homosexual behavior. Still others defend sexual reorientation therapy as a matter of free choice for the unhappy client, claiming that their treatments do not imply a negative judgment on homosexuality per se. They seek to provide what they describe as a treatment alternative for men and women whose homosexuality is somehow incongruent with their values, life goals, or psychological structures.

Of the articles to be examined in this review, few have addressed the question of how sexual orientation is defined. Such a definition seems necessary before one can describe how sexual orientation is changed. However, most research in this area offers a dichotomous view of human sexuality in which undesired homoerotic impulses can be eradicated through a program that replaces them with heterosexual competence. Few studies even rely on the relatively simplistic Kinsey scale (Kinsey, Pomeroy, & Martin, 1948) to make an attempt at assessing a subject's sexual orientation. Although a comprehensive discussion is well beyond the scope of this article, I began with a passing reference to what is meant by the terms *homosexuality* and *heterosexuality*.

From Douglas C. Haldeman, "The Practice and Ethics of Sexual Orientation Conversion Therapy," *Journal of Consulting and Clinical Psychology*, vol. 62, no. 2 (1994). Copyright © 1994 by The American Psychological Association. Reprinted by permission of The American Psychological Association and the author.

The data of Kinsey et al. (1948) suggested that as many as 10% of American men considered themselves to be primarily or exclusively homosexual for at least 3 years of their adult lives. His assessment was based on the subject's actual behavior as well as the content of the subject's fantasy life. Subsequent efforts to quantify sexual orientation have incorporated gender-based, social, and affectional variables (Coleman, 1987). Several complex questions involved in the defining of sexual orientation have been either reduced or overlooked in the literature on conversion therapy. For instance, those conversion therapy programs that claim the greatest success included more subjects whose behavioral histories and fantasy lives appeared to have significant heteroerotic components (Haldeman, 1991). Instructing a "homosexual" subject with a priori heteroerotic responsiveness in heterosexual behavior appears to be easier than replacing the cognitive sociosexual schema and redirecting the behavior of the "homosexual" subject with no reported heteroerotic inclinations. Nevertheless, both types of "homosexual" subjects are often included in the same treatment group.

Any definition of sexuality based solely on behavior is bound to be deficient and misleading. Sense of identity, internalized sociocultural expectations, and importance of social and political affiliations all help define an individual's sexual orientation, and these variables may change over time. The content of an individual's fantasy life may provide information that is not influenced by the individual's need for social acceptance, but even these are subject, in some women and men, to variations in gender of object choice, based on environmental or political factors. Social demand variables also figure in describing sexual orientation, given the frequency with which gay men and lesbians marry (Bell & Weinberg, 1978)....

The categories homosexual, heterosexual, and bisexual, conceived by many researchers as fixed and dichotomous, are in reality very fluid for many. Therefore, in addition to how sexual orientation is defined, one must also consider how it is experienced by the individual. For many gay men, the process of "coming out" may be likened to an internal evolution of sorts, a conscious recognition of what has always been. On the other hand, many lesbians describe "coming out" as a process tied to choices or social and political constructions. In this regard, many lesbians may have more in common with heterosexual women than with gay men, suggesting a gender-based distinction relative to the development of homosexual identity.

Questions about the complex nature of sexual orientation and its development in the individual must be addressed before change in sexual orientation is assessed. Many previously heterosexually identified individuals "come out" as lesbian or gay later in life, and some people who identify themselves as gay or lesbian engage in heterosexual behavior and relationships for a variety of personal and social reasons. How, then, are spontaneously occurring shifts in sexual orientation over the life span to be differentiated from behavior resulting from the interventions of a conversion therapist? Essentially, the fixed, behavior-based model of sexual orientation assumed by almost all conversion therapists may be invalid. For many individuals, sexual orientation is a variable construct subject to changes in erotic and affectional preference, as well as changes in social values and political philosophy that may ebb and flow throughout life. For some, "coming out" may be a process with no true endpoint. Practitioners assessing change in sexual orientation have ignored the complex variations in an individual's erotic responses and shifts in the sociocultural landscape.

Psychological Conversion Programs

The case for conversion therapy rests on its ability to understand who is being converted and its ability to describe the nature of the conversion taking place. Acknowledging the theoretical complexities and ambiguities left unaddressed by most conversion therapists, the first question is "Are these treatments effective?" In assessing the efficacy of conversion therapy, psychotherapeutic and religious programs will be reviewed. Those interested in reviews of medical therapies (drug or hormonal and surgical interventions) are referred to Silverstein (1991) and Murphy (1992).

Psychotherapeutic approaches to sexual reorientation have been based on the a priori assumption that homoeroticism is an undesirable condition. Two basic hypotheses serve as the foundation for most therapies designed to reverse sexual orientation. The first is that homosexuality results from an arrest in normal development or from pathological attachment patterns in early life. The second is that homosexuality stems from faulty learning. Therapies most closely associated with the first perspective are of the psychoanalytic and neo-analytic orientations.

Psychoanalytic tradition posited that homosexual orientation represented an arrest in normal psychosexual development, most often in the context of a particular dysfunctional family constellation. Such a family typically featured a close-binding mother and an absent or distant father. Despite the relative renown of this therapy, it is based solely on clinical speculation and has never been empirically validated. Subsequent studies have indicated that etiologic factors in the development of sexual orientation are unclear but that the traditional psychoanalytic formulations concerning family dynamics are not viable (Bell, Weinberg, & Hammersmith, 1981).

Psychoanalytic treatment of homosexuality is exemplified by the work of Bieber et al. (1962), who advocate intensive, long-term therapy aimed at resolving the unconscious anxiety stemming from childhood conflicts that supposedly cause homosexuality. Bieber et al. saw homosexuality as always pathological and incompatible with a happy life. Their methodology has been criticized for use of an entirely clinical sample and for basing outcomes on subjective therapist impression, not externally validated data or even self-report. Follow-up data have been poorly presented and not empirical in nature. Bieber et al. (1962) reported a 27% success rate in heterosexual shift after long-term therapy; of these, however, only 18% were exclusively homosexual in the first place. Fifty percent of the successfully treated subjects were more appropriately labeled bisexual. This blending of "apples and oranges" returns us to the original question: Who is being converted, and what is the nature of the conversion?

Another analytically based study reported virtually no increase in hetero-sexual behavior in a group of homosexual men (Curran & Parr, 1957). Other studies report greater success rates: For instance, Mayerson and Lief (1965) in-dicate that, of 19 subjects, half reported engaging in exclusive heterosexual behavior 4.5 years posttreatment. However, as in Bieber et al.'s study, those subjects had heteroerotic traits to begin with; exclusively homosexual sub-jects reported little change, and outcomes were based on patient self-report. As in other studies, an expansion of the sexual repertoire toward heterosexual behavior is viewed as equivalent to a shift of sexual orientation.

California psychologist Joseph Nicolosi has developed a program of repar-ative therapy for "non-gay" homosexuals, individuals who reported being un-comfortable with their same-sex orientation. Nicolosi stated, "I do not believe that the gay life-style can ever be healthy, nor that the homosexual identity can ever be completely ego-syntonic" (1991, p. 13). This belief erroneously presup-poses a unitary gay lifestyle, a concept more reductionist than that of sexual orientation. It also prejudicially and without empirical justification assumes that homosexually oriented people can never be normal or happy, a point refuted numerous times in the literature. Nonetheless, this statement is the foundation for his theoretical approach, which cites numerous studies that sug-gest that gay men have greater frequencies of disrupted bonds with their fathers, as well as a host of psychological concerns, such as assertion problems. These observations are used to justify a pathological assessment of homosexuality. The error in such reasoning is that the conclusion has preceded the data. There may be cause to examine the potentially harmful impact of a detached father and his effect on the individual's self-concept or capacity for intimacy, but why should a detached father be selected as the key player in causing homosexuality, unless an a priori decision about the pathological nature of homosexuality has been made and unless he is being investigated as the cause? This perspective is not consistent with available data, nor does it explain the millions of heterosex-ual men who come from backgrounds similar to those of gay men, or for that matter, those gay men with strong father–son relationships. Nicolosi does not support his hypothesis or his treatment methods with any empirical data.

Group treatments have also been used in sexual reorientation. One study of 32 subjects reports a 37% shift to heterosexuality (Hadden, 1966), but the re-sults must be viewed with some skepticism, because of the entirely self-report nature of the outcome measures. Individuals involved in such group treatments are especially susceptible to the influence of social demand in their own report-ing of treatment success. Similarly, a study of 10 gay men resulted in the ther-apist's impressionistic claims that homosexual patients were able to "increase contact" with heterosexuals (Mintz, 1966). Birk (1980) described a combina-tion insight-oriented-social-learning-group format for treating homosexuality. He claimed that overall, 38% of his patients achieved "solid heterosexual shifts." Nonetheless, he acknowledges that these shifts represent "an adaptation to life, not a metamorphosis," and that homosexual fantasies and activity are ongoing, even for the "happily married" individual (Birk, 1980, p. 387). If a solid hetero-sexual shift is defined as one in which a happily married person may engage in more than occasional homosexual encounters, perhaps this method is best described as a laboratory for heterosexual behavior, rather than a change of sexual orientation. A minority of subjects, likely with preexisting heteroerotic tendencies, may be taught proficiency in heterosexual activities. Eager to equate heterosexual competence with orientation change, these researchers have ignored the complex questions associated with the assessment of sexual orientation. Behavior alone is a misleading barometer of sexual orientation, which includes biological, gender-based, social, and affectional variables. No researchers who conducted conversion studies have displayed any such thoughtfulness in their assessment or categorization of subjects.

Behavioral programs designed to reverse homosexual orientation are based on the premise that homoerotic impulses arise from faulty learning. These studies seek to countercondition the "learned" homoerotic response with aversive stimuli, replacing it with the reinforced, desired heteroerotic response. The aversive stimulus, typically consisting of electric shock or convulsion- or nausea-inducing drugs, is administered during presentation of same-sex erotic visual material. The cessation of the aversive stimulus is accompanied by the presentation of heteroerotic visual material, supposedly to replace homoeroticism in the sexual response hierarchy. These methods have been reviewed by Sansweet (1975). Some programs attempted to augment aversive conditioning techniques with a social learning component (assertiveness training, how to ask women out on dates, etc.; Feldman & McCullogh, 1965). Later, the same investigators modified their approach, calling it "anticipatory avoidance conditioning," which enabled subjects to avoid electrical shock when viewing slides of same-sex nudes (Feldman, 1966). Such a stressful situation could likely inhibit feelings of sexual responsiveness in any direction; nevertheless, a 58% cure rate was claimed, with outcome criteria defined as the suppression of homoerotic response. Cautela (1967) reported on single subjects who were taught to imagine such aversive stimuli rather than undergo them directly. His later work focuses on structured aversive fantasy, in which subjects are asked to visualize repulsive homoerotic encounters in stressful circumstances (Cautela & Kearney, 1986). The investigators deny a homophobic bias to this therapeutic approach.

Other studies suggest that aversive interventions may extinguish homosexual responsiveness but do little to promote alternative orientation. One investigator suggests that the poor outcomes of conversion treatments are due to the fact that they "disregard the complex learned repertoire and topography of homosexual behavior" (Faustman, 1976). Other studies echo the finding that aversive therapies in homosexuality do not alter subjects' sexual orientation (McConaghy, 1981). Another study similarly suggests that behavioral conditioning decreases homosexual orientation but does not elevate heterosexual interest (Rangaswami, 1982). Methodologically, the near-exclusive use of self-report outcome measures is problematic, particularly in an area where social demand factors may strongly influence subjects' reports. The few studies that do attempt to externally validate sexual reorientation through behavioral measures show no change after treatment (Conrad & Wincze, 1976).

Masters and Johnson (1979) reported on the treatment of 54 "dissatisfied" homosexual men. This was unprecedented for the authors, as their previous works on heterosexual dysfunction did not include treatment for dissatisfied heterosexual people. The authors hypothesized homosexuality to be the result of failed or ridiculed attempts at heterosexuality, neglecting the obvious: that heterosexual "failures" among homosexual people are to be expected because the behavior in question is outside the individual's normal sexual response pattern. Despite their comments to the contrary, the study is founded on heterosexist bias. Gonsiorek (1981) raises a variety of concerns with the Masters and Johnson study. Of the numerous methodological problems with this study, perhaps most significant is the composition of the sample itself. Of 54 subjects, only 9 (17%) identified themselves as Kinsey 5 or 6 (exclusively homosexual). The other 45 subjects (83%) ranged from 2 to 4 on the Kinsey scale (predominantly heterosexual to bisexual). Furthermore, because 30% of the sample was lost to follow-up, it is conceivable that the outcome sample does not include any homosexual men. Perhaps this is why such a high success rate is reported after 2 weeks of treatment. It is likely that, rather than converting or reverting homosexual people to heterosexuality, this program enhances heterosexual responsiveness in people with already established heteroerotic sexual maps.

Evidence for the efficacy of sexual conversion programs is less than compelling. All research in this area has evolved from unproven hypothetical formulations about the pathological nature of homosexuality. The illness model has never been empirically validated; to the contrary, a broad literature validates the nonpathological view of homosexuality, leading to its declassification as a mental disorder (Gonsiorek, 1991). Thus, treatments in both analytic and behavioral modes are designed to cure something that has never been demonstrated to be an illness. From a methodological standpoint, the studies reviewed here reveal inadequacies in the selection criteria and the classification of subjects and poorly designed and administered outcome measures. In short, no consistency emerges from the extant database, which suggests that sexual orientation is amenable to redirection or significant influence from psychological intervention.

Religion-Based Conversion Programs

In a recent symposium on Christian approaches to the treatment of lesbians and gay men, one panelist said of his numerous unsuccessful attempts at sexual reorientation: "I felt it was what I had to do in order to gain a right to live on the planet." Such is the experience of many gay men and lesbians, who experience severe conflict between their homoerotic feelings and their need for acceptance by a homophobic religious community. This conflict causes such individuals to seek the guidance of pastoral care providers or Christian support groups whose aim is to reorient gay men and lesbians. Such programs seek to divest the individual of his or her "sinful" feelings or at least to make the pursuit of a heterosexual or celibate lifestyle possible. Their theoretical base is founded on interpretations of scripture that condemn homosexual behavior, their often unspecified treatment methods rely on prayer, and their outcomes are generally limited to testimonials. Nonetheless, these programs bear some passing examination because of the tremendous psychological impact they have on the many unhappy gay men and lesbians who seek their services and because of some psychologists' willingness to refer to them. Lastly, many such programs have been associated with significant ethical problems.

Gay men who are most likely to be inclined toward doctrinaire religious practice are also likely to have lower self-concepts, to see homosexuality as more sinful, feel a greater sense of apprehension about negative responses from others, and are more depressed in general (Weinberg & Williams, 1974). Such individuals make vulnerable targets for the "ex-gay" ministries, as they are known. Fundamentalist Christian groups, such as Homosexuals Anonymous, Metanoia Ministries, Love In Action, Exodus International, and EXIT of Melodyland are the most visible purveyors of conversion therapy. The workings of these groups are well documented by Blair (1982), who states that, although many of these practitioners publicly promise change, they privately acknowledge that celibacy is the realistic goal to which gay men and lesbians must aspire. He further characterizes many religious conversionists as individuals deeply troubled about their own sexual orientation, or whose own sexual conversion is incomplete. Blair reports a host of problems with such counselors, including the sexual abuse of clients.

The most notable of such ministers is Colin Cook. Cook's counseling program, Quest, led to the development of Homosexuals Anonymous, the largest antigay fundamentalist counseling organization in the world. The work of Cook, his ultimate demise, and the subsequent cover-up by the Seventh Day Adventist Church, are described by sociologist Ronald Lawson (1987). Over the course of 7 years, approximately 200 people received reorientation counseling from Cook, his wife, and an associate. From this ministry sprang Homosexuals Anonymous, a 14-step program modeled after Alcoholics Anonymous, which has become the largest fundamentalist organization in the world with a unitary antigay focus. Lawson, in attempting to research the efficacy of Cook's program, was denied access to counselees on the basis of confidentiality. Nonetheless, he managed to interview 14 clients, none of whom reported any change in sexual orientation. All but two reported that Cook had had sex with them during treatment. According to Blair, another homosexual pastor who used his ministry to gain sexual access to vulnerable gay people was Guy Charles, founder of Liberation in Jesus Christ. Charles was a homosexual man who had claimed a heterosexual conversion subsequent to his acceptance to Christ. Like Cook, Charles was ultimately disavowed by the Christian organization that sponsored him after charges of sexual misconduct were raised.

To date, the only spiritually based sexual orientation conversion program to appear in the literature has been a study by Pattison and Pattison (1980). These authors describe a supernatural healing approach in treating 30 individuals culled from a group of 300 who sought sexual reorientation counseling at EXIT of Melodyland, a charismatic ex-gay ministry affiliated with a Christian amusement park. The Pattisons do not explain their sampling criteria, nor do they explain why 19 of their 30 subjects refused follow-up interviews. Their data indicate that only 3 of the 11 (of 300) subjects report no current homosexual desires, fantasies, or impulses, and that 1 of the 3 subjects is listed as still being "incidentally homosexual." Of the other 8 subjects, several indicated on-going neurotic conflict about their homosexual impulses. Although 6 of these men have married heterosexually, 2 admit to more than incidental homosexual ideation as an ongoing issue.

Recently, founders of another prominent ex-gay ministry, Exodus International, denounced their conversion therapy procedures as ineffective. Michael Busse and Gary Cooper, co-founders of Exodus and lovers for 13 years, were involved with the organization from 1976 to 1979. The program was described by these men as "ineffective... not one person was healed." They stated that the program often exacerbated already prominent feelings of guilt and personal failure among the counselees; many were driven to suicidal thoughts as a result of the failed reparative therapy ("*Newsbriefs,*" 1990, p. 43).

The fundamentalist Christian conversion programs hold enormous symbolic power over many people. Possibly exacerbating the harm to naive, shame-ridden counselees, these programs operate under the formidable auspices of the Christian church, and outside the jurisdiction of any professional organizations that may impose ethical standards of practice and accountability on them. A closer look at such programs is warranted, given the frequency with which spiritual conversion programs seek to legitimize themselves with psychologists as affiliates.

An examination of psychotherapeutic and spiritual approaches to conversion therapy reveal a wide range of scientific concerns, from theoretical weaknesses to methodological problems and poor outcomes. This literature does not suggest a bright future in studying ways to reorient people sexually. Individuals undergoing conversion treatment are not likely to emerge as heterosexually inclined, but they often do become shamed, conflicted, and fearful about their homerotic feelings. It is not uncommon for gay men and lesbians who have undergone aversion treatments to notice a temporary sharp decline in their sexual dysfunction. Similarly, subjects who have undergone failed attempts at conversion therapy often report increased guilt, anxiety, and low self-esteem. Some flee into heterosexual marriages that are doomed to problems inevitably involving spouses, and often children as well. Not one investigator has ever raised the possibility that conversion treatments may harm some participants, even in a field where a 30% success rate is seen as high. The research question, "What is being accomplished by conversion treatments?" may well be replaced by, "What harm has been done in the name of sexual reorientation?" At present, no data are extant.

Ethical Considerations

We have considered the question of whether sexual orientations are amenable to change or modification by means of therapeutic interventions. Of equal, if not greater, import is the question of whether psychology should provide or endorse such "cures." Ethicists object to conversion therapy on two grounds: first, that it constitutes a cure for a condition that has been judged not to be an illness, and second, that it reinforces a prejudicial and unjustified devaluation of homosexuality.

The American Psychiatric Association's 1973 decision to remove homosexuality from its *Diagnostic and Statistical Manual of Mental Disorders* marked the official passing of the illness model of homosexuality. The American Psychological Association (APA) followed suit with a resolution affirming this anti-illness perspective, stating, in part, "... the APA urges all mental health professionals to take the lead in removing the stigma of mental illness that has long been associated with homosexual orientations" (APA, 1975). Homosexuality was replaced with the confusing "ego-dystonic homosexuality" diagnosis, which was dropped altogether in 1987. ...

Proponents of conversion therapy continue to insist, in the absence of any evidence, that homosexuality is pathological. This model was rejected because of a lack of such evidence, and its demise has been described by Gonsiorek (1991). This review underscores the faulty logic inherent in classic psychoanalytic theories of family dysfunction as etiologic of homosexuality. Researcher bias, as well as methodological inadequacies, characterize studies supporting the illness model. Psychological test data, from Hooker's (1975) study to present-day studies, have been reviewed and show no substantive differences between homosexual and heterosexual subjects.

Were there properties intrinsic to homosexuality that make it a pathological condition, we would be able to observe and measure them directly. In reality, however, there exists a wide literature indicating just the opposite: that gay men and lesbians do not differ significantly from heterosexual men and women on measures of psychological stability, social or vocational adjustment, or capacity for decision making. In fact, psychological adjustment among gay men and lesbians seems to be directly correlated to the degree that they have accepted their sexual orientation (Weinberg & Williams, 1974). In light of such evidence, the number of studies examining the pathogensis of homosexuality has diminished in recent years.

Davison (1976, 1978, 1991) has detailed many of the ethical objections to conversion therapies. A behavior therapist once well known for his program to change sexual orientation, Davison believes that a disservice is done to the gay or lesbian individual by offering sexual orientation change as a therapeutic option. In Davison's view, conversion therapy reinforces antigay prejudice. He asks, "how can therapists honestly speak of nonprejudice when they participate in therapy regimens that by their very existence—and regardless of their efficacy—would seem to condone the current societal prejudice and perhaps also impede social change?" (1991, p. 141).

In his paraphrase of Halleck (1971), Davison states that therapeutic neutrality is a myth and that therapists, by the nature of their role, cannot help but influence patients with respect to values. Davison suggests that the question of whether sexual orientation can be changed is secondary to the consideration that it should not be changed, because of the devaluation and pathologizing of homosexuality implicit in offering a "cure" for it. Because therapists operate from positions of power, to affirm the viability of homosexuality and then engage in therapeutic efforts to change it sends a mixed message: If a cure is offered, then there must be an illness. This point is echoed by Begelman, who stated that "(conversion therapies) by their very existence, constitute a significant causal element in reinforcing the social doctrine that homosexuality is bad; therapists ... further strengthen the prejudice that homosexuality is a 'problem behavior', since treatment may be offered for it" (1975, p. 180). Charles Silverstein (1977), points to social factors (e.g., rejecting families, hostile peer interactions, and disapproving society) as being responsible for people seeking sexual orientation change. These authors indicate that what were historically viewed as "ego-dystonic" responses to homosexuality are really internalized reactions to a hostile society.

Proponents of conversion therapy often deny any coercive intent, claiming that theirs is a valuable service for distressed lesbians and gay men who freely seek their services. However, the concept that individuals seek sexual orientation change of their own free will may be fallacious. Martin (1984) stated that "a clinician's implicit acceptance of the homosexual orientation as the cause of ego-dystonic reactions, and the concomitant agreement to attempt sexual orientation change, exacerbates the ego-dystonic reactions and reinforces and confirms the internalized homophobia that lies at their root" (p. 46). . . .

Discussion

Our understanding of human sexuality is entering a new era, one in which formerly sacrosanct assumptions and classifications are no longer applicable. A new generation of individuals, no longer self-identified as gay or lesbian but as "queer," is developing a perspective of sexual orientation more complex and fluid than what has historically been viewed along rigid lines. This new construction of sexuality, combined with the antiquated, unscientific hypotheses on which conversion therapy has been based, render traditional reorientation therapy anachronistic.

The lack of empirical support for conversion therapy calls into question the judgment of clinicians who practice or endorse it. The APA "Fact Sheet on Reparative Therapy" opens with the following statement: "No scientific evidence exists to support the effectiveness of any of the conversion therapies that try to change sexual orientation." A review of the literature makes it obvious why this statement is made. Psychologists are obliged to use methods that have some empirically demonstrable efficacy, and there is a paucity of such evidence relative to conversion therapy. Moreover, there is a need to understand fully the potentially damaging effects of a failed conversion treatment.

A next logical question, then, involves standards of practice for the treatment of lesbians and gay men that *are* compatible with scientific data. In 1991, the APA's Committee on Lesbian and Gay Concerns published the results of a survey on bias in psychotherapeutic treatment of lesbians and gay men. This survey is an initial step in providing the clinician with guidelines that are consistent with science and that promote the welfare and dignity of the gay or lesbian individual. More research is needed to refine these recommendations for the myriad of issues that gay people bring to therapy. It is the responsibility of psychologists to provide accurate scientific information, particularly as so much misinformation is currently being used to further stigmatize and justify, even legislate, discrimination against gay people. The current wave of antigay political activity is founded on the mistaken assumptions that homosexuality is a chosen way of life and an abnormal one at that. It may be impossible to understand why so many people would believe that lesbians and gay men would deliberately choose a way of life that puts them at risk for discrimination and violence. It is, however, well within psychology's purview to disseminate accurate information from our considerable database about homosexuality.

Even more significant than the practical considerations of conversion therapy are the ethical concerns. Psychologists are obliged to use methods that promote the dignity and welfare of humankind. Conversion therapies fail in this regard because they are necessarily predicated on a devaluation of homosexual identity and behavior. Some contemporary conversionists would claim a value-neutral stance, insisting that conversion therapy is simply a matter of the client's right to choose treatment, but what is the purpose of attempting to change sexual orientation if it is not negatively valued? How many dissatisfied heterosexual men and women seek a similar conversion to homosexuality? What message does psychology send to society when it affirms the normalcy of homosexuality yet continues to give tacit approval to efforts to change it? Murphy, summarizing his review of the conversion therapy literature, addressed this:

> There would be no reorientation techniques where there was no interpretation that homoeroticism is an inferior state, an interpretation that in many ways continues to be medically defined, criminally enforced, socially sanctioned, and religiously justified. And it is in this moral interpretation, more than in the reigning medical therapy of the day, that all programs of sexual reorientation have their common origins and justifications. (1992, p. 520)

This morality is at work in all aspects of homophobic activity, from the alarming increase in violent hate crimes against gay men and lesbians to the political and legislative agendas of antigay organizations. Perpetrators of violence and antigay political groups justify their actions with the same devaluation of homosexuality that is used by conversion therapists.

Given the extensive societal devaluation of homosexuality and lack of positive role models for gay men and lesbians, it is not surprising that many gay people seek to become heterosexual. Homophobic attitudes have been institutionalized in nearly every aspect of our social structure, from the government and the military to our educational systems and organized religions. For gay men and lesbians who have identified with the dominant group, the desire to be like others and to be accepted socially is so strong that heterosexual relating becomes more than an act of sex or love. It becomes a symbol of freedom from prejudice and social devaluation. Psychology cannot free people from stigma by continuing to promote or tacitly endorse conversion therapy. Psychology can only combat stigma with a vigorous avowal of empirical truth. The appropriate focus of the profession is what reverses prejudice, not what reverses sexual orientation.

References

American Psychological Association. (1975). Minutes of the Council of Representatives. *American Psychologist, 30,* 633.

Begelman, D. A. (1975). Ethical and legal issues of behavior modification. In M. Hersen, R. Eisler, & P. M. Miller (Eds.), *Progress in behavior modification* (pp. 175–188). San Diego, CA: Academic Press.

Bell, A., & Weinberg, M. (1978). *Homosexuality: A study of diversity among men and women.* New York: Simon & Schuster.

Bell, A., Weinberg, M., & Hammersmith, S. (1981). *Sexual preference: Its development in men and women.* Bloomington, IN: Indiana University Press.

Bieber, I., Dain, H., Dince, P., Drellich, M., Grand, H., Gundlach, R., Kremer, M., Rifkin, A., Wilbur, C., & Bieber, T. (Society of Medical Psychoanalysts). (1962). *Homosexuality: A psychoanalytic study.* New York: Basic Books.

Birk, L. (1980). The myth of classical homosexuality: Views of a behavioral psychotherapist. In J. Marmor (Ed.), *Homosexual behavior: A modern reappraisal* (pp. 376–390). New York: Basic Books.

Blair, R. (1982). *Ex-gay.* New York: Homosexual Counseling Center.

Cautela, J. (1967). Covert sensitization. *Psychological Reports, 2,* 459–468.

Cautela, J., & Kearney, A. (1986). *The covert conditioning handbook.* New York: Springer.

Coleman, E. (1987). The assessment of sexual orientation. *Journal of Homosexuality, 14*(1 and 2), 9–24.

Conrad, S., & Wincze, J. (1976). Orgasmic reconditioning: A controlled study of its effects upon the sexual arousal and behavior of male homosexuals. *Behavior Therapy, 7,* 155–166.

Curran, D., & Parr, D. (1957). Homosexuality: An analysis of 100 male cases. *British Medical Journal, 1,* 797–801.

Davison, G. (1976). Homosexuality: The ethical challenge. *Journal of Consulting and Clinical Psychology, 44,* 157–162.

Davison, G. (1978). Not can but ought: The treatment of homosexuality. *Journal of Consulting and Clinical Psychology, 46,* 170–172.

Davison, G. (1991). Constructionism and morality in therapy for homosexuality. In J. Gonsiorek & J. Weinrich (Eds.), *Homosexuality: Research implications for public policy* (pp. 137–148). Newbury Park, CA: Sage.

Faustman, W. (1976). Aversive control of maladaptive sexual behavior: Past developments and future trends. *Psychology, 13,* 53–60.

Feldman, M. (1966). Aversion therapy for sexual deviation: A critical review. *Psychological Bulletin, 65,* 65–69.

Feldman, M., & McCullogh, M. (1965). The application of anticipatory avoidance learning to the treatment of homosexuality: Theory, technique, and preliminary results. *Behavior Research and Therapy, 2,* 165–183.

Gonsiorek, J. (1981). Review of *Homosexuality in perspective,* by Masters and Johnson. *Journal of Homosexuality, 6*(3), 81–88.

Gonsiorek, J. (1991). The empirical basis for the demise of the illness model of homosexuality. In J. Gonsiorek and J. Weinrich (Eds.), *Homosexuality: Research implications for public policy* (pp. 115–136). Newbury Park, CA: Sage.

Hadden, S. (1966). Treatment of male homosexuals in groups. *International Journal of Group Psychotherapy, 16,* 13–22.

Haldeman, D. (1991). Sexual orientation conversion therapy: A scientific examination. In J. Gonsiorek & J. Weinrich (Eds.), *Homosexuality: Research implications for public policy* (pp. 149–160). Newbury Park CA: Sage.

Halleck, S. (1971). *The politics of therapy.* New York: Science House.

Hooker, E. (1957). The adjustment of the male overt homosexual. *Journal of Projective Techniques, 21,* 17–31.

Kinsey, A. C., Pomeroy, W. B., & Martin, C. E. (1948). *Sexual behavior in the human male.* Philadelphia: W. B. Saunders.

Lawson, R. (1987, June). *Scandal in the Adventist-funded program to 'heal' homosexuals: Failure, sexual exploitation, official silence, and attempts to rehabilitate the exploiter and his methods.* Paper presented at the annual convention of the American Sociological Association, Chicago, Illinois.

Martin, A. (1984). The emperor's new clothes: Modern attempts to change sexual orientation. In E. S. Hetrick & T. S. Stein (Eds.), *Innovations in psychotherapy with homosexuals* (pp. 24–57). Washington, DC: American Psychiatric Association.

Masters, W., & Johnson, V. (1979). *Homosexuality in perspective.* Boston: Little, Brown.

Mayerson, P., & Lief, H. (1965). Psychotherapy of homosexuals: A follow-up study of nineteen cases. In J. Marmor (Ed.), *Sexual inversion* (pp. 302–344). New York: Basic Books.

McConaghy, N. (1981). Controlled comparison of aversive therapy and covert sensitization in compulsive homosexuality. *Behavior Research and Therapy, 19,* 425–434.

Mintz, E. (1966). Overt male homosexuals in combined group and individual treatment. *Journal of Consulting Psychology, 20,* 193–198.

Murphy, T. (1992). Redirecting sexual orientation: Techniques and justifications. *Journal of Sex Research, 29,* 501–523.

Newswatch briefs. (1990, February 22) *Gay Chicago Magazine, 8,* p. 43.

Nicolosi, J. (1991). *Reparative therapy of male homosexuality.* Northvale, NJ: Jason Aronson.

Pattison, E., & Pattison, M. (1980). "Ex-gays": religiously mediated change in homosexuals. *American Journal of Psychiatry, 137,* 1553–1562.

Rangaswami, K. (1982). Difficulties in arousing and increasing heterosexual responsiveness in a homosexual: A case report. *Indian Journal of Clinical Psychology, 9,* 147–151.

Rist, D. Y. (1992). *Heartlands: A gay man's odyssey across America.* New York: Dutton.

Sansweet, R. J. (1975). *The punishment cure.* New York: Mason/Charter.

Silverstein, C. (1977). Homosexuality and the ethics of behavioral intervention. *Journal of Homosexuality, 2,* 205–211.

Silverstein, C. (1991). Psychological and medical treatments of homosexuality. In J. Gonsiorek & J. Weinrich (Eds.), *Homosexuality: Research implications for public policy* (pp. 101–114). Newbury Park, CA: Sage.

Weinberg, M., & Williams, C. (1974). *Male homosexuals: Their problems and adaptations.* New York: Penguin Books.

CHALLENGE QUESTIONS

Is Sexual Orientation Conversion Therapy Ethical?

1. Yarhouse bases his arguments on the notion that clients requesting sexual orientation conversion should be respected as autonomous individuals capable of making a free choice in this matter. What arguments can be made for and against the notion that the client is the most appropriate decision maker with regard to a particular clinical intervention?
2. Haldeman argues against sexual orientation conversion therapy on the premise that this treatment approach rests on homophobic ideology. What social forces might be at play in promoting people to value heterosexuality over homosexuality?
3. Imagine that you are a clinician consulting with a 21-year-old man who is distressed by his homosexuality because it runs counter to his strong religious beliefs. How would you develop a treatment geared to alleviating his distress while respecting his religious values?
4. Imagine that you are evaluating a study intended to assess the effectiveness of aversive conditioning (e.g., shock) in reducing homosexual responsivity in men exposed to homoerotic stimuli. What ethical issues would you raise about this proposed project?
5. The APA has been striving in recent years to develop guidelines for clinicians working with gay and lesbian clients. What aspects of therapy would you regard as especially important in this kind of clinical work?

Suggested Readings

American Psychological Association. (1998). Appropriate therapeutic responses to sexual orientation in the proceedings of the American Psychological Association, Incorporated, for legislative year 1997. *Americian Psychologist,* 53(8), 882–939.

Stein, T. (1996). A critique of approaches to changing sexual orientation. In R. P. Cabaj, & T. S. Stein (Eds.), *Textbook of homosexuality and mental health.* (pp. 525–537). Washington, DC: American Psychiatric Press.

Yeoman, B. (1999). Gay no more? Reorientation programs for homosexuals. *Psychology Today,* 32(2), 26(1).

ISSUE 19

Is the Abuse Excuse Overused?

YES: Alan M. Dershowitz, from *The Abuse Excuse: And Other Cop-outs, Sob Stories, and Evasions of Responsibility* (Little, Brown, 1994)

NO: Peter Arenella, from "Demystifying the Abuse Excuse: Is There One?" *Harvard Journal of Law and Public Policy* (Spring 1996)

ISSUE SUMMARY

YES: Law professor Alan M. Dershowitz criticizes the "abuse excuse," a legal tactic by which criminal defendants claim a history of abuse as an excuse for violent retaliation. He asserts that it is dangerous to the very tenets of democracy, which presuppose personal accountability for choices and actions.

NO: Law professor Peter Arenella argues that Dershowitz grossly exaggerates the extent to which the "abuse excuse" is actually used in criminal law by highlighting a few high-profile, exceptional cases.

For centuries experts in the fields of mental health and psychology have struggled to define the circumstances under which a person's criminal behavior should be excused on the basis of mental illness or justifying circumstances. The insanity defense has been used by defense attorneys who have argued on behalf of their clients that, because of a mental disorder, these individuals should not be held responsible for their criminal actions. Controversy with regard to the insanity defense exploded following the case of John Hinckley, a young man who attempted to assassinate President Ronald Reagan in 1981. At the time, Hinckley, who was obsessed with actress Jodie Foster, believed that if he killed the president, Foster would be so impressed that she would fall in love with and marry Hinckley. At the trial the jury concluded that Hinckley was insane, and he was subsequently sent to a mental hospital rather than a prison.

The public was outraged about the possibility that an assassin could get away with murder on the grounds of having a mental disorder. Soon thereafter Congress enacted significant changes in the law in order to tighten the standards of the insanity defense. Nevertheless, a number of legal cases subsequently emerged in which various legal defenses were mounted by lawyers trying to convince juries that their clients should not be held responsible for their criminal acts. Efforts to reduce criminal culpability in cases involving acts of violent retaliation became increasingly common in highly publicized cases. The Menendez brothers, Erik and Lyle, claimed that their brutal murder of both parents was the result of a history of awful childhood abuse at the hands of their father. Lorena Bobbitt claimed that cutting off her husband's penis could be excused on the grounds that he had abused her repeatedly during their marriage.

Alan M. Dershowitz is intensely critical of what he has termed the "abuse excuse," a legal tactic by which criminal defendants claim a history of abuse as an excuse for violent retaliation. In the following selection, he asserts that widespread acceptance of the abuse excuse is dangerous to the very tenets of democracy, which presuppose personal accountability for choices and actions. According to Dershowitz, abuse excuses are typically "politically correct" efforts that employ different criteria of culpability when judging disadvantaged groups; as such, these excuses endanger collective safety by legitimizing a sense of vigilantism.

In the second selection, Peter Arenella takes issue with Dershowitz and other prominent academics who have asserted that there is an epidemic of new syndrome excuse defenses swamping courtrooms. According to Arenella, these critics are attacking a strawman because the criminal law has not endorsed defenses that absolve victims from blame for their criminal acts, except in cases involving the insanity defense. He contends that there is a notion of widespread reliance on the abuse excuse because the media have spread misinformation about the workings of the criminal justice system by giving inordinate attention to exceptional cases such as those of the Menendez brothers and Lorena Bobbitt.

POINT

- More and more defense lawyers are employing the abuse excuse tactic, and more and more jurors are buying into it.
- The abuse excuse endangers Americans' collective safety by legitimizing a sense of vigilantism, which reflects society's frustration over the apparent inability of law enforcement to reduce rampant violence.
- The media, especially TV talk shows, have made abuse excuse defenses their daily fare, lending an air of credibility that legitimates these excuses in the minds of jurors.

- The prevalence of the abuse excuse endangers the credibility of legitimate defenses, such as those involving insanity or self-defense.

COUNTERPOINT

- Prominent academics have erroneously legitimated conventional wisdom that there is an epidemic of new syndrome excuse defenses.
- If the focus were placed on the killers who populate Death Row, observers would discover serious evidence of early abuse and victimization that did not diminish the killers' culpability in the eyes of the law.
- The media, especially network news shows, do not focus on ordinary prosecutions but on high-profile cases, which, by definition, are aberrational cases containing unique elements that capture attention.
- Criminal law has not endorsed abuse excuse defenses that absolve victims from blame for their criminal acts.

The Abuse Excuse

The "Abuse Excuse"—the legal tactic by which criminal defendants claim a history of abuse as an excuse for violent retaliation—is quickly becoming a license to kill and maim. More and more defense lawyers are employing this tactic and more and more jurors are buying it. It is a dangerous trend, with serious and widespread implications for the safety and liberty of every American.

Among the recent excuses that have been accepted by at least some jurors have been "battered woman syndrome," "abused child syndrome," "rape trauma syndrome," and "urban survival syndrome." This has encouraged lawyers to try other abuse excuses, such as "black rage." For example, the defense lawyer for Colin Ferguson—the black man accused of killing white commuters on the Long Island Railroad—has acknowledged that his black rage variation on the insanity defense "is similar to the utilization of the battered woman's syndrome, the posttraumatic stress syndrome and the child abuse syndrome in other cases to negate criminal accountability."

On the surface, the abuse excuse affects only the few handfuls of defendants who raise it, and those who are most immediately impacted by an acquittal or reduced charge. But at a deeper level, the abuse excuse is a symptom of a general abdication of responsibility by individuals, families, groups, and even nations. Its widespread acceptance is dangerous to the very tenets of democracy which presuppose personal accountability for choices and actions. It also endangers our collective safety by legitimating a sense of vigilantism that reflects our frustration over the apparent inability of law enforcement to reduce the rampant violence that engulfs us.

At a time of ever-hardening attitudes toward crime and punishment, it may seem anomalous that so many jurors—indeed, so many Americans—appear to be sympathetic to the abuse excuse. But it is not anomalous at all, since the abuse excuse is a modern-day form of vigilantism—a recognition that since official law enforcement does not seem able to prevent or punish abuse, the victim should be entitled to take the law into his or her own hands.

In philosophical terms, the claim is that society has broken its "social contract" with the abused victim by not according him or her adequate protection. Because it has broken that social contract, the victim has been returned to a "state of nature" in which "might makes right" and the victim is entitled to invoke the law of the jungle—"kill or be killed." Indeed, these very terms were used in a recent Texas case in which one black youth killed two other blacks in a dangerous urban neighborhood. The result was a hung jury.

But vigilantism—whether it takes the old-fashioned form of the lynch mob or the new-fashioned form of the abuse victim's killing her sleeping husband—threatens the very fabric of our democracy and sows the seeds of anarchy and autocracy. The abuse excuse is dangerous, therefore, both in its narrow manifestation as a legal defense and in its broader manifestation as an abrogation of societal responsibility

The other characteristic shared by these defenses is that they are often "politically correct," thus reflecting current trends toward employing different criteria of culpability when judging disadvantaged groups. In effect, these abuse excuse defenses, by emphasizing historical discrimination suffered by particular groups, seek to introduce some degree of affirmative action into our criminal-justice system.

These abuse-excuse defenses are the daily fare of the proliferating menu of TV and radio talk shows. It is virtually impossible to flip the TV channels during the daytime hours without seeing a bevy of sobbing women and men justifying their failed lives by reference to some past abuse, real or imagined. Personal responsibility does not sell soap as well as sob stories. Jurors who watch this stuff begin to believe it, despite its status as junk science. The very fact that Sally Jessy and Montel repeat it as if it were gospel tends to legitimate it in the minds of some jurors. They are thus receptive to it in the courtroom, especially when the defendant is portrayed as sympathetic, and his dead victim is unsympathetic. William Kunstler is quick to point to recent public-opinion polls that show that "two-thirds of blacks and almost half the whites surveyed recognize the validity of our [black rage] theory of Mr. Ferguson's defense."

But neither public-opinion polls nor TV talk shows establish the empirical or normative validity of such abuse-excuse defenses. The basic fallacy underlying each of them is that the vast majority of people who have experienced abuses—whether it be sexual, racial, or anything else—do not commit violent crimes. Thus the abuse excuse neither explains nor justifies the violence. A history of abuse is not a psychological or a legal license to kill. It may, in some instances, be relevant at sentencing, but certainly not always. . . .

The worst consequence of these abuse excuses is that they stigmatize all abuse victims with the violence of the very few who have used their victimization as a justification to kill or maim. The vast majority of abuse victims are neither prone to violence nor to making excuses. Moreover, abuse excuses legitimate a cycle of abuse and further abuse, since most abusers have themselves been victims of abuse. Thus, by taking the abuse excuse to its logical conclusion, virtually no abusers would ever be culpable. . . .

With very few exceptions, all crimes require not only a criminal act such as killing, but also a criminal state of mind, such as intent or premeditation (advance planning). Even if both the act (called *actus reas*) and the state of mind (called *mens rea*) are present, the law also provides for defenses such as "official justification," "self-defense," and "insanity."

For example, the official state executioner who places the condemned man on the gurney and injects a lethal drug into his veins has killed that man with intent and premeditation. Yet he is, of course, entirely innocent of any crime, because he—like the policeman or the soldier who acts lawfully—has official justification for his actions.

So, too, the person who kills in self-defense is innocent of any crime, despite the fact that he intentionally took the life of the aggressor. The law expressly authorizes a person to use deadly force, if necessary, to prevent his imminent death or serious injury.

More controversially, if a mentally ill person kills his father because he hears voices commanding him to do so, he may be innocent of murder by reason of insanity.

In addition to complete defenses, the law also provides for an array of mitigating factors that may either reduce the charge—say, from murder to manslaughter—or reduce the sentence—say, from death to life imprisonment. These factors include being provoked, for example, by finding your spouse in bed with another person, or, as another example, making an unreasonable mistake, such as believing that an obviously unarmed person poses an imminent threat to your life.

Defenses and excuses have existed since the beginning of time. Virtually from the day they can speak, children seem endowed with a repertoire of excuses calculated to mitigate parental wrath. "I didn't mean it." "I couldn't help it." "He did it to me first." "All the kids do it." "You didn't tell me I couldn't do it." "You do it." "He made me do it." "Mary's mother lets her do it." "You let my older sister do it." "I saw it on TV." Whether these excuses are copied from parents, or whether there is some kind of built-in human "excuse" mechanism, it is beyond dispute that excuses are part of the earliest human vocabulary....

The earliest recorded cases in Anglo-American legal history include ancient accounts of what has come to be called the insanity defense. As Justice Felix Frankfurter put it:

> Ever since our ancestral common law emerged out of the darkness of its early barbaric days, it has been a postulate of Western civilization that the taking of life by the hand of an insane person is not murder.

In 1956, the philosopher J. L. Austin wrote an influential essay entitled "A Plea for Excuses," in which he analyzed a wide range of excuses and justifications that have been recognized throughout history. The law has traditionally distinguished among "justifications," "excuses," and "mitigations." A justification, such as self-defense, not only results in a complete legal exoneration, but generally also in a total moral exoneration. If an act is justified, it is the right thing to have done and to do in the future. It is praiseworthy, or at least not blameworthy. You are supposed to kill an aggressor in self-defense. The law prefers the life of the defender to that of the aggressor.

An "excuse," on the other hand, may be a complete legal defense, but it is not generally a moral exculpation. Killing someone by accident does not generally result in criminal liability (at least absent a high degree of negligence), but it surely is not praiseworthy. The act is indeed deserving of condemnation, though the actor is excused. We don't want him to do it again, though we will excuse him from criminal responsibility this time.

A mitigating factor does not constitute a legal defense, though it may reduce the degree of legal (and moral) responsibility. A defendant who is provoked into killing may have the charges reduced from murder to manslaughter or may have his sentence reduced, but he is not excused.

These distinctions are not always susceptible to neat categorization. Insanity, which sounds like a mitigating factor, may be a complete legal excuse. A mistake about self-defense may sound like an excuse, but if the mistake is a "reasonable" one, the law treats it as a justification. (If it is an unreasonable mistake, it may be a mitigation.) But at its core, the distinction among justifications, excuses, and mitigations is an important one that is becoming unfortunately blurred by some recent excuses. For example, the battered woman syndrome is generally introduced as part of self-defense, which is a complete justification. Yet many believe it should be regarded as a mitigating factor or, at most, as an excuse, since we do not want to encourage abused women (or children) to take the law into their own hands. We may want to excuse the conduct in extreme cases, but we surely don't want to justify it.

Another excuse, which is a variation on the abuse excuse, is the "crime of passion" mitigation. When a person kills or injures a loved one, or more commonly a former loved one who has spurned his love, the claim is that he acted out of passion and that this explanation should mitigate or excuse his punishment. "Texas self-defense" refers to the frequent acquittals in the Lone Star State of husbands who have killed their wives upon finding them in bed with another man. More often, a claim of "passion" is enough to reduce murder to manslaughter on the ground that the killer was provoked. Indeed, some recent abuse-excuse cases are really passion-excuse cases dressed up in the language of the day. Lorena Bobbitt's mutilation of her husband seemed as much to reflect her anger over his desire to leave her as her fear of his continued abuse.

Often passion defies understanding. When Judge Sol Wachtler—one of our most distinguished and respected appellate court judges—was accused of creating a fictitious character to stalk and frighten his former mistress, the legal community was shocked. When O. J. Simpson was accused of murdering his former wife, his friends and fans couldn't believe that such a "nice person" was capable of such a brutal act. And the presumption of innocence requires that Simpson's plea of not guilty be credited unless the prosecution proves otherwise. But "nice" and "respected" people have engaged in crimes of passion since the beginning of history. At issue is not whether passion "explains" some crimes; it surely does. The question is whether or under what circumstances passion should excuse or mitigate a crime of violence.

Most of the abuse excuses that are criticized in this [selection] are raised in an attempt to fit the defendant's conduct into self-defense, provocation, or insanity....

There are a growing number of abuse excuses—and other excuses that are analogous—that have been raised or proposed. The list of "syndromes" which have been "discovered," "invented," "constructed," or "concocted" as excuses for crime is mind-boggling. A sampling follows:

Adopted child syndrome
American dream syndrome
Arbitrary abuse of power syndrome
Battered child syndrome
Battered woman syndrome
Black rage syndrome
Computer addiction
Distant father syndrome
Elderly abuse syndrome
"Everybody does it" defense
Failure-to-file syndrome
False memory syndrome
Fetal alcohol syndrome
Gangster syndrome
Holocaust survivor syndrome
Legal abuse syndrome
"The minister made me do it" defense
Multiple personality disorder
Parental alienation syndrome
Patient-therapist sex syndrome
"Pornography made me do it" defense
Posttraumatic stress disorder
Premenstrual stress syndrome
Rape trauma syndrome
Repressed (or recovered) memory syndrome
Ritual abuse (satanic cults) syndrome
Roid rage (violence caused by steroids)
Self-victimization syndrome
Sexual abuse syndrome
Sexually transmitted disease syndrome
Situational stress syndrome
Stockholm syndrome
Super Bowl Sunday syndrome
Sybil syndrome
"Television made me do it" defense
Tobacco deprivation syndrome
"Twinkies made me do it" defense
UFO survivor syndrome
Urban survival syndrome
Vietnam syndrome

Each of these syndromes and defenses shares in common a goal of deflecting responsibility from the person who committed the criminal act onto someone else who may have abused him or her or otherwise caused him or her to do it. Some of these excuses try to shift the blame to the abuser, others to a condition or circumstance. The likelihood of success increases if the finger of abuse can be pointed to the specific person whom the defendant killed or injured, allegedly to protect himself or herself.

One reason why the abuse excuse has become so popular lately is because it is often a vigilante defense that places the victim—who is usually dead and incapable of defending himself—on trial. If the dead victim can be painted in an unflattering light and the live defendant can be seen sympathetically, the jury may be persuaded that "he had it coming" and that his killer should not be held culpable....

The murder trial of the Menendez brothers for the cold-blooded shooting of their parents is a paradigm of the abusive and successful employment of the abuse excuse. Indeed, it was this case which led me to coin the term in a column about the Menendez and Bobbitt cases.

It is certainly possible—and in my view highly likely—that the Menendez brothers concocted out of whole cloth the entire story of sexual abuse by their father. The fact that while confiding their carefully planned killing to a trusted psychologist, they never even mentioned the alleged history of the abuse is strong evidence of its falsity. So is the fact that Erik chose to attend UCLA, which is near the Menendez home, rather than Berkeley, which is hundreds of miles away—at a time when he claimed to be trying to escape the ongoing abuse.

But even assuming that the story of abuse was entirely true, how does that justify, excuse, or even mitigate the culpability of Lyle and Erik Menendez for their carefully planned execution of both their parents and their lengthy cover-up of the killings? Their lawyers claimed self-defense, despite the ease with which the brothers could have left home, moved to another part of the country or the world, and escaped the alleged sexual abuse. Even if they believed that their father *and mother* would hunt them down and kill them, they could have sought police protection. Instead, they decided to take the law into their own hands, shopped for weapons, plotted a "perfect" double murder, executed a cover-up, and—perhaps—contrived an abuse-excuse defense in the event they were caught.

Despite what appeared to many knowledgeable observers of the criminal justice system to be an open-and-shut case of first-degree murder, and despite the trial judge's refusal to instruct the juries—they were tried together but to separate juries—that they could acquit the defendants on grounds of self-defense, each Menendez brother *won* a hung jury based on the abuse excuse. I use the word "won" advisedly, since in most criminal cases a hung jury is a clear victory for the defendant, giving the defense considerable leverage in negotiating a favorable plea bargain. In the Menendez cases this was a spectacular victory, since the evidence of guilt—both factual and legal—appeared so overwhelming.

If the defense had managed to persuade only a handful of jurors in each of the Menendez cases, observers might attribute this to the vagaries of jury selection or to the uniquely quirky character of California juries. But public-opinion polls and other measures of public attitudes strongly suggest that a large proportion of Americans throughout the nation bought the Menendez brothers' abuse excuse.

Why, in an age of ever-toughening attitudes toward law and order, could so many Americans be so sympathetic to two such cold-blooded parricides? The answer, I believe, lies in a number of factors, some more specific to the Menendez cases, others of an historical nature, and still others more general to the time in which we live. Ironically, although abuse excuses are *defenses* to crime, at another level they are also manifestations of our deep need to control our environment—to take the law into our own hands. They argue that since official law enforcement is incapable of protecting victims of abuse, these victims are entitled to engage in vigilante justice.

At the narrowest level, the prosecution in the Menendez cases made a serious tactical blunder—at least in retrospect. Had it tried the brothers *first* for the murder of their mother *only*, it would have been more difficult for the brothers to mount a sympathetic abuse excuse for killing *her*. She, after all, did not herself abuse the boys, even according to their highly questionable account. By putting the brothers on trial for killing both their mother and father, the prosecution made it easier for them to counter by putting their dead and defenseless father on trial for abusing them. And José Menendez was the perfect victim to place on trial. Whether or not he was guilty of the specific crime of sex abuse —and he was not there to defend himself against somewhat vague accusations of this very private crime—he was surely guilty of being an overbearing and over-ambitious parent. In the minds of several jurors and many observers of this widely watched trial, José Menendez "had it coming."

In contrast to the single-dimensional portrait of evil painted of José Menendez by the lawyers for the Menendez brothers, his killers were painted in a far more sympathetic and multidimensional light. Jurors cried more openly when Erik and Lyle described their lives with José than when photographs of the bullet-riddled bodies of the Menendez parents were passed around. In the midst of this after-the-fact attempt by the brothers to pin the blame for the killings on their father, Kitty Menendez got lost. Did she, too, "have it coming"? Did she pose an imminent threat to the brothers' lives? Why did she have to be killed as she was filling out college application forms for her younger son and eating strawberries?

Instead of focusing on the legal issues—primary among which was whether an alleged history of abuse can justify or mitigate a carefully planned "preventive" execution—the trial degenerated into an emotional blame-a-thon between two spoiled young men and their dead father and mother....

The battered woman syndrome and the rape trauma syndrome have many factors in common with the abused child syndrome. Among other things, they treat women like children. But there is at least one important difference. Since the battered woman syndrome and the rape trauma syndrome almost always involve a *female* abuse victim who killed or maimed a *male* abuser, a political dimension is added to these cases, which often degenerate into "men-versus-women," "we against them" show trials. The Bobbitt trials were a case in point.

In theory, it is difficult to imagine a clearer case of culpable criminal mayhem. Lorena Bobbitt willfully cut off her husband's penis while he was asleep. She claimed that he had raped her, though he was acquitted of that charge. Even if it were true, she had easily available options short of mayhem. She could simply have left him. There were no children. There were not even economic ties, since she held a good job. He had not threatened to harm her if she left. Indeed, he seemed anxious to be rid of her. She reported his alleged misconduct, but refused to take the next step toward securing legal relief. Instead, she struck with a knife.

Women throughout the world—not all but many—rallied to her "cause" and cheered her on. Her lawyers raised a defense of "temporary insanity," which combined elements of self-defense, rape trauma syndrome, and battered woman syndrome. She was acquitted by reason of insanity, sent to a mental hospital for observation, and quickly released when—as expected—the doctors found that there was nothing really wrong with her. The "insanity" defense had been a cover for the real defense of "the sexist son-of-a-bitch had it coming." The same feminists who rail against putting the victim on trial in rape cases cheered the tactic of putting John Wayne Bobbitt on trial in this case. (Nor did some feminists have much hesitation in putting Paula Jones's prior sexual history on trial after she filed a lawsuit against President Clinton.)

And John Wayne Bobbitt was also the perfect victim to put on trial. He made a terrible impression, both in and out of court. He was arrogant, unrepentant, sexist, and insensitive. He exploited his injury commercially on television and in magazines. His trial testimony was repeatedly contradicted by more believable witnesses. He was an utterly unsympathetic character. Lorena Bobbitt, on the other hand, made a very sympathetic impression. She cried, appeared remorseful, and created an impression of honesty. In the end, the jury decided that they liked Lorena better than John. And who can blame them for that! But a criminal trial should not be a popularity contest. The Bobbitt jury was hoodwinked into believing an "insanity" defense that had little medical basis, as evidenced by Bobbitt's quick release from the mental hospital. Bobbitt was an angry, vengeful woman who chose to exact revenge rather than exercise the option of leaving her abusive husband.

The tactic of putting the dead or maimed victim on trial and getting the jury to identify with the defendant can be dangerous. Recall the early days of the civil rights movement, when white juries in the Deep South routinely acquitted white sheriffs, Klansmen, and other assorted killers for murdering both black and white civil rights workers "who had it coming." Everyone loves vigilante justice when the vigilantes are on "our side," but they hate it when the vigilantes are on "their side."

That is why—as a *civil libertarian* and as a *defense attorney*—I am so concerned about the excesses of the abuse excuse. Taken to its current and projected extremes, it is a lawless invitation to vigilantism, both on the part of abuse victims and on the part of jurors who sympathize more with them than with those whom they have killed or maimed. It threatens to increase the cycle of violence, not only by women but also against women. It endangers civil liberties by substituting vigilante justice—which is an oxymoron—for courtroom justice, and the rule of man (and woman) for the rule of law. It endangers legitimate defenses—such as insanity based on mental illness, self-defense when there is no recourse, and diminished capacity—by expanding them to the point where a swing of the pendulum is inevitable. Charles P. Ewing, a psychologist and law professor, points to a jury trial following the Menendez and Bobbitt cases in which the jury deadlocked in a clear-cut battered woman syndrome case. He attributes this to a backlash caused by the media barrage in the Menendez and Bobbitt cases.

In light of this reality, it might be expected that civil libertarians, feminists, and defense attorneys would share my concern about the abuses of the abuse excuse. Some do, but others have virtually accused me of treason for criticizing the extremes to which the abuse excuse has been taken.

A prominent criminal-defense lawyer wrote an entire article in the *California Criminal Defense Practice Reporter* castigating me for "bashing juries that don't convict and bad-mouthing the lawyers" who raise the abuse excuse. I plead guilty to the former but not to the latter. No one should criticize any defense lawyer who honestly and ethically raises an available defense. What I am criticizing is the easy availability of the defense in cases like Menendez and Bobbitt and the foolish jurors who fall for the sob stories told by the lawyers. I strongly believe that these defenses do great damage to civil liberties by encouraging vigilante justice. That is why I believe they are popular in an age in which most Americans want to see us get tough on crime. Abuse-excuse defenses play right into the hands of those who do not trust our legal system to do justice. Lorena Bobbitt is a female version of "Dirty Harry," who is certainly no hero to civil libertarians.

Abusive defenses such as those employed by the Menendez brothers and Lorena Bobbitt also undercut the credibility of legitimate defenses in appropriate cases. Finally, they stigmatize entire groups of people—women, blacks, and others—who share characteristics in common with the criminals but who do not commit similar crimes.

That is why I criticize the abuse excuse *as a* civil libertarian, *as a* defense lawyer, and *as an* egalitarian. That is why I criticized vigilante defenses used by Southern lawyers in defense of Klan members who killed civil rights workers. Being a civil libertarian and a defense lawyer does not obligate me to favor *every* defense to crime, regardless of whether it hurts or helps civil liberties. The abuse excuse hurts civil liberties by undercutting personal responsibility and encouraging lawlessness.

NO ↩

Peter Arenella

Demystifying the Abuse Excuse:
Is There One?

Media accounts of some recent high-profile cases claim the criminal law has eagerly embraced a new "abuse excuse" defense; one that allows the defendant to negate his criminal responsibility by shifting blame from himself to the victim who "abused" him. Some prominent academics like Alan Dershowitz and Stephen Morse have legitimated this conventional wisdom by writing op-ed pieces and articles suggesting that "there is an epidemic"[1] of new syndrome excuse defenses swamping our courtrooms. Professor Dershowitz condemns this "defense" by pointing out how easily it can be fabricated by desperate defendants and sleazy defense counsel.[2] Even when claims of victimization are factually well founded, critics insist that most of these abused defendants are moral agents who should be held accountable for their criminal acts.[3]

If such an "abuse excuse" existed in theory or in practice, its factual and normative premises would indeed be indefensible. Being an *adult* victim of abuse, by itself, does not unduly impair one's moral capacities. Nor does victimhood abrogate one's moral duty not to use unnecessary violence against his victimizer. But the critics are attacking a strawman because the criminal law has not endorsed abuse excuse defenses that absolve victims from blame for their criminal acts.

Let us begin with the obvious. There is no such thing as an "abuse excuse" defense in the substantive criminal law. The only excuse defense that permits a defendant to use evidence of past or present victimization to negate his legal responsibility is the insanity defense. Very few defendants raise this defense[4] and even fewer are acquitted. When defendants claim insanity, juries usually find them sane[5] regardless of whether the defense relies on some traditional mental illness or on one of the new syndromes.

Far from making it easy to deny moral responsibility, the criminal law usually treats documented claims of early victimization that can erode an individual's moral capacities—for example, physical or sexual abuse by a parent or custodian, birth trauma generating neurological damage, or mental retardation—as irrelevant to issues of moral accountability. The sentencing authority may consider this type of evidence but is free to use it as an aggravating factor

From Peter Arenella, "Demystifying the Abuse Excuse: Is There One?" *Harvard Journal of Law and Public Policy*, vol. 19, no. 3 (Spring 1996). Copyright © 1996 by The Harvard Society for Law and Public Policy, Inc. Reprinted by permission.

suggesting the defendant's dangerousness, thus justifying a longer sentence or even death.[6]

While the insanity defense does not provide a very successful vehicle for abuse excuse theories, there are some *partial* defenses reducing murder to manslaughter that can rely on abuse-related claims to explain the defendant's motivation for the killing. For example, if the defendant killed because he unreasonably believed he was about to be killed or he killed in the heat of passion, he may raise imperfect self-defense or provocation. However, calling these *partial* defenses "abuse excuses" is misleading because they do not negate the defendant's criminal and moral responsibility for his actions. They simply permit the jury to return a verdict for a less serious homicide crime when the jury believes the defendant is less culpable than someone who killed without these culpability-reducing motivations. Fabrication and victim-bashing strategies may mislead jurors in such cases. These two risks, however, are the price we pay for a criminal justice system that believes the severity of homicide sanctions should depend, in part, on the killer's motivations.

Not only does criminal law theory reject abuse excuses, the system's practices hold most criminal defendants fully accountable for their criminal acts despite evidence of significant impairment of their moral capacities resulting from childhood victimization. Yet, the public believes our system unduly privileges abuse excuse defenses that dilute common sense notions of moral accountability.

What explains the dissonance between our actual legal practices and the public's perception of them? The simple answer is the public's dependence on the media, and especially television, for most of its information about how our criminal justice system functions. The network news does not focus on ordinary criminal prosecutions but on "high profile" cases which, by definition, are aberrational cases containing unique elements that capture our attention.

Only one of these aberrational cases—the prosecution of Lorena Bobbit for assaulting her husband—illustrated the abuse excuse in action. Despite the absence of any prior history of serious mental disorder, the jury found Bobbitt insane after listening to powerful testimony of how she had been abused by her husband.[7] No one should be happy with a verdict that transformed her willful, unjustifiable act of violent retaliation against her abuser into the irresistible impulse of a crazed woman. We should not excuse private vengeance. Nor does being a victim prevent one from becoming a victimizer. Her husband deserved state-sanctioned punishment for his prior assaults, not mutilation. Bobbitt should have been held accountable for her crime with her victimization being used to justify a lenient sentencing disposition.

This one clear example of an abuse excuse rationale motivating a successful insanity defense triggered a media feeding frenzy. Instead of reminding the public that the jury's acquittal of Bobbitt was the exception to the rule that insanity defenses are rarely successful,[8] the media highlighted those pundits who waxed eloquent about the erosion of moral norms. Commentators attacked the cultural theme expressed in talk shows and seemingly reflected in the Bobbitt verdict that everyone is a victim and no one is responsible for how they respond to their victimizer.[9] Professor Alan Dershowitz coined the term "abuse excuse" defense to describe the Bobbitt case and the media looked for new cases to illustrate this disturbing "trend."

Thanks to Professor Dershowitz and a willing media, the [Erik and Lyle] Menendez brothers became the new poster boys for the defense. Most of the American public believed they got away with murder when their first prosecution ended in a mistrial.[10] After all, the Menendez brothers intentionally and brutally slaughtered their parent and then lied about it. Few Americans credited their subsequent claims of abuse and most assumed these teenage boys did not need to kill their parents to solve their "problem." One could almost hear the sighs of relief across America when both brothers were convicted of first degree murder at their retrial.[11]

Despite the media's treatment of Menendez as Bobbitt redux, the two cases do not illustrate the same abuse excuse theme. Unlike Bobbitt's use of the insanity defense to package an abuse excuse theory, the Menendez defense conceded the brothers were criminally responsible for their parents' killing. The issue was whether they were guilty of murder or voluntary manslaughter. If the prosecution story that they killed for greed is correct, they are cold blooded murderers. If one accepts the defense's story, their prolonged abuse led them to misinterpret their parents' actions that fateful evening. They shot their parents based on the *unreasonable belief* that their parents were about to kill them. One does not have to believe their story to understand that their claim of imperfect self-defense[12] is not an abuse excuse defense because it concedes their criminal responsibility for the crime of voluntary manslaughter.[13] In short, imperfect self-defense is a partial excuse that reduces culpability but does not destroy it.[14]

If the media paid attention to ordinary criminal cases, they would find very few examples of successful abuse-related defenses that negated the defendant's criminal responsibility. For every Lorena Bobbitt there are a hundred Jeffrey Dahmers. Even if we consider abuse-related partial defenses such as imperfect self-defense and provocation, there are very few murder prosecutions involving battered children and battered women defendants that pose the same risk of fabrication as the Menendez case. Finally, if the media focused on the backgrounds of those killers who populate Death Row, they would discover serious and undisputed evidence of early abuse and victimization that did not diminish the killers' culpability in the eyes of the criminal law.[15]

I dealt with these developmentally disabled defendants every day as a young public defender. In my youthful arrogance and ignorance, I just labeled them dumb. It was a routine joke in the office that the police's clearance rate for serious felonies would be much lower if the average defendant had even a modicum of basic intelligence. They committed their crimes foolishly and impulsively and told transparent lies about their innocence. I saw them as slow and dimwitted. I did not understand anything about their developmental deficits. I did not realize how different they were from me.

But life has a way of teaching hard lessons. I have a ten-year-old son who is brain damaged. I now know firsthand how difficult life is for someone who does not have the basic cognitive skills and self-control capacities that most of us take for granted. My son is mildly retarded and suffers from Tourette's syndrome, a neurological disorder whose symptoms include tics and impulse control problems. Under the law's minimalist account of what capacities a person needs to qualify as a moral agent, my son will be one when he reaches the appropriate age. He is able to make rational choices about whether to comply with rules and he knows the difference between right and wrong. Although he has extraordinary difficulty controlling some of his impulses, he can do so on most occasions for some period of time.

Tragically, there are far too many children like my son who do not have intact families with the resources to take care of them. Some of these children are abused by their parents or guardian, neglected by underfunded social service agencies, ignored in the classroom because of their learning disabilities, and used by their more savvy peers in a manner that aggravates their preexisting problems. When these "at risk" children get in trouble with the law, few people in the juvenile justice system take their claims of victimization seriously. The few who do lack the resources to address their problems. When these "at risk" children develop into violent young "adult" offenders, the law treats them as fully accountable actors who *deserve* whatever punishment we give them. We judge them by our standards because we do not understand how fundamentally different they are from the rest of us.[16]

Should an enlightened criminal law excuse the developmentally-disabled offender? Hardly. When sane adults commit violent crimes, we must hold them legally accountable, despite their deficits, as an act of community self-defense. However, we should not indulge in the moral hypocrisy of insisting that when we punish and even execute this group of offenders, we necessarily are giving them their just deserts. When we punish the developmentally disabled and mentally retarded offender, we are simply protecting ourselves.

So do not lose too much sleep over the prospect that notions of moral accountability are being demeaned through the rampant use of abuse excuse defenses. The truth is just the opposite: the law privileges a minimalist view of what it takes to be a morally accountable agent to ensure that all but the most severely disabled offenders are held accountable for their crimes.

Notes

1. Stephen J. Morse, *The New Syndrome Excuse Syndrome* 14 CRIM. JUST. ETHICS, Winter/Spring, 1995, at 3, 4.

2. *See* Alan M. Dershowitz, *The Abuse Excuse*, S. F. EXAMINER, Jan. 16, 1994, at A15. In one of the first syndicated op-ed pieces in which he coined the phrase "abuse excuse," Professor Dershowitz wrote:

> Two clear messages have been sent. The first to victims of abuse: The legal system may excuse you if you take the law into your own hands instead of either leaving or reporting the abuse. This unfortunate message has been underlined by the outpourings of public support for abuse victims who kill or maim. The second message is directed to criminal defense lawyers: When neither the law nor the facts are on your client's side, argue abuse. It may get you an acquittal, a reduced charge or a hung jury. The popularity of the "abuse excuse" poses real dangers to our safety and to the integrity of our legal system. It is far

too easy for a desperate criminal to concoct a false history of abuse, for a disturbed criminal to imagine such a history or for a sleazy lawyer to manufacture such a defense.

Id. Professor Dershowitz's subsequent book, *see* ALAN M. DERSHOWITZ, THE ABUSE EXCUSE AND OTHER COP-OUTS, SOB STORIES AND EVASIONS OF RESPONSIBILITY (1994), about the abuse excuse received widespread media attention in part because it reinforced the public's perception that claims of victimization were being used by people in all walks of life to deny responsibility for their actions. *See, e.g.,* Tom Egerman, *Legal Expert Doesn't Buy Defensive 'Abuse Excuse,'* STAR-TRIB. (Minneapolis-St. Paul), Dec. 4, 1994, at 14F; Carolyn See, *An Angry Dershowitz Rails Against Our Nation of Wimps,* ROCKY MOUNTAIN NEWS, Dec. 25, 1994, at 78A; Richard E. Vatz & Lee S. Weinberg, *Making Excuses: Legal Media Hound's Latest Effort is a Poor Excuse for a Book on the Issue of Dodging Criminal Responsibility,* SUN-SENTINEL (Ft. Lauderdale, Fla.), Dec. 25, 1995, at 10D.

3. *See* Morse, *supra* note 1.

4. *See* J. S. Janofsky, M. B. Vandewalle, & J. R. Rappeport, *Defendant Pleading Insanity: An Analysis of Outcome,* 17 BULL. AM. ACAD. PSYCHITRY L. 203 (1989).

5. *See id.*

6. *See* Peter Arenella, *Convicting The Morally Blameless: Reassessing The Relationship Between Legal and Moral Accountability,* 39 UCLA L. REV. 1511, 1513 n.4 (1994).

7. *See The Unkindest Cut of All,* U. S. NEWS & WORLD REP., Jan. 31, 1994, at 14 [hereinafter *Unkindest Cut* (discussing the facts of the Bobbitt case).

8. Consider Jeffrey Dahmer, a killer who ate his victims' flesh and froze some of their body parts. Despite a documented history of severe mental illness and a consensus from experts about the impact of that illness on his actions, the jury found him sane. *See Found Sane,* TIME, Feb. 24, 1992, at 68.

9. *See* Andrea Sachs, *Now for the Movie,* TIME, Jan. 31, 1994, at 99; *Unkindest Cut, supra* note 7, at 14.

10. *See* People v. Menendez, No. SA002728 (L.A. County Mun. Ct. Jan. 28, 1994).

11. *See Menendez brothers found guilty of murder; Self-defense rejected in parents' slayings,* BALTIMORE SUN, Mar. 21, 1996, at 3A (reporting that the judge in the case refused to allow the use of the imperfect self-defense theory).

12. *See* Cal. PENAL CODE §§ 188, 192 (West 1995).

13. *See* People v. Christian S., 7 Cal. 4th 768 (1994) (holding that a finding of imperfect self-defense requires that a murder defendant be convicted of voluntary manslaughter).

14. The two juries in the first Menendez trial hung because they could not agree about whether the brothers had committed murder or voluntary manslaughter. Some of the jurors held out for murder, believing the brothers had fabricated their claims of abuse and their perception of imminent threat from their parents. Other jurors held out for murder because they did not understand the nature of the defense. They did not care whether the brothers were abused, because, in their view, abuse should not justify murder. These jurors did not appreciate that imperfect self-defense did not justify the killings but reduced the brothers' culpability in committing them. Several jurors held out for voluntary manslaughter because they had a reasonable doubt about whether the brothers unreasonably believed their parents were about to kill them that night. The media and Professor Dershowitz characterized those jurors holding out for voluntary manslaughter as irrational and untrustworthy. *See, e.g.,* James H. Andrews, *I May Be a Murder, But It's Not My Fault,* CHRISTIAN SCI. MONITOR, Sept. 19, 1994, at 13; Myron Beckenstein, *The Verdict Is In: The Jury Is Flawed,* SUN, Oct, 9, 1994, at 6F; David Markey, *Juries Are Guilty of Injustice,* TIMES UNION, Feb. 27, 1994, at E1; Mark Marvel, *The*

Law in a Whole New Light, INTERVIEW, Sept. 1994, at 118 (interviewing Professor Dershowitz). *But see* William A. Schroeder, *A No-Fault System of Justice?,* ST. LOUIS POST-DISPATCH, Feb. 23, 1994, at 7B (supporting the jury's decision in the Menendez case). On a Nightline special, Professor Dershowitz referred to some of the Menendez jurors as "fools" who might have watched too much daytime television. *See* Laura Gaston Dooley, *Our Juries, Our Selves: The Power, Perception, and Politics of the Civil Jury,* 80 CORNELL L. REV. 325, 330 n.21 (1995). This public trashing was completely unfair to the jurors, who were doing their job in good faith, and to the defense lawyers who presented powerful evidence of serious pathology in the Menendez family.

15. Studies that have examined the psychological profiles of death row inmates have found striking similarities: family histories of abuse, prenatal problems, premature birth, low birth weight, and a very high prevalence of low-average intelligence to slight mental retardation. *See* M. Feldman, K. Mallouh, & D. O. Lewis, *Filicidal Abuse in the Histories of 15 Condemned Murders,* 14 BULL. AM. ACAD. PSYCHIATRY L. 345 (1986); D. O. Lewis, J. H. Pincus, M. Feldman, L. Jackson & B. Bard, *Psychiatric, Neurological, and Psychoeducational Characteristics of 15 Death Row Inmates in the United States,* 143 AM. J. PSYCHIATRY 838 (1986); J. H. Panton, *Personality Characteristics of Death-Row Prison Inmates,* 32 J. CLINICAL PSYCHOL. 306 (1976).

16. Those who defend the law's minimalist view of the capacities one needs to qualify as a moral agent frequently remind us that the criminal law imposes very minimal standards of behavior that most of us can obey with ease. As Stephen Morse has written, "it is not hard *not* to kill, rape, steal, and burn, and the duty of care to avoid criminal liability for risky conduct is met easily." Morse, *supra* note 1, at 11. This statement certainly is true for many of the people who run afoul of the criminal law. But, there is a growing class of youthful criminal offenders whose impulsivity from a very early age suggests the standards imposed by the criminal laws are not so easily met.

CHALLENGE QUESTIONS

Is the Abuse Excuse Overused?

1. Dershowitz is intensely critical of abuse excuses, which he considers nothing less than legal maneuvers aimed at absolving individuals of responsibility for their violent behavior. What kinds of circumstances, if any, might Dershowitz agree could justify the excusing of a person's responsibility for a violent crime?
2. Dershowitz distinguishes the notions of "justifications," "excuses," and "mitigations." Imagine a legal scenario involving a violent crime, and apply each of these legal concepts to the behavior of an individual whose culpability is being evaluated.
3. Arenella contends that, because of media attention to a few aberrational cases, the public has been led to believe that there is an epidemic of cases involving the abuse excuse. What factors prompt the media to give so much attention to these kinds of cases?
4. Dershowitz points to several kinds of abuse excuses in which a woman asserts that her violent behavior against a man should be excused because of the man's abusive behavior toward her. Consider the role of gender issues in such cases, and discuss the ways in which these cases might be viewed differently if the genders of the characters were switched.
5. Arenella states that when developmentally disabled or "at-risk" youth get into trouble with the law, few people in the juvenile justice system take their claims of victimization seriously because they do not understand how fundamentally different these individuals are from the rest of society. What efforts might experts in the fields of law and psychology make to attend to the special characteristics of such youth?

Suggested Readings

Leeper, K. K., & Bruschke, J. (1995). The prevalence of the abuse excuse: Media hype or cause for concern? *Communications and the Law*, 17(4), 47–65.

Morse, S. J. (1995). The "new syndrome excuse syndrome." *Criminal Justice Ethics*, 14(1), 3–15.

Neuman, E. (1994). Abuse excuse goes on trial. *Insight on the News*, 10(13), 16–20.

Wilson, J. Q. (1997). *Moral judgement: Does the abuse excuse threaten our legal system?* New York, NY: BasicBooks, A Division of HarperCollins Publishers, Inc.

ISSUE 20

Is Electroconvulsive Therapy Ethical?

YES: Max Fink, from *Electroshock: Restoring the Mind* (Oxford University Press, 1999)

NO: Leonard R. Frank, from "Shock Treatment IV: Resistance in the 1990s," in Robert F. Morgan, ed., *Electroshock: The Case Against* (Morgan Foundation, 1999)

ISSUE SUMMARY

YES: Physician Max Fink asserts that electroconvulsive therapy (ECT) is an effective intervention whose use has been limited as a result of social stigma and philosophical bias, which have been reinforced by intimidation from the pharmaceutical and managed care industries.

NO: Physician Leonard R. Frank criticizes the use of ECT because of its disturbing side effects, some of which he personally has suffered, and asserts that its resurgence in popularity is economically based.

For more than six decades some psychiatrists have treated their patients with electroconvulsive therapy (ECT), an extreme intervention involving the administration of an electric shock with the aim of controlling disturbing emotional and behavioral symptoms. Most commonly used in cases of debilitating depression, ECT consists of a treatment in which electric shock is applied through electrodes attached to the head. The premise of ECT is that radical alterations in the brain's chemistry stimulate beneficial changes in neurons, thus reducing certain kinds of symptoms. ECT grew in popularity among American psychiatrists during the 1940s and 1950s, but so did criticisms of this procedure because it was so often abused as a means of disciplining and controlling disruptive patients in psychiatric hospitals. As a result of considerable controversy surrounding ECT, the method became infrequently used by the 1970s. In recent years, however, there has been renewed interest in this intervention, which some experts regard as an effective and efficient option, especially for severely symptomatic individuals who do not respond to medication or psychotherapy.

In the following selection, Max Fink asserts that ECT is an effective intervention whose use has been limited as a result of social stigma and philosophical bias against it. Fink views ECT as a safe treatment that has been demonstrated to be effective with a range of psychiatric disorders, including severe depression, mania, schizophrenia, and catatonia. In trying to explain the reluctance of American psychiatrists to recommend ECT, Fink contends that they are intimidated by the pharmaceutical industry, managed care companies, and political forces that have underfunded psychiatric care and research.

In the second selection, Leonard R. Frank speaks against ECT, not only in his role as a physician but also as a former patient who was given extensive treatments with ECT and its predecessor, insulin-induced coma treatments. Expressing alarm about the resurgence of ECT, he criticizes claims that it is effective and safe, and he contends that its current popularity is economically based. Highlighting a number of disturbing side effects, some of which he personally suffered, Frank speaks about this method as one that destroys "the memories and lives of those subjected to it."

POINT

- ECT is a safe and reliable form of treatment.

- ECT is not as widely used as it should be, because psychiatrists are intimidated by the pharmaceutical industry, managed care companies, and political forces that have underfunded psychiatric care and research.

- The antidepressant effects of ECT occur earlier and are more robust than those of antidepressant drugs.

- It is shameful that many agencies that are licensed to treat the mentally ill lack the facilities to give ECT.

- Many criticisms about ECT are based on references to problems that were associated with ECT when it was first introduced, which are wholly unwarranted today because modern practice has made ECT safe.

COUNTERPOINT

- The serious risks associated with ECT are consistently understated and overlooked.

- The increase in ECT, particularly in the psychiatric wards of general hospitals, has been due in part to the fact that costs are paid for by insurance companies, causing some hospitals to reap considerable financial benefits from their use of ECT.

- After 50 years of research on ECT, no methodologically sound study has shown beneficial effects of ECT lasting as long as four weeks.

- ECT is one of the most controversial treatments in psychiatry, and it has great potential for destroying the memories and lives of those subjected to it.

- The side effects associated with ECT are very serious and include amnesia, denial, euphoria, apathy, wide mood swings, helplessness, and submissiveness—effects that offset the problems that supposedly justified the use of ECT in the first place.

 **YES**

Electroshock in the 1990s

Within the past decade, clinical and research interest in ECT [electroconvulsive therapy] has revived. The resurgence has been most marked in the United States, where the greatest efforts are under way to improve its safety and its efficacy. Psychiatrists in other countries have sought to reintroduce ECT, but its use varies widely. ECT is an accepted part of psychiatric practice in the Scandinavian countries, Great Britain, Ireland, Australia, and New Zealand, and usage is similar to that in the United States. A stigma attached to ECT limits its use in Germany, Japan, Italy, and the Netherlands to a few academic medical centers. Low reimbursement rates hamper its use in Canada and Japan, and also affect its availability in the United States. The unavailability of modern equipment and the expense of the medicines for anesthesia prevent its use in Africa, Asia, and Eastern Europe, and many patients in these countries who do receive it are subjected to unmodified ECT, such as was delivered in the 1930s and 1940s.

ECT is mainly a treatment for hospitalized patients, although many institutions are developing programs for outpatient ECT. The equipment and trained personnel are, for the most part, in the academic hospitals. Academic leaders recognize the merits of the treatment; some even encourage research and teaching. ECT is ignored by the research scientists at the National Institute of Mental Health. Few of the state, federal, or Veterans Administration hospitals provide ECT, and where it is available its use is infrequent. While 8 percent to 12 percent of adult inpatients at academic hospitals receive ECT, fewer than 0.2 percent of adults at nonacademic centers do. Such a discrepancy reflects the continuing social stigma and philosophical bias against electroshock. Before the federal Medicare and the Hill-Burton legislative acts of the 1960s opened access for all patients to any hospital facility, such discrepancies may have been common. But now that the nation has adopted an open-admission policy to its psychiatric facilities, the discrepancy is unjustified. It is shameful that many agencies licensed to treat the mentally ill lack the facilities to give the treatment.

Effects of Research on Practice

When ECT was revived in the late 1970s, the principal concern was its effects on cognition and memory. Unilateral ECT won favor with many practitioners after demonstrations that it reduced effects on memory. But other practitioners reported that unilateral ECT required more treatments than, and was not as effective as, bilateral ECT. The seizures in unilateral ECT were often brief, with poorly defined EEG seizure patterns. Studies of the interaction of electrode placement, energy dosing, and current form show that unilateral treatments, even with precise energy dosing, are less efficient than bilateral ECT. As a result, bilateral ECT is now preferred. When unilateral ECT is considered, its use includes precise energy dosing. Sinusoidal currents elicited unnecessarily high degrees of EEG and memory effects, compared with brief pulse square-wave currents, so the former have now been discarded.

We have learned that monitoring the motor seizure is not sufficient to measure the adequacy of an individual treatment, so we now look to EEG measures as more reliable indices. By recording and displaying the seizure EEG, we rely on the seizure characteristics as a guide to an effective treatment. Practitioners depend more on these characteristics than on criteria based on the motor convulsion and the change in heart rate as measures of beneficial treatment.

The interseizure EEG has stimulated research interest. Studies in 1957 had shown that a good clinical response in ECT depended on the slowing of the frequencies in the interseizure EEG. The observation was confirmed in 1972 and again in 1996, and the interseizure EEG is once again used as a guide to an effective course of treatment.

The indications for ECT have been broadened. As we have seen, it has gone from being a last resort for unresponsive depressed and suicidal patients to being a treatment option for patients with delusional depression, mania, schizophrenia, and catatonia. ECT can also be useful in patients with parkinsonism and those suffering from neuroleptic drug toxicity. Treatment can be safely given in the presence of complex systemic disorders and mental retardation.

Yet research on ECT is limited. Most of the research is directed at determining which treatment—medication or continuation ECT—can best maintain the benefits of a course of ECT in patients with severe depression. Some scientists still believe that sophisticated brain-imaging methods will find evidence of persistent brain dysfunction after ECT. So far, such studies have yielded no new information about mental illness or about ECT. Others seek the benefits of ECT without a seizure by the use of rapid magnetic pulses instead of electrical ones. The method, called "rapid transcranial magnetic stimulation" (rTMS), has yet to be proven of benefit.

Future of Electroshock

Psychiatric care in the United States is in such turmoil that the problem of restoring the availability of electroshock seems nearly insignificant. American psychiatry lacks the leaders to stand up to the pharmaceutical industry and the managed care executives who are taking ever larger portions of the financial resources allocated to treating mental illness. State legislatures are cutting funds for mental health care, urging their mental hospital administrators to reduce patient admissions and shorten durations of stay. The state mental hospitals, which served as the ultimate haven for the mentally ill, are being closed and patients are being consigned to a motley collection of inadequate substitutions. The nonthreatening and passive homeless are on the streets; those who are more ill go in and out of the revolving doors of community centers and emergency wards or to hospitals equipped only for short-term care. Those who fall between end up in halfway houses and adult homes.

At one time the states supported research centers that were the jewels of the nation's mental health activities. Few institutes are still supported by the states, and even these are forced to compete for larger portions of their budgets from federal resources and private charity.

Academic researchers depend on industry to support increasing portions of their salaries. Industry sponsorship has taken over major aspects of the training of psychiatric residents by providing funds for lectures and seminars at medical schools and hospitals, and for national and international meetings. Industry employees organize carefully crafted symposia, and the ensuing discussions are published as supplements to freely distributed psychiatric journals. The opportunity for independent assessment and open dialogue about the efficacy and safety of psychoactive drugs, and especially comparisons with other treatments such as electroshock, has been virtually eliminated.

The leaders of the lay agencies that speak for the mentally ill are confused, torn between the promises of an industry hawking its products, state mental health agencies seeking to self-destruct, and managed care companies striving to limit expenditures for the care of the mentally ill. The lay agencies are sensitive to the stigma of electroshock and avoid mention of it for fear of losing members and financial support. For that reason, they do not encourage state and municipal legislatures to provide the treatment.

In this turmoil, few psychiatrists speak up in behalf of electroshock for their patients. The two U.S. manufacturers who make modern ECT devices and support educational efforts are too small to do more than survive. Although their new devices have highly sophisticated EEG-recording capabilities that can monitor electroshock treatments with great precision, these manufacturers can do little to ensure that their instruments are properly used.

In the brouhaha over the revival of ECT in the 1970s, the anti-ECT lobby tried to persuade the FDA to limit the sale and use of ECT devices in the United States. Their claim was that the devices were unsafe. In the early 1980s the FDA ruled that the devices in use were safe and reliable. The devices delivered energies with a fixed maximum under standard conditions, a maximum that had been set arbitrarily. Patients' seizure thresholds, however, rise with age, and many of the elderly need higher energies for effective treatment. The device manufacturers developed such devices, but when they applied to the FDA for modification of the standards, they were turned down and could not sell their equipment. The devices now sold in the United States are inadequate for effective treatment of some patients. Since the higher-energy devices are sold in the rest of the world, we have the awkward situation that patients in Canada, Europe, and Australia are being effectively treated while we in this country fail in treating some patients with similar conditions.

There is one opportunity on the economic horizon for a broader recognition of the merits of electroshock. The duration of inpatient treatment for patients receiving electroshock seems to be longer than for those receiving other treatments. But patients come to ECT after drug trials, often many trials, have failed. If the duration of inpatient care of patients given ECT is estimated from the day of the decision to use ECT, it is shorter and the costs are lower than the costs for psychotropic drugs. In one academic general hospital, of 19 depressed patients treated with ECT alone, the average hospital stay averaged 41 days, and for the 55 patients treated with tricyclic antidepressants (TCA) alone, the average stay was 55 days. The longest stay was for patients first treated with TCA and, when those failed, with ECT—an average length of stay of 71 days. The estimated cost of the stay for ECT treatment was $20,000 and for TCA alone it was $26,500, a savings of $6,500 for ECT over TCA. The same financial advantage is found when outpatient ECT is prescribed.

A study of patients discharged from general hospitals with a principal diagnosis of depressive disorder found that the initiation of ECT within five days of admission leads to shorter and less costly inpatient treatment than for those treated with drugs alone or delayed ECT. Other studies found that the antidepresssant effects of ECT occur earlier and are more robust than those of antidepressant drugs.

For the present, few managed care insurers recognize the merits of ECT, either as a relief for their insured ill patients or as a financial benefit to their shareholders. Payment for ECT is rarely approved for a patient with schizophrenia, so that patient must endure one drug trial after another. The most specious arguments are made about patients seen as catatonic, where neuroleptic drug trials are required, despite the evidence that neuroleptic drugs may precipitate the more acute state of neuroleptic malignant syndrome (NMS).

As managed care organizations assume a greater role in medical care, they reduce costs by limiting the conditions for which payments will be made, cutting professional fees and negotiating cheaper hospital costs. Once these measures have squeezed out of the system all the "excess" costs they can, the demand for the most efficient treatments will gain support. The advantages of ECT over medication should promote its greater use. Such an effect is already apparent in the expanding number of institutions seeking to develop qualified ECT facilities, in the interest of practitioners in obtaining education credits for ECT, and in the overt inclusion of electroshock as a valid treatment in algorithms now recommended for depression.

Many object to the revival of ECT by reminding others of the problems with electroshock when it was first introduced; at the time it was virtually the only effective treatment for the mentally ill. Such criticism is wholly unwarranted today; it is no more reasonable than to speak of the excesses in tonsillectomy, hysterectomy, pallidotomy, insulin coma, and labotomy that marked the enthusiastic reception of those procedures in earlier decades. Our appreciation of electroshock must be based on its present practice. We call on it because it is effective, often more so than alternate treatments, and because modern practice has made it safe.

Leonard R. Frank  **NO**

Shock Treatment: Resistance in the 1990s

Electroshock: Death, Brain Damage, Memory Loss, and Brainwashing

Since its introduction in 1938, electroshock, or electroconvulsive therapy (ECT), has been one of psychiatry's most controversial procedures. Approximately 100,000 people in the United States undergo ECT yearly, and recent media reports indicate a resurgence of its use. Proponents claim that changes in the technology of ECT administration have greatly reduced the fears and risks formerly associated with the procedure. I charge, however, that ECT as routinely used today is at least as harmful overall as it was before these changes were instituted. I recount my own experience with combined insulin coma–electroshock during the early 1960s and the story of the first electroshock "treatment." I report on who is now being electroshocked, at what cost, where, and for what reasons. I discuss ECT technique modifications and describe how ECT is currently administered. I examine assertions and evidence concerning ECT's effectiveness....

In October 1962, at the age of 30, I had a run-in with psychiatry and got the worst of it. According to my hospital records (Frank, 1976), the "medical examiners," in recommending that I be committed, wrote the following: "Reportedly has been showing progressive personality changes over past two or so years. Grew withdrawn and asocial, couldn't or wouldn't work, and spent most of his time reading or doing nothing. Grew a beard, ate only vegetarian food, and lived life of a beatnik—to a certain extent" (p. 63). I was labeled "paranoid schizophrenic, severe and chronic," denied my freedom for nine months, and assaulted with a variety of drugs and fifty insulin-coma and thirty-five electroshock "treatments."

Each shock treatment was for me a Hiroshima. The shocking destroyed large parts of my memory, including the two-year period preceding the last shock. Not a day passes that images from that period of confinement do not float into consciousness. Nor does the night provide escape, for my dreams bear them as well. I am back there again in the "treatment room;" coming out of that last insulin coma (the only one I remember); strapped down, a tube in my nose, a hypodermic needle in my arm; sweating, starving, suffocating, struggling to move; a group of strangers around the bed grabbing at me; thinking—Where am I? What the hell is happening to me?

Well into the shock series, which took place at Twin Pines Hospital in Belmont, California, a few miles south of San Francisco, the treating psychiatrist wrote to my father:

> In evaluating Leonard's progress to date, I think it is important to point out there is some slight improvement, but he still has all the delusional beliefs regarding his beard, dietary regime, and religious observances that he had prior to treatment. We hope that in continuing the treatments we will be able to modify some of these beliefs so that he can make a reasonable adjustment to life. (p. 77)

During the comatose phase of one of my treatments, my beard was removed—as "a therapeutic device to provoke anxiety and make some change in his body image," the consulting psychiatrist had written in his report recommending this procedure. He continued, "Consultation should be obtained from the TP [Twin Pines] attorney as to the civil rights issue—but I doubt that these are crucial. The therapeutic effort is worth it—inasmuch that he can always grow another" (p. 76).

Earlier, several psychiatrists had tried unsuccessfully to persuade me to shave off my beard. "Leonard seems to attach a great deal of religious significance to the beard," the treating psychiatrist had noted at the time. He had even brought in a local rabbi to change my thinking (p. 75), but to no avail. I have no recollection of any of this. It is all from my medical records.

> Genuine religious conversions are also seen after the new modified lobotomy operations. For the mind is freed from its old strait-jacket and new religious beliefs and attitudes can now more easily take the place of the old. (Sargant, 1957, p. 71)
>
> At the "Mental Health Center" [in Albuquerque] where I work, there is a sign on the wall near the inpatient wards that reads: "PATIENTS' RIGHTS: Patients have the right to religious freedom unless clinically contraindicated." (Jones, 1988, p. 2)

One day, about a week after my last treatment, I was sitting in the day room, which was adjacent to the shock-treatment wing of the hospital building. It was just before lunch and near the end of the treatment session (which lasts about five hours) for those being insulin-shocked. The thick metal door separating the two areas had been left slightly ajar. Suddenly, from behind the door, I heard the scream of a young man whom I had recently come to know and who was then starting an insulin course. It was a scream like nothing I had ever heard before, an all-out scream. Hurriedly, one of the nurses closed the door. The screams, now less audible, continued a while longer. I do not remember my own screams; his, I remember.

> [The insulin-coma patient] is prevented from seeing all at once the actions and treatment of those patients further along in their therapy... As much as possible, he is saved the trauma of sudden introduction to the sight of

patients in different stages of coma—a sight which is not very pleasant to an unaccustomed eye. (Gralnick, 1944, p. 184)

During the years since my institutionalization, I have often asked myself how psychiatrists, or anyone else for that matter, could justify shocking a human being. Soon after I began researching my book *The History of Shock Treatment* (1978), I discovered Gordon's (1948) review of the literature, in which he compiled fifty theories purporting to explain the "healing" mechanism of the various forms of shock therapy then in use, including insulin, Metrazol, and electroshock. Here are some excerpts:

> Because prefontal lobotomy improves the mentally ill by destruction, the improvement obtained by all the shock therapies must also involve some destructive processes.
> They help by way of a circulatory shake up . . .
> It decreases cerebral function.
> The treatments bring the patient and physician in closer contact. Helpless and dependent, the patient sees in the physician a mother.
> Threat of death mobilizes all the vital instincts and forces a reestablishment of contacts with reality. . . .
> The treatment is considered by patients as punishment for sins and gives feelings of relief.
> Victory over death and joy of rebirth produce the results.
> The resulting amnesia is healing.
> Erotization is the therapeutic factor.
> The personality is brought down to a lower level and adjustment is obtained more easily in a primitive vegetative existence than in a highly developed personality. Imbecility replaces insanity. (pp. 399–401)

One of the more interesting explanations I found was proposed by Manfred Sakel, the Austrian psychiatrist who, in 1933, introduced insulin coma as a treatment for schizophrenia. According to Sakel (cited in Ray, 1942, p. 250):

> [W]ith chronic schizophrenics, as with confirmed criminals, we can't hope for reform. Here the faulty pattern of functioning is irrevocably entrenched. Hence we must use more drastic measures to silence the dysfunctioning cells and so liberate the activity of the normal cells. This time we must *kill* the too vocal dysfunctioning cells. But can we do this without killing normal cells also? Can we *select* the cells we wish to destroy? I think we can. [italics in original]

Electroshock may be considered one of the most controversial treatments in psychiatry. As I document below, the last decade has witnessed a resurgence of ECT's popularity, accompanied by assertions from proponents concerning its effectiveness and safety—assertions which deny or obscure basic facts about the historical origins of ECT, the economic reasons behind its current popularity, as well as its potential for destroying the memories and lives of those subjected to it. . . .

Electroshock Facts and Figures

Since 1938, between ten and fifteen million people worldwide have undergone electroshock. While no precise figure is available, it is estimated that about 100,000 people in the United States are electroshocked annually (Fink, cited in Rymer, 1989, p. 68). Moreover, the numbers appear to be increasing. Recent media accounts report a resurgence of ECT interest and use. One reason for this is the well-publicized enthusiasm of such proponents as Max Fink, editor-in-chief of *Convulsive Therapy*, the leading journal in the field. Fink was recently cited as saying that "[ECT should be given to] all patients whose condition is severe enough to require hospitalization" (Edelson, 1988. p. 3).

A survey of the American Psychiatric Association (APA) membership focusing on ECT (APA, 1978) showed that 22% fell into the "User" category. Users were defined as psychiatrists who had "personally treated patients with ECT" or "recommended to residents under their supervision that ECT be used on patients" during the last six months (p. 5). If valid today, this figure indicates that approximately 7,700 APA members are electroshock Users.

A survey of all 184 member hospitals of the National Association of Private Psychiatric Hospitals (Levy and Albrecht, 1985) elicited the following information on electroshock practices from the 153 respondents (83%) who answered a nineteen-item questionnaire sent to them in 1982. Fifty-eight percent of the respondents used electroshock (3% did not use electroshock because they considered it to be "inappropriate treatment for any illness").

The hospitals using ECT found it appropriate for a variety of diagnoses:

100% for "major depressive disorder," 58% for "schizophrenia," and 13% for "obsessive-compulsive disorder." Twenty-six percent of the ECT-using hospitals reported no contraindications in the use of the procedure.

Darnton (1989) reported that the number of private free-standing psychiatric hospitals grew from 184 in 1980 to 450 in 1988. In addition, nearly 2,000 general hospitals offer inpatient psychiatric service (p. 67). While the use of ECT in state hospitals has fallen off sharply over the last twenty years, the psychiatric wards of general hospitals have increased their reliance on ECT in the treatment of their adult inpatients (Thompson, 1986).

In cases of depression, an ECT series ranges from six to twelve seizures—in those of schizophrenia, from fifteen to thirty-five seizures—given three times a week, and usually entails four weeks of hospitalization. In 72% of the cases, according to the APA (1978, p. 8) survey cited above, electroshock costs are paid for by insurance companies. This fact led one psychiatrist to comment, "Finding that the patient has insurance seemed like the most common indication for giving electroshock" (Viscott, 1972, p. 356). The overall cost for a series of electroshock in a private hospital ranges from $10,000 to $25,000. With room rates averaging $500 to $600 a day, and bed occupancy generally falling, some hospitals have obtained considerable financial advantage from their use of ECT. A regular ECT User can expect yearly earnings of at least $200,000, about twice the median income of other psychiatrists. *Electroshock is a $2–3 billion-a-year industry.*

More than two-thirds of electroshock subjects are women, and a growing number are elderly. In California, one of the states that requires Users to report quarterly the number and age categories of electroshock subjects, "the percentage 65 and over" being electroshocked increased gradually from 29% to 43% between 1977 and 1983 (Warren, 1986, p. 51). More recently, Drop and Welch (1989) reported that 60% of the ECT subjects in a recent two-year period at the Massachusetts General Hospital in Boston were over 60 years and 10% were in their eighties (p. 88).

There are published reports of persons over 100 years old (Alexopoulos, Young, and Abrams, 1989) and as young as 34½ months (Bender, 1955) who have been electroshocked. In the latter case, the child had been referred in 1947 to the children's ward of New York's Bellevue Hospital "because of distressing anxiety that frequently reached a state of panic.... The child was mute and autistic." The morning after admission he received the first of a series of twenty electroshocks and was discharged one month later. "The discharge note indicated a 'moderate improvement' since he was eating and sleeping better, was more friendly with the other children, and he was toilet trained" (pp. 418–419).

Children continue to be electroshocked. Black, Wilcox, and Stewart (1985) reported on "the successful use of ECT in a prepubertal boy with severe depression." Sandy, 11 years old, received twelve unilateral ECTs at the University of Iowa Hospitals and Clinics in Iowa City. He "improved remarkably" and "was discharged in good condition. Follow-up over the next eight years revealed five more hospitalizations for depression" (p. 98).

Some of the better known people who have undergone shock treatment include: Antonin Artaud, Thomas Eagleton, Claude Eatherly, Frances Farmer, Zelda Fitzberald, James Forrestal, Janet Frame, Ernest Hemingway, Vladimir Horowitz, Bob Kaufman, Seymour Krim, Vivien Leigh, Oscar Levant, Robert Lowell, Vaslav Nijinsky, Jimmy Pearsall, Robert Pirsig, Sylvia Plath, Paul Robeson, Gene Tierney, and Frank Wisner.

In the early 1970s electroshock survivors—together with other former psychiatric inmates/"patients"—began forming organizations aimed at regulating or abolishing electroshock and other psychiatric practices which they believed were harmful. In 1975, one group, the Network Against Psychiatric Assault (San Francisco/Berkeley), was instrumental in the passage of legislation that regulated the use of electroshock in California. Since then, more than thirty states have passed similar legislation.

In 1982, the Coalition to Stop Electroshock led a successful referendum campaign to outlaw ECT in Berkeley, California. Although the courts overturned the ban six weeks after it went into effect, this was the first time in American history that the use of any established medical procedure had been prohibited by popular vote.

The Committee for Truth in Psychiatry (CTIP), all of whose members are electroshock survivors, was formed in 1984 to support the Food and Drug Administration (FDA) in its original (1979) classification of the ECT device in the high risk category of medical devices, Class III, which earmarks a device of its related procedure for a safety investigation. To prevent an investigation of ECT, the APA had petitioned the FDA in 1982 for reclassification of the ECT device to Class II, which signifies low risk. After many years of indecision, the FDA proposed in 1990 to make this reclassification—but has not yet done so....

Claims of Electroshock Effectiveness

Virtually all the psychiatrists who evaluate, write about, and do research on electroshock are themselves Users. This partially explains why claims regarding ECT's effectiveness abound in the professional literature—while the risks associated with the procedure are consistently understated or overlooked. User estimates of ECT's effectiveness in the treatment of the affective disorders (i.e., depression, mania, and manic-depression) usually range from 75% to 90%. Two important questions, however, need to be addressed: What is meant by effectiveness, and how long does it last?

Breggin (1979, p. 135; 1981, pp. 252–253) has proposed a "brain-disabling hypothesis" to explain the workings of electroshock. The hypothesis suggests that ECT "effectiveness" stems from the brain damage ECT causes. As happens in cases of serious head injury, ECT produces amnesia, denial, euphoria, apathy, wide and unpredictable mood swings, helplessness and submissiveness. Each one of these effects may appear to offset the problems which justified the use of ECT in the first place.

Amnesia victims, having forgotten their problems, tend to complain less. Denial serves a similar purpose. Because of their embarrassment, ECT subjects tend to discount or deny unresolved personal problems, as well as ECT-caused intellectual deficits. With euphoria, the subject's depression seems to lift. With apathy, the subject's "agitation" (if that had been perceived as part of the original problem) seems to diminish. Dependency and submissiveness tend to make what may have been a resistive, hostile subject more cooperative and friendly. In hailing the wonders of electroshock, psychiatrists often simply redefine the symptoms of psychiatrogenic brain damage as signs of improvement and/or recovery.

Electroshock advocates themselves unwittingly provide support for the brain-disabling hypothesis. Fink, Kahn, and Green (1958) offered a good example of this when describing a set of criteria for rating improvement in ECT subjects: "When a depressed patient, who had been withdrawn, crying, and had expressed suicidal thoughts, no longer is seclusive, and is jovial, friendly and euphoric, denies his problems and sees his previous thoughts of suicide as 'silly' a rating of 'much improved' is made" (p. 117). Two additional illustrations are given below; see Cleckley (cited in Thigpen, 1976) and Hoch (1948).

On the question of duration of benefit from ECT, Weiner (1984)—in one of the most important review articles on ECT published during the last decade —was unable to cite a single study purporting to show long-term, or even medium-term, benefits from ECT. Opton (1985) drew this conclusion from the Weiner review: "In this comprehensive review of the literature, after fifty years of research on ECT, no methodologically sound study was found that reported beneficial effects of ECT lasting as long as four weeks" (p. 2). Pinel (1984), in his peer commentary on the Weiner article, accepted Weiner's conclusion that "the risks of ECT-related brain damage are slight" and then added, "it is difficult to justify any risks at all until ECT has been shown unambiguously to produce significant long-term therapeutic benefits" (p. 31).

The following excerpt from an article in *Clinical Psychiatry News* reveals the short-range outlook of many ECT Users:

> The relapse rate after successful treatment for affective disorders is very high, from 20% to 50% within six months after a *successful* course of ECT, according to Dr. Richard Abrams [a well-known ECT proponent]. "I think it is reasonable and appropriate to always initiate maintenance in the form of a tricyclic [an antidepressant drug] or lithium" he said. For patients who relapse despite adequate drug therapy, maintenance ECT [periodic single electroshocks, spaced several weeks or months apart] has been used successfully. (Klug, 1984, p. 16) [italics added]

The underlying assumption of this approach is that affective disorders are for the most part chronic and irreversible. There is a popular saying among psychiatrists, "Once a schizophrenic, always a schizophrenic." While not a maxim, "Once a depressive, always a depressive" is nevertheless a core belief among many ECT Users. It "explains" so much for them. From this perspective, there are hardly any ECT failures, only patients with recurring depressive episodes who require ongoing psychiatric treatment, intensive and maintenance by turns.

Proponents also claim, but cannot demonstrate, that ECT is effective in cases of depression where there is a risk of suicide. They often cite a study by Avery and Winokur (1976) to support their position. But this study makes no such claim, as we can see from the authors' own conclusion: "In the present study, treatment [ECT and antidepressants] was not shown to affect the suicide rate" (p. 1033). Nevertheless, Allen (1978), in the very first paragraph of his article on ECT observed, "Avery and Winokur showed that suicide mortality in patients afflicted with psychotic depression was lower in patients treated with ECT than in those who were not" (p. 47)....

Electroshock Modifications

In recent years, to allay growing public fears concerning the use of electroshock, proponents have launched a media campaign claiming, among other things, that with the introduction of certain modifications in the administration of ECT, the problems once associated with the procedure have been solved, or at least substantially reduced. These techniques center around the use of anesthetics and muscle relaxants, changes in electrode placement, and the use of brief-pulse electrical stimulation.

However, investigation and common sense indicate that while these modifications may offer some advantages—for example, muscle relaxants prevent the subject's thrashing about, thereby greatly reducing the risk of bone and spinal fractures, and making the procedure less frightening to watch—the basic facts underlying the administration of electroshock have not changed at all. The nature of the human brain and that of electricity are the same today as they were more than fifty years ago when ECT was introduced. Whatever may be the ameliorating factors of the newer delivery techniques, when a convulsogenic dose of electricity is applied to the brain, there is going to be a certain amount of brain damage, some of which will be permanent.

There is even evidence that the drug modifications make ECT more destructive than ever because the central nervous system depressants, anesthetics and muscle relaxants raise the subject's convulsive threshold which, in turn, makes it necessary to apply a larger dose of electricity to set off the convulsion. And, the more current applied, the more amnesia and brain damage. As Reed (1988) noted, "The amnesia directly relating to ECT depends on the amount of current used to trigger the generalized convulsion" (p. 29).

Other problems are associated with the use of premedications in ECT. In his study of 254 ECT deaths, Impastato (1957) reported that thirteen of sixty-six persons from the "cerebral death" group had received muscle relaxants and that these "appear to play a major role in the death of some of these patients" (p. 42). There were also five other patients who died immediately after receiving muscle relaxants but before being given the electric shock. These figures are from a period when muscle relaxants were not widely used. More recently, Ulett (1972) concurred with Impastato on the danger of muscle relaxants in ECT: "The objection to the use of muscle relaxants is that, although decreasing the rate of fracture complication, they unquestionably increase the change of fatal accident" (p. 284). Given the paucity of ECT-death studies in recent years, it is difficult to gauge the extent of this problem in current practice.

Another modification, unilateral ECT, has received much attention since its introduction in the late 1950s but has not replaced—and is not likely to replace—bilateral ECT as the standard technique. According to the APA survey on ECT (1978, p. 6), 75% of the Users reported using bilateral electrode placement exclusively. In bilateral ECT, the electrodes are placed on the subject's temples so that the current passes through the brain's frontal lobe area. In unilateral ECT, one electrode is placed on a temple and the other just above the back of the neck on the same (usually the nondominant) side of the head. Unilateral placement, proponents claim, results in less memory loss. But proponents of bilateral ECT assert that unilateral ECT is less effective and therefore requires more treatments (Gregory, Shawcross, and Gill, 1985).

Cleckley (cited in Thigpen, 1976) offered this explanation for the ineffectiveness of unilateral ECT: "My thought about unilateral stimulation is that it fails to cure. I think this failure to cure is in direct proportion to the avoidance of memory loss" (p. 40). During his interview with Abrams (1988b), Kalinowsky made this comment about unilateral ECT: "My experience is completely negative and if patients improve at all, it's probably due to the repeated anesthesia induction with methohexital" (p. 38).

Given the need for "somewhat more current to produce a seizure" in each treatment session (Fink, 1978, p. 79) and for more treatment sessions per series, unilateral ECT may be more brain damaging in some cases than bilateral ECT.

The problems associated with brief-pulse stimulation, another innovation in ECT adminstration, are similar to those associated with unilateral ECT. While brief-pulse stimulation may cause less amnesia than the routinely used sine-wave stimulation, the newer technique "may be insufficient to induce an adequate generalized seizure" (Reed, 1988, p. 29).

What Ulett (1972) wrote about unidirectional current stimulation—a supposed advance in ECT technology introduced by Liberson (1948)—may also apply to brief-pulse stimulation, and to unilateral ECT as well: "[I]t is often necessary to give a greater number of these milder treatments to achieve the desired therapeutic result" (p. 287)....

Conclusion

Mystification and conditioning have undoubtedly played an important role in shaping the public's tolerant attitude toward electroshock. But it is not only the uniformed and misinformed public that has stood by silently during the electroshock era. There has hardly been a voice of protest from the informed elite—even when one of its own has been victimized.

While undergoing a series of involuntary electroshocks at the famed Mayo Clinic in 1961, Ernest Hemingway told visitor A. E. Hotchner, "Well, what is the sense of ruining my head and erasing my memory, which is my capital, and putting me out of business? It was a brilliant cure but we lost the patient. It's a bum turn, Hotch, terrible." (cited in Hotchner, 1967, p. 308).

A few days after his release from the Mayo Clinic following a second course of ECT, Hemingway killed himself with a shotgun. With all that has been written about him since his death, no recognized figure from the world of literature, academia, law religion or science has spoken out against those responsible for this tragedy. As might have been expected, the psychiatric professional has also been silent. Not only did the psychiatrist who electroshocked Hemingway escape the censure of his colleagues, but a few years later they elected him president of the American Psychiatric Association.

Since ancient times, physicians have been trying to cure epilepsy. One might therefore think that they would object to the use of artificially-induced seizures as a method of treatment. But no such objection has been forthcoming. On the contrary, the medical profession's passive acquiescence to the use of electroshock has recently turned to active support:

The AMA [American Medical Association] has endorsed the use of electroconvulsive therapy (ECT) as an effective treatment modality in selected patients, as outlined by the American Psychiatric Association.... [The AMA] recognized ECT as a safe procedure in proper hands. (ECT, Animal Rights, 1989, p. 9)

ECT User Robert Peck titled his book *The Miracle of Shock Treatment* (1974). Antonin Artaud (cited in Sontag, 1976), the French actor and playwright, who was electroshocked in the early 1940s, wrote afterwards: "Anyone who has gone through the electric shock never again rises out of its darkness and his life has been lowered a notch" (p. 530). In which perspective—or at what point between these two perspectives—is the truth to be found? This is no trivia question. For some, it will be the gravest question they will ever have to answer.

References

Abrams, R. (1988b). Interview with Lothar Kalinowsky, M.D. *Convulsive Therapy, 4,* 25–39.

Alexopoulos, C. S., Young, R. C., and Abrams, R. C. (1989). ECT in the high-risk geriatric patient. *Convulsive Therapy, 5,* 75–87.

Allen, M. R. (1978). Electroconvulsive therapy: An old question, new answers, *Psychiatric Annals, 8,* 47–65.

American Psychiatric Association. (1978). *Electroconvulsive Therapy.* Task Force Report 14. Washington, D.C.: American Psychiatric Association.

Avery, D., and Winokur, O. (1976). Mortality in depressed patients treated with electroconvulsive therapy and antidepressants. *Archives of General Psychiatry 33,* 1029–1037.

Bender, L. (1955). The development of a schizophrenic child treated with electric convulsions at three years of age. In C. Caplan (Ed.), *Emotional Problems of Early Childhood* (pp. 407–425). New York: Basic Books.

Black, D. W., Wilcox, J. A., and Stewart, M. (1985). The use of ECT in children: Case report. *Journal of Clinical Psychiatry 46,* 98–99.

Breggin, P. R. (1979). *Electroshock: Its Brain-Disabling Effects.* New York: Springer.

Darnton, N. (1989, July 31). Committed youth. *Newsweek,* pp. 66–72.

Drop, L. J., and Welch, C. A. (1989). Anesthesia for electroconvulsive therapy in patients with major cardiovascular risk factors. *Convulsive Therapy, 5,* 88–101.

ECT, animal rights among topics discussed at AMA's Dallas meeting. (1989, January 20). *Psychiatric News,* p. 9;23.

Edelson, E. (1988, December 28). ECT elicits controversy—and results. *Houston Chronicle,* p. 3.

Fink, M. (1978). Electroshock therapy: Myths and realities. *Hospital Practice,* 13, 77–82.

Fink, M., Kahn, R. L., and Green, M. (1958). Experimental studies of electroshock process. *Diseases of the Nervous System,* 19, 113–118.

Frank, L. R. (1976). The Frank papers. In J. Friedberg, *Shock Treatment is not Good for Your Brain* (pp. 62–81). San Francisco: Glide Publications.

Frank, L. R. (1978). *The History of Shock Treatment.* San Francisco: Frank.

Gordon, H. L. (1948). Fifty shock therapy theories. *Military Surgeon,* 103, 397–401.

Gralnick, A. (1944). Psychotherapeutic and interpersonal aspects of insulin treatment. *Psychiatric Quarterly,* 18, 177–196.

Gregory, S., Shawcross, C. R., and Gill, D. (1985). The Nottingham ECT study: A double-blind comparison of bilateral, unilateral and simulated ECT in depressive illness. *British Journal of Psychiatry,* 146, 520–524.

Hoch, P. H. (1948). Discussion and concluding remarks. *Journal of Personality,* 17, 48–51.

Hotchner, A. E. (1967). *Papa Hemingway.* New York: Bantam.

Impastato, D. (1957). Prevention of fatalities in electroshock therapy. *Diseases of the Nervous System,* 18 (supplement), 34–75.

Jones, T. (1988, June). Letter. *Dendron* (Eugene, Oregon), p. 2.

Klug, J. (1984, June). Benefits of ECT outweigh risks in most patients. *Clinical Psychiatry News,* p. 16.

Levy, S. D., and Albrecht, E. (1985). Electroconvulsive therapy: A survey of use in the private psychiatric hospital. *Journal of Clinical Psychiatry,* 46, 125–127.

Liberson, W. T. (1948). Brief stimuli therapy: Physiological and clinical observations. *American Journal of Psychiatry,* 105, 28–39.

Opton, E. M., Jr. (1985, June 4). Letter to the members of the panel. National Institute of Health Consensus Development Conference on Electroconvulsive Therapy.

Peck, R. E. (1974). *The Miracle of Shock Treatment.* Jericho, New York: Exposition Press. Philadelphia Psychiatric Society. (1943). Symposium: Complications of and contraindications to electric shock therapy. *Archives of Neurology and Psychiatry,* 49, 786–791.

Pinel, J. PJ. (1984). After forty-five years ECT is still controversial. *Behavioral and Brain Sciences, 7,* 30–31.

Ray, M. B. (1942). *Doctors of the Mind: The Story of Psychiatry.* Indianapolis and New York: Bobbs-Merrill.

Reed, K. (1988). Electroconvulsive therapy: A clinical discussion. *Psychiatric Medicine, 6,* 23–33.

Rymer, R. (1989, March-April). Electroshock. *Hippocrates,* pp. 65–72.

Sargant, W. (1957). *Battle for the Mind: A Physiology of Conversion and Brainwashing.* Baltimore: Penguin.

Thigpen, C. H. (1976). Letter. *Convulsive Therapy Bulletin,* 1, 40.

Thompson, J. W. (1986). Utilization of ECT in U.S. psychiatric facilities, 1975 to 1980. *Psychopharmacology Bulletin, 22,* 463–465.

Ulett, G. A. (1972). *A Synopsis of Contemporary Psychiatry.* St. Louis: C. V. Mosby.

Viscott, D. (1972). *The Making of a Psychiatrist.* Greenwich, Connecticut: Faucett.

Warren, C. A. B. (1986). Electroconvulsive therapy: "new" treatment of the 1980s. *Research in Law, Deviance and Social Control, 8,* 41–55.

Weiner, R. D. (1984). Does electroconvulsive therapy cause brain damage? *Behavioral and Brain Sciences, 7,* 1–22 (peer commentary section, pp. 22–54).

CHALLENGE QUESTIONS

Is Electroconvulsive Therapy Ethical?

1. Fink views ECT as a safe intervention that has been underutilized partly because of ideological and financial pressures to use drugs instead. What kind of research study could be designed to compare the therapeutic effectiveness of ECT with the benefits of medication?
2. Frank criticizes ECT as an intervention that involves very serious and lasting side effects. Given the fact that this intervention is typically recommended for seriously impaired individuals, what steps should be taken to ensure that patients are protected from being given a treatment that involves considerable risk?
3. Imagine that you are a clinician treating a suicidal woman who is incapable of eating and for whom antidepressant medications have had no therapeutic effect. What arguments for and against ECT could be made with regard to the treatment of this client?
4. Psychopharmacological medications work by bringing about changes in brain chemistry. Consider the assumptions about what makes ECT effective. In what ways are the two interventions similar and different?
5. Fink contends that much of the negativity associated with ECT stems from its misuse in earlier decades and from the unfavorable presentation of ECT in the movie *One Flew Over the Cuckoo's Nest*. What aspects of these historical issues may account for the continuing negativity about ECT, even decades later?

Suggested Readings

Breggin, P. R. (1997). *Brain disabling treatments in psychiatry: Drugs, electroshock, and the role of the FDA*. New York, NY: Springer Publishing Company.

Fink, M. (1997). The decision to use ECT: For whom? When? In A. J. Rush (Ed.), *Mood disorders: Systematic medication management. Modern problems of pharmacopsychiatry, vol. 25*. (pp. 203–214). Basel, Switzerland: Karger.

Fink, M. (1997). Prejudice against ECT: Competition with psychological philosophies as a contribution to its stigma. *Convulsive Therapy*, 13(4), 253–265.

Salzman, C. (1998). ECT, research, and professional ambivalence. *American Journal of Psychiatry*, 155(1) 1–2

Contributors to This Volume

EDITOR

RICHARD P. HALGIN is a professor of psychology in the Clinical Psychology Program at the University of Massachusetts–Amherst. He is coauthor, with Susan Krauss Whitbourne, of *Abnormal Psychology: Clinical Perspectives on Psychological Disorders*, 3rd ed. (McGraw-Hill, 2000) and coeditor, with Whitbourne, of *A Casebook in Abnormal Psychology: From the Files of Experts* (Oxford University Press, 1998). His list of publications also includes more than 50 articles and book chapters in the fields of psychotherapy, clinical supervision, and professional issues in psychology. He is a board-certified clinical psychologist, and he has over two decades of clinical, supervisory, and consulting experience. At the University of Massachusetts, his course in abnormal psychology is one of the most popular offerings on campus, attracting more than 500 students each semester. In recent years, he has also offered this course at Amherst College and Smith College. His teaching has been recognized at the university and national level: he was honored with the University of Massachusetts Distinguished Teaching Award and was recognized by the Society for the Teaching of Psychology of the American Psychological Association.

STAFF

Theodore Knight   List Manager
David Brackley   Senior Developmental Editor
Juliana Poggio   Developmental Editor
Rose Gleich   Administrative Assistant
Brenda S. Filley   Production Manager
Juliana Arbo   Typesetting Supervisor
Diane Barker   Proofreader
Lara Johnson   Design/Advertising Coordinator
Richard Tietjen   Publishing Systems Manager
Larry Killian   Copier Coordinator

AUTHORS

NANCY C. ANDREASEN holds the Andrew H. Woods Chair of Psychiatry at the University of Iowa School of Medicine, and she is editor in chief of the *American Journal of Psychiatry*. She is internationally respected for her research contributions to psychology and psychiatry focusing on the biological bases of human behavior in mental illnesses, particularly schizophrenia, and she has authored many related articles and books, including *The Broken Brain: The Biological Revolution in Psychiatry* (HarperCollins, 1984).

E. JOANNE ANGELO is an assistant clinical professor of psychiatry at Tufts University School of Medicine, and she maintains a private psychiatry practice in Boston, Massachusetts. She is a corresponding member of the Pontifical Academy for Life, and her published writings have focused on abortion.

PETER ARENELLA, a professor of law in the University of California, Los Angeles, School of Law, is a criminal law scholar who has served as a consultant to congressional committees and the national media.

THOMAS ARMSTRONG, a former special education teacher, is a consultant on learning and human development in Sonoma County, California. He has published several articles and books, including *The Myth of the A.D.D. Child* (E. P. Dutton, 1995).

JOYCE ARTHUR is a social activist for abortion rights, evolution education, and wildlife preservation, topics on which she has written numerous articles.

RUSSELL BARKLEY is a professor of psychiatry and neurology at the University of Massachusetts Medical Center. He has authored or edited numerous articles and books on attention deficit hyperactivity disorder and related topics, including *Taking Charge of ADHD: The Complete Authoritative Guide for Parents* (Guilford, 1995) and *Child Psychopathology* (Guilford, 1996).

JONATHAN BIRD is associated with the Burden Neurological Hospital and the University of London Institute of Psychiatry.

JEFFERY P. BRADEN is a faculty member in the Department of Educational Psychology at the University of Wisconsin–Madison. He serves on the editorial boards of *School Psychology Quarterly, Journal of Psychoeducational Assessment,* and *School Psychology Review,* and he does research in assessment, aiding youths in urban schools, and deafness. His publications include the book *Deafness, Deprivation, and IQ* (Plenum, 1994).

PETER R. BREGGIN is the founder of the International Center for the Study of Psychiatry and Psychology, a nonprofit organization concerned with the impact of mental health theory and practice on individuals. He is the author of several books, including *Talking Back to Ritalin: What Doctors Aren't Telling You About Stimulants for Children* (Common Courage Press, 1998) and *Beyond Conflict: From Self-Help and Psychotherapy to Peacemaking* (St. Martin's Press, 1995).

ANDREW CHRISTENSEN is a professor of psychology at the University of California, Los Angeles. He is coauthor, with Neil S. Jacobson, of *Integrative Couple Therapy: Promoting Acceptance and Change* (W. W. Norton, 1996).

ALAN M. DERSHOWITZ is the Felix Frankfurter Professor of Law at Harvard Law School. A prominent figure in the media's coverage of criminal law and civil liberties, his numerous publications include *Just Revenge* (Warner Books, 1999) and *Reasonable Doubts* (Simon & Schuster, 1997).

ALBERT ELLIS, founder of rational-emotive therapy, is president of the Institute for Rational-Emotive Therapy in New York City. He has authored or coauthored more than 600 articles and over 50 books on psychotherapy, marital and family therapy, and sex therapy, including *Why Some Therapies Don't Work: The Dangers of Transpersonal Psychology*, coauthored with Raymond Yaeger (Prometheus Books, 1989), and *How to Control Your Anxiety Before It Controls You* (Carol Publishing Group, 1999).

RHEA K. FARBERMAN is associate executive director for public communications at the American Psychological Association. She is also executive editor of the *APA Monitor.*

MAX FINK is a professor of psychiatry and neurology at the State University of New York at Stony Brook. He has been studying electroconvulsive therapy (ECT) since 1954, and he is the founding editor of the scientific journal *Convulsive Therapy.* He is director of the ECT Service at University Hospital at Stony Brook and executive director of the International Association for Psychiatric Research. His publications include *Electroshock: Restoring the Mind* (Oxford University Press, 1999).

MICHAEL B. FIRST is a research psychiatrist at the New York State Psychiatric Institute and in the Department of Psychiatry at Columbia University. He is coauthor of *Am I Okay? A Layman's Guide to the Psychiatrist's Bible* (Simon & Schuster, 2000); *DSM-IV Guidebook* (American Psychiatric Press, 1995); and *DSM-IV Casebook: A Learning Companion to the Diagnostic and Statistical Manual of Mental Disorders,* 4th ed. (American Psychiatric Press, 1994).

ALLEN FRANCES is a professor of psychiatry at Duke University Medical School. He has published extensively in the field of psychiatry, particularly on issues pertaining to the *DSM-IV.* His books include *Am I Okay? A Layman's Guide to the Psychiatrist's Bible* (Simon & Schuster, 2000); *DSM-IV Guidebook* (American Psychiatric Press, 1995); and *DSM-IV Casebook: A Learning Companion to the Diagnostic and Statistical Manual of Mental Disorders,* 4th ed. (American Psychiatric Press, 1994).

LEONARD R. FRANK is an honorary staff member of the Bristol Hospital in Bristol, Connecticut. A former editor of the *Madness Network News,* he is an outspoken critic of the use of electroconvulsive therapy. He is the editor and publisher of *Influencing Minds: A Reader in Quotations* (1994) and *The History of Shock Treatment* (1978).

JONATHAN L. FREEDMAN is a professor of psychology at the University of Toronto.

LINDA GANZINI is a psychiatrist at the Oregon Health Science University in Portland, Oregon, and director of genetic psychiatry at the Portland Veterans Affairs Medical Center.

SOL L. GARFIELD is a professor emeritus of psychology at Washington University. He has authored many articles and books in the field of psychotherapy, including *Psychotherapy: An Eclectic-Integrative Approach,* 2d ed. (John Wiley, 1995).

HOWARD H. GOLDMAN is a professor in the Department of Psychiatry at the University of Maryland at Baltimore. He is also codirector of the Institute of Psychiatry and Human Behavior, and he has been scientific editor for the surgeon general's report on mental health.

DOUGLAS C. HALDEMAN is a counseling psychologist in private practice in Seattle, Washington. He previously served as president of the American Psychological Association's Society for the Psychological Study of Lesbian, Gay, and Bisexual Issues.

EDWARD M. HALLOWELL is a child and adult psychiatrist on the faculty of Harvard Medical School and an authority on attention deficit disorder. He is coauthor, with John J. Ratey, of *Answer to Distraction* (Bantam Books, 1996) and the author of *Connect* (Pantheon Books, 1999).

L. ROWELL HUESMANN is a professor of psychology and communication at the University of Michigan as well as a senior research scientist at the Research Center for Group Dynamics at the Institute for Social Research. He is also president of the International Society for Research on Aggression. His publications include *Development of Aggression from Infancy to Adulthood* (Westview Press, 1999).

NEIL S. JACOBSON was a professor of psychology at the University of Washington prior to his recent death. His research interests included depression as well as marital and family therapy. He coauthored, with John M. Gottman, *When Men Batter Women: New Insights into Ending Abusive Relationships* (Simon & Schuster, 1998).

PHILIP C. KENDALL is a professor of psychology at Temple University, and he has served as editor of the *Journal of Consulting and Clinical Psychology.* His publications include *Handbook of Research Methods in Clinical Psychology,* coedited with James N. Butcher and Grayson N. Holmbeck (John Wiley, 1999).

STUART A. KIRK has worked as a psychiatric social worker and as editor in chief of *Social Work Research.* He is coauthor, with Herb Kutchins, of *Making Us Crazy: DSM—The Psychiatric Bible and the Creation of Mental Disorders* (Free Press, 1997) and *The Selling of DSM III: The Rhetoric of Science in Psychiatry* (Aldine de Gruyter, 1992).

RICHARD P. KLUFT is a psychiatrist who brought international attention to the diagnosis of dissociative identity disorder during his tenure in the Department of Psychiatry at the Institute of Pennsylvania Hospital. He is the editor of *Childhood Antecedents of Multiple Personality Disorder* (American Psychiatric Press, 1985) and coeditor, with Catherine G. Fine, of *Clinical Perspectives on Multiple Personality Disorder* (American Psychiatric Press, 1993).

TERRY A. KUPERS is a forensic psychiatric consultant and the author of *Revisioning Men's Lives: Gender, Intimacy, and Power* (Guilford, 1993).

HERB KUTCHINS is a professor of social work at California State University, Sacramento. He is coauthor, with Stuart A. Kirk, of *Making Us Crazy: DSM— The Psychiatric Bible and the Creation of Mental Disorders* (Free Press, 1997) and *The Selling of DSM III: The Rhetoric of Science in Psychiatry* (Aldine de Gruyter, 1992).

DAVID B. LARSON is president of the National Institute for Healthcare Research and a former assistant director of planning at the Department of Health and Human Services in Washington, D.C. His publications include *The Forgotten Factor in Physical and Mental Health: What Does the Research Show?* coauthored with Susan Larson (National Institute of Healthcare Research, 1994).

ELIZABETH F. LOFTUS is a professor of psychology and an adjunct professor of law at the University of Washington. An expert on human memory, eyewitness testimony, and courtroom procedure, she has also served as president of the American Psychological Society. One of her books, *Eyewitness Testimony,* coauthored with Gary Wells (Cambridge University Press, 1984), won a National Media Award from the American Psychological Foundation.

PAUL R. McHUGH is a professor of psychiatry at the Johns Hopkins School of Medicine. He has a long list of publications, including *The Perspectives of Psychiatry,* coauthored with Phillip R. Slavney (Johns Hopkins University Press, 1986).

JESSICA MOISE is a graduate student in the interdepartmental Ph.D. program in mass communication at the University of Michigan.

FRED OVSIEW is an associate professor of clinical psychiatry at the University of Chicago.

HAROLD ALAN PINCUS is director of the American Psychiatric Association's Office of Research and coauthor of *DSM-IV Case Studies: A Clinical Guide to Differential Diagnosis* (American Psychiatric Press, 1996) and *DSM-IV Guidebook* (American Psychiatric Press, 1995).

FRANK W. PUTNAM is a psychiatrist who is an expert on multiple personality disorder. His list of publications includes *Diagnosis and Treatment of Multiple Personality Disorder* (Guilford, 1989).

RUTH ROSS is managing editor of the *Journal of Practical Psychiatry and Behavioral Health.* She is coauthor of *DSM-IV Guidebook* (American Psychiatric Press, 1995) and *DSM-IV Case Studies: A Clinical Guide to Differential Diagnosis* (American Psychiatric Press, 1996).

DIANA E. H. RUSSELL is a professor emeritus of sociology at Mills College in Oakland, California. A leading authority on sexual violence against women and girls, she has performed research and written articles and books on rape, incest, the misogynist murder of women, and pornography for 25 years. Her publications include *Against Pornography: The Evidence of Harm* (Russell, 1994) and *Making Violence Sexy: Feminist Views on Pornography* (Teachers College Press, 1993).

VICTOR D. SANUA is an adjunct professor of psychology at St. John's University. He is also the author of *Fields of Offerings: Studies in Honor of Raphael Patai* (Fairleigh Dickinson University Press, 1983).

MARTIN E. P. SELIGMAN is a professor in the Department of Psychology at the University of Pennsylvania and is well known for his formulation of the learned helplessness model. He has served as president of the American Psychological Association, and he has published many books, including *What You Can Change and What You Can't: The Complete Guide to Successful Self-Improvement* (Alfred A. Knopf, 1994) and *Helplessness: On Depression, Development, and Death* (W. H. Freeman, 1992).

ROBERT J. STERNBERG is the IBM Professor of Psychology and Education at Yale University and a fellow of the American Academy of Arts and Sciences, the American Association for the Advancement of Science, the American Psychological Association, and the American Psychological Society. His research on human intelligence focuses on "successful intelligence," or people's ability to use what capabilities they have, given the sociocultural context in which they live. His list of over 600 publications includes *Successful Intelligence: How Practical and Creative Intelligence Determines Success in Life* (Dutton/Plume, 1997) and *Intelligence, Heredity, and Environment* (Cambridge University Press, 1997).

NADINE STROSSEN, a professor of law at the New York Law School, is the first woman to become president of the American Civil Liberties Union. She writes and lectures extensively on constitutional law, civil liberties, and international human rights.

MARK D. SULLIVAN is an associate professor in the Department of Psychiatry and Behavioral Sciences at the University of Washington. He has written extensively on the topics of pain, death and dying, and physician-assisted suicide.

E. FULLER TORREY is a psychiatrist and an ardent spokesperson for the appropriate treatment of people with mental illness. He is executive director of the Stanley Foundation, for which he serves as president of the Treatment Advocacy Center and chair of the Research Program on Serious Mental Illness, and he is also the founder of the National Alliance for the Mentally Ill Research Institute. His many publications include *Out of the Shadows: Confronting America's Mental Illness Crisis,* 2d ed. (John Wiley, 1998) and *Surviving Schizophrenia: A Manual for Families, Consumers and Providers,* 3rd ed. (HarperTrade, 1995).

FRANK T. VERTOSICK, JR., is a neurosurgeon in private practice at Western Pennsylvania Hospital in Pittsburgh, Pennsylvania. He is also the author of *When the Air Hits Your Brain: Tales of Neurosurgery* (W. W. Norton, 1996), which is an account of his training in surgery.

THOMAS A. WIDIGER is a professor of psychology at the University of Kentucky. In addition to serving on a number of editorial boards, he is a member of the National Institute of Mental Health's clinical psychopathology review committee, and he was a member of the American Psychiatric

Association task force that developed the *DSM-IV.* He is coauthor of *DSM-IV Case Studies: A Clinical Guide to Differential Diagnosis* (American Psychiatric Press, 1996).

MARK A. YARHOUSE is an assistant professor in the Regent University School of Psychology and Counseling, where he specializes in marriage and family therapy, human sexuality, ethics, and the integration of psychology and theology.

STUART J. YOUNGNER is a professor of biomedical ethics, medicine, and psychiatry at Case Western Reserve University, where he has served as director of the Center for Biomedical Ethics and associate director of Clinical Ethics. He serves on the editorial advisory boards of the *Journal of Medicine and Philosophy* and the *Kennedy Institute of Ethics Journal.* He is coeditor, with Renee C. Fox and Laurence J. O'Connell, of *Organ Transplantation: Meanings and Realities* (University of Wisconsin Press, 1996) and coeditor, with Maxwell J. Mehlman, of *Delivering High Technology Home Care: Issues for Decisionmakers* (Springer, 1991).

Index